Life of the Party

Also by Christopher Ogden

MAGGIE: An Intimate Portrait of a Woman in Power

Life of the Party

THE BIOGRAPHY OF
PAMELA DIGBY CHURCHILL HAYWARD HARRIMAN

Christopher Ogden

LITTLE, BROWN AND COMPANY

A *Little, Brown* Book

First published in Great Britain in 1994
by Little, Brown and Company

A CIP catalogue record for this book
is available from the British Library.

ISBN 0 316 91188 7

Printed in England by Clays Ltd, St Ives plc

Little, Brown and Company (UK)
Brettenham House
Lancaster Place
London WC2E 7EN

Contents

Author's Note

THIS IS an unauthorized biography, although it draws on the extensive access that I had to Pamela Harriman for six months in 1991 after she asked me to write her autobiography. At the time, I was chief diplomatic correspondent for *Time* magazine, traveling the world with Secretary of State James Baker and writing about the Bush administration's foreign policy.

Mrs. Harriman approached me in June 1991 through an intermediary. She liked a biography I had written of British prime minister Margaret Thatcher. Advisers and friends had told her that I knew the British scene from several journalistic postings in London and understood Democratic party politics, her then passion, from having been *Time*'s White House correspondent during the Carter administration.

Hers was a wonderful story, a saga of a determined young English aristocrat, bored with rural life, who went to the big city, married into the Churchill family at the outset of World War II and, through a subsequent series of targeted liaisons and marriages to rich and famous men in Europe and the United States, parlayed her ambition and talents into a vast fortune and major political clout.

She had lived one of the most fascinating lives of the century, but no one had told the story at book length and depth. I was interested, but my concern was that if I were to write it for her, the story had to be honest and complete. Some of her relationships with powerful men were sensitive. The story did not have to be salacious and sensationalistic, I told her, but it had to be real. Otherwise, she should seek another writer. Plenty were available.

Mrs. Harriman insisted that she wanted me and offered me an exceptionally generous 50 percent of whatever publisher's advance was acceptable. We began talking in July and continued until November. In September, we received from a distinguished publisher a very lucrative offer, so high that Mrs. Harriman panicked. For that much money — $1,625,000 — she and I would have to produce a full memoir. That was fine with me. It was only on that condition that I had agreed to participate in the first place. But as she thought more about what she was getting into, Mrs. Harriman got colder and colder feet. Declining to sign the publisher's contract, she pulled out of the project in December. I was never paid a penny, not even for expenses.

Referred to her lawyers, I was first ignored and then rebuffed by them as I sought for six months to reach some sort of fair settlement. As a writer, and not a litigator, I did not want to sue. Litigation was bound to be a negative experience; because Mrs. Harriman had inherited one of America's great fortunes and I had left my full-time job at *Time* to write her story, it was certain to be a financially painful experience for me as well. Instead, I decided to write the story anyway.

I had tapes of some forty hours of my interviews covering her life — copies of which I sent her as a courtesy — and no contractual obligation to confidentiality. Interviews with nearly two hundred other sources with close knowledge of Mrs. Harriman at each stage of her life fleshed out a more comprehensive portrait. What you are about to read comes from all those sources plus, as noted in endnotes and the bibliography, a substantial amount of additional primary and secondary source material.

A few words about attribution: I have not quoted Mrs. Harriman from my interviews nor attributed to her material from our sessions together. That is because, as a journalist, I deal regularly with information in accordance with traditional sourcing rules and understandings. They include, on-the-record, background material, where the information may be used but the source is not specifically identified, and, off-the-record, material that may not be used. My interviews with Mrs. Harriman were understood by the two of us from the outset to be "on background," with her right reserved to clear quotes or direct attribution. What she told me off the record is not included here.

That said, it should be clear that while this is an unauthorized biography, it has an insider's perspective tempered by the reality checks of well-informed outsiders. The story has been told with no malice or rancor. To have allowed such sentiments to creep in would have been foolish, shortsighted and could have distorted an extraordinary life. On the contrary, I am grateful to Mrs. Harriman for the opportunity she gave me to explore firsthand and at length her character, motivations and experiences. No writer could ask for more.

To

Agnes Bennett Ogden
Michael Joseph Ogden
my parents

Margaret Crosby May
John Wesley May
my in-laws

wonderful teachers, all four

Introduction

SECRET SERVICE war wagons, those black, high-riding, fuel-injected Chevy Suburban four-by-fours, crammed with cases of Uzi submachine guns, heart defibrillators and secure communications gear, choked N Street in the heart of Georgetown. Blue-and-white squad cars barred entry from Wisconsin Avenue, a shopping street which divides the historic, tree-lined Washington, D.C., neighborhood where John Kennedy lived until moving to the White House in 1961. The temperature hovered just above freezing, but matrons in furs, residents and the curious in parkas and knit Redskins caps stood, breath visible, on front steps and on the uneven brick sidewalk behind yellow plastic tapes marked Police Line: Do Not Cross.

Buffed brass numerals — 3038 — reflected the television lights bathing the black door of the 1830 Federalist house on the street's south side. Inside, a trench-coated agent pressed his hand to his ear. "One minute," he said, half-turning to Clive Whittingham, the butler in black tie. "One minute," Clive repeated to the honey-haired woman standing in the foyer. She nodded and shifted from one Manolo Blahnik–clad foot to the other, fingering a gold saxophone pin fixed above her right breast. Designer Kenneth Jay Lane sent it personally, along with a note: "You really should be able to blow your own horn."[1]

Behind her, the buzz from ninety guests trailed off. Street noise rarely penetrates the "petit salon" and living room where the van Gogh, Matisse and Picasso hang, but the Doppler staccato of shrieking police sirens approaching the house was too much for even these cushioned chambers.

At a signal, the door swung inward as the armored limousine pulled up. The crowd applauded. Photographers jostled and shouted, strobe lights flashing. Hillary and Bill Clinton turned and waved, then headed for the low, double-step entry. "Hi, Pamela," said Clinton, embracing her. "Hello, Mr. President, and welcome," replied Pamela Digby Churchill Hayward Harriman, her eyes flashing and her throaty voice rising girlishly. "I'm so glad you could come this evening."

Seventeen days earlier, on November 3, 1992, Bill Clinton had been elected president of the United States. This was his first trip to Washington, D.C., since he toppled George Bush and ended a twelve-year Republican hold on the White House. For many Democrats, including the Old Guard gathered in Pamela's drawing room, the wait had been double that, nearly a quarter century.

Jimmy Carter had not counted for them. He wasn't a real Democrat, not by their definition. The former Georgia governor and peanut farmer won his single term in 1976 by running against Washington and his own party's establishment. In office, little changed. Carter couldn't stand the establishment or the Georgetown set of career diplomats, spies, heiresses and writers. They were dying to be embraced, but when Carter rejected them, the party panjandrums reciprocated. The president came in an outsider and would leave one. He was NOC,D — not our class, dear. The last one who understood and appreciated this crowd was Lyndon Johnson, who left office in 1969, mired in Vietnam.

For the Democratic Old Guard, desperate to be back in the power loop, Clinton was a throwback as well as a savior. He had gone to Georgetown University, only eight blocks west from Pamela's doorway. He was from Arkansas, but he was no outsider, no rural hick. He was Oxford, a Rhodes scholar, and Yale Law.

He was as establishment as he wanted, or felt he had to be. Clinton courted the satraps, phoned and schmoozed them, played them like gut-hooked Ozark lake bass.

Now he was headed to the White House and these preening dinner guests would be insiders. Some would hold Cabinet or White House staff jobs. Pamela would be named U.S. ambassador to France, one of the most prestigious and glittering appointments a president can offer. A few would be tapped despite sneers from the quick, hard-edged Clinton campaign staff that the Old Guard were "fossils," relics of a bygone age. All that, of course, would play out later in the transition and the opening months of the new administration.

Right now, Clinton was taking a victory lap. He was in the capital for only three days to talk with still-president George Bush, see leaders of the Senate and House and be guest of honor at two dinner parties. The first was a small, select affair at the northwest Washington home of Ann Jordan and Vernon Jordan, the new president's transition chief, a millionaire lawyer-lobbyist who did not take a job in the administration.

The jockeying for invitations had been brutal, but Jordan, the country's most powerful African American, was resolute. Only forty attended and some of those who had not made the cut left town, or said they had, to avoid embarrassment. The second dinner was at Pamela's. A guest at Jordan's, she too wanted a tiny gathering but had been beaten down by the crush of Democrats frantic to be part of the celebration marking the end of their long exile in the political wilderness. It was harder for Pamela to keep her list down because she knew far more people.

Katharine Graham, neighbor and chairman of the Washington Post Company, was there, ready at seventy-five to hand off her title as America's most powerful woman to Hillary Rodham Clinton. So was Bob Strauss, once Washington's premier power broker, a former Democratic party chairman who had just up and quit as Republican Bush's ambassador to Moscow to fly home for the festivities. Clark Clifford, a tarnished prince indicted (but never brought to trial) for his alleged involvement in a banking scandal, was absent, but everybody else who was anybody in the Democratic party was in the Harriman home. Speaker of the

House Tom Foley huddled with Senate majority leader George Mitchell and Lee Hamilton, head of the House Foreign Relations Committee.

Lawyer Warren Christopher, Senator Lloyd Bentsen and Congressman Les Aspin grinned and told guests they didn't know if they would be named secretary of state, treasury and defense. Less than a month later, they were.

Over by *The Blue Hat*, painted by Matisse in 1944, stood one of Pamela's own foreign policy advisers, Washington lawyer Samuel "Sandy" Berger. Within days, Clinton named him deputy national security adviser. Joseph Biden, chairman of the Senate Judiciary Committee, that gaggle of out-of-touch men who botched the hearings of U.S. Supreme Court nominee Clarence Thomas, lobbied new senator Dianne Feinstein to join his panel and get outraged Anita Hill supporters off his back. She said she would, and did.

Over by *Mother and Child*, a 1922 Picasso, was Evangeline Bruce, widow of diplomat David Bruce, America's postwar ambassador to France and a special envoy for President Kennedy. Holding court near the fireplace was the Reverend Jesse Jackson, whom Clinton had stiff-armed throughout the year-long campaign for the White House. In victory, Jackson was in the fold. He was off to Arkansas on the weekend to preach in Little Rock and talk with the president-elect, maybe get a sense of what he might expect, if anything.[2]

Clutching the president-elect's hand, Pamela led Clinton from room to room, her own aura parting the crowd, past the artwork for which museum directors slaver, past the seven-foot-tall sterling torchères and huge vases of tulips and potted amaryllis on a Louis XIV porcelain jardinière, past the Gardner Cox portrait of her late husband Averell Harriman and the silver-framed photographs of him with Stalin and Churchill at Yalta, past the eighteenth-century hand-painted Chinese wallpaper removed with meticulous care from an English estate and flown to Washington, past the muted chintz sofa with the needlepoint pillow that read: "Be reasonable. Do things MY way."

Pamela and the president glided, smiling and laughing, from

Senators Joe Lieberman and Bob Graham to Dale Bumpers, Barbara Mikulski and D.C. mayor Sharon Pratt Kelly and on through a progression of congressmen and congresswomen and top party operatives. Clinton knew almost everyone. The few he didn't, Pamela introduced. These high and mighty were all her friends.

She had known Vangie Bruce since the 1940s, when Pamela was living in France with Gianni Agnelli, later head of the Fiat auto empire and Europe's most prominent businessman. Kay Graham had been a pal from the 1960s. Pam and then-husband Leland Hayward, the theatrical agent and Broadway producer of such hits as *Gypsy* and *The Sound of Music*, had flown to Washington for visits in Leland's plane, the showman at the controls. Shortly after Leland died in 1971, Kay hosted a dinner party at her Georgetown home which reunited Pam and multimillionaire statesman Averell Harriman, a recent widower then almost eighty.

That Averell was twenty-eight years her senior meant nothing to Pam. Within three months she married the former railroad titan, ambassador to Moscow and London and 1952 and 1956 presidential candidate. Their age spread felt wider in 1941 when she was twenty-one, daughter of an English baron and married to the only son of British prime minister Winston Churchill, and Harriman was forty-nine, married and in Britain to run the Lend-Lease program for Franklin D. Roosevelt.

With the German Luftwaffe pounding London, the evening they met they sought refuge in each other's arms in Harriman's ground-floor suite in the Dorchester Hotel at the first blare of the air raid sirens. Comforted and stimulated by the statesman, she found irresistible the invitation to spend the night under his down coverlet. Their two-year wartime affair gave extra meaning to the so-called Special Relationship that bound the United States and Roosevelt to Britain and Churchill.

Pamela knew most of the other politicians mingling in the house from the 1980s when she chaired her own PAC, or political action committee, an organization that raises money for like-minded candidates for office. She launched "Democrats for the 80's," promptly dubbed PamPAC, in 1980 just after Ronald Reagan trounced Jimmy Carter so badly that the Democrats lost control of the U.S. Senate for the first time since 1954. Rarely had the party's fortunes seemed so desperate, its future so bleak. "Those were the dark, dark days," said Speaker Foley.[3]

Elder statesman Averell was by then eighty-nine, deaf, partially crippled and fading. Mentored by Strauss and Clifford, Pamela picked up Averell's baton and opened her house for thousand-dollar-a-plate dinners at which leading Democrats discussed with contributors from around the country an entire spectrum of policy issues, from defense spending to welfare reform. Over the next decade, she collected close to $12 million which she carefully doled out to candidates, many of whom sought help in the same living room Bill Clinton was working this night.

Most of the money had gone to Democrats seeking Senate seats. Smaller amounts were set aside for candidates for the U.S. House of Representatives and governors' mansions. Pamela rarely became involved in presidential races, until Clinton. As governor of Arkansas, he had been an early member of the PamPAC board of directors. But Clinton was not Pamela's original candidate for president in 1992. She doubted that he could win. She found him very bright, but also slick, just as his critics claimed, and too facile. His zipper problem would keep him out of 1600 Pennsylvania Avenue, she had told some of those same friends who were reaching out in her living room to grab his hand and pat his back.

By November 20, 1992, the night of her buffet reception for the new president, Pamela was far more than the enormously wealthy widow of Averell Harriman. The plump redhead who played cards late into the night with Winston Churchill, the captivated father-in-law she called "Papa," was now, a half century later, on the arm of the president of the United States. She had triumphed.

She looked fabulous, almost breathtaking, in an understated black Bill Blass dress and sporting, in addition to her saxophone pin, a modest double strand of pearls and slightly flashier pearl-and-diamond earrings. She was seventy-two but looked in her mid-fifties and had the energy of a forty-year-old. Her posture was regal. Her rich, now-blond hair had not a strand out of place but brushed up and out of her face still managed to look soft.

Her complexion was ivory with just a hint of blush, so impeccable that her very light makeup looked natural. Her smile can appear too practiced, but tonight it was wonderfully wide and guileless. Her voice is erogenous and can skip across the scales of an aural keyboard, one moment sounding like the clink of polished sterling on a Waterford goblet, the next, like the soft, popping bubbles of the Pol Roger inside.

Tonight, her voice was low, with a sexy, croaky catch that had guests leaning close to digest every practiced syllable. The eyes shone with twinkles. She was having great fun. Pamela comes alive with powerful people and these were the most powerful anywhere. It was her home; she was hosting and they were all there because of what she and her guest of honor had accomplished. She was absolutely vibrant.

Of course, she was more than a hostess. Call her that and the blue eyes blanched gray like a North Sea ice storm and her lips flattened tight against her teeth. She considered herself a woman of substance and, in recent years, she had earned the sobriquet.

Notepad and silver pen in hand, she had sat to the bitter end of every policy conference, no matter how arcane or boring the discussion or overheated the room. She had led private delegations to Russia and China, met senior officials and returned home and written op-ed page articles for the *New York Times* and *Washington Post*. At least her byline ran over the pieces. She was a member of the prestigious Council on Foreign Relations.

Historians, political scientists and writers graced her weekend estate in Virginia's hunt country and her vacation homes in Sun Valley, Idaho, and Barbados. Sometimes, members of Averell's family would be invited, usually when she was not there. Not Leland's offspring, though. Too painful. Too much bitterness lingered from those past ties.

But here, with the president-elect on her arm, she was precisely where she had always wanted to be — at the center of the best political action she could find. For her years of unremitting labor in the Democrats' dark political wilderness, President Clinton thanked her and raised a gold-rimmed crystal champagne flute: "To Pamela, the First Lady of the Democratic Party." Hear-hears echoed through the house. Hillary smiled and applauded with everyone else.

Pamela tossed her head back in delight. Her eyes crinkled at the corners and her teeth gleamed. She was thrilled. She had every right to be. What a night she was having. What a life she'd had.

CHAPTER ONE

🗿 🗿

Everard and Jane

DORSET is the rural England of romantic epics, a verdant, sensuous county of mystic heaths, baronial estates and family lineages traced to the Roman Conquest. Dorset is the river Stour and meandering brooks, cutting through pastures of fat cows and lilacs and past earthwork tombs from the neolithic age. Dorset is the weekend shoot and hunt balls with liveried servants unpacking guests' satin or tulle gowns, black dinner jackets and starched white collars.

Dorset is Thomas Hardy country, home of the novelist who interlaced the tangled Victorian lives of local families with the brooding, primeval landscape. The ring at Casterbridge in *The Mayor of Casterbridge* was the ancient Roman amphitheater in Dorchester, Dorset's largest city and railhead. Weatherbury Farm in *Far from the Madding Crowd* was Waterston Manor, "a hoary building of the Jacobean stage . . . the manorial hall upon a small estate." Miss Charmond's Hintock House in *The Woodlanders* was Minterne Magna.

"To describe it as standing in a hollow would not express the situation of the manor house; it stood in a hole, notwithstanding that the hole was full of beauty," Hardy wrote in 1887. "The front of the house exhibited an ordinary manorial presentation of Elizabethan windows, mullioned and hooded, worked in rich, snuff-colored freestone from local quarries." So serenely did the house occupy its hollow that sheep grazing on the hillside "as they ruminated looked quietly into the bedroom windows."[1]

If they could have seen inside, they might have spotted a plump little girl with a captivating smile and a head of red curls, for Dorset and Minterne Magna is where Pamela Digby grew up in the idyllic years between the two World Wars. Minterne nestles in a lush valley in the heart of Dorset between Dorchester and Sherborne. Two miles south of the estate, above the tiny town of Cerne Abbas, is one of the county's most famous sights: The Giant, a four-thousand-year-old drawing of a man with a nine-foot erection cut from the springy turf into the chalk hillside, a prehistoric fertility symbol engraved like modern graffiti. As a child, Pamela used to leap the phallus on her horse. " 'God, it's big,' she would say," recalled Lady Edith Foxwell, a riding friend from childhood. "She couldn't have been more than twelve."[2]

Minterne dates to the fourteenth century. The Church of St. Andrew at the entrance gate to the Digbys' manor house lists rectors from Walter Hudd in 1350 through Derek Jackson in 1989. The house belonged to the monastery at Cerne, which in 1551 turned it over to the warden of Winchester College. The college leased the property to a succession of obscure tenants until the early 1600s, when it was sold, in what would later be considered quite a coincidence, to London lawyer John Churchill.

The Churchills were royalists in the 1642–49 Civil War in which Puritan leader Oliver Cromwell overthrew the monarchy and Parliament ruled Britain. Parliamentary fines ravaged the family coffers during the war, but John's son fought bravely for the Crown against the Roundheads and was knighted: the first Sir Winston Churchill, the great-great-great-great-great-great-great-grandfather of the World War II leader. He expected Charles II would restore the family treasures. When only a fraction were returned, he adopted as the family motto: *Fiel pero desdichado*, or "Faithful but unhappy."

The first Winston had four children. John, who became the

Duke of Marlborough, was Britain's leading military commander. Not only was he undefeated in ten campaigns on the Continent, he was never repelled from a single fortress to which he laid siege. In 1704, he commanded his younger brother Charles, an infantry general, along with the combined English, German, Dutch and Danish armies to victory over the forces of France's Louis XIV at the Battle of Blenheim on the Danube in Bavaria.[3]

Charles rose to distinguished heights himself. His reputation as one of Europe's best commanders of foot soldiers led to his being named general of the army, governor of Brussels and of the island of Guernsey. Third son George became a Royal Navy admiral, while the sole daughter, Arabella, was mistress to King James II and mother of the king's bastard son.

When he died in 1688, Winston left Minterne Magna to Charles, much to the annoyance of John, who, according to a three-hundred-year-old family joke, had to make do with Blenheim Palace, named for his victory, where in 1874 the modern era's Winston Churchill was born.

The Digbys took over Minterne in 1768. Admiral Robert Digby, younger son of the seventh Baron Digby of nearby Sherborne Castle, bought the estate from Charles Churchill's executors. The Digbys were a colorful clan, a captivating collection of handsome nonconformists, heroes and heroines, villains and swashbuckling adventurers. The family traced its ancestry to Edward the Confessor, the Saxon king who ruled England for a quarter century until his death in 1066.

John Digby served as King James I's ambassador to Spain in the early 1600s. As a reward for "services to the Crown," he was permitted to buy Sherborne Castle, whose owner, Sir Walter Raleigh, was convicted of treason for attempting to kill the king.

Ironically, another Digby was trying to do the same thing, quite independent of Raleigh. The family's blackest sheep, Sir Everard Digby, was a Catholic convert who conspired with Guy Fawkes to blow up the House of Lords and King James I at the State Opening of Parliament in 1605 with thirty-six barrels of powder hidden under the chambers.

Raleigh, who was not involved in the Gunpowder Plot, was thrown into the Tower of London, eventually reprieved and released, only to be executed years later. Sir Everard's fate was sealed more quickly. Captured and also sent to the Tower, the twenty-eight-year-old was hanged, drawn and quartered. Legend has it that when the executioner plucked out his heart and gave the traditional cry to the crowd, "Here is the heart of a traitor," the dead lips of the unyielding Everard replied, "Thou liest."[4]

Everard's son was Kenelm Digby. Nearly three hundred years later, Pamela's father was named for him. The original Kenelm was three when his father was executed, only the first of a succession of hurdles he battled to overcome. For his Catholicism at Oxford in the 1620s, a religion his namesake would shun, he was ostracized, forbidden to wear academic gowns and prohibited from pursuing an academic degree. He was intelligent, though, and became a favorite of his teachers, one of whom bequeathed him a library of rare manuscripts. As a teenager, Digby fell in love with the beautiful and older Venetia Stanley, who had a reputation for being "sanguine and tractable and of much suavity."

The widowed Lady Digby tried to break off the romance by sending young Kenelm off to the Continent. In France, Marie de Medici, the forty-seven-year-old queen, developed such a crush on the teenager that Kenelm, in an effort to end her pursuit, spread the rumor that he had died. He fled to Italy and studied art and science in Florence, where Galileo befriended him. Venetia, who heard and believed the stories of his death, became the mistress of a married man and bore a child.

Kenelm returned to England and, over the protests of his mother, married Venetia anyway. Unlike many of his contemporaries, Digby did not regard bridal chastity as an imperative. "What discreet man," he asked, "ever threw away a fair and rich garment for having a small spot in one corner?"

An adventurer and a poet, he sailed to Syria, was knighted by the king his father tried to kill and jailed as a royalist during the Civil War. Like so many Digbys, Kenelm had a knack for promotion. He ended a full life best known for touting the "powder of substance," a balm supposed to heal wounds without direct application to the skin.

"Something in all the Digbys caused them to win renown by being at odds with society," wrote Kenelm's biographer, R. T.

Petersson. "The Digbys possessed a power of illusion within and a flair for theatricality without which made them seem, at moments, to be heroes in the world. In reality, they were not heroes but players in subordinate roles. They acted not so much greatly as grandly, always appearing, somehow, where important things were happening."[5]

The first "Lord" Digby, kin to Kenelm, was an elder Robert than the one who took over Minterne Magna. This Robert was created an Irish peer, of Geashill, in 1620. Digbys were not British peers until the seventh baron was ennobled in 1765, a distinction of major import to other peers, genealogists and the parents of marriageable aristocrats, if few others. The Robert Digby who purchased Minterne did not have the title, but he did set a family precedent that would be followed a century later by Lord Randolph Churchill, father of Britain's wartime leader. He married an American — Eleanor Elliott, daughter of the governor of New York — whom he met while commanding the Royal Navy's North American fleet. His share of the prize money his frigates captured from French and Spanish treasure ships gave him the stake to buy and rebuild Minterne.

The estate was in terrible condition when Robert bought it in 1768. He was so unenthusiastic about the property that it is unclear why he bothered to make the purchase. A good-sized mansion by any standard, but not a grand house by British baronial measure, the property's attraction may simply have been that it was cheap and close to the relatives at Sherborne Castle, only a few miles north.

For the landed gentry, it was a golden era. Twenty years earlier, Henry Fielding had captured the rollicking spirit in his masterful novel *Tom Jones,* a ribald tale of country squires, bawdy servants and intrigue over inheritances. (When the book became the movie which won the 1963 Academy Award for Best Picture, exterior shots were filmed at Minterne Magna.)

There was little boisterousness in Robert when he first saw the property. "The estate compact, but naked and the trees not thriving," he wrote. "The house ill-contrived and ill-situated." The Churchills had owned the house, but not the freehold on the property. Appearances notwithstanding, Digby bought it all and within weeks he became a committed fixer-upper. He landscaped, planted beeches and, in the kind of frustration that can be heard from any modern-day estate owner from Beverly Hills to the south of France, lamented that he was "determined to get rid of my gardener as soon as possible."[6]

By the end of the eighteenth century, the property was transformed. Two puny fishponds became a lovely lake and the meadows were turned into grazing land. A gracious stone bridge was built and a waterfall created to aerate the stream. Digby moved the main road west and refashioned the house, which was then an irregular horseshoe shape with a north-south alignment, to a more symmetrical design laid out on an east-west line and straddling the valley.

There were no children from Robert and Eleanor's marriage, so in 1815 Minterne passed to Robert's nephew Sir Henry Digby. Like Robert, Henry was an admiral, but the similarity ended there. He did little to improve the estate. On land, Henry was at sea.

Thomas Creevey, a well-known diarist of the Regency period, called Henry "a dull dog at dinner," yet he was anything but dull aboard ship. By the time he moved to Minterne Magna, Henry had had a phenomenal career. He was one of Nelson's captains at Trafalgar, the 1805 battle which destroyed France's fleet and ended Napoleon's sea power. Nelson's words at the beginning of the battle against the allied French and Spanish fleets — "England expects that every man will do his duty" — became immortal.

Henry did pretty well himself. Commanding the sixty-four gun *Africa*, the smallest ship in the battle, he accidentally made a wrong turn in the middle of the fleet, baffled the enemy and took out the most powerful warship, the 140-gun *Santissima Trinidada*.

Gunships were glory and Parliament gave him a gold medal. But Henry's specialty was treasure ships and gold in larger measure, by the ingot and bag. Robert launched the plunder business. By Trafalgar, Henry had made it an art. He joined the navy at fifteen. By twenty-five, he commanded the frigate *Aurora*, which seized dozens of ships, earning a large share of the spoils for himself and his crew.

He was sailing aboard the *Alcimene* between Portugal and the Azores in 1779 when he heard a disembodied, insistent voice,

"Digby, go north." Henry ignored the suggestion, but in the middle of the night, unable to sleep, he ordered the helmsman to change course. At dawn, he captured a silver-laden Spanish galleon and, in no time, two Spanish frigates.

By the time he was thirty, Henry had amassed a fortune. Sailors, normally press-ganged into service, fought to join Henry's crew and gain a share of his loot. He obliged with fifty-seven trophies, or seized ships, the richest of which was Spain's *Santa Brigada*, enroute to the Americas laden with gold coins when Henry captured it in 1799.

Henry was known until then as "the Silver Captain." His nickname did not change, but his gold plunder, according to family members, was the largest sum ever captured by the Royal Navy. Henry's share was forty thousand pounds sterling, $10 million at current exchange rates, one-third of his career spoils. The family kept a bag of the coins at Minterne until 1914, when they donated all but one doubloon to the World War I effort.

Henry's seamanship filled the family coffers and burnished the Digby name in Britain, but it was his daughter Jane who put the family on tongues in every corner of the Empire. Jane Digby was to the nineteenth century what Pamela Digby would be to the twentieth. Jane's love life titillated and scandalized Victorian Britain.

Like Pamela's, her husbands and lovers were rich, famous, exotic and scattered all over the map. Unlike Pamela, she paid her own way. Pamela loves Jane's story and never tires of telling — and retelling — the tale. On holidays, sitting on a terrace or by the pool, she has been known to pull out a biography of Jane and read it aloud. Some guests muttered that sure, it was a good story, but they had heard it before. In some cases, several times.

For Pamela, though, there was no such thing as too much of Jane. To her, growing up and staring at pictures on the back stairs of Minterne of a lovely red-haired woman on a white horse, Jane was a wonder. Pamela is terribly proud of her and loves hearing comparisons with this ancestor with whom she has shared so much.

There were no early hints of what lay in store for Jane. Her childhood was much like that of any young aristocrat in George

IV's regency. Born in 1807, she grew up with ponies and dogs, cosseted by nurses, domestics and governesses. Unschooled but a natural beauty, Jane was married off at seventeen to the earl of Ellenborough, twice her age and, on paper, a great catch.

The marriage was a disaster, a remarkable precursor to what would happen a century later to Pamela and Randolph Churchill. "Blasé, prematurely middle-aged and cynical," the unpopular Ellenborough was a run-around who so neglected his young bride that she found companionship elsewhere.[7]

At nineteen she had her first affair, with a twenty-seven-year-old cataloguer from the British Museum. He was entranced, but did not last long, out of place in Jane's aristocratic social circle. She dumped him and took up with her cousin, an Army colonel. They were seen everywhere around London, where gossip about the two was incessant.

Not that adultery and musical beds were uncommon diversions in those years. Among patricians, promiscuity was rampant, but it did have rules. Ladies, who were identifiable by their clothes, hairstyle, bearing and manner of speech, were always under observation, especially in London. Discretion mattered. As Mrs. Patrick Campbell once explained famously, "It doesn't matter what you do in the bedroom as long as you don't do it in the street and frighten the horses."[8]

Because there was little privacy in the city, dalliances tended to take place on weekends at country houses. Some affairs were long-standing and well known and hostesses took care when making room assignments to insert the proper namecards into the small brass frames on each door. Putting known lovers at opposite ends of sleeping quarters would never do. Nor was an eligible single man knowingly assigned a room on a corridor housing wives who were believed to be sleeping with their husbands.

When the lights went out, figures could be spotted gliding through the halls seeking regular or new companions for the night. An hour before dawn, a butler would appear in the corridor, strike a gong once and depart. Within minutes, shadowy figures would reappear in the hallway, making their way back to their original rooms. Pamela took a lighthearted view of such escapades. "They went to bed a lot with each other, but they were all cousins, so it didn't really count."[9]

When Jane was sharing her favors outside the bounds of even distant family, society was in ferment. The Industrial Revolution was imminent and a precursive sense of change could be felt. The arts were in full flower. Blake, Coleridge and Keats wrote. Constable and Turner painted. However indulgent the age, Jane crossed the line when she fell desperately in love with Prince Felix Schwarzenberg, assigned to Austria's embassy in London. Not only did her carriage sit for hours outside his Harley Street house, but they were spotted at the Norfolk Hotel in Brighton. Each incident was an absolute violation of aristocratic etiquette.

The gossips had a field day. "Anything so impudent as she, or so barefaced as the whole thing, I never beheld," wrote diarist Creevey.[10]

The prince inadvertently introduced a new word to the language: cad. Wits noted that a horse named Cadland had beaten the favorite, Colonel, in the Derby just as Schwarzenberg had nipped Lady Ellenborough's cousin, the colonel.

The earl sued for divorce, a procedure so expensive and complex, involving a private act of Parliament, that on average only two a year were granted. Jane had produced an heir, by whom no one was certain. The prince was reassigned to Paris. Jane pursued him. She was "Passion's Child," like Haidee in Byron's masterpiece "Don Juan," which was published in 1824, the year Jane married Ellenborough.

Exiled from Britain for an incestuous love affair with his half-sister, Byron created the Romantic Age's new hero, a proud, passionate lover who broke the rules which constrained spirits.[11] According to Margaret Fox Schmidt, Jane's biographer in *Passion's Child*, "it was this hero Jane sought all her life, little realizing that she was the female counterpart."

In Paris, Jane was infamous, a star. The whiff of scandal about her fascinated Parisian society. Jane had two chidren by Schwarzenberg before the prince's passion waned. Her divorce from Ellenborough came through. But the prince was Catholic. His career could be threatened. His family warned him to break off the relationship and he did, the cad.

His departure was made easier by Jane's own flowering. Because she and Schwarzenberg were unmarried, Jane was often barred from social events. Left alone, this pretty and charming English aristocrat with a past found it easy to infiltrate the intellectual crowd. She saw Hugo, Dumas, and Balzac, who slept with Jane and wrote her character into *La Comédie Humaine*.

Abandoning her children, she quit Paris for Munich, where she became the mistress of King Ludwig of Bavaria. He was excited by Greece and introduced her to classic, Hellenic art. They remained close even after Jane took up with his son Otho, king of Greece. Back in England, Jane's exploits horrified the Digbys, who turned her picture to the wall at Minterne and forbade that her name be spoken.

They would be so outraged that when they inherited her diaries, which Jane wrote in English, French and Latin, they pulled out and burned all but the first and last twenty pages. Pamela was not allowed to read them as a child but later loved to pore over the bits that survived, reading the English excerpts so often that she could recite some passages verbatim.

Pamela gets a dreamy, distant look in her eye when considering the diaries. Sometimes, the stories feel familiar, almost as though she had lived her own life once before. Jane's recorded thoughts before she married her final husband resonate in Pamela. In one passage, Jane mused how she had had so much, so many great moments and great loves, yet each time she thought she was finally settled with the one great love of her life, the affair soured and the relationship collapsed. In near lament, she wrote of wondering what would happen next. Several days later, her innate optimism had returned. Forget the disappointments. All that mattered was to love and to hope. Each new love that came along would be the love of her life.[12]

Pamela shares Jane's philosophy. Her siblings call Pamela today's Jane, but the real Jane's immediate family were neither romantics nor amused by their daughter's carryings-on.

It was a relief for them when, in 1832, Jane married one of Ludwig's courtiers, Baron Carl-Theodore von Venningen, and settled down — briefly. She had two children by Venningen, who adored her, but in no time she was bored with life as a Munich matron.

At a court ball where Ludwig entertained the newly crowned Otho and his Greek courtiers, she met Count Spyridon Theotoky, a dashing Byronic figure. The predictable affair followed, capped by a duel in which Jane's husband shot her lover in the chest. The wound appeared fatal until Jane dried her tears and nursed Theotoky back to health with the kind of devotion Pamela would later expend on two husbands.

Jane took off again for a new life and marriage with Theotoky in Paris and Greece, where King Otho resumed his pursuit. Children and monogamy did not matter to Jane. Men and horses mattered. She was the delight of Athens to all but Otho's Queen Amalie, who, perhaps understandably, was jealous.

When Jane's fourteen-year-old son by Theotoky sleepwalked out the window and accidentally killed himself, the marriage was destroyed. Otho replaced Theotoky as aide-de-camp with an Albanian general, Xristodolous Hadji-Petros, with whom Jane next lived. He was penniless, but as well as paying her own way Jane paid, when necessary, her lover's.

The Albanian liaison ended when Jane discovered that the general was more interested in her money than her love. Pressing east, she sailed to Syria, ostensibly to buy an Arabian horse. The one she found was attached to a sheikh, Abdul Medjuel el Mezrab, who fell in love with Jane while consummating the sale.

The mistress of kings made a deal. She agreed to pay full price for the animal and marry Medjuel if he gave up his harem. She would be sole wife for three years. After that, the contract could be renewed or abandoned. He agreed and they lived together with the bedouin in the desert and in Damascus. Her Arabian horses accompanied her everywhere and wherever she stayed, Jane planted an English garden.

The Honorable Jane Digby el Mezrab, as she was known, became fluent in Arabic, her ninth language, and was respected as a tribal queen, a role her descendant Pamela would one day play. Medjuel was faithful when Jane was present and she responded with adoration. Like a chameleon, she completely assumed the characteristics of her latest love and environment.

She rode with Medjuel into battle, her eyes blackened desert-style with kohl. In their tent, she cooked his food, washed his hands and feet, and stood and waited while he ate. In short, she ran a wonderful home for her exotic, sun-burnished lover and, to the astonishment of Arabs and English alike, the arrangement worked. For more than twenty years they remained married, until her death and burial in Damascus in 1881.

She returned to England only once to see the family at Minterne and meet her lawyers to put Medjuel in her will. She had written wonderful letters but had not been home in thirty years, since the Schwarzenberg affair. The family was astonished. Despite spending so much time in the desert sun, Jane's skin was soft, unlined and creamy white. Her teeth looked like pearls. With no recourse to the still uninvented wonders of plastic surgery, she looked but half her age.

She had fared better than Minterne, which her older brother Edward inherited in 1863. He did little to improve the estate, but by the 1880s, the pace of activity at Minterne picked up. The last years of the nineteenth century were glory days for Dorset. Seventeen families each owned more than 7,000 acres and, all told, controlled 218,000 acres, more than one-third of the county. The Digbys were not among them. They were comfortable on their then 2,000 acres, but Henry's gold was gone and the Digbys were not in the top rank of wealthy landholders. Still, they were not far off.

An 1872 survey, midway through the reign of Queen Victoria, showed that 80 percent of British land belonged to fewer than seven thousand people, a category which did include the Digbys.[13]

Near the apex of Empire, Britain's influence extended everywhere. The Hooker expedition to the Himalayas brought rhododendrons to Minterne, the start of a collection which made the Digby gardens famous in the twentieth century. Rare seedlings from 1903 expeditions to China and Tibet thrived, the result of a peculiar local ecosystem which deposits forty-two inches of rain a year on Minterne's valley, ten inches more than on neighboring properties.

The renown of the gardens was not matched by the quality of the manor house. Minterne had deteriorated by the turn of the century. In early 1902, Emily Digby, wife of the tenth baron, wrote in her diary that "a horrible smell turned up in the middle of last night which we think must be a dead rat in the wall, but we cannot trace it."[14] Worse than rodents, dry rot was diagnosed. The manor house was demolished and while 130 workmen labored daily on reconstruction for the next five years, the Digbys moved to their London townhouse on Belgrave Square, returning regularly to supervise.

Rebuilt on the same site from apricot-colored local stone, the new Minterne Magna displayed a dreary Gothic north side when the family returned for good in 1907. Little sun struck the ashlar walls where the drive entered the property. At first sight today from the entrance, the four-story manor house squats like a large toad on the end of a diving board. No vegetation breaks the harsh line where wall meets the packed ground. Like a shallow cave, the entrance door is recessed under an arch, forbidding on winter days.

Better to arrive on foot through copses of bluebells to the south, where light bathes the softer Elizabethan facade, or in the moonlight, when cries of Hardy's nightjar spill across the garden to the pond at the foot of the hillside.

CHAPTER TWO

❦ ❦

Pansy and Carnation

PAMELA BERYL DIGBY lived a fairytale childhood at Minterne Magna. The valley was small, green and snug. The property was ancient and redolent with history, but the house itself was almost new, fresh and clean. In contrast to the formal and forbidding interiors of many large country houses, Minterne was airy, yet also warm and cozy. Light poured in through windows on the east and south fronts and while the house was well furnished, it was with an eye more to comfort than to ostentation. The exception was a spectacular set of four Dutch and French tapestries given to Charles Churchill when he was governor of Brussels and left behind when the house was sold to the Digbys.

Pamela was not born at Minterne. Her parents were living just south of London in Kent at Farnborough when she was born on March 20, 1920, the first of four children. She was wrapped in heated towels and placed in the bottom drawer of a chest of drawers which served as a temporary crib until she moved to Minterne, where a nursery, toys, starched linens and cottons and a nanny awaited. Her parents had married on July 1, 1919, eight months and three weeks previously.

Father was Edward Kenelm Digby, a twenty-five-year-old captain in the Coldstream Guards who stayed in the army at the end of World War I. He was stationed at Farnborough, just a few miles from the Biggin Hill airfield. Ken Digby, as he was known then, was a much-decorated soldier, a legitimate war hero. He looked the part. Slat-thin, ramrod-straight and six feet one inch tall with red hair and piercing blue eyes, in 1914 he was sworn into the elite infantry force whose members don red coats and bearskins and guard Buckingham Palace.

The following year, Digby was commissioned a lieutenant when the other officers in his unit were killed in France by German troops and he assumed command. At that time, he was the youngest ever to lead a Coldstream battalion, a situation brought about by an extraordinary number of officer fatalities in the war. The Oxford University graduates of 1913 suffered a 31 percent casualty rate and the 20 percent death toll among the peerage was the highest since the fifteenth-century Wars of the Roses.[1]

Digby moved up to captain in 1917 and eventually became a Coldstream colonel with such decorations as a Distinguished Service Order, the French croix de guerre and a double military cross. Although he survived without serious injury, the war took its toll.

Digby was so emaciated when he returned to Dorset from the trenches in Flanders that doctors informed him that he would die within months if he did not force himself to eat. He heeded them, later becoming quite the portly squire with a ruddy complexion and paternal smile, though even these did not invite excessive familiarity with his staff or children.

Mother was The Honorable Constance Pamela Alice Bruce, the youngest daughter of three girls and three sons of the second Baron Aberdare, a wealthy peer who owned coal-mining rights in the Aberdare valley in Wales. Pansy, as friends called the elder Pamela, had no formal schooling and met Ken during the war when she worked as a nurse in Middlesex Hospital. She was five feet five inches tall and full figured, with brown hair, a firm jaw and prominent nose. Steel-gray eyes bore into mischievous children, warning that maternal instructions were to be followed without hesitation.

The year Pamela was born, Ken Digby's father died. As the eldest son, he inherited Minterne as well as a seat in the House of Lords, which was then dominated by conservative land-owning aristocrats much like himself. The three Digbys moved into the ancestral seat, but not for long. Death duties had been in effect before the First World War, but the need to finance four years of bloody fighting on the Continent meant that tax rates on everyone, especially the upper class, began shooting up in 1915. Taxes more than quintupled between 1914 and 1918 — from 8 percent to 43 percent — on those making over ten thousand pounds a year. The wealthy paid only 15 percent taxes on unearned income of ten thousand pounds or more before the war; 50 percent when it was over.

Taxes were far more worrisome to the aristocracy than the Bolshevik Revolution which had just toppled the Czarist monarchy in Russia. Socialism was a future threat; taxes, a current agony which menaced not only inherited fortunes but the political power inherent in wealth. The duke of Devonshire, whose Chatsworth was one of Britain's finest estates, packed with treasures and great master paintings, felt such postwar tax pressure that he sold the family's house on London's Piccadilly for a million pounds to preserve the country acreage. The purchasers planned to build a cinema, dance hall and tea room complex, a signal of how quickly times were changing in the capital.

Death duties on estates struck the coldest fear into aristocratic hearts when they skyrocketed to 40 percent.[2] There were tax advantages to working overseas, so in 1921 the new eleventh Baron Digby signed on as military secretary to Lord Forster, the governor general of Australia. Pamela was not quite eighteen months old when she sailed through the Suez Canal on the six-week voyage to Australia. In the absentee fashion common to well-to-do English families, who spent little time with their children, the Digbys did not sail with their daughter. Pamela went with a nanny; they traveled independently via Japan.

The Digbys stayed Down Under for two and a half years, mostly in Melbourne, and moved to Sydney each summer. A loquacious white parrot taught Pamela her first words and established a gift for mimicry that she called on later to emulate the rolling cadences of Winston Churchill and the butter-rich Italian inflections of business mogul Gianni Agnelli. She took her first riding lessons at the age of three under the tutelage of the Ashton brothers, polo players who rode with her father.

A chance event in Australia had an enduring influence on her. One day, leaving Government House with her daughter to ride in their first car, Pansy Digby was unable to open the garage door. She apologized to Pam and explained that the trip would have to be postponed. Pamela would have none of it. She pouted, refusing to budge from the car. She wanted the ride then and there. There was no one in the garage, no one outside. But perhaps hearing the same voice that a century earlier had advised Henry Digby to sail north, Pam told her mother that a man would come and solve their predicament.

Not a chance, darling. There is no one here.

A defiant Pam was insistent. She did not know how or why, but she was positive that a man would arrive to assist them.

Suddenly, a policeman appeared around the corner. He had heard a noise. Could he help? Pansy looked astonished. Pamela squealed with delight. As an adult, she felt certain that an intrinsic faith in men was ingrained in her that day: somehow, whenever she needed help, she felt confident that a man would turn up to lend a hand.

Her sister Sheila, eighteen months younger, was born in Australia. When their father's assignment ended in late 1923, the two children and nanny sailed back to England. Ken and Pansy returned by way of New Zealand and China, part of a pattern of separation which continued once they returned to Dorset.

Although she was less than four years old on the return trip, Pamela can still feel the heat of the voyage to Cape Town and steaming up the coast of West Africa. In days long before air conditioning, grapes turned to raisins in the cabin fruit basket. Sirens blared one night. A crewman, crazed by the heat below deck, had leaped overboard. The ship was stopping to pull him out.

Disembarking during a refueling stop in Cape Town, she sank her teeth into the leg of a black man on the quay. She had never seen a dark person before and thought he was made of chocolate, like the Easter bunnies she had eaten in Australia. She was hustled back on board while nanny made awkward apologies.

Each day after breakfast, ladies took turns walking the promenade deck with the ship's captain, a striking six-foot-six officer in gleaming whites with a twirled and waxed mustache. They chatted, laughed and seemed to be having an interesting time. After watching for several days, young Pamela could no longer bear being left out. Attention was important to this little girl, who was not getting much notice.

Pamela took matters into her own hands. She walked up and tugged on the captain's sleeve. Would he walk with her too? Of course he would. She reached up to put her arm on his, imitating several of the ladies, and they proceeded soberly around the deck, nodding and greeting the amused passengers. Pamela was delighted. Everyone was watching her. It was much nicer being smiled at than ignored; much more interesting being escorted by a handsome older man that it was playing with the other children on board.

Even at that age, her contemporaries did not interest Pamela. They were dull. They did not defer, think she was special or even pay particular attention to her, so when they weren't looking she threw their toys over the side. When the trip ended, the ship's officers gave her a silver napkin ring for being the best baby aboard.

Nanny knew otherwise and told Pamela she did not deserve the reward. She had seen how Pamela treated the other boys and girls and played up to the officers. Pamela didn't care what nanny or the children thought. She kept the prize.

With the family back at Minterne in 1924 Pamela's only brother, Edward, was born. Four years later, Jacquetta made it three girls. The age gap between Pamela and Jacquetta was only eight years, not much of a spread in many families. But it was enough for Pamela to convince herself that the separation in years plus the onset of war while Jacquetta was still a preteen explained why she and her youngest sister were never close. The arrival of the fourth child completed this Digby generation and, for the most part, a content family it was. The 1920s were glorious years to grow up in rural Britain, an idyllic decade, the last that the country would enjoy.

The nation had suffered terribly in World War I. The empire had lost three million subjects, including nearly a million in Britain alone. Another two million Britons had been wounded. The Island Kingdom had lost 15 percent of its assets and owed $11 billion to European allies and $5 billion to the United States, which the war had transformed into a global power.

War's end brought an increasing number of Americans to Britain, reversing a trend among the wellborn. British nobility had been trolling for years in the American upper classes, especially when family balance sheets needed a boost.

The eighth duke of Marlborough married American Lily Hammersley, a wealthy heiress whose dowry helped repair the roof of Blenheim Palace. The ninth duke also went bride shopping in the United States and brought home Consuelo Vanderbilt, daughter of William Kissam Vanderbilt, the railroad heir and yachtsman. Her prewar dowry was an estimated two million pounds. The marriage contract gave the duke twenty thousand pounds a year plus income from a five-hundred-thousand-pound fund.[3]

In 1915, a German submarine had sunk the British liner *Lusitania* and killed 128 Americans, putting the brakes on the rising transatlantic traffic. But by the early 1920s, Americans were headed back to Europe in force, packing new ocean liners like the speedy and luxurious *Mauretania,* which set a crossing record of twenty-six knots in 1924. Once in Britain, some new arrivals bought fine art or property while others acquired husbands and reputations as resourceful hostesses.[4]

The immediate prospects for Britain after World War I were uncertain. The war was a cosmic divide, but the British upper classes found it difficult to acknowledge the inevitability of change. Instead of confronting a new world order, Britain tried to ignore the reshaped political landscape and looked back with nostalgia and hope that prewar life could be salvaged. George V, who was king throughout Pamela's childhood, held his first postwar levee, a formal court reception for men, the month she was born. "It was refreshing," the relieved monarch noted in his diary, "to see the old full dress uniform again."[5]

Reminiscence took precedence over reality. "Left or right, everybody was for the quiet life," said Sir Robert Vansittart, permanent undersecretary at the Foreign Office. At Oxford University in 1933, the Union debating society caused a national uproar when it resolved 275 votes to 153 that "this House would in no circumstances fight for King and country."

Controversy aside, pacifism was the prevailing mood, inspired in part by books about the horrors of modern war published in the late twenties and early thirties, including Richard Aldington's *Death of a Hero* and Siegfried Sassoon's *Memoirs of an Infantry Officer*.[6]

Pacifist James Ramsay MacDonald, Britain's first Labour party prime minister, was in 10 Downing Street when the Digbys returned from Australia. His successor, Stanley Baldwin, was a caricature of the era's mood: kindly, patient, hating anything that smacked of confrontation. Baldwin felt life was to be savored and enjoyed, watching the sun set, contemplating the serenity of a meadow with the peal of village church bells echoing in the distance.

Few families were more in tune with that mood than the Digbys of Minterne Magna. On their fourteen hundred acres in central Dorset, they lived an upper-class country life, isolated from the bustle and cares of the city. Sherborne was the nearest town, nine miles north. Dorchester was ten miles south, bigger than Sherborne and boasting the train station to London, which was four hours away by rail. For children, London might as well have been the far side of the moon, it seemed so far away. The roads to Minterne were unpaved in the 1920s. The national speed limit was twenty miles an hour and in dry weather clouds of white chalk dust billowed up from passing cars. For the most part, the children did not stray far from the estate.

They grew up isolated and protected, surrounded by a staff that made Minterne not only the biggest local employer, but a self-sufficient complex comprised of the Big House and village. More than twenty domestics worked inside the house: a cook, two kitchen maids and three scullery maids; a separate sweets cook for desserts and jams; a butler, two footmen, a hallboy and valet; Lady Digby's maid, Louisa, a head housemaid and four or five helpers. For the nursery on the fourth floor, where all the children slept, there was a nanny and two nursery maids, fat Cathleen and thin Cathleen. Outside, there were six stable boys, four in the dairy, four more in the laundry, six who dealt with cows and as many as twelve working the garden and fields. Everyone in the the tiny village outside Minterne's stone-and-iron gate worked for the Digbys. Men and boys worked in the garden or stables; women and girls worked inside the house in the kitchen or as upstairs or ladies' maids.

There were separate dining rooms for senior and junior staff. Servants who accompanied guests for the extended weekends were fed and housed according to their own rank. The numbers were phenomenal, but huge numbers of domestics worked in houses throughout Britain. The 1931 census showed that 1.3 million women and 80,000 men were working as household servants, an increase of 100,000 over 1911.[7] Wages rose after the war but were still remarkably low, ranging from twenty-five to fifty pounds a year for parlormaids and cooks.

Because of the age difference, Eddy and Jacquetta were on different schedules with different nannies. Pamela spent most of her time with Sheila. They shared a top-floor room. Exotic dolls in kimonos and other native dress from around the world filled shelves. The sisters kept a box of tortoises from Venice on a window ledge until one evening when their mother came by with houseguests to say good night. One guest warned Pansy that a child's room was no place for the tortoises. Thin Cathleen removed the beasts to a garden hothouse. The next morning, when the girls raced down to check their precious pets, they were horrified. Each had flipped on its back and died. Mixed with the girls' tears was anger that Mummy had not hesitated to side with the guest and had ignored their protestations against the pets' removal.

When Pamela was twelve and Sheila ten, the girls smuggled a pony into an elevator and up to the nursery. The staff was appalled; the governesses, chagrined. Stableboys were summoned to carry the terrified animal down the four flights of stairs. The girls were sent to bed without dinner.

Nine or ten dogs, including Dutch barge dogs, greyhounds and

Labradors, padded around the house and grounds. Pamela's favorite was an Irish wolfhound named Creina, "Darling" in Gaelic, which she took on hour-long walks before breakfast. Walks anywhere, preferably in hills, would be a lifelong pleasure for Pamela, who was exhausting much younger hiking companions when she was well into her seventies.

After dog walking, breakfast for the girls was at 8 A.M. As soon as they finished, there was a quick stop to bid good morning to Mummy and Daddy, who were sitting up in bed having tea and cookies, a wake-me-up before their breakfast at 9:30 A.M. The girls were tutored in English, math, history and sewing until 12:30 or 1 P.M. After lunch, there was usually an afternoon walk or a ride with a stable groom.

On Tuesdays and Fridays in the years 1930 to 1934, Pamela and Sheila, accompanied by Whitelock, the stud groom, would foxhunt with the adults. Dinner for the children was early in the schoolroom, while Lord and Lady Digby dressed for dinner every single night whether there were guests or not: a fresh stiff collar, tie and suit for Ken; a long dress with a high neck but little ornamentation for Pansy. Pamela and Sheila donned starched smocks and joined their parents downstairs for formal tea shortly after 5 P.M. Mummy would read aloud — Kipling, Dickens, Walter Scott — before the girls were hustled off upstairs to bed. Lights-out was at 7 P.M.

On holidays, the children were sometimes taken to Scotland to visit Pansy Digby's sister, Eva, Lady Rosebery, who had a house with a private golf course at Dalmeny, just west of Edinburgh. Accompanied by a lady's maid and nanny toting wicker food baskets, Pansy took the children north by train, filling the wood-paneled first-class compartment. Ken Digby rarely went along. While Pansy was off visiting her family, he went shooting with men friends.

Pansy and the children would also motor around the highlands and lochs and visit her other sister, Margaret, Countess Bradford, whose husband, the fifth earl, was one of Britain's largest landholders. Pamela loved the touring much more than the time with her aunt. Countess Bradford was stone deaf and was forever shouting at the children to speak up, which terrified them.

Countess Bradford's outbursts appear to have helped make Pamela more aware as an adult of the importance of listening carefully and modulating her own voice, a technique that became one of her best-known characteristics. "An eloquent listener" is how the columnist Joseph Kraft described her decades later when asked to define her appeal.[8]

Among the children was Pamela's cousin Lavinia, Eva's eldest daughter, who later married the sixteenth duke of Norfolk, Bernard Marmaduke Fitzalan-Howard. The largely Roman Catholic Norfolks became earls of Arundel — the seat of one of Britain's most spectacular castles, which they own along with fifteen thousand acres — in 1139 and became holders of Britain's oldest dukedom in 1483.[9]

The popularity of golf soared in Scotland in the late 1920s and early 1930s. Sporting friends of the Roseberys gave the girls clubs cut down to their size and lessons which Pamela hated. Forced to play, but frustrated by having little natural hand-eye coordination, she was bored to tears and never took up the sport again.

Scotland was also where Pamela learned to swim. She hated that too. The local instructor was a lifeguard whose technique was to tie a leather belt with a hook around the swimmer's waist, then toss the student out of a rowboat into the numbing cold water of the Firth of Forth. Those who failed to swim were yanked out by a pole which hooked into the belt hook. Pamela learned, but grudgingly, and thereafter restricted her outdoor swimming to heated pools, the south of France, millionaires' yachts in the Aegean and the sun-baked beach alongside her Barbados estate.

On rare occasions, the family visited Ireland. Digbys had owned property there since the early seventeenth century, thanks to King James I. Beginning in 1607, he stepped up pressure to Anglicize the Irish, a process his predecessors Henry VIII and Elizabeth I began a century before. James seized the estates of Irish Catholic earls and handed out huge tracts to English and Scottish colonizers. By 1640, he had seeded Ireland with a hundred thousand Protestant crown royalists, among them the Digbys.

The trip to the Geashill property was always an ordeal. It meant taking a train to Holyhead in western England, switching to a boat for the four-hour journey across the choppy Irish Sea to Dublin, overnighting there in a hotel on the bank of the Liffey, breakfast and finally a car ride to Offaly in central Ireland. Ken Digby often made the journey alone to shoot or handle property matters.

The land was heavily forested and timber sales provided the family with considerable income. In earlier days, when faced with exceptional bills or sudden death duties, the family sometimes sold a patch of the Irish property. None of the family lived there. In 1921, during the struggle for Irish independence, the Irish Republican Brotherhood, forerunner of the Irish Republican Army, burned down the Geashill castle.

Pamela never liked the place. In one sense, she was delighted the castle had been reduced to ruins. Had it not been, she feared that she might have been forced to spend a lot more time in what to her was the middle of nowhere. A few days' stay in the home of the property manager was always plenty. In another sense, though, the destruction of the castle angered her because it meant that the Irish Republicans had destroyed her family's property. The experience left her with a nagging animus toward Ireland. Sheila never felt it and lives in Ireland to this day in Mallow, County Cork, but Pamela has never visited her.

She felt differently about a separate piece of Irish family property, a section of a salmon-fishing river called the Glenamoy in County Mayo in the northwesternmost corner of the Republic. That was gorgeous, an area of great natural beauty inland from the rocky cliffs above the Atlantic, where no malevolent historic spirits permeated the land. Lord Digby and Eddy, Pamela's brother, visited several times a year to fish. Lady Digby and the girls usually went once in the summer, staying in the rural inn at Belmullet, where they ate freshly grilled trout and gamebirds shot on the nearby moors.

Pamela learned a pragmatic lesson from the way her father maintained the secluded property. Poaching almost denuded the property of game until he hired the region's most successful poacher as his gameskeeper. Thereafter at Glenamoy, there were always salmon in the river and grouse on the heath. Ken's refusal to be victimized was a life strategy that Pamela adopted. Later, when she ran houses and built her own English gardens, or had to deal with difficult contractors, thankless stepchildren or re- calcitrant political donors, Ken's daughter recalled the homily from the Irish countryside: Don't sit back and be taken advantage of. Playing victim would never be her style. She preferred taking offensive action to holding back.

Ken and Pansy were almost lampoon characters, the quintes- sential country squire and his tweedy corseted lady, the types featured in *New Yorker* and *Punch* magazine cartoons. English to the core, with a powerful sense of propriety, responsibility and a perpetually stiff upper lip, they were strict with the children and very close and devoted to one another, an upright — and up- tight — country couple. There are no tales of Pansy and Ken Digby corridor-creeping in and out of others' rooms during long shoot- ing weekends.

A teetotaler who got his sugar from an addiction to chocolate, Lord Digby enjoyed riding, shooting, fly-fishing and tending his exotic garden. Those who did not call him "the Milkman," for the family's extensive dairy farming interests, knew him as "Car- nation" Digby for the oversized, fresh, hothouse-raised red car- nation he wore in his lapel whenever he went out.

His interest in gardening and in the land was deeply ingrained, the passion of his life, and he was prominent and expert in each area. He was active for decades in the Royal Horticultural Society and was vice-president of the International Dendrology Union, which studied the science of trees and shrubs. Late in life, he was awarded the Victoria Medal of Honor in horticulture, Britain's top award in a field which consumes large segments of the nation's interest. Another national passion revolved around animals. Digby was up to the top of his Wellington boots in that category as well. Three times president of the National Horse Show, he also headed the National Pony Society, the National Light Horse Breeding Society, the British Society of Animal Production, the English Guernsey Cattle Society and was the only British repre- sentative on the European Zoo Federation, an animal research group.

A shrewd judge of horseflesh from childhood, as a young man he picked two horses to win the 1914 Derby. When the first was disqualified, his second choice was declared the winner. At the 1938 Grand National, he was the sole winning ticket holder of the daily double and pocketed 6,025 pounds, nearly $30,000 at the then rate of exchange, which he used to restore the Minterne chapel and to buy a maroon Buick and a Ford station wagon, colossal vehicles measured against midprice British car models of the day.[10]

His interest in flora, fauna and in maintaining the Minterne estate took up a tremendous amount of time, but in addition, Ken Digby was fully involved in tending to all the duties expected of a landowning peer of the realm. He regularly went to London to attend debates in the House of Lords, where his red-leather seat was only feet away from the spot where his ancestor Sir Everard Digby helped position the gunpowder barrels to blow up the Upper House.

He was a bedrock Conservative, or Tory, genetically as well as by disposition, but a sense of duty far outweighed his limited interest in politics. He felt an enormous responsibility to his nation and monarch, but unlike his eldest daughter in later years, he was far less interested in government and party matters.

Digby's reading was limited almost exclusively to periodicals on horticulture and horses. He had scant time for or interest in history, biography or even the newspapers. He rarely rose to speak in the House of Lords and there were never political discussions — or much general talk at all that involved the children — around the Digby dinner table, not even in the 1930s when the winds of war began swirling over Europe.

"Duty" and service were different from politics. As admirals, generals and the heads of feudal estates, Digbys had been inbred for centuries with the very essence of noblesse oblige, that obligation to honorable and responsible behavior expected from families of high birth or rank and on which the government depended for good order.

A half century later, a similar attitude would be manifest in Pamela when she married Averell Harriman, a railway magnate and patrician Democrat. It was the reason, she said, she was not a Republican. "For me, the Tory party and the Democratic Party were very much alike," she once explained. "You took care of people and you were compassionate."[11]

For a dozen years until his death in 1964, Lord Digby also served as lord lieutenant of Dorset, the queen's representative in the county, responsible for all major ceremonial functions, especially when she visited. The ultimate old boys' network, the concept of lord lieutenancy was instituted by the Tudors to "uphold the dignity of the crown." Five centuries later, the monarch's men still come almost exclusively from the ranks of the upper class and senior military.[12]

Ken's background and temperament made him the obvious choice for what was all part of an ancient code. As Roy Perrott wrote in *The Aristocrats*, "The person inhabiting the Big House in any rural locality, whether sensitive, paternal-minded gentleman or impervious dunderhead, has automatically assumed local leadership without any special need for the central government to jog him into it. The villagers and tenantry have just as automatically accepted it."[13]

For Ken Digby, the responsibility was no burden, but a charge he carried with pleasure and a sense of high honor. In recognition of his devotion and service, Queen Elizabeth II in 1960 created him a Knight of the Garter, the nation's highest honor. Selection to the chivalric order founded in 1348 as a reward for masterful jousting was solely at the monarch's pleasure and membership at any one time was limited to twenty-six persons. When Digby was tapped, he joined Winston Churchill in the coveted circle. That meant Pamela, having married Winston's son, was one of the few women in Britain outside the royal family to have had a father and father-in-law as Garter Knights.

That honor might have meant more to her had she felt closer to her father. Pamela respected him, but even after factoring in the normal separation of upper-class parents from their children, she resented his frequent absences from home and from her life. She had nothing in common with her father and it took her a long time, deep into her adult years, before she began to appreciate him.

A gentle man to outsiders, preoccupied with his flowers and

duties, he was severe and aloof to Pamela, literally distant: a shooting, hunting man's man whom his eldest daughter found almost unapproachable. Some of her contemporaries remain convinced, however unscientifically, that the absence of a strong male figure who focused on her in childhood helps explain why she later sought so assiduously the company of powerful men.

The children saw more of their mother, but not all that much more. An aristocrat in her own right, Mummy too believed in the hands-off approach to child-rearing. She stood back from them for another reason: she was totally dedicated to her husband. That trait made her a strong role model for Pamela, whose trademark in later life would be an overwhelming devotion to the important men in her life. Pansy traveled with Ken, but she also had her own work befitting the lady of the manor and served as a Dorset magistrate.

While Pamela would never burst in on Daddy in his study, she felt no inhibitions about interrupting her mother, who was a much bigger influence on young Pamela than her father. Which is not to suggest that Pansy was a bundle of love and joy. She was humorless, demanding and well stocked with English reserve. "A very, very formidable woman," was the assessment of the duke of Devonshire, who is exactly Pamela's age and who visited the family at Minterne.[14] "Very, very strong" was how Pamela herself described her mother.[15]

Pansy set the behavior standards and meted out punishment that was not dispensed by nannies. Reading aloud to the girls was the closest she came to striking mental sparks. Only by comparison to Daddy was Mummy stimulating. Otherwise, Minterne was an intellectual wasteland, filled with a staff of forelock tuggers saying "m'lord" this, "m'lady" that.

In her isolation, Pamela did not know how much she didn't know. There is no evidence, for example, that she felt any compulsion to read adult books or asked to be taken to the library at Dorchester to expand her horizons. Several reasons suggest that she did not, including the fact that, as an adult, she showed little appetite for books that did not relate to her personally. Also, reading is a private pleasure, and one thing Pamela did not want to be was alone. She wanted to be out and around other people,

people who were fun, not like Sheila, who was almost her only companion.

The two older sisters were constantly together, but proximity had little impact on affinity. They were total opposites. Sheila was dark, shy and introverted. Pam was red-haired, freckled and gregarious. Sheila was Miss Thin; Pam, Miss Fat. When summoned to greet visitors, Pam bounded downstairs, eager to meet anyone new. Sheila, moaning that she wanted to be left alone, had to be coaxed from hiding in her room and ordered to shake hands.

Sheila was Daddy's girl; Pam was Mummy's. Sheila liked to shoot, hunt and ride alone through the forest. Pamela was uninterested in shooting and preferred the glamour of the show ring, ideally with plenty of spectators on hand to applaud. She was a skillful, controlled and brave rider. Winning her first show ribbons at the age of seven gave her a taste for the spotlight she relished the rest of her life. Neither sister liked the other. More than sixty years later, Pam takes pride in a letter from their mother which said how wonderful all the children were except Sheila.[16]

Sheila does not respond directly. Publicly, she is diplomatic, with just a hint of barbed edge when asked about her sister. "Pamela decided early on that she was going to turn herself into a very glamorous person," Sheila explained in 1988. "She had a lot of ambition."[17]

Pamela was ten when that ambition turned into a drive to get out of Minterne. She was literally bored to tears. Other than Sheila, she had no playmates. Given her attitude about Sheila, that meant virtually no friends at all. Pamela was not one to hang out with the children of the staff. Growing up did not change her attitude about her contemporaries. At Christmas and Easter, various cousins would show up, but like her experiences with the children on shipboard returning from Australia, such visits usually meant more fighting than fun. Those she did enjoy were invariably older, people who would indulge her, talk to her and pay her attention.

There was dancing class and a few local birthday gatherings, but they produced no fond reminiscences. She was lonely and longed — ached — for her parents' weekend parties, when grown-ups would arrive at Minterne, trailed by ladies' maids and valets trundling luggage packed with tweeds for shoots, pinks for hunts, dinner jackets and three long dresses — one for each night's dinner — loaders for shoots and horse vans.

More than two hundred hunts were established in Britain in the mid-1930s, each with a boundary as fixed as those for a parish or county. Ken Digby was master of foxhounds for the Cattistock hunt while Pamela was growing up and hunting weekends were a fixture on the family's calendar from November to March, "the open season hailed with delight when ditches are visible and woods diaphanous."[18] Dozens of riders gathered in the Minterne forecourt, while up to forty Welsh hounds snuffled, anxious to get out into the trees etched against the pale blue-and-mauve sky and to the field gallops among the gorse, rich green fern and flocks of bleating sheep.

Hedge artists traversed the country, transforming jagged bushes into clean, pruned walls and teaching local landowners how to lay hedges and trim the stakes on which the quickthorn, black-thorn and hazel wattle grew so that no sharp points stuck up to gut a horse or injure a rider. When they were older, Pamela and Sheila rode with the guests, scrambling and splashing after hunt master Digby, ducking branches of ancient oaks and elms as blasts from the brass horn, baying hounds and the snorting of lathered horses echoed across the meadows.

On the weekend evenings, after guests bathed, dressed and finished a dinner of steaming soup, roasted game and beef topped off with pudding or trifle, Pamela was allowed to stay up late. While Sheila remained in her room, Pam stood entranced in the minstrel's gallery overlooking the two-story medieval-style main hall and gazed, a captivated romantic, at the couples in formal dress milling about below or in the adjacent drawing room with its pink silk curtains and vases filled with matching roses and gladioli.

In London, fancy-dress parties had been fashionable since the First World War. There were Mozart parties with period dress and featuring the composer's music and Pharaonic revels commemorating the 1922 discovery of Tutankhamen's tomb in the Valley of the Kings by English archaeologist Howard Carter. At one bash, an entire house was redecorated to evoke Imperial Russia. A

Negro band armed with drums, rattles and bells played jazz until just before dawn, when the guests left the dance floor and moved to St. George's Baths for a swimming party, which caused a mini-scandal when the papers picked up the story and questioned the propriety of white girls in long-sleeved and beskirted bathing costumes being entertained by black musicians.

The Minterne parties were nowhere near as elaborate, but they were the epitome of glamour as far as Pamela was concerned. Sometimes guests brought ukuleles and led group singing. Pam tapped her feet when they turned on a gramophone and listened to early thirties blues, big band sounds or tunes from West End or Broadway shows. The gayest event of the year was the annual hunt ball, at Minterne or the estate of another prominent Dorset family. At that, a dance band allowed guests to experiment with some of the latest steps, including the Jog Trot, the Camel Walk, the Shimmy and, of course, the Charleston.[19]

Pamela's favorite visitors were Americans, the Higginsons, who were originally from Massachusetts. A. Henry Higginson was a well-known foxhunter — president of the Master of Foxhounds Association of America — who moved in 1912 to Dorset, where he became the only U.S. master of an English hunt, the Cattistock, and a good friend of Lord Digby's. He had an interesting pedigree. Higginson was the grandson of Louis Agassiz, the renowned naturalist and geologist who wrote some of the earliest studies about the Ice Age and who revolutionized science teaching in nineteenth-century America.

Pamela liked him because he was fun and far less stiff-necked than her own father. Hig loved dinner parties, at which he would blast on his hunting horn to summon servants with the next course, a practice that amused Pansy and Ken, but not one they emulated at Minterne.

His third wife was an American actress named Mary Newcomb, who entranced Pamela. She was glamorous and funny and Pamela, especially in her preteen years, had an enormous crush on her. Mary was a fine actress who performed at the Royal Shakespeare and Old Vic companies throughout the 1930s, starring in comedies and drama. She was the most fashionable woman Pamela had ever met, completely in vogue with the latest dress and hair sytles formulated not only by Paris designers but increasingly by American film stars. No sooner did Katharine Hepburn wear a shallow-crowned boater with streamers at the back in *Little Women* than Mary was wearing a similar hat in Dorset. The 1934 Alexander Korda film *The Private Life of Henry VIII* with Charles Laughton, the first British film to score a commercial success in the United States, started a craze for looped and padded sleeves. Pamela missed the film but saw the styles on Mary, who also appeared once in the demure velvet "Juliet frock" made popular in the film version of *Romeo and Juliet*.[20]

Both Higginsons had spunk and personality. They were the first Americans Pamela had met and they made a huge impression. Mary was Hig's third wife; he was her second husband. Associating with stage people was still new. Barriers between the stage and society had only recently fallen, giving an added zing to such friendships. Mary and Hig were quick to share London and theater gossip and were much more liberated, freewheeling and interesting than anyone Pamela had known. She could sit for hours, her mouth agape, listening to Mary's stories and her devastating mimicry.

Soon after the Higginsons arrived on the scene, she met the Ruxtons, another well-to-do American couple. Talley Ruxton rode with her father. His wife was known as Tops. They too bought a Dorset home, a lovely Jacobean estate which Tops set about renovating. Pamela would burst into giggles when Tops told how she was having difficulty conversing with workmen. Her bedroom needed two closets, but for English builders, that meant a water closet, a toilet. They were baffled by this American who wanted two toilets in her bedroom.

For the first time, Pamela learned that, common language notwithstanding, there were fascinating differences between the Americans and the English. One trait she found appealing and adopted was the Americans' inclination to look ahead instead of her family's tendency to live in the past. Like the Higginsons, the Ruxtons seemed far more chic and glamorous than the straitlaced citizenry of upper-crust Dorset. Their clothes were brighter with bigger buttons and cut more fashionably. In London, square shoulders were dropped in 1934 in favor of sloping shoulders and wide necks for a softer effect. Wider belts for women emphasized a greater tendency toward slim waists, while sleeves began to be cut looser and more bell-shaped. In the city, debate raged over the propriety of plucking eyebrows. In tradition-steeped Dorset there was no new look nor much discussion of fashion until the Americans arrived, complete with exotic snake-skin and crocodile shoes and the latest accessory — sunglasses.[21]

The Ruxtons each had children from prior marriages and constantly baffled the locals by referring to one or another's child as being his or hers, never theirs. Some of the local gentry criticized the Ruxtons for being too flashy and a bit garish. Tops even smoked, using a long, elegant cigarette holder! Pamela never took up smoking, but she was anything but critical. She thought Dorset's newest residents were wonderful, far more stimulating than anyone she knew in England.

Getting to know the Higginsons and Ruxtons as an adolescent began Pamela's lifelong fascination with Americans and also got her thinking about the world beyond Minterne. Until then, she had little notion of what was out there. She knew nothing about the depression which was pushing unemployment in England up from two to three million. The rise of Fascism and Socialism were totally foreign to her.

In interviews in later years, she maintained that she had been political all her life, but the claim was a spurious bit of revisionism. Unlike, for example, Margaret Thatcher, who was five years her junior and whose childhood conversations with her family centered on politics and economics, Pamela developed political awareness only after she left home.

Conversation at home was no less sterile than education at home. Governess lessons initially taught her little beyond the conventions of English class life. Her first governess, a Scot named Johnny Johnson, was less a teacher than a disciplinarian who insisted Pamela complete her rote memory work before jumping on a pony. As far as it went, the training worked. In her seventies, Pamela could still recite line after line of Kipling and, for that matter, at least one obscure Australian poet.

A bigger impact came when the girls outgrew Johnny and

Pansy hired a Swiss governess to teach them French. Sheila disliked her, but Pamela was intrigued. She knew about art and geography and cities like Paris, which she described in such lush detail — the arts, fashions, architecture and bright lights — that Pamela's determination to experience it all herself grew. Notwithstanding the trip to Australia, the rest of her life had been circumscribed by the estate at Minterne Magna. Her parents and Johnny scarcely spoke of topics beyond Dorset. She was beginning to realize there was a great deal more to see and do.

Walking Creina in the hills in the morning, Pamela thought more and more, "When I am grown up, I will leave this place and will live in a city."[22] She would sit under an oak tree at the top of the valley and look down on the manor house with all its security and comforts, scratch her dog's ears and plan her escape. She was bored to tears and could not wait to get away and not come back. It hardly mattered where she went, just as long as there were other people and things to see and do.

🌀 🌀

CHAPTER THREE

George and Adolf

IN 1932, Pamela's brother Eddy turned eight and was sent off to the junior boarding school which would prepare him for Eton. Her father had studied there before going on to the Royal Military College at Sandhurst. Pamela was twelve and begged to be sent away too, but Pansy and Ken said no. Girls did not go to boarding school so early. Upper-class "gels" were intentionally taught poorly and trained to be docile and helpless in an effort to guarantee a good marriage. Education was power, but aristocratic English women were raised to breed, not to be powerful. Marriage was imperative. Nannies, governesses and spinster aunts were all reminders of what happened to girls who did not marry.[1] It was important, however, that Eddy be educated. As the family's only boy, he would inherit the title and Minterne when Daddy died.

Pamela had no chance of getting the estate. She was the eldest child, but according to the practice of primogeniture, inheritance rights went to the eldest son. He would become a baron and Lord Digby; his wife, Lady Digby. Pamela was not even Lady Pamela. As the daughter of a baron, she was The Honorable Pamela Digby.

The destiny of an upper-class girl child of the 1920s was basic schooling, finishing on the Continent, presentation at court as a debutante, then marriage to a suitable young aristocrat, preferably an eldest son. Not inheriting the estate did not faze Pamela, though it did mean she would have to find some means of support. What horrified her was the prospect of being shut away forever on some estate in the hills of Shropshire, or some other place like Dorset, with a husband like her father.

She launched a campaign to be sent to the nearby Sherborne Girls School, but was turned down again by her parents. Sherborne was considered an intellectual school, too brainy for the Digby girls then, although Jacquetta went there during World War II when gasoline rationing limited the distance families could travel. After two more years of pleading, Pamela and Sheila were finally sent in 1934 to Downham School in Hatfield, Hertfordshire, "a girls' school of the sort grandmothers describe as a 'genteel seminary.' "[2]

Pamela refers to the school in conversations, on her résumé and in her *Who's Who* listing as Downham College, where she says she received a "B.," for "Bachelor," Domestic Science–Economy.[3] Her hope seems to be that people will assume she is a college graduate.

(On the official biography which she submitted on March 19, 1993, to the Senate Foreign Relations Committee for her nomination to be ambassador to France, however, she listed it as Downham School. Why the switch? The FBI checks out biographical data as part of the background investigation it conducts of presidential appointees. Failing to tell the truth could have posed a problem.)

She further refers to her finishing school study in Paris as "postgraduate work at the Sorbonne."[4] Then there is her honorary doctor of laws degree from Columbia University.

In fact, she left Downham at sixteen, having studied home economics for two years. Her "postgraduate work" took place while she was sixteen and seventeen. According to the Sorbonne archivist, Monsieur Péycere, no one named Pamela Digby is on record as having received any degree or diploma from that institution, nor is there a record of any coursework that she may have studied. Her honorary doctor of laws degree was granted after Averell Harriman gave $11.5 million to Columbia University to endow the W. Averell Harriman Institute for the Advanced Study of the Soviet Union.

Pamela maintains that she was "head girl" at Downham, the top honor at any school. "I was always the girl picked out to be prefect, head girl, all that nonsense," she said.[5] Not quite. Classmates say that actor David Niven's first wife, Primula Rollo, was head girl during Pamela's year. According to a longtime friend who likes but does not always trust Pamela: "With Pamela, it's always hard to find where truth lies."[6]

Pamela stretches the truth about her education because as an adult it bothers her that she has had so little. She arrived at Downham at fourteen with no geometry, no algebra and no Latin. What else she had was not very good and she had to scramble academically, which was not easy. The advantages of being away from Minterne far outweighed the initial scholastic struggle. On her way to Downham, she stayed overnight in London for the first time and saw her first play. It was all she had hoped for, new experiences and the start of a great adventure.

She loved school, got along well with her teachers and by her second year was chosen a prefect, a senior student monitor. The position allowed her to punish misbehaving students, usually by making them memorize poetry. One of her victims was a girl named June Osborne, a girl who had been whispering during morning prayers. Pamela gave her a selection of Milton's "Paradise Lost" to memorize. Years later, when June succeeded her as the second Mrs. Randolph Churchill, Pamela told the story to the retired Sir Winston Churchill. The old lion smiled at his former daughter-in-law. After living with Randolph, he suggested, June could by then likely recite "Paradise Regained."

Pamela left Downham in 1936, a watershed year for Britain. In January, a week after the country was plunged into grief at the death of Rudyard Kipling, King George V died after a quarter-century reign. His eldest son succeeded him as Edward VIII, the first bachelor to ascend the throne since George III, the monarch who lost the American colonies. That spring, just after Pamela turned sixteen, the new king gave a dinner party in London at

St. James's Palace to which he invited an American couple, Wallis and Ernest Simpson, and Prime Minister and Mrs. Baldwin. "It's got to be done," the king wrote. "Sooner or later my Prime Minister must meet my future wife."

Shortly after the dinner, Mrs. Simpson began proceedings to divorce her husband. Britons, Americans, Europeans and nearly everyone in the Empire with access to a newspaper spent the rest of the year mesmerized by the clash between the monarchy and Baldwin's government over whether the king could marry Mrs. Simpson and keep his throne. On December 10, the king informed the world that he was abdicating. The following night, he left Britain to spend much of the rest of his life in France.

Pamela was in Paris when the ex-king became the duke of Windsor. She heard the news of the abdication on a scratchy radio and was horrified. Part of the denouement was very romantic: the king could not go on without the support of the woman he loved. The finality of his giving up the throne and leaving the country, on the other hand, shocked her. She had not met him nor the duchess, which Wallis Simpson became when they married in France in June 1937. But she would later.

At that point, Pamela was still a country girl from the shires, wide-eyed and curious, with ringlets of red curls and only just embarked on the "finishing" process which was designed to transform uneducated aristocratic girls into marriageable young women.

French was the international language of the day and the language of culture. Paris, the capital of elegance and art, was the most popular destination. Britain was still shaking off the impact of depression in the mid-30s but Paris was alive. Picasso was painting; Cocteau was writing and making films; Josephine Baker was singing; and Gertrude Stein, who had hosted in the twenties such "lost generation" writers as Ernest Hemingway and F. Scott Fitzgerald, still maintained her extraordinary salon.

Pamela met none of them, but she picked up the scent of liveliness in the air. Everyone had a sense of style, even the lower-class French women she passed on the street. It was not only that their dresses looked smarter than anything she saw in England, but that they wore their outfits with a certain insouciance that she found very appealing. Sometimes they just added a pin or the latest fashion accessory, an artificial flower, which seemed to say, "Look at me." That was what she wanted and her Downham classmates had sometimes joked about how hard she tried. When the girls were all in bed and the lights went out, Pamela could be heard moving in the dark, putting curlers in her hair to enhance her appearance, then waking early to hide them.

There was far more color and verve in Paris, whether it was silk fabric draped on elegant shop window mannequins or pyramids of fancy pastries and chocolates or the strange but intriguing new smells trailing out of bistros and boulangeries. Young men her age looked her in the eye instead of ducking away like awkward English boys.

The ambience was heady, but Pamela's first experience in France was restricted. The girls in Paris studied language and French history, visited cathedrals and museums and attended the opera. Some studied fine sewing of satin and lace; others, including Pamela, who soaked up everything she saw, learned about antiques and paintings at the Sorbonne or the Louvre in small classes, some lasting only a few weeks and designed specifically for young English ladies. Academic demands were minimal.

The overall experience was designed to give them "a light dusting of culture — how to tell a Manet from a Monet — the rudiments of feminine skills like arranging flowers, and, most important of all, introduced them to a selection of well-bred foreign girls."[7] Not everyone went to France. Some were finished in Italy or Germany. If a girl were lucky, she got to two countries. Pamela was lucky.

Various stories about Pamela in later years described how she attended boarding schools in Paris and Munich, but the education was not as formal as the term suggests. In France, she was one of four English girls living with a family in Arcueil, on the southern edge of Paris. Two daughters in their early twenties taught French to their paying guests, who included Daisy Fellowes, the daughter of an heiress to the Singer Sewing Machine fortune, and a girl named Ann Spencer. The girls were well mannered and well groomed but otherwise completely unsophisticated when they arrived. They had been overprotected by nannies and parents and were so naive sexually that escort by chaperones was normal practice.

Pamela was a late developer, fourteen and a half when she hit puberty. She was told only that menstruation had something to do with growing up and that she could not ride her pony or swim for five days, an unexplained nightmare. She never discussed sex with her mother and would not have dreamed of mentioning the subject with her father.

These girls were nothing like modern teenagers landing in Paris. Midteens only in years, they were schoolchildren and, at least for a while, did what they were told. Before World War II, no English girl from a proper aristocratic family was allowed to be alone with a young man, no matter how respectable he might be. There was no "dating," nor even opportunities for young men and women to have a meal alone together. There was no fooling around at that age by such girls. Which is not to suggest that they did not flirt madly, mostly by responding to teasing by the boys, if they did not initiate it themselves. Pamela joined in with enthusiasm. The boys liked her because she was so gregarious and obviously interested in them. But she also still felt very much a country girl and slightly out of her depth in the city. She didn't remain that way for long.

After a year in Paris, Pamela came home to join her parents on a trip to the United States and Canada, where Lord Digby had been asked to judge at the Royal Winter Fair horticulture exposition in Toronto. The three Digbys left Southampton on October 30, 1937, in second-class accommodations on the SS *Britannic* and arrived eight days later in New York, where they stayed at the home of the William Woodwards, a huge house on the corner of Fifth Avenue and Eighty-sixth Street.

The Woodwards were serious New York society, with strong ties to Britain. Shortly after graduating from Harvard in 1902, William Woodward became secretary to the U.S. ambassador to the Court of St. James's. He returned to America in 1910 and inherited the giant Hanover Bank, and the three-thousand-acre Belair Farm, the nation's oldest racing stud and home to Triple

Crown winners Gallant Fox and Omaha. Benjamin Franklin had visited Belair and six fawns from its deer park had been given to George Washington for his Mount Vernon home.[8]

Breeding and racing thoroughbreds were Woodward's passions. He raced often in England and tried unsuccessfully for years to win the Derby, which is how he met horseman Digby. In manners, dress and Edwardian formality, Woodward acted British, a pose the English usually find off-putting. But Woodward had been a friend of King Edward VII, the son of Queen Victoria, which allowed him more leeway in this regard than most Americans. In addition, he and Ken Digby shared too many interests for "posing" ever to be an impediment.

On the contrary, the Woodward mansion overlooking Central Park and the Metropolitan Museum of Art could not have been more inviting. The house was fully staffed, from footmen to parlormaids, smelled of rich beeswax furniture polish and had fresh-cut flowers — violets, camellias and daisies — everywhere. Elsie Cryder Woodward knew how to run a home.

She was not to the manner born, but she was practical and clever and it took her little time to adapt. She was one of the famous Cryder triplets, who had been models for a set of Gibson Girls, those icons of aristocratic beauty and social refinement drawn for *Harper's* and *Colliers Weekly* by illustrator Charles Dana Gibson. "We were poor and we weren't pretty," she conceded, "but my mother was very publicity-conscious and dressed us alike so we were pretty well-known."[9]

Married to Woodward in the society wedding of the year in 1904, by the 1920s Elsie was running one of the foremost social salons in New York, a putative rival of those led by the Astors and Vanderbilts. For decades she employed an exceedingly formal English butler, Arthur Putz, who dressed in white tie and patent leather shoes, remembered everyone's name and their preferred drinks, a technique which the adult Pamela adopted and perfected herself. During their visit, Pamela watched transfixed at dinner as Putz orchestrated the movements of white-gloved footmen, some holding candelabra, by some unseen or unheard signal. Only by finally asking did she learn that he did it all by discreetly raising or lowering his chin.[10]

[In 1955, the same Woodward family was involved in one of society's greatest scandals. *Life* magazine called it "The Shooting of the Century" when the Woodwards' eldest son, Billy — owner of the great bay colt Nashua, which won two legs of the 1955 Triple Crown — was shot to death at home by his beautiful wife, Ann, a former model who had a fling with the playboy Prince Aly Khan. The killing had taken place just after they returned home from a party in honor of the duchess of Windsor.[11]]

Ethel, the youngest Woodward daughter, was put in charge of Pamela. Ethel was twenty-one and Pamela, for the first time, felt that she was being treated as a grown-up. Or almost. Her clothes were an embarrassment. Pansy refused to allow her daughter to wear anything sophisticated. Pamela was not permitted to wear black, which was what she craved. The only evening apparel she had from England was light-colored party dresses worn by schoolchildren. Ethel gently mocked her young charge. Was it common in England to wear chiffon in winter? Pamela blushed. She knew she had a lot to learn, not least about dressing.

Her embarrassment did not last long. There were too many wonderful things to do in New York in 1937. In Paris, her life had been limited by chaperones and an allowance. In New York, she had only to cross Fifth Avenue to wander through the Metropolitan Museum and marvel at the variety of exhibits, from ancient Egyptian sarcophagi to French Impressionists. She was thrilled by her first Broadway show, Harold Rome's *Pins and Needles*, a new and popular musical about Franklin D. Roosevelt. The year before the president had swamped Alf Landon in the nation's biggest election landslide and the show captured the magic of the Roosevelt revolution, an emotion Pamela found almost addictive.

She felt a palpable sense of excitement in the United States that autumn. Others sensed it too. The New Deal was working and America was moving out of the Depression era. Nightclubs were jammed, but the visiting Digbys had no problem getting in. Pansy and Ken had met Prince Serge Obolensky, the White Russian proprietor of the nightclub at the St. Regis Hotel, in Australia, where he bounced baby Pamela on his knee.

Obolensky's ancestors were princes of Kiev and his family had put together the art collection at the Hermitage in St. Petersburg. When he left Russia just after the 1917 revolution, he came to New York, married Alice Astor and went to work for her brother Vincent, who owned the St. Regis. The Digbys knew Vincent through his English relatives, the Astors of Cliveden. The ties were interesting, but Pamela did not need them to feel comfortable. She was having a ball.

The party in the roof nightclub was Pam's first of many. Society columnist Elsa Maxwell was there, holding court. Years later, they would meet often. Everyone was so glamorous, so beautiful in evening dresses and dancing a new step called the Big Apple. They taught it to Pamela, who had never had so much fun. She thought the whole evening was breathtaking, just what she hoped the world beyond Minterne would be like. (In this regard, Sheila Digby may not have been so different from her sister. She married industry executive Charles Arthur Moore, who had been married to Sarah Woodward, one of Elsie and William's three daughters, immediately after World War II, a move which ruffled relations between the Digbys and the Woodwards as well as between Pansy and Sheila.)

After five magical days of new experiences in New York, the family moved on to Toronto and into a large suite at the Ritz. They linked up with the Eatons, also hunting friends from England, who owned a department store. The Eatons hosted a hunt, quite different from any Pam had known in that it took place in the snow and journalists were present, which marked her first exposure to publicity. That in itself was a bit risqué. At the time, upper-class women traditionally appeared in newspapers three times in their life — at birth, on their wedding and at death. A photograph of Pamela leaping high over a snow-dusted hedgerow, in perfect control of her horse, grinning broadly and with curls flying, appeared in Toronto's newspaper the *Globe and Mail*, captioned ENGLISH RIDER THRILLS TORONTO HUNT.

Pamela thrilled one hunter in particular, none other than the newspaper's proprietor, George McCullagh. McCullagh was a dynamo, a real-life Horatio Alger who started selling newspapers on the streets of Toronto at nine and by thirty-one had merged the *Globe* with the *Mail and Empire* into Canada's most powerful and influential newspaper, a position it still holds. When Pamela met him, McCullagh was thirty-two and married, with two children. Vigorous and outspoken, he flirted with the delighted seventeen-year-old visitor and invited her to ride at his farm.

Neither Pamela nor McCullagh mentioned the invitation to her parents, but Ken Digby heard about the offer from another Canadian, who told him McCullagh was more than a powerful publisher. He had quite a reputation as a womanizer and for Pamela to go anywhere with him unescorted was completely inappropriate. Lord Digby forbade his darling daughter to see McCullagh, but she was already slipping out of his and Pansy's control.

Boys had been sniffing around from her earliest teen years, but this was the first time any interesting man had paid attention to her and Pamela was dazzled. McCullagh was rich and important and not only talked to her, but listened to her opinions. His reputation and unsuitability intrigued her all the more. Jane's genes were kicking in. She sneaked out of the Ritz to meet him.

Her parents discovered what happened and were furious, but there is no evidence Pamela was chastened by the experience. It is unclear whether sex was involved, but McCullagh began sending the teenager bouquets of flowers and orchid plants. The gifts upset her parents even more. They could hardly wait to get out of Canada and head back to England, which, within several more days, they did.

Pamela saw McCullagh again a few years later when he visited London and Max Aitken, Lord Beaverbrook, the Canadian-born British press baron who was a Winston Churchill intimate and who would have tremendous influence on Pamela. When she left Canada, the flirtation was over. But the appeal of forbidden fruit and the lure of older, powerful and dynamic men — no matter if they were married — had only started.

After Paris and her trip to New York and Toronto, Pamela moved to Munich with Pauline Winn, the daughter of Olive, Lady Baillie, who owned Leeds Castle in Kent. The girls stayed at the home of Gräfin Cucca Harrach, a regular hostess for English predebs who were being "finished" in Germany. The experience was meant to add a touch more polish, like another coat of lacquer on a Rolls-Royce. Germany was thought to offer a finer-grained sheen than France, a patina with the added ingredients of Goethe, Schiller and Wagner.

How much Pamela learned in Germany is not clear, but Munich would have been difficult for her under the best of circumstances. For one thing, she had studied French at Minterne, but she did not speak German at all. Even girls who had graduated from English schools with certificates of proficiency in German were dismayed to discover how little they understood once they arrived.

Secondly, the atmosphere in Germany in early 1938 was more frightening than alluring. Hitler opened the notorious Dachau concentration camp just north of Munich in 1933, reincorporated the Saar in 1935 and the following year occupied the Rhineland and formed the Axis with Italy's Mussolini, but still predeb English girls were dispatched to Germany as if nothing had happened.

By 1937, however, stormtroopers were stopping pedestrians at random and ordering them to shout "Heil Hitler." Girls began returning home to Britain scared. "The children of the family I was living with were fervent members of the Hitler Youth Movement and did their best to make me feel lazy, unhealthy and decadent," said one girl who studied in Munich in 1937. "Their meetings and other outdoor activities were strenuous and repetitious and I was not a little frightened of their much vaunted violence."[12]

The fact that Pamela was sent off in early 1938 to Munich, the headquarters of Hitler's National Socialist or Nazi party, was an indication of how out-of-touch politically the Digbys were. Ken Digby commuted to London for debates in the House of Lords. He was a World War I veteran with a strong dislike of what he and his Tory contemporaries called The Hun. He heard Winston Churchill in the House of Commons fulminating about the Nazis. Still, he saw no problem with his daughter going to Germany. Neither did Pamela, who knew almost nothing about events unfolding on the Continent.

The Digbys were hardly unique. Much of the British upper

class agreed with Neville Chamberlain, who became prime minister in 1937, that Germany should be appeased — not opposed — to keep Hitler away from the island kingdom. Nancy Astor, the first woman member of Parliament, gathered like-minded thinkers — the so-called Cliveden set — at the family's country house, Cliveden, to promote a conciliatory approach to the Axis. Chamberlain was among the participants. The Mitford clan fell in thrall in varying degrees to Hitler, mesmerized by the illusion that he was transforming Germany from chaos and poverty to order and prosperity. In late October 1937, the week before the Digbys left for the United States, the duke and duchess of Windsor had tea with Hitler while touring Germany. If Germany was good enough for the former king, it seemed good enough for the Digbys.

Pamela has limited recollection of her academic experiences in Munich which, unlike her time in Paris, she did not list for the FBI. She does have fond memories of going out at night with Bavarian opera singers and upsetting her chaperones. Finding Jane Digby's portrait in a museum gallery honoring Munich's most beautiful women especially thrilled her, as did the guide's characterization of her ancestor as a wicked lady over whom a tremendous number of duels had been fought.

Her father's experiences in World War I may have made him very anti-German, but Pamela was not put off by phalanxes of infantry troops goose-stepping through the Bavarian capital. Nor was she anti-German enough to avoid Hitler. Like other contemporaries and her seniors, Pamela wanted to meet the Nazi leader. Unity Mitford, the youngest of the Mitford sisters and so pro-Nazi that she became a friend of Hitler's, set up the meeting one Friday afternoon over tea in Munich's Englischer Garten.

Even for a girl as uninvolved politically as Pamela was at the time, it is surprising how slight an impression Hitler made on her. In later years, Pamela told interviewers that she felt he was made of tinfoil, a one-dimensional character who was nervous and obviously unfriendly, although the very description was a cliché. It was lost from memory whether he was with propagandist Joseph Goebbels or Luftwaffe chief Hermann Goering, at least one of whom usually accompanied the chancellor and party boss.

She recalls nothing that was discussed nor did she make any notes about the experience. Nor was there any indication that she ever discussed the Hitler experience later with her father-in-law, Sir Winston Churchill, who had reason to be curious about his adversary. In 1977, she was quoted as saying that meeting Hitler had made her more politically aware and that she returned to England that year with "an urge to get out the word that Germany was going to attack."[13] Maybe so, but there are holes in the story that raise some question as to whether she actually met the Nazi leader.

Pamela has difficulty recalling precisely the dates of her stay in Munich but fixes the trip generally in the period following the November 1937 trip to the United States and Canada and ending in March 1938, when Hitler occupied Austria and her parents summoned her home. Therefore, it would have been midwinter — only weeks before the *Anschluss* — that the seventeen-year-old met the German chancellor in the open-air riverside garden. (Or perhaps the meeting took place in Hamburg, where other friends recall her saying — implausibly — that she was introduced to the Führer.)

Sarah Norton Baring, one of her closest friends, who saw Hitler in 1936 in Munich but was not introduced, doubts that Pamela did meet the Führer. Although they were friends before and throughout the war, Pamela never mentioned such a meeting. "I wonder if she really did meet him," Baring said later. "Isn't it awful, but it is rather doubtful." Other than Unity Mitford, who was always around, by 1938, Baring said, "Hitler didn't entertain [English girls] that way."[14]

If the meeting did not take place, why might Pamela have invented it? Because being involved would become very important to her. Because Averell Harriman, the statesman who would become a key figure in her life, later lamented that the one important leader he never met was Hitler. Because Britons did see Hitler in Munich in the 1930s, and for her to have been present in the city and not have met the Führer would have meant that she missed something, a difficult admission for her to make once she became politically active in the 1970s.

*   *   *

Pamela was back in England in time for her "season," the 1938 round of debutante parties, the final stage in the ritualistic process devised to move girls with bearing, but not much education, into the marriage market with boys of some education, if not about women. Although there was plenty of gaiety, the season had a more serious purpose than simple fun. Strip away the music, champagne, gowns and white ties and the ritual was all about breeding and preserving or improving bloodlines.

Two or three different balls and dinners took place every night from late May through June. Daytimes could mean a stop at Royal Ascot for the horse races or Henley for the rowing. Girls and their mothers arrived at a dinner hostess's house at 8 P.M., dressed usually in satin or tulle, complete with an evening bag and cape or fur wrap. Garlands of crimson and pink tulips and roses were a favorite decoration. The debs sipped orange juice or sherry, the mothers a cocktail before sitting down a half hour later for a dinner of fish and chicken. The dances were often scheduled to begin at 10 P.M., but savvy debs arrived late so as not to be confronted by the overly eager and thus less suitable young men who arrived first. The dancing was in full swing by 11 P.M. and continued, after a midnight-to-1 A.M. break for "supper," until 4 or 5 A.M.

Because a girl and her mother often did not return home until the first streaks of dawn were breaking over the dome of St. Paul's, the season was an endurance test, a social obstacle course which taught grace and discipline under pressure and constant scrutiny to determine whether a daughter was "clever" or "agreeable." She did not have to be the first; those deemed not to fall into the second category, however, were failures.

One of the most nerve-racking experiences for shy or unattractive girls was dealing with the dance card which listed the evening's fox trots ("You Leave Me Breathless" and "My Heart Is Taking Lessons") and waltzes (each simply noted as "Viennese") and the numbered spaces next to each dance for writing in the name of one's partner. Some wrote in names of boys anyway to avoid the embarrassment of having too many blanks. Presentations at court required drilling in the full court curtsy as taught by Madame Vaccani, who insisted that the deb sink as low to the floor as possible while keeping her back straight. "Throw out your little chests and burst your little dresses," she instructed.[15]

There are no good records for the 1938 season, but in 1939, the final prewar season, some two hundred to four hundred girls took part, about a hundred of them announcing their dances in the *Times* of London's weekly social column and thus comprising the inner circle of debdom. Coming out was expensive, costing about two thousand pounds, or about the same cost as renting a modest house in London for four years. But these families could afford it. In 1937, the top 1 percent of the rich held 56 percent of the nation's wealth.[16]

When Pamela came out, Pansy rented a house in London's Mayfair district for two months. Staying in hotels or eating in restaurants was not how Lady Digby's friends lived. As a result, hotels and restaurants — more forbidden fruit — became magnets for Pamela. Despite the French, American and German experiences, she had little confidence in herself during the 1938 season. She argued with her mother constantly about clothes.

Pansy never wanted to pay more than eight pounds, about thirty-five dollars then, for an evening dress. Pamela looked at the more sophisticated dresses of her best friends, Pauline Winn, Lady Baillie's daughter, and Sarah Norton, and felt like a country bumpkin.

"Those people I met in London were very sophisticated. It scared me because I couldn't compete. My friends were all going to Hartnell, the man who did the sequins [and was the queen's couturier]. I had all the beautiful ponies I wanted, but what I wanted was one expensive dress. When you're young and lack confidence, clothes make a great difference."[17]

Not having the right clothes was only part of a larger problem. Pamela wore the traditional ostrich plumes in her hair for presentation at court and she made a friend in fellow deb Kathleen "Kick" Kennedy, daughter of the American ambassador, but she hated being a deb.

Six months after her experience with George McCullagh, she

still could not stand the boys her age, although she was not immune to smuggling up to her room some young men who visited her at Minterne.

What, if anything, happened up there is unclear, but she never found conversation to be the strong suit of her male contemporaries. She lamented that they had nothing exciting to say beyond yacking in self-absorbed fashion about the hunting, shooting and fishing that she despised. One or two vague "beaux" emerged, including a Scot who would die in the war. But they were so fleeting and had such little impact that their names have been forgotten.

The most exciting part of the season for Pamela was sneaking away with other girls from a ball after midnight and racing to a nightclub, the Four Hundred or the Kit Kat, for a glass of champagne or a closer, slower dance in a darker room. The trick was getting back before parents or chaperones discovered you were missing. Some girls were reluctant to sneak off, given the predatory instincts of some boys. The debs had their own code for well-known offenders; some were NSIT, Not Safe in Taxis, or MTF, meaning they Must Touch Flesh.

When the season ended, the Digbys gave up the London rental and packed Pam off back home to Dorset. Siberia would have been no worse. The days dragged at Minterne. Riding, walking, playing silly board games, talking to family — everything was boring. She had to get out.

In the late summer of 1938, she returned to the Continent to stay with Daisy Fellowes at her parents' huge house in Paris and their even bigger estate in the south of France. Her French was becoming quite good and the parties with Daisy and Coco Scaparelli, another friend, were fun. But they were only a diversion. Pamela was spreading her wings and killing time, but for just what, she did not know.

At eighteen and uninterested in any of the young English lords who might have pulled her away from Minterne and dropped her into an identical life elsewhere, Pamela was in a rut. Three things got her out: the war, a half-American mentor and a dark green 2.4 Jaguar.

CHAPTER FOUR

Olive and David

PAULINE WINN, Popsy to her chums, brought Pamela to Leeds Castle to meet her mother and a few family friends — some of the biggest names in politics, industry, show business and the arts. The introduction changed the life of a country girl who came from a good family but who was neither rich enough nor sufficiently well born to be guaranteed access to the highest social strata.

For the better part of a year during 1938 and 1939, Pamela spent most weekends at Leeds Castle obtaining the full-immersion graduate education she never would have received in the best university seminars at Oxford or Cambridge. The mentors who took her under their wing shifted her onto a faster track and Pamela never looked back.

Popsy was a Munich pal and a '38 deb. She was named for her grandmother Pauline Whitney, one of the fabulously wealthy American Whitneys. The elder Pauline's father was William Whitney, a prominent New York lawyer, sportsman and social scion who served as secretary of the navy under President Grover Cleveland. Her husband was Lord Queenborough, whose grandfather, the Marquess of Anglesey, commanded the British cavalry at the Battle of Waterloo. When Pauline died young, her American-British daughter Olive inherited a hefty chunk of Whitney money with which she bought Leeds Castle in 1926.

An hour's drive south of London in Kent, Leeds Castle is England's oldest and perhaps most romantic stately home. Its walls and battlements rise up from a large encircling lake like a legendary Arthurian fortress. Such is the ambience that visitors can be forgiven for half-expecting to see the court of Camelot proceeding across the lake bridge to the castle or to spot Sir Lancelot courting Arthur's Queen Guinevere in the surrounding oak forest.

"Wonderful in manifold glories," wrote Lord Conway, the castle historian, "are the great castle visions of Europe; Windsor from the Thames, Warwick or Ludlow from their river sides, Conway or Canarvon from the sea, Amboise from the Loire, Aigues Mortes from the lagoons, Carcassonne, Coucy, Falaise and Château Gaillard — beautiful as they are and crowned with praise, are not comparable in beauty with Leeds, beheld among the waters on an autumnal evening when the bracken is golden and there is a faint blue mist among the trees — the loveliest castle, as thus beheld, in the whole world."[1]

Built first in wood in the ninth century by the Saxon chief Leed, then in stone by a Norman baron during the reign of Henry I, the son of William the Conqueror, Leeds became Crown property in the late thirteenth century. For the next three hundred years it served as a "ladies' castle" for eight of England's medieval queens, from Eleanor of Castile to Ann Boleyn, whose husband, Henry VIII, constructed the castle's banquet hall.

The castle was empty and the thirty-two-hundred-acre surrounding estate was in poor condition when Olive bought the property. By strange coincidence, or perhaps one of those inexplicable cosmic links, Lady Baillie, as Olive became, had ties to Henry VIII on both sides of her family. Whitney ancestors were members of Henry's household; one had been dubbed a knight in honor of the king's marriage to Ann Boleyn. Henry VIII had also knighted and made secretary of state an ancestor of Lord Queenborough's.

Whether the blood ties influenced Lady Baillie's purchase is unknown. What is clear is that she loved the castle from the moment she laid eyes on it, captivated by its beauty and setting. Everyone loved Leeds Castle; Olive had the means to buy and restore it. She did it with vigor, imagination, hundreds of workers and hundreds of thousands, if not millions, of dollars. Until she died in 1974 and gave the castle to the nation, Leeds was her life's work.

She completely renovated the basic structure and restored the Gloriette, site of the royal apartments in Tudor times. Surrounding the castle were the remains of a medieval park, which had been overgrown with brush and pocked with rabbit warrens. The land was cleared and a nine-hole golf course, a swimming pool and tennis courts were constructed.

Olive created the lovely wood garden, a traditional naturalistic English garden of wildflowers and shrubbery, bordered by the small streams of the Riven Len, which formed the lake where the castle sat on two islands. From around the world, she shipped in rare birds and animals — zebras, llamas, Australian parakeets and storks — for the lake and gardens.[2]

To restore the interior, she went first-class and chose the incomparable Stephane Boudin. The American decorator Mark Hampton said that Boudin "for over forty years created and supervised the execution of rooms all over the world that were considered the height of taste and grandeur by royalty and the very rich everywhere."[3]

Boudin defined French refinement and perfection. Chips Channon, the American expatriate and diarist who chronicled British society throughout the thirties and forties, called him simply "the greatest decorator in the world." The Channons hired Boudin to design the dining room of their Belgrave Square home, which featured silver-gilt carvings and was modeled on a room in Munich's eighteenth-century Amalienburg pavilion. "It will shock and perhaps stagger London and it will cost us over 6,000 pounds," or nearly thirty thousand dollars, an astonishing price, Channon wrote in 1934 after his first meeting with the decorator.[4]

A decade before, in 1923, at the age of thirty-five, Boudin went to work for what was then the greatest interior decorating firm in the world, Jansen, on Paris's rue Royale. Over the course of a brilliant career, he worked for a succession of very wealthy clients: the Ronald Trees at Ditchley; the duke and duchess of Windsor; the Winston Guests; the Charles Wrightsmans; Stavros Niarchos; the Gianni Agnellis and Jacqueline Kennedy, who brought Boudin to Washington early in the Kennedy administration to restore portions of the White House.

For no client did he labor as long or as diligently as for Olive, Lady Baillie. The complete Leeds Castle renovation took Boudin nearly thirty years. Into a medieval environment, he brought the best English and French furniture, mostly eighteenth-century pieces crafted in the reigns of Louis XV and Louis XVI, the husband of Marie Antoinette. Luxury and extreme grandeur, with an extensive use of rich crimsons and gold and a mix of French and English furniture, were the hallmarks of a Boudin work. He brought in bed hangings and heavily detailed draperies to add literal and figurative warmth to the drafty castle rooms.

Coloring and making new walls look antique were other Boudin specialties. He used steel brushes to bring out the grain in new boiserie, or wood panels, painted them with gesso or three or four coats of thin glaze, rubbed in tints and covered the final coloration with wax. He taught painters to imitate marble loosely instead of using the overly detailed style common to English painters and kept them redoing a room until he was satisfied it was right.

The results in Olive's bedroom were so superior, said Leeds historian David Cleggett, that "it is difficult not to believe that the bedroom is not covered with panels removed from a Louis Quatorze Parisian town house."[5] Boudin also supervised the installation of a French parquet floor in the bedroom and the construction of an adjoining boudoir which featured ornate gilded paneling taken from the walls of the dismantled billiard room.

A distinguishing feature of Boudin's work was his preference that each room have an individual color and motif, a style perhaps best displayed in the early 1960s, when he redid the Blue, Red and Green public rooms of the White House and the oval yellow drawing room in the private quarters. His "color schemes based on one color intensified the hierarchical mood of the house," said Mark Hampton.[6] An exceptional example at Leeds Castle was the pale robin's egg blue dining room, which featured blue-and-white Chinese porcelains mounted on slender brackets.

The essential renovations were completed by the early 1930s. By the time Pamela arrived with Popsy, Leeds Castle had been restored to glory and Lady Baillie was running the most stimulating salon in Britain. Glamorous friends and international visitors flocked to intimate weekend parties to ride, shoot, play bridge, golf or swim in the luxurious pool filled with filtered moat water. Alfonso XIII of Spain came. So did Edward VIII before he abdicated. A movie buff, Lady Baillie loved inviting American stars passing through Britain. A fun-filled weekend in a castle was more than enough inducement for Errol Flynn, Clark Gable, Jimmy Stewart and Douglas Fairbanks Jr.

The "Leeds set" rivaled, then surpassed, Nancy Astor's "Cliveden set" in diversity and talent. It was not as well known because Lady Baillie, unlike the Astors, hated publicity. Newspaper owners were asked not to write about her and were invited to the castle on the strict understanding that everything about the gatherings would be off-the-record.

Sir Adrian Baillie, a member of Parliament and Olive's third husband, was a marginal figure around the castle. His parliamentary constituency was in Scotland, where he often traveled to conduct "surgeries," office hours for members of his district. He did not own the castle; Olive bought it before she married him.

Despite the size of the estate and the fact that Sir Adrian was frequently absent, Olive was never lonely. She was surrounded by a small group of regular courtiers and "admirers," in the felicitous phrase of the day, whose constant attendance did not appear to stop at the entrance to the spectacular bedroom Monsieur Boudin had designed for her. Two were of particular significance and influence.

David Margesson had been the chief whip in the House of Commons for seven years when Pamela met him in 1938. The chief whip holds one of the most important jobs in government, controlling the majority through organizational skill, discipline and charm. Margesson had all the required attributes in great supply, so much so that he held the job under four prime

ministers — MacDonald, Baldwin, Chamberlain and Churchill —
the last of whom made him secretary of war in 1940.

A striking figure, Margesson was tall, handsome and immac-
ulately tailored. He was forty-eight years old, thirty years older
than Pamela when she met him. He was separated from his wife,
Frances Leggett, another American heiress, and involved with
Olive Baillie. He read. He thought. He was articulate. He had
enormous drive, exceptional courtesy and sense of fairness, great
common sense and an incisive, often profane, sense of humor.
"A charmer, but a somewhat bromidic one," said Chips Channon,
who would not have found him as alluring as the women, young
and older. Still, Channon conceded, "he has undoubtedly as
much power as anyone in the land."[7]

Margesson knew everything that was going on. He knew the
details of every political initiative and the strengths and foibles
of every politician in every party. He knew who was loyal, who
was smart, who had a drinking problem, and the telephone numbers of mistresses in the event an errant MP had to be summoned
for a vote.

Geoffrey Lloyd was, at thirty-six, a dozen years younger than
Margesson, and still a political golden boy. While in his twenties,
he had been private secretary to Sir Samuel Hoare, a future foreign
secretary, then became parliamentary private secretary to Prime
Minister Stanley Baldwin. All his life, he was devoted to Olive
Baillie.

"A gentle, unassertive man of ability," according to Churchill's
private secretary John Colville, Lloyd was also an information
addict and a shrewd analyst. When Chamberlain succeeded Baldwin in 1937, Lloyd became number two at the Home Office,
which oversees domestic affairs. A rumor could scarcely be whispered in a Home Office corridor without Lloyd's hearing it within
minutes.[8]

There could hardly have been a better-informed pair in the
country than Lady Baillie's foremost admirers. They shared their
insights and information in surprising detail. Pamela liked Geoffrey Lloyd, but David Margesson was mesmerizing. She also found
him incredibly attractive.

Margesson was everything that Ken Digby was not. Margesson

was always at Leeds Castle on weekends, holding court with Olive and Lloyd, guiding conversations, gossiping and charming guests. Increasingly, Pamela showed up too, the newest and youngest Leeds groupie. "She was a pretty face," said Douglas Fairbanks Jr., who saw Pamela there frequently. "She was engaging, intelligent, charming and nice."[9]

And unattached. Usually ten or twelve guests stayed the weekend, a small enough group for conversation to be substantive and lively. With fresh news and gossip constantly circulating, Pamela became an even better listener and soaked up information. What she heard was not prattle, the inanities she heard from boys her own age. These men were experts who knew what they were talking about. She was impressed.

She learned more than politics. Pamela had an eye and good taste from her upbringing at Minterne, but with Boudin in and out of the castle, her sense of style became increasingly refined. What she learned at Leeds Castle, coupled with her early experience in Paris, provided the foundation on which she would build her own reputation as a sophisticated arbiter of home decoration.

Literally at Olive's feet, she heard Boudin articulate his ideas and monitored Lady Baillie's reactions. His advice on color, for example, extended beyond the paint on the panels, the gilding on the lambrequins or the velvet chair coverings to include the floral arrangements in each room.

The tone and placement of the arrangements were made not merely in accordance with the color scheme in the particular room in which they were positioned, but also with how they related to the view into the next room and its tints and how the entire pattern fit together.[10]

Pamela watched Olive plan weekends, put guest lists together, then make her guests comfortable and never allow them to feel intimidated by the castle or the cast of characters in residence. Olive was strong-willed in a school-mistressy sort of way and some visitors arrived expecting to be daunted. "Something about her frightened people," Douglas Fairbanks recalled. "She seemed very cross and very stern, but she was actually very soft and kind and good."

So any possible expectations of intimidation went unfulfilled.

In the most wonderful surroundings, Olive made everyone invariably feel at home in her home, encouraging visitors to take full run of the place and, in the evening, galvanizing but not dominating conversations. Pamela absorbed everything. She was not an original thinker, but she did have an excellent memory. She could always recall conversations, as she could poetry, and parrot what she had been told.

War was on everyone's mind. In September 1938, Chamberlain flew to Munich and signed an agreement allowing Hitler to dismember Czechoslovakia — as long as he stopped there. Hitler made the deal with a smile. Chamberlain returned home to proclaim in tragic error, "I believe it is peace for our time." Outside 10 Downing Street delighted crowds sang "For He's a Jolly Good Fellow."

In the House of Commons, Chamberlain's chief critic, Winston Churchill, called the Munich agreement "a total and unmitigated defeat." "In the depths of that soul," he said of Chamberlain, "there is nothing but abject surrender."

Inside Downing Street and in the House of Commons, Margesson saw and heard all.

Margesson became more than Pamela's mentor, more like a guardian. He essentially took over the role of her father. Margesson was never condescending and Pamela respected his confidences. Lady Baillie became her unofficial godmother and took over more and more of Pansy's role, teaching her about etiquette, relationships with men, party planning, decorating, card playing and her future.

The Digbys were not happy with the turn in Pam's life, although they had inadvertently provided the catalyst. The small Jaguar her father gave Pamela when she turned nineteen had become a getaway car. The Jag gave her independence and ended her isolation. Every weekend and sometimes during the week, she would take a maid and drive to London or straight to Leeds.

Ken Digby, immersed in his own squiredom of flowers, horses and civic duties, had little or no idea about what was going on at Leeds Castle. Pansy had a slightly better notion, but it was not fully formed. Pansy was quite innocent. She did not want to understand everything, but she understood enough to disapprove of Pam's lifestyle. More straitlaced than her husband, Pansy thought the Leeds set was awful. She worried that the environment was too dangerous for her daughter, but her anxiety came too late.

Pamela didn't care what her parents thought. She was becoming aware of another characteristic that would endure throughout her life and throughout all her relationships. She did not care one damn if people were upset with what she was doing. Like her ancestor Jane Digby, if she wanted to do something, she did it. If it seemed okay to Pamela, it was no one else's business. Not her parents', her siblings', her friends' or her elders'. She did not care what anyone thought.

Pansy had plenty of reason to be concerned. Leeds was a fast crowd for a nineteen-year-old girl. There was gambling, drinking and lord knows who slept where. Corridor creeping was hardly unknown at Leeds Castle. The protocol was that creepers knew where they were going and were expected. But that wasn't always the case.

Randolph Churchill used to boast that he often slipped into bedrooms of unaccompanied strangers at weekend parties in other country homes simply to determine whether anyone was available. Alan Pryce-Jones, the eminent English writer and Randolph's schoolmate at Eton, heard him tell the story to their mutual friend, Lady Mary St. Clair-Erskine. "You must get a lot of rebuffs," she said. "I do," Randolph said, guffawing, "but I get a lot of fucking too."[11]

Pamela, however, was not getting any sex at that point, at least according to one authoritative version of events. Prewar mores, as well as chaperones, unreliable birth control and a ban on abortions limited freewheeling behavior by teenage daughters of aristocrats. Her life was more exciting and glamorous once she began spending most of her time in London and at Leeds Castle, she admitted, but she was still very naive. She was a flirt, but that was as far as she went.

If she indeed was still a virgin, said one girlfriend, she was a virgin on the verge. "Pam was terribly sexy and very obvious," said one of her 1938 debmates who was also a Leeds visitor. "She was very plump and so bosomy we all called her 'the dairy maid.'

She wore high heels and tossed her bottom around. We thought she was quite outrageous. She was known as hot stuff, a very sexy young thing."[12]

Sexy enough to attract another older man, Fulke Warwick, the earl of Greville, who was twenty-eight to Pam's nineteen when they met at Leeds Castle in 1939. Pamela's hormones were raging by then, possibly inspired by Popsy Winn's entanglement with another of her mother's beaux, a charming gambler named John Hallett, or possibly just watching Olive Baillie juggle Margesson, Lloyd and Sir Adrian. Warwick inherited an earldom at seventeen, was married at twenty-two and had a son. When he met Pamela, he was recently divorced, still rich and dashing, and had a lot of time for a sexy nineteen-year-old with tight red curls, high heels and a tossing bottom.

One weekend, Pam drove to London to stay with Sarah Norton and her mother, Jean, on Grosvenor Square, as she often did when she did not go to Leeds Castle. No sooner had she arrived than she disappeared. Jean Norton asked her daughter where Pam had gone. Sarah didn't know. By 1939, Pam was often disappearing without explanation. Maybe home to Minterne, Sarah said. Maybe to Leeds Castle. No one knew until Monday, when Pam suddenly reappeared.

"And where have you been?" Sarah asked.

"My dear, I've been to Paris with Fulke Warwick," Pam responded.

"Oh my goodness," said Sarah later. "I was absolutely stunned. Fulke Warwick was a friend of my father's. I thought it was very, very odd indeed and frightfully daring. Talk about crossing the Rubicon."[13]

"Crossing the Rubicon" was deb talk for going all the way. It seemed plausible to some contemporaries. Warwick paid for the trip, the first of many trips Pamela would accept from older men. She also returned with a pair of beautiful long jade earrings that Warwick had given her in Paris. They stayed in separate places. He stayed at the Ritz. She may have stayed with the family of Ann Spencer, her friend from the school days in Paris. They each sneaked away, met and went to a nightclub. With the possible exception of helping her put on her new jade earrings, he never touched her. Although he certainly could have, he didn't even try.

They were spotted in the nightclub. Word got back to Olive Baillie, who gave Pamela holy hell for fooling around with Fulke Warwick. He was too old for her and a run-around. She would ruin her reputation if she kept up that kind of behavior. Pamela didn't mind. She had had a wonderful time. Olive Baillie's own complicated love life gave her little authority to preach. In this area, she didn't care what Lady Baillie thought any more than she cared about how her mother would react.

Pansy, however, did not know about the Paris jaunt. Soon after, she told Jean Norton how proud she was of Pam's managing her allowance of four pounds a week so well. "She's frightfully clever getting along on two hundred a year." Sarah Norton almost laughed out loud. If Pansy Digby really thought Pam was living the life she was living on her allowance, Sarah knew that Lady Digby did not have a clue about just what kind of life Pamela was beginning to live. "She was somewhat naive about Pam," said Sarah. "Pam was, to use a delightfully old-fashioned word, fast. She wasn't wild, but she was a terrific flirt and bored with boys her own age."[14]

Fulke Warwick panicked after Paris. Pamela was sweet, but he was not interested in a relationship that would get them both in trouble. The incident also worried Jean Norton. As a good friend of Pansy's, she had accepted responsibility for the Digbys' daughter when she offered to let Pam stay with them in London. But Jean, who was herself tied up in a long-term affair with press baron Lord Beaverbrook, was getting nervous about the increasingly adventurous Pam.

"My mother thought she had taken on more than she really wanted to," said her daughter, now Mrs. Sarah Baring. Sarah also felt the gap widening with her best friend. "She became too grown up for me. From 1939, she started having older men friends and those of us her age got left behind."

The final months before Britain joined the war against Germany were a jumble for Pamela. She was reaching out as far and as fast as she could. In May, she went to the Epsom races, where Lord Rosebery, her uncle, won his first English Derby with his popular favorite, Blue Peter.

Pam won there, but in Scotland later that summer lost a hundred pounds — six months' allowance — at the track. She went screaming to her father, who reimbursed her. One more man who came to help, just like the policeman in Australia.

She gambled at Leeds too. One weekend she insisted on playing poker with the men and lost big. She did not pay. Instead, said Lord Harlech, Pamela "cried all night until the debt was forgiven."[15]

In June, the duke and duchess of Windsor dined at the German embassy in Paris. Nazi soldiers saluting and bellowing "Heil Hitler" greeted them at the entrance. The duke did not return the stiff-arm *Hitlergruss* salute that evening, but he had in the past, notably during his honeymoon in Germany.

Other Britons were preparing for war. Winston Churchill took a short August holiday in Normandy to paint. Packing away his easel and brushes after only a few days, the soon-to-be First Lord of the Admiralty predicted "this is the last picture we shall paint in peace for a very long time."

Days later, the Hitler-Stalin nonaggression pact was signed. The agreement allowed Germany to attack Poland without fear of fighting an Eastern Front war against the Soviet Union. Britain and France had guaranteed Poland's independence. With the invasion, Britain declared war on Germany on September 3, 1939. In Munich, Unity Mitford went to the Englischer Garten and shot herself. The bullet lodged in her skull but did not kill her. Hitler arranged her evacuation home through Switzerland.

Britain mobilized. Streetlights were extinguished and blackout rules took effect. Railings from the front of Buckingham Palace, Brooks's (a club on St. James's) and other buildings were removed to be melted down into arms. Hundreds of thousands of Londoners moved to the country to avoid bombing raids. Among the first to flee London was the defeatist American Ambassador, Joseph P. Kennedy.

Kennedy had been enthusiastically received when he, his wife, Rose, and their nine children arrived in London in 1937 to represent the United States at the Court of St. James's. But his repeated predictions that Germany would defeat Britain turned the Boston Irishman into a despised figure in London. Franklin Roosevelt, who appointed him, was disgusted when Kennedy abandoned the capital and withdrew him in 1940.

King George VI and Queen Elizabeth made a point to stay put even as bombs began to drop on Buckingham Palace. That decision plus the concern they showed by arriving in bombed neighborhoods while the rubble was still shifting forever endeared them to their subjects. During the first days of the Blitz, the king showed up in London's East End early one morning with no advance notice. He trudged through the debris from still-burning houses and talked quietly to some of the families trying to cope with their losses.

"You're a great king," a Cockney cried out.

The monarch looked at the man and smiled. "You're a great people."[16]

In Dorset, the Digbys joined the war effort. Pamela's father was named an honorary bodyguard of the king in 1939. From 1940 to 1942, he served with the rank of general as assistant inspector of infantry at the War Office and from 1942 to 1944 as inspector of infantry training establishments. Pansy signed up too and served in Dorset as chief commandant of the Auxiliary Territorial Service.

Sheila joined the army, but Pamela wanted no part of military life. She was not afraid of war, but she was afraid of returning to Dorset and getting shoved into the army with Sheila. She told David Margesson that under no circumstances was she going home. Could he find her a job in London? Margesson found an opening at the Foreign Office, which hired her for six pounds a week as a French translator. Her son Winston later claimed that she also translated German, but Pamela's German was not good enough for her to be a translator.

She needed a place to live. The Nortons were no longer willing to put her up on Grosvenor Square. Pamela wanted more independence anyway. She knew the world was changing. She wanted flexibility and the freedom to change as well.

All entertaining stopped at Leeds Castle. After 850 vessels evacuated nearly 350,000 Allied troops from Dunkirk in late May and early June 1940, it was thought that Kent might be a German invasion route. Much planning for the defense of the English Channel ports and the south coast was conducted in the early days of the war from Leeds Castle and Dover Castle, just as it had been in the eleventh century. When the threat of invasion passed, Lady Baillie turned over the castle to the government for use as a military hospital.[17]

For two and a half pounds a week, Pamela rented an apartment near Victoria Station from Lady Mary Dunn, whose sister-in-law Brigid was a friend of Pam's. The month before the war began, Brigid went to Bavaria to marry her boyfriend, Peter Metternich. He was killed early in the war and she was stuck, an English widow, in Germany.

Mary Dunn's husband, Philip, had already left to join his regiment and Randolph Churchill was in hot pursuit of Mary. Mary Dunn was used to being pursued. Then twenty-seven, she was the daughter of the fifth earl of Rosslyn and had been Lady Mary St. Clair-Erskine before marrying Dunn. Two years before, the young mother of two had become involved briefly with William S. Paley, who would later create the CBS television network. Paley had proposed that they marry and run away to India.[18]

Randolph Churchill was pursuing others at the time. Whenever he could, he slept with a vaudeville actress named Clare Luce, no relation to the writer and politician Clare Boothe Luce. But when he returned to London on a pass the week after war was declared, Miss Luce was busy. Pushing through the revolving door at the Ritz Hotel on Piccadilly, Winston Churchill's only son spotted Lady Mary coming out the other side. Could she have dinner with him? She didn't want to have dinner with Randolph. She was dining with Randolph's friend Alan Pryce-Jones and his wife, but she did have a backup.

As she told Pryce-Jones, "I've got a red-headed tart up my sleeve. A girl coming to stay with me called Pamela Digby. She will do for Randolph." "I remember the phrase," Pryce-Jones said. " 'She will do for Randolph.' And so she did."

Mary Dunn was back in the apartment when Randolph called, but Pamela picked up the phone.

"This is Randolph Churchill. Who are you?"

"Pamela Digby. Do you want to speak to Mary?"

"No, I want to speak to you."

"But you don't know me," Pamela replied.

"Mary Dunn said I could invite you out to dinner. What do you look like?" he demanded.

"Red-headed and rather fat, but Mummy says that puppy fat disappears," Pamela responded, according to a version Randolph told his cousin, biographer Anita Leslie.[19]

"Will you come to dinner with me?" he asked. Mary Dunn had walked toward Pam during the conversation, nodding her head vigorously. "Do go out with him," she said. "I can't."

Pamela agreed, hung up the phone and turned back to Mary. "What's this all about?"

"He's an old friend of mine," Mary explained. "He's great fun, a bit too fat and drinks too much, but very amusing. I told him I would try to persuade you to dine with him. Please do — you'll have a very good time."

Pamela met Randolph at 7:30 P.M. at Quaglino's, a restaurant-nightclub near Piccadilly. He was then working as a London *Times* journalist. Other friends of his were there and Pamela joined the group. Randolph almost completely ignored her, but she was intrigued nonetheless.

He was nine years older than she and handsome, two important qualities for Pamela. What next impressed her was Randolph's total confidence that Britain would win the war. It would be very bloody, but Britain would certainly win, he said, thumping his hand on the table. He was the first person she had talked to who had not the slightest doubt how it would turn out.

Randolph's assurance was very inspiring to a nineteen-year-old who had been hearing nothing but pessimism from her contemporaries. Until then, "I found it all so depressing," she said. "Anytime one went to the Four Hundred [club] whoever you were with, instead of asking Rossi, the head-waiter to keep his whisky bottle until the next visit, as was the custom, would end the evening by presenting the bottle to the head-waiter and saying, 'Take this, I won't be coming again — I'm going out to get killed.' I was getting terribly upset by seeing all my friends going off, as they dramatically thought, to be killed. I thought how marvelous it was to be going out with somebody about whom I didn't give a damn who was, by contrast, so irrepressibly optimistic."[20]

Although he scarcely spoke to her at dinner, Randolph asked Pamela what she was doing the following night. She was free, so they went to dinner again, this time alone. At the end of the evening Randolph suggested they get married. Pamela was startled, but she barely hesitated. Yes. Why not? It was an impulsive response. All her life she has relied on her instincts and, not always but often, her intuition has been correct. She had thought about marriage, just not to Randolph until he mentioned it. Marriage was a passport to a new life. It would guarantee her break from Minterne and her parents.

She had never been in love, but in the abstract, love in marriage was less important for Pamela than freedom from worry that she might one day have to return home or marry some upper-class twit her age. Randolph might or might not survive the war, and she might or might not ever love him, but in the meantime, he had plenty of attributes that Pamela liked. He was good-looking, well known, politically connected and her emancipator, offering entrée into an entire new and activist social circle. They were near strangers, but each had very good reasons for marching down the aisle.

Then everything became very complicated.

❧ ❧

CHAPTER FIVE

Randolph, Winston and Clemmie

BRITAIN had been at war with Germany for ten days when Randolph proposed to Pamela. Within another two weeks, they were formally engaged. The intervening days were chaotic for the country and the couple.

In London, by the Knightsbridge Barracks, steam shovels bit into the soft turf where the Household Cavalry rode, and dumped the earth into trucks which took it away to fill sandbags. Barrages of balloons were sent aloft to confuse enemy planes. Special yellow paint which changed color in the presence of poison gas was splashed on scarlet royal mail boxes. Gas masks were issued by the thousands. The BBC calmly interrupted its evening Promenade concerts with instructions to motorists and expectant mothers about what to do during air raids. Police halted incoming traffic to London and the evacuation of the capital by car and rail began. Squadrons of troop-transport planes filled the skies.[1]

Just as quickly, friends of Pamela and Randolph mobilized on hearing the engagement news. Everyone Pamela knew tried to talk her out of what they all figured would be a terrible mistake.

Lady Baillie and David Margesson were furious when she

informed them. They told her that she knew nothing about Randolph. He was insufferable: a drunk and a troublemaker; totally unsuitable. She had no idea how bad his reputation was. The whole idea of marrying him was ridiculous. "Oh dear me, what a pity," said Jean Norton when she heard the news.[2] Even one of Randolph's closest friends, Ed Stanley, tried to talk her out of it. He called Pamela to complain that she had stood him up for dinner.

"And I find you dining with Randolph Churchill. He's a very, very bad man and you shouldn't go out with people like that."

"But he's one of your best friends," Pamela retorted.

"Yes, he is one of *my* best friends," Stanley replied, "but that doesn't mean he should be one of *yours*."[3]

Randolph had proposed to eight girls since the war began, he continued, including three in one night. But instead of being warned off, Pamela became more determined to marry him. It was *her* life, not theirs and she would live it the way she wanted. It is unclear precisely how much she knew about Randolph. She has told some people that she had no idea who he was and scarcely knew anything of Winston. Her contemporaries and friends consider that nonsense.

That might have been true if she were just the pony-loving teenager from Dorset, but by the outbreak of war she was no longer a naïf. The Leeds Castle experience ensured that she knew what was happening politically. According to Julian Amery, Pamela's good friend from childhood, "In the run-up to the war, politics was the only thing on everyone's agenda," including Pamela's.[4] To suggest that she was politically involved but unaware of the significance of the Churchills who, after all, also had a Minterne Magna connection, was an effort by Pamela to suggest that she was less calculating about her suitor than she in fact was.

By September 1939, Winston Churchill's name was on everyone's lips. The day war was declared, Neville Chamberlain named him First Lord of the Admiralty, the post he first held in 1911. "Churchill in the Cabinet," said Luftwaffe chief Hermann Goering when he heard the news. "That means war is really on."[5] Not only were the newspapers filled with reports that WINSTON'S BACK, the Leeds Castle political talk leading up to and immediately following Chamberlain's declaration of war would have centered on Winston. Eight months after war began he would be prime minister.

His only son, Randolph, was widely known among the upper class, on the nightclub circuit and certainly by the savvy politicians at Leeds Castle, the entire circle trying to dissuade their young friend from marrying him. Randolph was no callow twenty-eight-year-old: he had already been a candidate for Parliament; his newspaper articles were noteworthy. If anything, Randolph was hard to miss.

Randolph was Winston's golden boy. A beautiful child, an Adonis with golden hair, bright eyes and sculpted looks, he was also precociously intelligent and a natural orator, with an excoriating wit. His looks and intelligence could not disguise the fact that he was also a complete terror who lost friends quicker than he could make them.

From his youngest days he was tough and pugnacious. He readily admitted to pranks he had not committed to demonstrate that he could take whatever punishment was meted out. When a nanny had enough of his obstreperousness and filled his mouth with hot mustard, Randolph screamed, but swallowed it. He persuaded his cousin Johnny to toss the contents of a chamber pot out a window without telling him that Prime Minister Lloyd George was seated below.[6]

He was a handful for his teachers. "A quick boy, at times too quick as he is apt to answer before he thinks," said W. M. Hornby, the headmaster of Sandroyd, of his eleven-year-old charge. When he sent his heir off to Eton at the age of thirteen in 1924, Winston Churchill asked that Randolph be spared corporal punishment. Almost immediately, Randolph was being beaten regularly for being "bloody awful all around."[7]

The analysis of his teachers at Eton was prescient. "Obstinacy appears to be one of his more prominent characteristics," concluded mathematics instructor H. G. Babington Smith. "He has shown himself to be possessed of a natural capacity in many directions, but he does not take kindly to being taught."

By the time Randolph was seventeen, another teacher, C. R. N. Routh, determined that while his ambitions outran his capacities, he was blessed with enthusiasm. "He is overflowing with ideas. He has passionate likes and hates. He is as courageous as they make them in defending his theories and he has a dialectical skill which is often needed if he is going to get out of some of the holes into which he gets himself." But also, Routh went on, "he is too quarrelsome. He likes being in a minority and enjoys, not rubbing people up the wrong way, but the result of having rubbed them the wrong way."[8]

Winston's own father, Lord Randolph, had been distant and cold, a selfish parent. "Immersed in his own brand of rebellious Tory politics [Lord Randolph] seldom wrote or spoke to his elder son except to chide him," wrote Winston's private secretary John Colville.[9] "Randolph actually disliked his son," said Churchill's biographer William Manchester.[10]

In speaking of his father to the writer Frank Harris, Winston said, "He wouldn't listen to me or consider anything I said. There was no companionship possible to me and I tried so hard and so often. He was so self-centered, no one else existed for him. My mother was everything to me."[11]

Determined to do better for his son, Winston erred in common fashion. He forever spoiled, indulged and forgave Randolph. Success was not enough for his only son. He wanted him to succeed spectacularly. He groomed him from childhood for politics, once explaining that "politics is like prostitution and piano-playing. The earlier you start the better."

In an effort to showcase his pride and joy, Winston frequently silenced cabinet ministers so Randolph could speak. His hopes may have been best displayed at a stag dinner he hosted at Claridge's for Randolph's twenty-first birthday. The great men of the day and their sons were all invited, including Lord Hailsham and Quintin Hogg, a future lord chancellor, and the great newspaper barons, Lords Camrose, Rothermere and Beaverbrook. The evening's theme was "passing the lamp" of power to the next generation.[12]

In Randolph's case, the lamp was never seized. It would be another quarter century before Winston stepped away from power in 1955. By then, as a result of alcoholism and his own abusive nature, Randolph had dropped every one of the endless opportunities handed him.

Although many of his contemporaries predicted that Randolph would never live up to his early promise, his ultimate fate was obviously unknown when Pamela met him in 1939. After the coming-of-age dinner, he used his contacts and considerable writing skill to become a journalist of some renown. He made a successful lecture tour in the United States. He covered the early Nazi rallies in Germany and filed dispatches predicting that "the success of the Nazi party sooner or later means war."

He bellowed support for his father's campaign to re-arm Britain to counter Hitler's military buildup throughout the 1930s. But his father was a political outcast who had not been in the Cabinet for a decade. The Baldwin and Chamberlain governments wanted no part of Winston Churchill, with his enormous ego and sharp tongue. To centrist Tories who cringed at his denunciation of the Munich pact, Winston was a wild-eyed militant, a scaremonger and warmonger.

Randolph's strident condemnation of appeasement made him an outcast as well. However correct Randolph would prove to be about Germany, he was his own worst enemy, living proof of the adage he often repeated himself: "Beneath the mighty oak, no saplings grow." His talents were outweighed by endless bouts of drunkenness and public brawling, gambling and chasing women.

Even his father felt compelled on occasion to upbraid him. In 1931, Winston wrote to protest a six-hundred-pound gambling debt that Randolph ran up betting on that year's election. The father agreed to pay, but warned, "I grieve more than it is worth setting down to see you with so many gifts and so much good treatment from the world leading the life of a selfish exploiter, borrowing and spending every shilling you can lay your hands on and ever increasing the lavish folly of your ways. But words are useless."[13]

They were. Criticism, even from the father he adored, rarely interrupted Randolph's march to self-destruction. When sent in 1935 to write about a by-election in a constituency near Liverpool, Randolph instead decided to join the fray as a rival to the

Conservative already contesting the seat. He succeeded only in splitting the vote for the Conservatives while the district sent a Labour party politician to the House of Commons for the first time. His father was livid.

Enough of Randolph's foibles were brought to Pamela's attention after his proposal that she immediately had second thoughts. She sensed that she was about to make a mistake, but she could not make a clear decision. She felt muddled.

She had cut herself off from home. She might have had a fairytale upbringing at Minterne Magna, but there was no warmth for her there or advice she respected. Pamela loved interesting people, loved to talk and listen. Randolph was older, no longer the perfect sylph, but still handsome and intriguing. He had a prodigious memory and recited to her verse by Hilaire Belloc and John Betjeman. She was frightened about war, but he was not. And while she understood that he could be beastly, he had been only charming and scintillating to her. Rarely was there a bigger charmer than Randolph when he was sober.

She was unable to assess the horror stories about his drinking and gambling. Her father was a teetotaler; her mother drank only an occasional sherry. Pamela had seen drinking and gambling at Leeds Castle as well as guests who had obviously drunk too much. She didn't take these diversions seriously. They seemed reasonable recreations, not addictions. Still, the warnings were dire. Ed Stanley told her directly to get out of it while she could. He advised that she call Randolph and tell him she was not going through with the marriage.

She called. Randolph came over from his flat in Westminster Gardens and they walked to Victoria Station, where Randolph drank a large brandy in the railway restaurant while they talked. He told her that she had no guts. He was going off to war and she was playing with his life. She'd be sorry at the mistake she was making. Pamela was more confused than ever. His pursuit was terribly romantic. She loved all the fuss and attention; it was better than the riding ring. Randolph did intrigue her. She put him off and bolted to Leeds Castle to talk to Lady Baillie. She did not consult Pansy. Randolph promised to call. He hoped she had enough spine to speak with him.

Randolph went to Tidworth, near Stonehenge in Wiltshire, to rejoin his regiment. The year before, in 1938, acting on the alarms he was helping sound, he had joined his father's old regiment — the Fourth Hussars — as a reserve officer. When Britain declared war in September, he was serving three weeks' annual duty.

He was not doing much. The Fourth Hussars were a cavalry regiment which had been officially mechanized in 1937. The unit no longer had horses, but neither had replacement tanks arrived.[14] With time on his hands, he repeatedly phoned Pamela. Summoning his formidable debating skill, after a five-day break in the engagement, he cracked the nineteen-year-old's faltering resolve. Pamela learned firsthand about Randolph what the world was about to discover about Winston: the Churchills could out-talk anyone.

When she changed her mind back, Pamela gave the first overt indication of how ambitious and calculating she could be. Until then, she had shown an independent streak in leaving home for the bright lights. Marrying Randolph would not only guarantee her freedom from Dorset but would move her into another league completely.

She had no idea how the war would play out, but she knew the world was changing and she did not want to be left behind. The Churchill name would ensure that she was not. "She was determined," said Sarah Baring. "She knew what she was doing."[15] Pamela has acknowledged as much herself.

Leeds Castle had been an almost addictive experience. Celebrities gave her a rush. By September 1939, no one had a better chance of being more prominent than Winston Churchill. Becoming a Churchill would open, according to the duke of Devonshire, "endless new vistas, a whole new world to her."

Going into it, Pamela did not have much faith that the marriage would last. But so what? If the marriage failed, her situation would be no worse. If it did not work, she told Lady Baillie matter-of-factly, she could always get a divorce. Pansy would have been horrified by such a cold-blooded scheme, although Pamela could have cited the Jane Digby–Lord Ellenborough precedent. Olive, who had been divorced twice, stopped arguing. The bridge player had been trumped.

The decision made, both sets of parents were informed. At Minterne, the Digbys were opposed. "She's too young," they said. "They don't have any money or anywhere to live. They don't even know each other."[16]

Randolph was on his best behavior, but he was not their real concern. Nor was their opinion of his father a significant hurdle, although they were not Winston backers. The Digbys were very traditional Tories and Winston Churchill was anything but traditional. In fact, one other reason that regular Tories mistrusted Winston was that for a period of twenty years he had defected from the party and been a Liberal.

To Pansy and Ken Digby and his mainstream Conservative friends in the House of Lords, Winston throughout the thirties was an aberration, a defunct politician and an irritant to Tory governance. His brilliance did not make an impact on the Digbys. When they thought about him at all, which was not often, they considered him unstable.

Their objections, however, were parental, not political. They felt that the young couple should wait a little. They did not press their case. Pamela was certain that they had given up on her by then. They knew she would do what she wanted.

They were right. They had long ago ceased to have influence and she did ignore their objections. For his part, Lord Digby withheld an unspecified amount of Pamela's dowry, although the stipulated reason was the uncertainty of war. Randolph took Pamela to Chartwell, Churchill's bucolic country sanctuary twenty-five miles southeast of London overlooking the Weald of Kent.

Used to a much bigger estate in Dorset, she was not impressed with the sixty acres and modest red-brick house that Churchill had purchased for five thousand pounds in 1922. It had no grand ballroom or massive library, no art collection and was neither city nor the kind of country living she knew. With considerable condescension, she thought it suburban.

She liked Winston enormously from the first moment, when he walked up from his studio wearing a long black painter's smock which set off his pink, scrubbed face.

"He knew more about my family than I did," Pamela recalled.[17]

"You're no longer Catholic," he said, removing his cigar from his mouth. "You had your heads chopped off in the Gunpowder Plot."

He knew all about the first Winston Churchill being buried at Minterne Magna and appeared to take an immediate liking to Pamela. "She's a charming girl," he told a friend.[18]

Clementine Churchill opposed the marriage but did not tell Pamela. To her young visitor and potential daughter-in-law, she was correct and reserved.

Clementine knew how much trouble Randolph was. Their relationship was always strained. Randolph told Pamela that his mother hated him. Once when he was nine and attending Sandroyd preparatory school, Clementine had come to visit him on a Saturday. She slapped his face in front of the other boys. From that moment he knew that she hated him.

Pamela thought it was ridiculous to draw such a conclusion, but the extreme chill between mother and son was well known — and the precise reverse of what his father had experienced. Randolph's younger sister Mary saw the problem: "As his personality developed, it produced features of character and outlook too dissimilar from his mother's whole nature and attitude to life. This lively boy manifestly needed a father's hand; but the main task of controlling him fell almost entirely upon Clementine and so right from the early days she and Randolph were at loggerheads."[19]

According to Lord Norwich, "That was one of the reasons he was such a nightmare. He never got any maternal love at all. Clemmie hated Randolph all his life."[20] The best Clementine could hope for — and she doubted it would happen — was that marriage might settle Randolph down.

Winston could not have offered a warmer welcome to Pamela. He brushed aside every argument against the marriage. "Nonsense. All you need to be married are champagne, a box of cigars and a double bed." He confided to Pamela that forty years before, when he was with the Fourth Hussars in India, he had once almost married a Pamela — Pamela Plowden, who later became a countess. He thought Pamela Digby was charming and pretty. He liked that in girls.

Pamela, in turn, was very solicitous of him as she always was and would be with interesting, powerful men. Soon she was calling him Papa, playing bezique, a pinochle-like sixty-four-card game, with him into the night and helping light his cigar. She cared greatly for him, but she was also cementing a personal relationship parallel to that with Randolph.

There was an extra incentive for Winston to welcome the teenager to the family. "I expect that he will be in action in the early spring and therefore I am very glad that he should be married before he goes," he wrote of Randolph to the duke of Westminster five days before the wedding.[21]

Marrying immediately gave Randolph time to sire a child. The question of succession was important. Winston was sixty-four. If his only son died without a male heir, the Churchill line ended.

No one was more aware of that responsibility than Randolph. He took Pamela with him to Southampton to see off his friend, the American journalist John Gunther, who was returning to the States. The engagement had not yet been announced and Gunther had never met Pamela before. That didn't stop Randolph, who, after introducing them, was typically blunt saying that "he was about to marry Pamela and that he must have a son and heir as soon as possible since he was convinced that he would soon be killed."[22]

Randolph was not shy about telling the same story around London. Having a child was much more important than having a wife or even being in love. Pamela's parents realized that a child, not a stable relationship, was Randolph's whole goal. "Digby said to me that Randolph had to have an heir," said Piers Dixon, a former MP and Churchill in-law.[23]

There was no one else who filled the bill as well as Pamela. Randolph was in love with Laura Charteris, whose sister would later marry the author Ian Fleming. But Laura was married to Lord Long and while she liked Randolph, she didn't love him nor care to have his child. Other girlfriends, like Clare Luce, were available for sex, but not for procreation. Pamela had all the requisite qualities.

She was young, healthy, pretty, willing, came from an acceptable family and was, more often than not, charmed by her fiancé. As Lady Mary Dunn had predicted, Pamela would indeed do for Randolph. Randolph was ready to assume his duties as a sire the second time he took Pamela to dinner and brought her home to her apartment, but she withstood his advances for the remainder of the truncated courtship.

The wedding took place on October 4, 1939, at St. John's Church in Smith Square near the Houses of Parliament. German bombs hit the lovely Christopher Wren church later in the war, but on the day of the ceremony, the biggest disruption came from crowds who had gathered to cheer Winston, whose prescience about Nazi Germany was only recently appreciated.

Outwardly, both bride and groom appeared jubilant, but Randolph was more optimistic about their prospects than Pamela because his expectations were lower. An English male, he did not have lofty ambitions about the romantic aspects of marriage. His father, his club, going off to war and continuing the line were what mattered to Randolph. Marrying Pamela made sense because it solved a problem. Whatever else might be involved in cementing a relationship could be dealt with after the war. If he survived. Because Randolph doubted he would, there was little reason to be concerned about solid foundations.

A much greater romantic, Pamela had higher hopes. She had heard others talk about dying in the war, but Randolph's optimism had eliminated most thoughts from her mind that he might actually be killed. No one close to her had died. Death was a concept, but unreal.

And while he was single when he went off to war, her own father had survived, returned home and enjoyed a successful marriage to her mother. So the portents were brighter for Pamela. Still, she was not blind to some early warning signs, triggered by Randolph's periodic disappearances. When they happened, she found herself saying, "This is absolutely idiotic."[24]

Whatever doubts she had, she concealed during the ceremony. She wore a deep blue coat trimmed with dyed fox fur over a dress of the same color. Her blue velvet beret-shaped hat sported a quill and she wore a spray of pink and white orchids. Randolph wore his uniform. Both looked plump. Pamela would become more attractive; Randolph, less.

They exited the church under an archway of raised swords

carried by Randolph's fellow Fourth Hussars. The guests all carried gas masks. The rector who performed the ceremony arrived with his mask in a special scarlet sack. A small reception for relatives and friends followed at Admiralty House on Whitehall, where the state rooms were opened for the occasion.

After the party, the newlyweds drove to Belton near Grantham to stay at the home of Lord Brownlow, equerry to the duke of Windsor. The four-day honeymoon almost doomed the marriage at the outset. Randolph insisted on reading aloud in bed to his teenage bride from Edward Gibbon's *Decline and Fall of the Roman Empire*.

Repeatedly, he stopped to ask: "Are you listening?"

"Yes, I am." Pamela sighed.

"Well, what was the last sentence?"

After the honeymoon, Pamela went with Randolph to Beverley in Yorkshire, where the Fourth Hussars were stationed. Contrary to Randolph's expectations, he was not sent overseas immediately. They settled in for what for Pamela was a miserable winter. Cold, snowy, icy. "It was ghastly," she said.[25]

Other units were dispatched abroad, but not the Hussars. Some regiment members believed that the unit was held back so Winston's son could be kept from harm's way. When Randolph asked to be given a more active war role, Winston confided to John Colville that if Randolph were killed he would be unable to carry on his work. He denied he played a role in holding his son's unit back, but suspicions remained.

"All the sergeants' wives were saying, 'Of course, we have nothing to worry about as long as Mr. Churchill's son is in the regiment — none of our husbands will be sent abroad,' " Pamela recalled.[26] The waiting was hard on Randolph. He was desperate to head off for the fighting. His frustration increased with each passing day, which led to more drinking, greater volatility and increasing abuse of his wife.

The season did not help anyone's mood. In addition to horrible weather, the winter of 1939–40 was the so-called "phony war." Air attacks were anticipated, but did not happen. Nerves grated on edge. The French government feared making any move that might incite the Wehrmacht, which was holding behind the Siegfried Line. In Britain, the Chamberlain government was pleased with the status quo. No fighting meant no bloodshed, which meant perhaps the government could hang on to office.

There were different tensions for Randolph and his regiment. His problem was that the Fourth Hussars was a regular army unit. Unlike territorial regiments which his friends from White's in London had joined, Randolph's regiment had junior officers ten years younger than he. They had nothing in common and taunted him endlessly about the miserable shape he was in and who he was, a replay of the jibes he suffered at Eton. Randolph, never one to walk away from a fight, mocked them back.

They bet him fifty pounds that he could not walk the 108 miles to Hull and back in twenty-four hours. Randolph trained for weeks, rubbed his feet with alcohol to toughen them and began the walk at 3 A.M. On the final stretch, his blisters were so bad that he removed his boots and walked in socks. The hike was agony. Pamela followed him the entire way with soup and coffee in the car, honking if he went below four miles an hour or faster than six. They beat the deadline by less than half an hour, but the junior officers, whooping derisively, refused to pay.

Pamela was furious at their behavior and Randolph's impotence to change it and remained bitter a half century later, cursing Randolph's tormentors. The passage of time did nothing to soften her memory of them as a bunch of rotten bastards.

She also felt sorrow for Randolph and anguish over his humiliation. Part of the incentive for making the hike was winning the fifty pounds. They needed the money. Randolph told Pam repeatedly how many bills they could pay off once he collected. "In fact," she said, "it wouldn't have paid off a tenth of them."[27] The bill problems in Beverley were only a hint of trouble to come.

The phony war ended in April 1940, when Hitler launched blitzkrieg attacks against Denmark and Norway. Admiralty chief Churchill had chafed through the winter, trying to persuade the Cabinet and Prime Minister Chamberlain to land British troops in Narvik in northern Norway. The plan was for them to cut inland to the iron mines at Gallivära in Sweden, which supplied ore for Hitler's weapons production. After cutting that pipeline, the troops would join the Finnish resistance, which had been battling Stalin's Red Army since the Soviet invasion on November 30, 1939.

Hitler learned of the stratagem and moved first. Denmark fell in hours. Norway proved tougher and gave King Haakon VII time to flee north from Oslo with twenty-three tons of gold. Britain had landed nearly twenty-five thousand Allied troops in Norway, but their equipment was limited, London's planning was weak and they were soon evacuated — along with the King and Norway's treasure. The German success, and Britain's failure to prevent the invasion, increased the strain on Chamberlain. "We have been completely outwitted," snorted Churchill.[28]

The pressure on the government peaked when, on May 7, Leo Amery rose in the House of Commons to address the prime minister with the same words that Oliver Cromwell used to dismiss Parliament three centuries before. "You have sat too long for any good you have been doing. Depart, I say, and let us have done with you. In the name of God, go!" Chamberlain took the advice. On May 10, the Nazis stormed into Belgium and France. Chamberlain resigned and, by evening, Winston Churchill was prime minister. Pamela was four months pregnant with his grandchild.

Britain was ready for leadership. Britons had watched countries on the Continent toppling like dominoes into neutrality or Nazi control. With Winston, they had the perfect match of leader and historic moment. Like no other, he was the right man at the right time. He put it gracefully. It was "the nation and the race dwelling all round the globe that had the lion's heart. I had the luck to be called on to give the roar."[29]

Roar he did. Seven months earlier, Chamberlain had abandoned Czechoslovakia to the Nazis, bleating that theirs was "a quarrel in a faraway country between people of whom we know nothing." Churchill, though, took office with one of history's most stirring pledges: "I have nothing to offer but blood, toil, tears and sweat. You ask, what is our policy? I will say: it is to wage war . . . with all the strength that God can give us. That is our policy."

Throughout the defeat of France, the Dunkirk evacuation and the first weeks of air raids against Britain, the Churchills stayed in Admiralty House. In mid-June they moved to 10 Downing

Street, the prime minister's office and official residence, and took over Chequers, the official country house.

Until then, Pamela had stayed with Randolph. But with the bombing of Britain picking up in intensity, talk of German invasion increasing and her pregnancy advancing, she moved in with the Churchills.

Pamela had been living with Randolph for nine months by then, long enough to be acutely aware of the problems she had taken on. Randolph was like the little girl with the curl in the nursery rhyme: when he was good, he was very, very good; but when he was bad, he was horrid.

Randolph's drinking embarrassed her. Winston drank. A Johnny Walker Red whisky and soda or Hine brandy or a flute of Pol Roger champagne seemed as close to hand as his omnipresent Romeo y Julietas cigars. But Winston was a careful drinker, not a heavy drinker. Pamela never saw Winston the worse for drink. But it was not only she who could attest to his boast that "I have taken more out of alcohol than alcohol has taken out of me." Writer Robert Sherwood confirmed that "anyone who suggested that he became befuddled with drink obviously never had to become involved in an argument with him on some factual problem late at night. He was really Olympian in capacity."[30]

Randolph was a different story. Randolph was the kind of abusive drinker that his father was referring to when he said, "We all despise a man who gets drunk."[31] One time at White's, Randolph became so offensive that his clubmates physically ejected him. "They kicked his backside right down the front steps," said Douglas Fairbanks Jr., who was present.[32]

When the young Churchills went out to dinner and Randolph was drinking, he invariably became argumentative. Often he stormed out of whatever house they were visiting, leaving Pamela to sit there in agony. She never knew what to do, whether to leave with him or stay. Sometimes he challenged her at the table. As conversation halted and the scene escalated, he demanded to know whether she was coming with him or not. She wanted to vanish into the upholstery. Sometimes he left, then returned to retrieve her; on other occasions, he disappeared.

He got in a screaming row one night soon after war was declared at dinner at the house of Lord Kemsley, the owner of the Sunday *Times* and the *Daily Sketch* newspapers, when Lady Kemsley urged that everyone forget about Hitler and concentrate instead on getting richer.

Randolph rightly exploded. It was people like the appeasing Kemsleys who got Britain into this problem in the first place, he shouted, his face turning red. They were quislings. Pamela agreed with Randolph, but she was mortified at having to flee the dinner table. She put up with similar behavior at home. Randolph did not hit her, but he frequently unleashed torrents of verbal abuse, stomped around, kicked furniture and hollered.

The newlyweds' other serious problem involved the bills that Randolph was accumulating. Her Minterne upbringing taught her that bills were paid when they came in. If you could not afford something, you did not buy it. Pamela had perhaps forgotten her Leeds gambling debt and her misfortune at the Scottish racetrack. Nonetheless, there was no question that the Digbys paid their bills on time.

Randolph did not, a situation made worse by the fact that sheaves of bills tumbled in over the transom. In the thirties, men's establishments allowed their customers to run up tabs. Gieves and Hawkes, the tailors; Hilditch and Key, the shirtmakers; Berry Brothers, the wine merchants; and White's, the gentlemen's club billed quarterly or semiannually. Accounts that Pamela had never heard of arrived. The number of invoices and totals due were staggering, far more than Randolph's income.

Randolph was unconcerned and blithely told Pamela not to worry. It was wartime. Creditors could wait another six months. Panicky, Pamela went to Clementine, who turned over the all too familiar problem to Winston. He told Pamela that he would cover the bills, but was she sure that was the end of them? In good faith, she thought so. Winston paid. Three months later an entirely new batch of invoices arrived. While shopping in Harrods, Pamela's charge privileges were revoked for nonpayment. She fled from the store in tears, shaking with humiliation.

Time and again she took her concerns to Clementine, who tried to be comforting, but no one was more aware of Randolph's capacity for trouble than his mother. Already her only son had infuriated the prime-ministerial staff.

"One of the most objectionable people I have ever met; noisy, self-assertive, whining and frankly unpleasant," was how Churchill's private secretary John Colville described his first meeting with Randolph. "He did not strike me as intelligent. At dinner, he was anything but kind to Winston, who adores him."[33]

Pamela talked to Clementine more openly than she talked to her own mother. Mrs. Churchill was considerate and tried to be helpful, but she lived in constant fear of Randolph embarrassing Winston.

She told Pamela that she had had to decide early in her own marriage whether she would devote her entire life to Winston or have some independence. She cited Diana Cooper, the youngest child of the duchess of Rutland and the beautiful wife of diplomat Duff Cooper, as the kind of woman who had personal friends and pursued her own intellectual, artistic and social interests. Clemmie, however, had decided to focus all her strength totally on Winston.

The decision meant that she spent a tremendous amount of time alone. Even before he was prime minister, Winston often hosted or attended four or five stag dinners a week. When he was not with his male friends, he was working, writing, traveling or, in prewar years, painting. Pamela became convinced that Clementine Churchill had more dinners on a tray alone in her room than she ever did with Winston or company and probably spent as much as 80 percent of her life alone.

Eating alone became such a habit that on weekends at Chequers, she often sent Pamela a note saying she would not be coming down for dinner and would Pamela please host instead. Thus did Pamela meet some of Britain's and the world's most powerful movers and shakers.

Part of Clementine's reticence was that she did not like many of Winston's friends and was frightened that they would ruin or embarrass her husband. Many were rich, but Clementine always felt pinched for money. She worried that Winston would be seduced by their wealth or the sybaritic pleasures they could offer. Winston spent so much time with them, she was jealous.

Clementine was also jealous of Randolph. She resented his constant intrusions between her and Winston and feared the damage that he, more than any cabinet minister, might cause his father.

When a tearful Pamela approached Clementine for help very early in the marriage, the older woman advised that she simply had to learn how to handle such things. She had had to develop a thick skin to deal with Winston's irascible behavior and Randolph's repeated disappointments. Pamela would have to learn to do the same. She advised her daughter-in-law to leave home for three or four days to give Randolph a scare and to pull him back into line. It was important for Pamela to demonstrate that she could exert influence.

If she chose not to use pressure, then Pamela got what she deserved. If she tried and there was no response, then perhaps the relationship was hopeless. But one had to try. Don't tell Randolph where you're going, she advised. Just leave a note that you have left. She had left Winston several times and once stayed in a hotel for two or three days. When she returned, everything was fine again.

Pamela adopted a variation of the advice by moving in with Clementine and Winston. That was more than fine with the Churchills. They urged her to stay with them. By seeking the tighter embrace of family, Pamela also secured her safety net. If the marriage failed, and it looked more likely by the day that it would, she would have her own links to the Churchills independently of Randolph and their baby.

As long as Randolph was away and she was living in Downing Street or at Chequers, Pamela felt secure. She was a cheerful young woman, pretty and solicitous of her in-laws, and the Churchills were very fond of her. It helped that they felt guilty about Randolph. They knew all too well what she had to endure from their son.

She quickly became part of the family in the way that Diana and Sarah Churchill's husbands — Duncan Sandys and Vic Oliver — had not. She learned how Randolph inherited his enthusiasm for battle from Winston when she asked him what she and Clemmie should do if the Germans landed. His determination was not a pose. There was nothing mock heroic about Winston.

"If the Germans come, each one of you can take a dead German with you," he said. Pamela could tell that he was not joking. "He was in dead earnest and I was terrified," she said later. How could she do that? "I don't know how to fire a gun," she told him. "You could go into the kitchen and get a carving knife," he recommended.[34]

During air raid alerts, Pamela slept underground in the former wine cellar, which had been converted into a shelter for the Churchills. At one end of the cellar, there was a small room where bunk beds were installed; at the other end, a room with a single bed. Clemmie took the single. Pamela shared the bunks with Winston. She and "Baby Dumpling," as she referred to her swelling stomach, slept on the bottom tier.

"We used to have dinner at 8 P.M. because, most evenings, the [air raid] sirens would start at 9 P.M. and I would immediately be sent below. I would fall sound asleep until 1 or 1:30 A.M. when Papa would come down and climb the narrow ladder into the top bunk," Pamela said. "That was the end of my sleep because within two minutes of arriving in his bunk, he would be snoring. He would snore most of the night and Baby Dumpling would kick for the rest of it. So between the two of them, the only sleep I got was before Winston arrived and after about 6 A.M. when he got up and went back to his own bed when the raids were over."[35] In bed, she joked, she had one Churchill inside her and one on top of her.

It may have been a mixed blessing, but the one Churchill she did not have in her bed was Randolph. On August 4, 1940, when she was seven months pregnant, Randolph came to Downing Street on forty-eight hours' leave. Pamela had not seen her husband in several weeks and was delighted to have him back. There was a small, jolly family dinner with Clemmie and Winston, but her pleasure was short-lived.

After supper, Winston returned to the Cabinet room to work. Clemmie retreated upstairs. Randolph said he wanted to drop by the Savoy Hotel to see an old friend, journalist H. R. "Red" Knickerbocker, with whom he had reported the Spanish Civil War. He would not be long, Randolph reassured her. Just a quick drink. He left. Pamela waited. And waited. She became upset and angry, then worried and miserable.

At 6:30 A.M., Randolph staggered in. He was so drunk Pamela had to undress him and put him to bed. An hour later, a maid arrived with a note from Clementine. Pamela's presence was urgently required in Clemmie's bedroom, which was always separate from Winston's, with its small, single bed and simple wash basin.

The young woman began to tremble. Her stomach was swollen. Despite the hour, the August heat and humidity were already rising off Horse Guard's Parade and swirling through the partially open windows of Number 10. She forced herself down the corridors of walls painted pale pistachio green and salmon pink, as panic rose in her gorge.

She arrived to find her mother-in-law sitting up in bed wearing white gloves. Pamela's eyes flickered around the room, past the chintz flowered draperies, the Sickert sketches and Nicholson still lifes. Clementine's voice sliced through the heavy air.

"Where was Randolph last night?" she snapped. "Do you have any idea what has happened?"

Pamela's hands covered her eyes and she burst into tears. No idea at all, she sobbed.

Inspector W. H. Thompson, Winston's personal bodyguard, had reported that Randolph arrived in Downing Street at 6:10 A.M., tumbled out and left classified military maps behind in Pamela's car. He had committed a terrible offense, a security breach, Clementine explained. That Downing Street was a public, not a private, house made it a worse transgression.

Clementine was insistent. "What is going on?"

Pamela cried harder. She did not know. She hated this criticism. Worse, she hated the disorder in the marriage and the threat to her relationship with her in-laws. She had scarcely slept, angry and frightened by Randolph's disappearance. Her stomach was heaving.

Clementine ordered Randolph out of the house. He had to move immediately to White's.

Randolph was repentant. Ashen-faced, bleary-eyed, his breath stinking, he explained to Pamela that he had met Knickerbocker. They drank until closing the Savoy bar at midnight, then went to Knickerbocker's room, where the Pulitzer Prize–winner goaded Randolph about his speech-making capabilities. He could not hold a candle to his father in the oratory department, the American taunted. Stung, Randolph paced back and forth making extemporaneous speeches — so he told Pamela — until dawn. He had consumed one, or possibly two, bottles of brandy.

Profusely apologetic, he repeated the explanation to his father, who was fuming. Randolph promised he would never drink again, a pledge both men knew would never be kept. Pamela believed him. She always believed Randolph when he promised to quit. She was the only one who did.

She sympathized to a certain extent with Randolph. She knew that the last thing Randolph wanted to do was embarrass or anger his father. She also understood how Knickerbocker could have pushed her husband out of control. Randolph was so easy to incite.

Instead of being angry, Pamela blamed herself. He was her husband and it was her problem. She had not yet given up on him. She still wanted to watch out for him. She felt responsible for helping to cause Randolph's behavior. She thought there was something wrong with her.

Today, she would be called an enabler. But in 1940, this twenty-year-old felt only that if she were older and more mature, she would be more helpful and could stop his ruinous behavior. She wanted to do all she could to keep the marriage alive. One of the reasons she married him was that he was overpowering. Now he was overpowering her again.

Randolph was rarely down for long. The following month, a Conservative MP died and Randolph was chosen to fill his seat. According to a wartime truce among the political parties then serving in a coalition government, openings in Parliament were not contested. Making Randolph an incumbent, his father's colleagues hoped, would make it easier for him to defend the seat in a real contest after the war.[36]

Randolph had already tried three times to win a seat and failed. He tried three more times after the war. Every election he contested he lost. "The reason always advanced for his failure to be elected was that he was rude to one and all," was Diana Mitford Mosley's explanation.[37] According to his youngest sister, Mary, Randolph was "throughout his life, an easily aroused and explosive person."[38]

Almost anything could set Randolph off. He fought with the conductor on the train ride to his constituency. He fought with his political manager. He fought with his constituents. The Preston seat he was handed unopposed in October 1940 was the only "victory" for the man who had once boasted that there was no reason why he, like William Pitt the Younger, should not be prime minister by the age of twenty-five.

Within ten days of the family debacle at Number 10, the Battle of Britain began, the fight for control of the nation's skies to prepare the way for an invasion by 260,000 German ground troops. The first massive bombing raids began on August 13, 1940, when some fifteen hundred Luftwaffe planes raced across the Channel to batter Royal Air Force airfields in southern England.

For weeks, while Britons stared up at aerial dogfights, the Nazi air force returned every day, to be met by heroic RAF defenders. The British were badly outnumbered. Luftwaffe chief Goering had fourteen hundred bombers and a thousand fighters under his command compared with nine hundred fighters for the RAF defenders.

On Sunday afternoon, September 15, Winston left Chequers with Pamela to visit Uxbridge, headquarters for the twenty-five fighter squadrons which were the bulwark of southern England's defenses against the Luftwaffe's bombing raids. They went fifty feet underground into a theaterlike command post, where they sat in the balcony, overlooking a map table where aides used sticks, like casino croupiers, to shift discs showing the positions of the invading Junker and Heinkel bombers and defending Spitfires and Hurricanes.

On a wall, a light-bulb display showed which of the British fighters from Kent, Essex, Sussex and Hampshire were on the ground, in the air or headed home. The room was still when they arrived, but within minutes, reports came in that a wave of German bombers was headed across the English Channel.

One after another, the bulbs on the wall lit up. Only the bottom row of lights, those signifying units held in reserve, remained dark. There were no units in reserve. Every fighter had been thrown into the battle. After an hour, the lights showed all the British planes back on the ground, unprotected while they re-fueled and re-armed.

Winston and Pamela stared at the display, hardly breathing. If a second wave of German bombers came in, England's air defenses were completely vulnerable.

There was no second wave. The "croupiers" showed the Luft-waffe flying home. A few minutes later, the "all clear" sirens sounded as Winston and Pamela climbed from the bunker. "Winston was exhausted," she recalled, "almost as though he had used his own willpower to turn the Germans back." On the drive back to Chequers, he barely spoke. As they neared the residence, he finally broke the silence. "There are times when it is equally good to live or to die."[39]

Later on, the courage of the RAF defenders inspired Churchill to comment that "never in the field of human conflict was so much owed by so many to so few."

Pamela had intended to have her baby at Middlesex Hospital in London, but because of the bombing, Winston moved her to Chequers in the Buckinghamshire countryside. The Coldstream Guard had moved in and set up anti-aircraft guns to defend the house. A cousin, Ronald Scott, was a Coldstream captain and occasionally dropped by to visit. Otherwise, but for staff, Pamela was alone weekdays during her final month of pregnancy. Weekends were different. Winston and Clementine arrived with a private secretary, often John Colville, and Lieutenant Commander C. R. "Tommy" Thompson, a naval aide.

Her doctor, Carnac Rivett, came almost every night, staying for dinner and overnight, which made Pamela first embarrassed and then angry. He seemed to be using her to avoid the bombing of London. His excuse was that the baby was overdue and could be born at any moment. Clementine upbraided her about the doctor's constant presence, and said it was awkward since Chequers was an official house.

Pamela knew Clemmie was right but said she could not control Rivett's visits; he just kept coming. Others used her for access to Winston. American columnist Virginia Cowles, another of Randolph's friends from the Spanish Civil War, came to see her on weekends, but Pamela felt the writer usually made the journey to see her father-in-law. If visitors really wanted to see her, they could have come during the week when she was alone.

On October 8, Randolph took his seat in the House of Commons, introduced by a proud Winston. A very pregnant Pamela drove in from Chequers with Clementine and with a tank of laughing gas anesthesia in the car in case she went into labor. Two days later, Pamela gave birth to a boy in one of Chequers's four-poster beds.

Randolph was in London but nowhere to be found during the four hours of labor that ended at 4:40 A.M. He later confessed that he was in the arms of Diana Tauber, wife of the singer, composer and conductor, Richard Tauber.

That news did not dampen for long Pamela's ecstasy at having produced a boy. Having a boy had become almost a sacred mission. Throughout the delivery she asked the beautiful Navy nurse what she was having. When she emerged from the anesthetic, she could hear the young woman saying, Five times I've told you. A boy. Please believe me. It can't change now.

After Pamela, no one was more thrilled than Winston. He often walked from his office to watch the baby nursing. He was determined that the child be named for him, but a slight problem had arisen. In July, the wife of his cousin the duke of Marlborough had given birth to a boy whom they named Winston Spencer-Churchill.

When Pamela heard the news from Clementine, she did what she had been doing with increasing frequency — and success. She ran to Winston and sobbed. She begged him to ask Mary, the duchess, to change the name of her son, who had already been christened and his name registered. Winston's grandson, not his nephew, should bear the name of the man on whom all Britons were counting.

Winston needed little convincing. He telephoned Mary and said that the name was his. He wanted it reserved for his grandson.

No pushover, the duchess correctly noted that Pamela had not yet given birth and that — in the days before amniocentesis — no one knew whether her child would even be a boy.

"Of course it will," the prime minister replied. "And if it isn't this time, it will be next time." The Duchess finally gave in and renamed her child Charles.[40] When Pamela's son was born, there was no question what he would be named. Nor did anyone stop to consider what a burden such a name could be.

Winston Spencer Churchill was christened on December 1, 1940, at Ellesborough, in the parish church near Chequers. The godparents were Lord Beaverbrook, the press baron, who had just been named minister for aircraft production; Brendan Bracken, Winston's parliamentary private secretary and later minister of information; Lord Brownlow, a former equerry to the duke of Windsor, and journalist Virginia Cowles.

The lunch at Chequers, Diana Cooper later wrote, included "champagne and tenantry on the lawns, the nannies and cousins and healths drunk, all to the deafening accompaniment of aeroplanes skirmishing, diving, looping and spinning in the clear air."[41]

Circumstances limited the usual gaiety. Living with the Churchills, observing firsthand the to-ings and fro-ings of the senior military staff and discussing the latest news over the dinner table, Pamela was exceptionally well informed. As they stared up at the early winter sky, she confided to Diana Cooper that "invasion was fully expected" at almost any moment.

German armies stood ready at ports across the English Channel, only twenty-two miles from British soil. The occasion was difficult for the prime minister, who had turned sixty-six the day before. Virginia Cowles said that she had always heard that Winston was emotional and that "at times he could be as sentimental as a woman." This was one of those times.

Throughout the christening ceremony, tears streamed down his cheeks and she could hear him murmuring, "Poor infant, to be born into such a world as this." Later at lunch, Beaverbrook toasted the prime minister, reminding the guests that they were in the presence of a man who would be remembered "as long as the civilized world existed." As he rose to reply, Winston wept and in a shaky voice replied, "In these days, I often think of Our Lord." Then he sat down abruptly, lost in his own thoughts.[42]

Once the baby was born, Pamela and Randolph decided it was time to move into a house of their own. Bracken, who served on the Church of England's ecclesiastical commission, found them an old Queen Anne rectory near Hitchin, about thirty miles north of London, that they could rent indefinitely for a pound a week, a virtual gift for a very pretty village house with paneled library, dining and living rooms, a walled garden and two bathrooms.

All it lacked was heat, a deficiency noted by the visiting wife of Ivan Maisky, the smirking and unpleasant Soviet ambassador, who wore her overcoat for warmth at the dining table. Cecil Beaton photographed Pamela and young Winston for a *Life* magazine cover story which appeared in late January 1941. Pamela had quickly slimmed down after pregnancy and was in great spirits.

She loved having the baby, living in her own house and, once again, being able to fit into her nicest dresses — even if, for the time being, she had no place to wear them. She wrote to Randolph, "Oh Randy, everything would be so nice if only you were with us all the time . . . oh my darling, isn't it rather thrilling — our own family life — no more living in other people's houses."[43]

Randolph showed less interest in living in Hitchin or remaining with his wife once his son was born than in seeing military action. War had been underway for more than a year and he had yet to be involved. At White's, he heard that Lieutenant Colonel Robert Laycock was recruiting officers for a commando unit.

Many of his drinking and gambling friends from White's were joining, including Philip Dunn, Pamela's former London landlord; Peter Fitzwilliam, who was Kathleen Kennedy's boyfriend; and the writer Evelyn Waugh, the acid-penned Truman Capote of his era.

Randolph was so eager to fight and so intrigued by the thought of night landings and guerrilla operations that he asked for an immediate transfer. He was astonished to discover that the Fourth Hussars were delighted to be rid of their aged and abrasive lieutenant. "What a shock it was to be told that the other officers disliked him, that they were fed up with his diatribes and could hardly wait for him to get some job elsewhere," said his cousin Anita Leslie. "Randolph, who had thought he was well-regarded, burst into tears."[44]

Number 8 Commando consisted of ten squadrons of fifty men each and was training at Largs, a seaside town near Glasgow. The five hundred men comprised an odd combination of serious, tough soldiers from various guards and marine units, and the playboys and dandies from White's. Discipline was initially strict, but by the time Randolph arrived in late 1940, the training had turned farcical. Uniforms were rarely worn and officers' quarters were in the Marine Hotel, where wives and girlfriends had flocked to join their heroes. The scene was wild and chaotic, a long-running fraternity party.

"The smart set drink a very great deal, play cards for high figures, dine nightly in Glasgow and telephone their [racehorse] owners endlessly," wrote Evelyn Waugh. "The standard of efficiency and devotion to duty, particularly among the officers, is very much lower than in the marines. There is no administration or discipline. . . . The indolence and ignorance of the officers seemed remarkable."[45]

The long hair and cigars of the officers were a source of contempt for the more serious soldiers, who called Randolph's crowd "scum." Night landings practice was ludicrous. Peter Beatty, son of a World War I Admiral of the Fleet and a Randolph crony, was instructed to send his landing craft ashore at 3 A.M. At the appointed hour, nothing happened. An hour later, still nothing, and Beatty was asked why. "It was dark," he explained feebly. "I couldn't see my watch." Daytime training proved equally slapstick, with troopship tenders repeatedly running aground off the coast of the Arran Islands.

Notwithstanding Winston's denials that he had interfered, as soon as Randolph left the Fourth Hussars, they were shipped out. They went to Crete, where they were almost annihilated. In the meantime, the Commandos were delighted to receive their orders to go to the Middle East. The waiting was over. Randolph was exuberant. He did not even mind the prospect of being killed, now that he had a son. Pamela was pleased because Randolph was finally getting his wish. Randolph told her that the separation would be terrible, but at least they could get their finances in order.

He reckoned they would live on his army pay. They could pay off their debts with the thirty pounds a week that Beaverbrook continued to pay him during the war as an *Evening Standard* journalist. The plan made sense to Pamela. Once again, she believed him.

In early February 1941, Randolph sailed aboard the *Glenroy*, one of three troopships bound for Egypt to fight the German and Italian forces commanded by Field Marshal Erwin Rommel. German submarine activity in the Mediterranean forced the convoy to sail the long way around by the Cape of Good Hope and the Suez Canal.

When Randolph left, Pamela invited his elder sister, Diana Sandys, and her children to move into the Hitchin cottage. Pamela volunteered at a communal kitchen in Hitchin, scrimped and stuck to a tight budget. To save money, she turned off the gas fire at 6:30 P.M. and went to bed under a pile of blankets.

Three weeks later, her little world collapsed. A telegram from Randolph arrived from Cape Town, followed by a letter. Catastrophe had befallen him on the voyage along the west coast of Africa.

Militarily, the journey on the overcrowded troop ship had been uneventful. Some younger soldiers underwent makeshift training during the day, but the older officers had no duties of significance. Randolph spent most of his time during the day reading *War and Peace* for the first time. At night, the officers gambled, endless games of chemin de fer and poker.

Randolph had been a gambler at White's where, *Connoisseur* magazine noted in 1754, "There is nothing, however trivial or ridiculous, which is not capable of producing a bet."[46] He and his friends were not above wagering on which of two raindrops would slide down the pane first and hit the window frame. Losing bets that he could ill afford to wager had contributed in no small way to the financial hole in which Randolph and Pamela found themselves. But this news made those lapses seem piddling.

Killing time by gambling on the long, slow trip aboard the

Glenroy, Randolph informed Pamela that he had lost three thousand pounds, some fifteen thousand dollars, the equivalent of two years' salary and an absolute fortune. He was ashamed and upset and remorseful.

He also needed Pamela's help. Under no circumstances was she to tell his parents what happened. He needed her to make arrangements so he could pay the debt off in increments of five or ten pounds a month.

The news was the final straw on the already concave back of their marriage. The bills, drinking and abusive behavior were bad enough. But this folly was a whole new ball game. Randolph's stupidity would thrust twenty-year-old Pamela and young Winston into a financial abyss for years. As Evelyn Waugh trenchantly wrote his wife, Laura, after watching Randolph lose night after night at high-stakes poker and chemin de fer, "Poor Pamela will have to go to work."[47]

Sitting there in the cottage staring at the telegram, it struck her. The marriage was over. She and young Winston were on their own. She had no money, no resources to make money, and she was terrified. For the first time — but not the last — she realized how important money was.

Pamela made a vow to herself never to feel so helpless again, a promise that, when finances were involved, became an obsession. She was too scared to dwell then on her anger. She had been through the angry stage. She cried but knew that sobbing would solve nothing this time. Now was the time to act, calculate and cut her losses.

The telegram arrived in the morning. She called Lord Beaverbrook in London and asked to see him right away. She jumped in her Jaguar, drove straight to his offices at the Ministry of Aircraft Production and explained what happened. She did not know what to do. Would he advance Randolph a year's salary? Beaverbrook said no. She was astonished. It never occurred to her that he would not. He would not dream of advancing Randolph his journalist's pay, but if she wanted him to, he would write her a check right then and there for the entire three thousand pounds. It would be a present from him to Pamela.

Pamela froze. She knew Max quite well through her husband

and father-in-law, and thought he was wonderful. But Randolph had also warned her about him. He was one of the most powerful men in Britain, perhaps second only to Winston. Before he was thirty, he had made an early fortune in Canada in a succession of shady business deals that prompted critics to call him "Beavercrooks" and later "Lord Been-a-crook."

Within six months of arriving in Britain in 1910, he had assaulted the bastions of aristocracy and become a Tory MP. He helped overthrow Prime Minister Herbert Asquith during World War I, transformed the *Daily Express* into the largest-circulation newspaper in the Empire as well as a house organ for the Conservative Party, bought and sold the Rolls-Royce company and won a peerage — all in a half dozen years.

At this point in his career, he was Winston Churchill's best friend, godfather to the prime minister's grandson, and was performing miracles as minister of aircraft production, the nation's most crucial wartime ministry, which had played a huge role in the RAF's historic victory in the Battle of Britain. Beaverbrook was also an all-world master of backroom political intrigue and manipulation. Information and influence were his currencies of choice.

Pamela's antennae twitched. She sensed danger. Randolph had told her that Beaverbrook was a dominator who liked nothing more than having people under his control. Never get in such a situation, Randolph had warned. Max would own you forever. His admonition ringing in her ears, Pamela refused Beaverbrook's offer.

Instead, she sold all her wedding presents and jewelry, some through the auction house Phillips. Among the latter was a pair of diamond earrings given her by Lady Baillie. Olive had inquired what kind of gems she would like for her present. Pamela asked for diamonds. Because they were white, she thought they would be less expensive than green or red stones, emeralds and rubies. And here it turned out they were the most expensive. What a surprise.

Whether Pamela actually did reject Beaverbrook's offer of money is open to question. She displayed no pattern — until then or later — of turning down the offer of money from a rich, powerful man. In writing about the incident three decades later, her son Winston fudged her specific reaction to Beaverbrook's offer but said she sold jewelry and that "we eventually got it all paid."[48] Richard Hough, author of *Winston and Clementine*, wrote that Beaverbrook "presented her with a check strictly as a present."[49]

Beaverbrook biographers Anne Chisholm and Michael Davie state that while Randolph was in the Middle East, "Beaverbrook was helping Pamela meet her profligate husband's debts."[50] If she took none of the money, Pamela did accept Beaverbrook's offer to send young Winston and his nanny to live at Cherkley, his country estate, while she moved back to London in search of a job. Just as David Margesson had helped eighteen months before, Max said that of course he would help.

Pamela drove back to Hitchin to plot the next phase of her own life and that of The Child, as she referred to young Winston. She was already pregnant with a second child. She was hoping for a girl and wanted to name her Jennie after old Winston's mother, Jennie Jerome. With all the tension, she lost the baby.

She rented out the rectory house for three pounds a week, triple what she had been paying, to one of the many nursery schools which had been forced to evacuate from London by the bombing. She moved as quickly as she could to the city, where she took a top-floor room at the Dorchester Hotel on Park Lane for six pounds a week.

Everyone who could get into the Dorchester wanted to stay there. The only hotel built with steel-reinforced concrete, the Dorchester was thought capable of withstanding all but a direct hit by German bombs. The hotel was jammed except for the vulnerable top floor. Up there with Pam was Clarissa Churchill, her former Downham classmate, who was now a relative by marriage.

During bomb raids, guests pulled their mattresses into the corridors. Pamela and Clarissa ran downstairs and slept in an inner foyer in the first-floor suite of Australian prime minister Robert Menzies. The charismatic Menzies was in London attempting to negotiate with Churchill a means of conducting the war without destroying the Empire, a negotiation that so deeply divided the two that Menzies made a futile effort to oust Churchill from office.

Almost immediately after moving into the Dorchester, Pamela lunched at 10 Downing Street. She was uncertain what to tell Clemmie and Winston if they asked why she had given up her infant son and house and moved to London. Her plan was to say that she felt she had to do more for the war effort than hide out in the country. But they did not ask, so she did not raise the subject. Never explain, never complain, was her philosophy, a motto that Henry Ford II popularized in the 1970s when arrested on a drunk-driving charge with a woman not his wife.

At lunch, she sat next to the minister of supply and told him that she needed a job. Within twenty-four hours the astute minister had the prime minister's daughter-in-law working in the ministry's royal ordnance factory hostel department, a division erecting accommodations for ammunition and bomb workers who were being moved from the south to the north of England. Her boss was Oliver Franks, who later became British ambassador to the United States.

Her six-pound weekly bill at the Dorchester included breakfast, but the rest of the time, Pamela was on her own. She usually ate lunch at the ministry cafeteria or went out for a bite with a coworker. In the evening, she had to hustle for an invitation. On occasion, she joined the Churchills at Downing Street, but she was careful not to overuse her entrée. Nor did she want to deal with questions about Randolph. Wednesdays were the one night she did not have to worry.

Every Wednesday, Emerald, Lady Cunard, hosted a dinner in the Dorchester for friends. Emerald was not a real aristocrat, nor was Emerald even her real name. She changed it from Maud, which she thought common, to the sparkling gem, which better suited her personality. Tiny, with brilliant blue eyes and heavily made up, she chattered endlessly. "A twittering, bejeweled bird," was Chips Channon's description, at whose soirees "the great met the gay, statesmen consorted with society and writers with the rich."[51]

Emerald was one more lively American with spectacular continental tastes in whom Pamela found a kindred spirit. Originally from San Francisco, she spent her youth traveling through Europe with her mother in search of excitement.[52] Her title came from a long-abandoned marriage to Sir Bache Cunard, grandson of the shipping line founder, but her great love was the dynamic conductor Sir Thomas Beecham, who founded the London Philharmonic and directed the Covent Garden Opera.

An urban Lady Baillie who specialized in café society, Emerald staged enchanting meals at her London home at a circular table of lapis lazuli which reflected the candlelight and the gilt epergne of the naked nymphs and naiads centerpiece. Her guests were an eclectic mixture of handsome men, social wits, clever women, writers, musicians, diplomats and politicians.

"Conversation was what is known as 'brilliant,' but as everyone was afraid of being a bore, they never stuck to a point long enough to follow a train of thought," said writer Kenneth Clark, a frequent guest. "It was a diet of hors d'oeuvres."[53]

Sometimes a bit of raw meat was dropped. Emerald loved to shock and one prewar evening, stunned her table into silence by cooing at the German ambassador, Joachim von Ribbentrop, "Tell us, dearest Excellency, WHY does Herr Hitler dislike the Jews?"[54]

With the onset of the Blitz, she shut up her house and table, but the gatherings continued when she moved into the Dorchester.[55] Her hotel salon was packed with so much valuable French furniture — a welter of velvet and gilt, busts by Houdon and Mestrovic — that it looked as though Sotheby's were using Emerald's quarters as a storeroom.

Pamela, young, pretty and well connected, was always welcome. She had learned a great deal from observing Emerald entertain, as she had from Olive. In March 1941, within days of her twenty-first birthday, she was in high spirits walking down the Dorchester corridor to Lady Cunard's suite. She felt independent and could not help but feel that her life was about to change totally.

Tugging a wrinkle from the shoulderless, gold-colored evening dress, Pamela walked into the suite. She had just washed her hair; her creamy skin glowed. Emerald hugged her and took her straight across the room to meet two Americans who had just arrived in London: John Gilbert Winant, the incoming U.S. ambassador who had succeeded the disgraced Joe Kennedy, and Averell Harriman, Franklin Roosevelt's Lend-Lease expediter. Harriman smiled at the young beauty. She stared back. He was the most beautiful man she had ever seen.

CHAPTER SIX

Averell I

AVERELL WAS JUST BEAUTIFUL. He was absolutely marvelous looking with his raven black hair. Very athletic, very tan, very healthy."[1] Pamela thought back and sighed, her memory fresh and unselective. Averell was as handsome as he was distinguished. Photos from the period bear out her recollection. In one publicity still for Sun Valley, the lean, six-foot-one Harriman stands on a mountain on skis, his shirt open at the neck and sleeves rolled up, better-looking than Gary Cooper and a good match for Cary Grant.

Pamela looked awfully good to Averell too. Her rich auburn hair reflected light from the room's crystal chandelier. She had lost her puppy fat, her double chin and the weight she had put on during pregnancy but not her full bosom. Her skin was untanned and her cheekbones newly prominent above a more sculpted jaw, but it was not only her striking physical looks that impressed Emerald's guest.

There was a serious, mature look in Pamela's eyes that belied her years and reflected the pain of her marriage and the gravity of being a Churchill at war and living in Downing Street. There was also an endearing warmth in her allure. Pamela had a tendency to touch people she liked, a bit of pressure on a hand or arm that Chips Channon called "her affectionate, conspiratorial way."[2] As dinner proceeded, Pamela leaned over more than once to touch the envoy's forearm and shoulder.

Averell said that he met Pamela for the first time at Chequers when he went to visit Winston, but he was covering up the real start of their extraordinary relationship, which began that night in the Dorchester Hotel.[3] Pamela had never heard of Harriman when Emerald Cunard sat them side by side for dinner. All Pamela knew was that as Franklin Roosevelt's special emissary, he would be influential in determining whether Britain survived or fell to the Nazis.

Nearly thirty years older than Pamela and three years older than her father, Averell was the son of E. H. Harriman, the ruthless and much vilified railroad magnate who built the Union Pacific Railroad and one of America's biggest family fortunes. E.H. was a stockbroker who moved into railroads in the 1880s. He was a charter member in the golden era of robber barons, of which trainmen were a particularly thuggish bunch.

E.H. pushed the breed to new lows and Theodore Roosevelt listed him among the "malefactors of great wealth."[4] E.H. took over the Southern Pacific system and precipitated a financial panic and legal battle that went to the Supreme Court when he tried to seize control of Northern Pacific and, in effect, monopolize the national track system. E.H. lost.

His son Averell graduated from Yale in 1913 but deliberately avoided military service in World War I. With the same single-minded drive that characterized his father's approach to business, he formed the country's biggest commercial shipping fleet before he was thirty. To finance his maritime interests, Averell had founded his own investment banking house, W. A. Harriman and Company, just as he turned twenty-eight years old.

In the 1920s, he displayed an intense business pragmatism but little of the sensitivity for the national interest that dominated the second half of his life. He completely ignored domestic political sentiment to negotiate a shipping agreement with Germany before the Great War's final armistice was signed.

He then chased a manganese concession from the Soviet Union, although the United States had yet to grant diplomatic recognition to Lenin's Bolshevik government. Condemned for being excessively expedient if not unpatriotic, Harriman was unapologetic. Both ventures, he said, were great opportunities for America.

He returned from a 1926 trip to Moscow claiming that the Socialist revolution was solidly in place and that the peasants had more freedom than they had under the czars. Stalin, he said, was "not a dictator in any sense of the word," but rather "a political boss" in the Tammany Hall mold.[5] Harriman had no intention of criticizing a leader who might do him some concessionary good.

Averell displayed few solidly held political beliefs in his early years. He supported Warren G. Harding in 1920 out of belief that the Republican would push harder in the immediate postwar period to make the United States the world's leading maritime power. But when the Republicans turned isolationist, Averell's international interests tugged him toward the Democrats, who were always happy to welcome the patrician wealthy.

His influential sister Mary Rumsey nudged him to support New York's Catholic governor Al Smith for the presidency in 1928. He backed Franklin D. Roosevelt in 1932 as a protest against high tariffs, prohibition, the Depression and the incumbent Republican Herbert Hoover, who he believed had mismanaged the economy.[6]

A loner in business, Averell was cold, brusque and aloof as well in his private life. An excellent bridge player at Yale, he later took up polo because it was the appropriate sport for a rich young man and also because he could apply to it the same intense focus that he brought to business. Taking your eye off the ball in polo could cause problems, including serious injuries.

He was not a natural on a pony or with a mallet, but he was tenacious. "He went into any game lock, stock and barrel," said Robert Lovett, Harriman's childhood friend, fellow Yalie and later secretary of defense. "He would get whatever he needed — the best horses, coaches, equipment, his own bowling alley or croquet lawn — and work like the devil to win."[7]

Such tenacity in polo earned him an eight-handicap out of the maximum rating of ten and, after he scored four of the U.S. team's seven goals against Argentina in the 1928 world polo championships, he was ranked among the top five players in the nation.

A similar discipline and plenty of lawn at his estates at Arden, on the edge of the Catskills, and Sands Point, New York, helped him become one of the nation's top croquet players. Persistence, he insisted, was the key. Egotism was another factor. He drove other players to distraction by taking up to twenty minutes to study a shot. "Subtle game," he would murmur.

His 1915 marriage to Kitty Lanier Lawrance collapsed after fourteen years. Averell had been away a great deal and Kitty was frail, but the basic reason the marriage failed, friends felt, was that both were so stodgy and introverted. That was far from the case with Marie Norton Whitney, with whom Averell had fallen in love while she was married to Cornelius Vanderbilt "Sonny" Whitney, a fellow polo player and Yale man.

Marie was seventeen years older than Pamela but every bit as beautiful in her twenties, when Averell had met her, as the young Englishwoman. Marie had mischievous violet-blue eyes and a voluptuous figure that turned men's heads, including that of bootlegger Al Capone, who met her once in Bimini when Marie was still married to Sonny. Whitney had enjoyed discussing horse racing with the gangster, but became upset, albeit carefully, when he realized that Capone's attention was aimed more at the striking Marie.[8]

What really set Marie apart was her personality. Brash, flippant, witty, imaginative — Marie Harriman was everything Averell was not. She was intolerant of his pomposity and often snorted caustically, "Oh, knock it off, Ave," when he turned too stuffy. Marie had studied art history and was a fine judge of painting, particularly that of post-Impressionists. They scoured galleries during their honeymoon in Paris and bought a variety of canvases, including van Gogh's magnificent still life *White Roses*, for which Averell paid seventy-two thousand dollars, half of it given by his mother as a wedding present.

Back home, Marie opened up his world. When Averell started the Sun Valley ski resort in Idaho in 1935 to romanticize train travel and build revenue for the Union Pacific, Marie and her friend Marjorie Duchin, wife of bandleader Eddy Duchin, helped decorate the resort lodge, which became a mecca for some of Hollywood's biggest stars.

In New York, Marie introduced Averell to café society, although he was dull and often had such difficulty keeping up with the repartee in a witty crowd that he rarely bothered to try. He usually ended up a wallflower at his own party. It was Marie who brought life to Arden, the gloomy, forbidding mansion an hour's drive north of Manhattan that looked like a Dracula movie set, where Averell was raised on twenty thousand acres.

In the belief that at least once a year the house should be filled, Marie pressed into service Alexander Woollcott, the writer and critic, to compile guest lists for an annual Thanksgiving party that lasted all weekend. A mixed bag of actors, literati, New Dealers, art dealers, croquet and polo players showed up, including Charlie MacArthur and Helen Hayes, Dorothy and Bill Paley, Madeline and Robert Sherwood, Tommy Hitchcock, Harpo Marx and Harry Hopkins.

One weekend, newspaper columnist Heywood Broun, a perpetual champion of the underclass, bowled in his stocking feet in the basement bowling alley against Diana Cooper, the quintessential English aristocrat, who was wearing an evening gown.[9]

Some of Averell's habits Marie could not change, notably his personal cheapness. He almost never carried cash, paid for taxis, picked up restaurant tabs or for the Arden Thanksgivings had more than one butler on hand — "Woods, the poor slave," the guests called him — to minister to the forty or so visitors.[10]

By 1940, Harriman was best known as a humorless American patrician, a handsome, wealthy sportsman who developed Sun Valley, set speed records with his Union Pacific trains and, thanks to his wife, welcomed interesting people to his estate. A less well known trait, though hinted at in his reaction to Stalin, was that Averell loved powerful people, almost regardless of who they were. He collected meetings with important people the way other people collected stamps.[11] He was so worried about being left out if he backed the wrong candidate in the 1940 presidential election that he contributed twenty-five thousand dollars each to Roosevelt and to Wendell Willkie, his Republican challenger.[12]

In the thirties, Averell had links to the New Deal because of his seat on the Business Advisory Council at the Department of Commerce in Washington. But it took the onset of war in Europe to turn him into a political activist. He wanted to get more involved for several reasons. One was that he knew that U.S. mobilization would help his rail and shipping businesses. Secondly, he was embarrassed by his decision to duck the First World War. Finally, never an isolationist, Harriman felt strongly that the United States had to step in to help Europe stop Germany.

President Roosevelt wanted to act, but a powerful lobby in Congress was determined to keep the United States out and held him in check. The America First group had aviator Charles Lindbergh as its figurehead and argued, as did many isolationist Republicans, that Roosevelt was a "warmonger." Roosevelt did not want to give the anti-interventionists extra ammunition against him because he had also decided to run for a third consecutive term, which in itself was highly controversial.

By the end of May 1940, though, with the U.S. election still six months away, Britain's situation was precarious. The German army had captured France and was poised on the Channel coast. Winston Churchill had nowhere to turn but to the United States.

In mid-May, within days of becoming prime minister, and still living in Admiralty House, Churchill was shaving one morning when he discussed his plans with Randolph. "I think I see my way through."

"Do you mean avoid defeat or beat the bastards?" Randolph asked.

"Of course, I mean we can beat them," Winston snapped, waving his foam-covered razor at his son.

"Well, I'm all for it, but I don't see how you can do it," said Randolph.

Winston wiped his face and turned to Randolph. "We shall drag the U.S. in."[13]

Churchill begged Roosevelt for help, specifically for fifty World War I destroyers mothballed in U.S. dockyards. Roosevelt was unwilling to abandon neutrality until Congress dropped its objections and his November reelection was behind him.

Once he swamped Willkie in November, by 449 electoral votes to 82, Roosevelt had much more freedom to maneuver overseas, a development few appreciated as well as Churchill did. After the election, Roosevelt went on holiday in the Caribbean. Churchill waited for him to rest and relax, then, hoping to catch the president in a more responsive mood, wrote him a letter detailing Britain's needs.

In the letter, which he later called "one of the most important I ever wrote," Churchill analyzed how his island's supply lines were being strangled by Germany's sinking of hundreds of thousands of tons of merchant ships monthly and that Britain urgently needed the delivery of aircraft and ammunition.[14]

Roosevelt mulled over the latest request with his top aide Harry Hopkins in December 1940.

"You know, a lot of this could be settled if Churchill and I could just sit down together for a while," Roosevelt said. It was difficult to arrange a meeting at that moment because the United States had no ambassador in London.

"How about me going over, Mr. President?" asked Hopkins, his eyes gleaming.[15]

Roosevelt turned him down then, citing the work required on his third inaugural address, the new budget and State of the Union speech. Immediately after New Year's, he changed his mind. On January 5, FDR announced he was sending Hopkins to Britain to see Churchill. Five days later, the president announced the Lend-Lease program to supply Britain and whoever else needed help to fight Germany.

Within an hour of the first announcement, Averell was on the phone, begging to go along with Hopkins, whom he had known since the early 1930s and who was a fellow croquet player on Long Island. "Let me carry your bag, Harry," he implored. "I've met Churchill several times and I know London intimately."

Hopkins refused, but in late February, Roosevelt asked Harriman to administer the supply pipeline to Britain, circumventing the red tape, bureaucracy and disorganization of Cordell Hull's state department. "I want you to go over to London," said Roosevelt, "and recommend everything we can do, short of war, to keep the British Isles afloat." Harriman's title would be expediter.[16]

Averell arrived in London on March 17, 1941, without Marie.

She had opened her own high-quality art gallery on East Fifty-seventh Street, the Marie Harriman Gallery, and stayed behind to run it. She also had severe eye problems. A retina operation so immobilized her that she was forced to lie flat on her back for a while with her head braced between sandbags.

The night Averell arrived, he was rushed to Chequers for a late dinner with Churchill. He needed to know exactly what Britain required, he told the prime minister, so the United States could be of maximum assistance. "We accept you as a friend," Churchill replied. "Nothing will be kept from you."[17]

Winston was as good as his word. But the one who would really keep Averell informed throughout the war was the twenty-one-year-old sitting next to him several nights later at Emerald Cunard's. He asked Pamela to tell him who was who at the party. Emerald had already explained who wasn't there. Foreign secretary Anthony Eden was among the no-shows. "Oooh, poor Anthony," Emerald commiserated. "Left in that terrible Foreign Office. How can he know what's going on?"

The guests laughed, but Emerald was serious. Eden's influence was limited and he deferred thoroughly on foreign policy to Churchill. There was better information available at Emerald's, as Averell had been advised, and far more appealing sources.

As Averell's glance traveled across Pamela's bare shoulders, up the line of fine hair on the side of her pale neck and into her amused blue eyes, he recalled how Harry Hopkins had briefed him about her. "Hopkins told me that she had more information than anyone in England," Harriman said.[18] He had also told Averell that she was delicious-looking.

Having met her father-in-law, Harriman this night was primarily interested in Pamela and in learning as much as he could about who was who in the war effort, especially about her son's godfather, Lord Beaverbrook, a fellow expediter as well as another opportunistic millionaire. Averell knew that in addition to his formal ministry post as head of aircraft production, Beaverbrook's job was also to cut red tape.

Harriman was aware that the Beaver, as he was known, had exceptional influence with Churchill. But Averell knew little about him professionally and almost nothing about him personally. He understood that Beaverbrook was not easy, that he was temperamental, a mischief-maker, someone who could be so blunt as to deny Harriman the diplomatic flexibility he might need. What could Pamela tell him about Max? What could she tell him about Winston?

Pamela was astonished at how little Averell knew. Here was President Roosevelt's new special envoy and his knowledge about the various brains behind Britain's war effort could be put in a teaspoon. Some statesman! At least he had the good sense to ask her. She has good instincts and right away determined that, while he might be naive, he was trustworthy. She knew just what he needed and was delighted to tell him in as much detail as he chose to absorb. Averell could not have had a better source.

They talked through dinner and ignored most of the other guests, including the new U.S. ambassador. Pamela was not interested in Gil Winant. Clementine would almost adopt the shy, quiet ambassador and preferred him to Harriman. Clemmie would play serious croquet at Chequers with Averell, but to her, the expediter was one more rich businessman and icily ambitious maneuverer who would isolate her more from her husband.[19]

[Eleanor Roosevelt understood Clementine's reservations about Averell. On a wartime visit to England, she was warned by Harry Hopkins to skip the ambassador and deal with Averell, who did have more power. The First Lady, who always had qualms about Harriman's personal ambition but liked Winant, did just the opposite.][20]

Pamela took an instant dislike to Winant, a former governor of New Hampshire whose deep-set eyes, dark, jutting features and habit of wearing unpressed shiny suits made him look — some said deliberately — like Abraham Lincoln. She found him dour and unattractive, a rather pathetic case. In fact, Winant became a highly popular envoy with the people of Britain. Informal and compassionate, Winant refused to move into the monumental ambassadorial residence at 4 Grosvenor Gardens vacated by the Kennedys, preferring an apartment on Grosvenor Square near the American embassy.

In the midst of night bombings, Winant could be spotted walking the streets, trying to lift the spirits of residents and instill confidence.[21] Pamela was also right about his being a sad case. Called on once to give a speech to a group in London, Winant got to his feet and stood there in dead silence, licking his lips for two or three minutes. "It was horribly embarrassing," said James Parton, aide to Lieutenant General Ira Eaker, commander of the Eighth Air Force. "Finally, he said, 'I guess I shouldn't have gotten up,' and sat down."[22]

Churchill and Roosevelt frequently cut Winant out of their direct communications. When they didn't, Averell often did. Unhappily married, Winant fell in love with Pamela's sister-in-law, Sarah Churchill, but the relationship went nowhere, although Sarah was separated from her husband, Vic Oliver. He resigned the ambassadorship in 1946, returned to his home in New Hampshire and, depressed with the realization that a lifetime of public service was over, soon after committed suicide.

After Emerald's dinner, Averell suggested that Pamela come back to his suite so they could keep talking. She accepted without hesitation. He said that he wanted to meet Beaverbrook as soon as possible. That was easy for Pamela to arrange. She called from Averell's room. Max was home and asked her to bring him to dinner Saturday at Cherkley.

Beaverbrook was thrilled at the prospect of early, private contact with Roosevelt's envoy. "He couldn't resist seducing men in the way he seduced women," Prime Minister Harold Macmillan once said of Beaverbrook. "And once a man was seduced by him, he was finished."[23]

No sooner were the plans made than the air raid sirens erupted. Much of the German bombing of London initially targeted the shipping docks in the East End. Recently, the Luftwaffe had shifted focus to the West End. Two weeks before, on March 8, a bomb had crashed through the roof of the Café de Paris, killing eighty-three patrons and wounding more than a hundred more.

On this night's attack, the bombers seemed to come straight up Park Lane over the roof of the Dorchester. Detonations could be heard close by in Mayfair. There was no way Pamela could return to her sixth-floor apartment. But there was no need to huddle in Prime Minister Menzies' foyer. Averell had a safe ground-floor suite and asked her to stay with him.

They looked at each other when he made the offer. The evening had been wonderful and Emerald's gathering seductive from the outset: luxuriant in food, drink and dress; high-powered in guests and conversation; invigorating in the realization that Harriman and Winant's presence meant the United States was getting closer to joining the war effort. They could feel the nearby bomb blasts shaking the hotel and sense the flat glare of flares through the suite's blackout curtains. Their adrenaline was surging.

Both knew what acceptance meant. Averell wanted Pamela to stay. For all his public stodginess, he loved glamorous women and had a powerful libido and virility that would last well into his eighties. During his first marriage, to Kitty Lawrance, he had a long affair with a sultry New York actress-singer named Teddy Gerard, who was famous enough in the 1920s to number Winston Churchill among her fans.[24] He would have others, including a rumored fling with actress Lillian Gish, but right then, far from home, flushed with anticipation over his assignment and suddenly under fire, he wanted Pamela.

She wanted him too. Her sex life with Randolph had left much to be desired. He was a womanizer, but in the sense of wanting to dominate women. When it came to sex, Randolph, like some other Churchill men, did not seem all that interested. It did not help that he drank too much to perform well or often.

Even being in the same bedroom with Randolph was a difficult proposition. "I came to regard with dread the approach of night," said his commando unit roommate, the Earl of Birkenhead, "for Randolph proved an unnerving bedfellow, and his thunderous snores and other even less pleasing eructations precluded sleep."[25]

Nor did Randolph's conceit, heightened by the English clubman's traditional approach to women as chattel, vanish in the bedroom. He was selfish, a chauvinist, and, if that were not enough for Pamela to entertain other offers, he was also in Egypt. Pamela was just as ready as Averell.

She was happy to accept. She helped Averell peel off her dinner dress and their own Special Relationship began immediately.

Affairs were common during the war. London was "a romantic place, very romantic," said Bill Paley. "It was sort of like the normal, conventional morals of the time were just turned on their ear because of the urgency. . . . The normal barriers to having an affair with somebody were thrown to the winds. If it looked pretty good, you felt good, well what in Hell was the difference?''[26]

Nowhere was life as frenetic as in London in 1941. The city was beleaguered — just before New Year's, ten thousand fire-bombs fell, destroying the Guildhall and eight Wren churches — but London had not fallen like Paris. There was a frenzied sense of living on the edge and for the moment. Bands played and, despite rationing, liquor flowed. Behind blackout curtains, res-taurants and nightclubs continued to operate in light too dark to see anything and too bright to do anything.

In West End theaters, the show went on. Two months after the Café de Paris bombing, a bomb fell on the Palace of West-minster which gutted the chamber of the House of Commons and destroyed the deanery of Westminster Abbey. At about the same time, Noel Coward's new play, *Blithe Spirit*, opened at the Pic-cadilly Theater, which had also been scarred by bombs. In the audience with actress Bea Lillie, Lord and Lady Mountbatten and Diana and Duff Cooper was Pamela Churchill.

Pamela and her friends spoke of "living for the day; fearing for the night." She suddenly had less reason to fear the night, but hers was not just any affair. Hers was a strategic relationship of the highest order. Word of her involvement with Harriman spread instantly. The first one to notice was Beaverbrook, when they arrived at Cherkley for dinner.

Max was a dozen years older than Averell, but he too had a powerful appetite for younger women. The writer Rebecca West was an early conquest and his long-term mistress Jean Norton was twenty years his junior. There was no evidence that he had sampled Pamela and it was unlikely that he would have, given his intimacy with Winston. But Max was all too familiar with the signs. Picking up on the intimate gestures and body language of his guests, the discreet touches on each other's arm and the lingering looks, Max was delighted. Averell had been in Britain only a matter of days and already he was compromised.

Not in a pejorative sense, as if he were an enemy. Quite the opposite. But the result was the same. To have FDR's personal representative, the man charged with keeping Britain safe, sleeping with the prime minister's daughter-in-law was a wonderful stroke of luck. The United States was not yet in the war and would not be until after Pearl Harbor, nine months later. But it was imperative for Britain, as Churchill had said, to drag the United States in. Pamela had talked with her father-in-law about the Americans, felt every bit the same as he and was ready to help her country.

The historic moment looks different in hindsight. What is obvious now — that the United States would join the battle, Hitler would be crushed and Churchill would attain fame as one of England's greatest sons — was anything but certain in early 1941. Churchill's own political position was far from impregnable. His own Conservative party continued to harbor doubts about its maverick.

A powerful current of jealousy flowed barely beneath the surface of relations between a United States in the ascendancy and a Britain on the wane. The United States had raised an economic challenge to Britain in the 1920s and its political isolationism in the 1930s had made many Britons skeptical of its intentions and commitment. "It is always best," Neville Chamberlain had said before leaving office, "to count on nothing from the Americans except words."[27]

Even in its great hour of need, Roosevelt did not "give" Britain the goods it needed. Rather, Washington made a deal for leases on British territorial possessions in the Americas on which the United States could build military bases to defend itself.[28]

The Averell-Pamela link was a very important tie that bound. Beaverbrook, who was every bit as eager as Churchill to pull in the United States, knew that their affair could only help the cause. "Max used everybody and Pamela was his catalyst on a hot tin roof," said Tex McCrary, an American journalist and friend of Beaverbrook's whom the press baron tried to hire to run one of his papers. "Beaverbrook was committed to getting closer to Harriman" and Pamela was his link. "She passed everything she knew about anybody to Beaverbrook," said McCrary, who was also an Eighth Air Force colonel during the war. "Beaverbrook was a gossipmonger and Pamela was his bird dog."[29]

Why did she do it? She was a full-fledged apostle to the cause.

Whether or not Pamela took Beaverbrook's three thousand pounds, or fifteen thousand dollars, in early March is far less relevant than the fact that she was totally committed to Winston and Max. She loved Winston for substance, what he was doing to lead Britain; she loved Max for style, how he did what he did. Both men were father figures. Winston was an icon. Max, more approachable, more her type, became a friend.

His wealth and generosity were only minor aspects of his appeal. She loved the fact that Beaverbrook was so cunning and devious, that he operated compulsively in such a miasma of intrigue. She loved the skillful way Max manipulated people, including Averell, teasing him with information, always trying to trade up. Max had an almost hypnotic effect, sometimes even on Winston. The two men were quite different, but both fascinated her. She would have done anything for either one of them.

Linking up with Averell, though, was no chore. If she did take Max's money, it was to get out of debt. No payment was necessary to do anything Winston or Max asked, especially to sleep with Averell. Her attraction to President Roosevelt's envoy was real. He was more than a wartime fling to her. He was a man for whom she honestly cared, although she did not allow herself to think then about any possible future. In the meantime, though, he fit all her criteria: Averell was famous, attractive, wealthy, older, powerful and plugged in. The fact that he — and she — were each married to others did not bother Pamela in the slightest. Such an inconvenience was little more than a minor nuisance to Pamela, best ignored — certainly in war — when conventional morality had gone by the boards.

For a master of intrigue like Beaverbrook, who regularly bought information and influence, the news about Pamela and Averell was priceless. Still, his awareness that an affair had begun was only a small part of the equation. Managing the affair properly for the long term was crucial because there was no better conduit than Pamela. She could pass to Winston and Max what the Americans were thinking and planning. She could pass on to the Americans through Averell whatever spin Britain wanted delivered.

Pamela was a willing student, eager to do more. "Pamela was a learner," McCrary said. "She really inhaled."[30] Throughout the war, Pamela was on call to both men. Max spoke to her constantly. Winston, or "Papa," often phoned her apartment late in the evening. He would dispatch an armored car to pick her up for games of bezique and gossip for hours into the night. "We would be sitting around after dinner," said Bill Walton, the *Time* magazine correspondent, "and the phone would ring and Pamela would come in and say, 'I have to go. He's calling me now.' "[31]

Pamela knew exactly what she was doing and what was going on. She was privy to everything, not only the most highly classified information, but also the bouts of depression — Winston called it his "Black Dog" — that struck the prime minister. She learned early to be extremely careful about what she said and to whom outside the Winston-Max-Averell circle, understanding that the wrong word at the wrong time could easily cost a general his job or worse.

She was constantly on guard, a cautious posture she maintained the rest of her life. She never bragged about her role, but she was not modest about it either. She knew that Averell, and the government he represented, would never have had the same close relationship with Churchill and Beaverbrook without her. She had insinuated herself into the very nexus of what was about to become the Special Relationship between Britain and the United States. She could not have been more delighted. This was better than being close to the action; she was part of the action.

Pamela knew that Max understood all about the affair instantly. Max understood the ramifications far better than Averell, not least because he was smarter than Harriman, a fact he did not attempt to conceal. Speaking to John F. Kennedy in 1958, Beaverbrook said of Averell, "Never has anyone gone so far with so little."[32]

In 1941, Max did not try to disguise how pleased he was. She was also aware that Harry Hopkins and Franklin Roosevelt quickly learned of the affair. Harry may even have set it up. She knew that was the way Hopkins operated.

She had met the president's aide on his first trip in January and found him tremendously appealing. Thin, wispy-haired, sickly, Hopkins was an old friend of Averell, who had introduced him to Roosevelt. A former social worker, Hopkins had little interest in nor much use for the British Empire until 1939 when he met King George VI and Queen Elizabeth during their trip to the United States. He loved their unaffected natures, their joy in chomping into hot dogs at Yankee Stadium. Hopkins was so entranced that he became a committed Anglophile.

He had a similar experience with Churchill. From listening to Churchill's dissents throughout the thirties, Hopkins first thought the prime minister might be full of hot air. He changed his mind once he saw how Churchill rallied Britain after the fall of France. From then on, Britain had no greater champion in the United States than Hopkins. To Churchill, Hopkins was the symbol that Britain was no longer alone.

During his visit, Hopkins attended a stag dinner with the prime minister and Beaverbrook. Speaking briefly, the envoy stood and quoted from the Book of Ruth: "Whither thou goest, I will go; Even unto the end." Eyes at the table moistened. Knowing looks were exchanged.

Franklin Roosevelt had fired Joseph Kennedy from the ambassador's post two months earlier. Winant had yet to arrive, but everyone in the room knew immediately that Hopkins had signaled a dramatic shift in U.S. policy. Word of his remarks flashed around London. "Lord Beaverbrook told me years later," said Hopkins's biographer Robert Sherwood, "that Hopkins' warmhearted sympathy and his confidence and conviction provided more tangible aid for Britain than had all the destroyers and guns and ammunition that had been sent previously."[33]

To Pamela, Harry Hopkins was a ray of sunshine breaking through the darkest clouds.

Harry had an amazing facility for making Winston think that he was working for him even though Winston knew he was Roosevelt's top aide. Hopkins — like Max, like Averell — was one of those people who knew how to get things done. He had no secretary, no staff, not much backup from the U.S. embassy in London, preferring to work instead out of his own hip pocket, using his unmatched access to Roosevelt. For the New Deal, Hopkins concentrated on putting Americans back to work. And succeeded spectacularly. Now he was specializing in winning the war any way he could.

On January 10, 1941, Hopkins and Churchill held their first meeting. Knowing of Hopkins's history as a social worker and his role in organizing Roosevelt's work-relief programs, Churchill started to speak of his plans to arrange a better life for the "cottagers" after the war. Hopkins interrupted sharply. "I don't give a damn about your cottagers. I came here to see how we can beat this fellow Hitler."[34]

The descendant of the duke of Marlborough and the son of a Sioux City, Iowa, harness maker sat through lunch until 4 P.M. discussing the war and how America could help. The Great Hall at Chequers was so cold that, for the first of many times, the frail Hopkins sat with his coat on, a briefcase filled with pill bottles by his side. Later in the war, he grinned impishly at Churchill one night and promised that if they beat Hitler, he would personally ensure that the American people gave Chequers a central heating system.

In his diary, Colville noted that the two were "greatly impressed with each other" in their first meeting. Churchill soon nicknamed Hopkins "Lord Root of the Matter."[35] In his report to FDR, Hopkins described Churchill as "a rotund, smiling, red-faced gentleman with a clear eye and a mushy voice" who showed him "with obvious pride the photographs of his beautiful daughter-in-law and grandchild."[36] He met the daughter-in-law during that visit and he discovered that she was not only attractive but wonderful company, quick and confident.

Hopkins knew that Averell, behind the facade of patrician reserve, had a roving eye for women. Hopkins knew about singer Teddy Gerard and other temptations to whom Averell had succumbed. Harry knew Averell cold. Hopkins, whom Pamela adored, had set the stage perfectly. As the relationship developed, she and Hopkins talked openly about it. Hopkins told her that Roosevelt knew all about the affair. The president, Harry said, got a big kick out of it.

Pamela was uncertain what the Churchills thought. She never discussed the Averell relationship with Clementine, nor in its early stages with Winston, but that wasn't really necessary. Much in British life is understood without being discussed. This was one of those cases. Pamela had discussed her Randolph problems with his sister Sarah, her closest confidante within the family, but she had not specifically discussed Averell.

John Colville recognized what was afoot. As he noted in his published diaries, Winston's private secretary had observed Pamela and Averell in the early morning of April 17, 1941, walking together across Horse Guards Parade to examine bomb damage. A year or so later, Winston mentioned that he was hearing quite a bit about Averell and Pamela. Pamela shrugged it off. Some people had nothing better to do than gossip. He agreed.

Pamela never had a sense that Winston and Clemmie disapproved. They never blamed her for infidelity to Randolph because they understood how difficult their son was. They knew as early as 1940 — before young Winston was born — that the marriage was ill-fated. They could have hindered Pamela's relationship with Averell had they wished, but they never did. If anything, Winston made it easier for the two to see each other outside London by inviting both to Chequers nearly every weekend.

It made perfect professional sense that Averell spend as much time as possible with the British leader, so the expediter always accepted with alacrity. Of his first eight weekends in Britain, he spent seven with the Churchills and Pamela, either at Chequers or at Ditchley, the estate of MP Ronald Tree near Oxford, where the prime minister went to avoid air attack when there was a full moon. Winston was delighted that their relationship seemed to be drawing the United States and Britain closer together.

Beaverbrook put extra effort into nurturing the affair. He kept young Winston and his nanny up at Cherkley for most of the war and gave Pamela and Averell virtual carte blanche to come and go whenever they wished. He gave Pamela money for clothes to beef up her wardrobe as well as checks for young Winston, ostensibly for his infant godson to further his religious instruction. The clincher came when Max persuaded Averell to bring his daughter Kathleen to London. Kathy was a daughter by Kitty Lawrance, not Marie Whitney, with whom Averell had no children. Kathy had just graduated from Bennington and wanted to come to Europe to see her father.

Averell thought it would be a good idea if she came. Many British families were sending children to Canada or the United

States to get away from the bombing and possible invasion. Averell believed that Kathy's presence would be seen as a symbol of American confidence.[37] Beaverbrook was a step ahead. Kathy was two years older than Pamela. It would be natural if the two young women became friends. Averell would have cover. Kathleen Harriman could be a beard for her father and an alibi for Pamela.

Beaverbrook asked McCrary to take Kathy on as an assistant. Max would pay her salary. Having a job made it possible for Kathy to get a passport for the war zone from the State Department. The British visa was easy with help from the minister of aircraft production. Two months after the Dorchester sleepover, in mid-May 1941, Averell's daughter arrived by flying boat via Bermuda, the Azores and Lisbon.

Kathy had not initially planned to stay long, but she was fascinated by the London scene and mood. The air was filled with defiance, romance, intrigue and drama. She was struck too by the importance of her father and his job. "He literally knows everyone of note," she wrote Marie a few days after arriving, "everyone who has a constructive part in the workings of the war and they all love him."[38] Kathy took over a sitting room in Averell's Dorchester suite. Pamela moved back to her room on the sixth floor.

The two women hit it off right away, just as Averell and Max had hoped. Pamela thought Kathy was wonderful. She was what Pamela imagined every typical American college girl was — attractive, long-legged, energetic, curious about everything and everybody. Kathy was even more impressed by Pamela, who was charming and jolly and confident and who had, in Evelyn Waugh's words, "kitten eyes full of innocent fun."[39]

Two weeks after arriving, Kathy wrote her older sister Mary that she was looking for permanent housing for Averell and was being helped by Randolph Churchill's wife, "a wonderful girl, my age, but one of the wisest young girls I've ever met — knows everything about everything, political and otherwise." When she wrote Averell's wife about how helpful Pamela was, Marie sent presents for young Winston.[40]

After two months of staying close to the Churchills in Britain, Averell decided it was time to explore other parts of the war zone.

Greece had fallen to the Germans in April and fifty thousand British troops were forced to evacuate. Some withdrew to Crete, which succumbed in late May after ten days of vicious fighting, including a German airborne assault.

Another evacuation took the British forces to Egypt, but they were still in harm's way. Rommel had seized Libya and Churchill was worried that the Afrika Korps would sweep all the way to the Suez Canal. Winston asked Averell to go to Cairo, which was the center of British operations in the Mediterranean, and assess the situation with an eye to shipping American equipment directly to the region.

Because Pamela was taking such good care of Averell in London, Churchill had Randolph detailed to escort Harriman in Egypt. "Darling Randolph," Winston wrote his son on June 8, 1941, "Averell Harriman is traveling out to the Middle East and I take the opportunity of sending you a line. Harriman's daughter, who is charming, and Pamela have made friends and are going to take a small house together while he is away. It seems a pity that the house that was furnished at Ickleford [the Hitchin house] is not available. Still, you are getting a very good rent. . . . I see Pamela from time to time and she gives me very good accounts of Winston. I have not seen him as he is living in Max's domains. . . . I hope you will try to see Averell Harriman when he arrives. I have made great friends with him and have the highest regard for him. He does all he can to help us."[41]

With the Mediterranean blocked to shipping, Cairo was the great jumping-off place for the Middle East and virtually all points east. Politicians, diplomats, military commanders, journalists, spies, entertainers — high-lifes and low-lifes — everybody flew in and out of Cairo either to visit the British Middle East command or to press onward to Russia, India and Australia. Cairo's embassies, hotels, clubs and bars buzzed with intrigue. Randolph loved the city and brought to it all his gusto and considerable journalistic talent. He had been promoted at one fell swoop from lieutenant to major and was named press relations officer at command headquarters.

He had arrived at headquarters "like a hot gusty wind," wrote Alan Moorehead, a war correspondent for the *Daily Express*. "He was an unabashed reflection of his father, whom he always referred to as Winston. He was aggressive, headstrong, opinionated, full of rushing energy and he went around GHQ [General Headquarters] mortally offending one brass hat after another. He was a notable figure with his heavy leonine head, his thick greying hair, his husky voice and big shoulders. . . . He had a habit of riding rough-shod over everyone he could. He disliked advice. Inevitably he made many enemies and many mistakes. But that limp, lifeless and pathetic thing we called British propaganda in the Middle East suddenly revived under his impulsion. He got things done."[42]

Randolph also enjoyed to the hilt the hedonistic pleasures of the Egyptian capital. The fact that his wife was involved with Averell raised little sympathy in London for Randolph who, as usual, behaved far worse. Randolph had a long-term affair in Cairo with Momo Marriott, who was the wife of Major-General Sir John Marriott of the Scots Guards. Daughter of an American financier, Momo was a rich, well-known, intelligent hostess who, rather like Emerald Cunard, ran witty soirees for her friends.

When he wasn't with Momo, Randolph had a succession of girlfriends, some of them prostitutes, with whom he drank in the bar of Shepheard's Hotel or sometimes brought, creating a minor scandal, to the exclusive Mohammed Ali Club.[43]

When Anthony Eden passed through, the foreign secretary saw Randolph and cabled his father that "he is looking fit and well. He has the light of bottle in his eye." The line confused Winston until Eden returned home and explained that the cypherist got one letter wrong.[44]

Randolph and Averell got along well during the expediter's visit. Randolph was not easily impressed, but he found himself sharing much the same high regard for Harriman that his father and wife held. "I have been tremendously impressed by Harriman and can well understand the regard which you have for him," he wrote his father. "In ten very full and active days, he has definitely become my favorite American. . . . He clearly regards himself more as your servant than Roosevelt's." No one would have been happier at hearing that assessment than Max.

The same day Randolph wrote Pamela about Averell so that

his visitor could carry the letters back to London: "I found him absolutely charming & it was lovely to be able to hear so much news of you & all my friends. . . . He spoke delightfully about you & I fear that I have a serious rival."[45]

Little did Randolph know. But he would soon. While Averell was gone, Pam and Kathy found an apartment in London at 3 Grosvenor Square, across the landing from Gil Winant, and a weekend cottage named Petersfield Farm near Dorking in Surrey. The two-hundred-year-old stone cottage sat in the middle of a field of wildflowers and seemed a lifetime away — not twenty miles — from the bomb rubble of London, where the homeless slept in subway stations.

The farm was near the Biggin Hill airfield. On weekends, the two girls would go over to see the eighteen- and-nineteen-year-old fighter pilots before their missions. They called the boys "beaux," but they really weren't. They were young and spirited and brave and eager to talk and the girls found them good company. Except sometimes they returned the next day to discover half of the men they'd been talking to had not returned from missions. Then they would drive back in tears to the cottage.

When Averell and Kathy moved into the apartment, Pamela joined them. The explanation was that Harriman was gone so much, it made sense that the women stay together. No one discussed why Pamela was spending so little time with The Child, though the rationale was that he had to be kept away from the city during the night bombing and while his mother worked. Clementine Churchill frequently mentioned to Pamela how nice it must be for her to have Kathy as a friend. But Kathy had quickly figured out that she was not Pamela's only friend in the Harriman family.

The issue became unavoidable in April 1942 when Averell became very ill. Pamela nursed him in the apartment until it was clear that he was getting worse. She called Beaverbrook's Welsh doctor, Sir Daniel Davies, who determined that Averell had caught typhoid fever from drinking well water on a trip to Northern Ireland. He summoned three American nurses from a field hospital near Oxford to take over the nursing chores. The sensitivity and tenderness Kathy's young English friend had shown while caring for her father — a nursing touch that Pamela would display time and again with the men in her life — bespoke more than friendship.

Kathy never mentioned the subject until months later when the two women were driving to the country one Friday evening. Something prompted the subject and Averell's daughter explained that she was not a total fool. She had spotted the affair soon after arriving in London. Once she did, she had to decide whether to stay and deal with it intelligently or go home to America. She was not shocked. She knew of her father's fondness for pretty women. She had a good, friendly relationship with him, more collegial than parental. She called him Ave or Averell, not Dad.[46]

Kathy got along with Marie Harriman, but Marie was her stepmother and they were not very close. She did not feel the emotional tug to defend Marie's welfare that she might have had it been her mother, Kitty, in the same situation.

For that matter, Marie was fooling around herself. When her best friend, Marjorie Duchin, died following the birth of Peter in 1937 — soon after the two of them had so much fun decorating the Sun Valley lodge — Marie Harriman began a long affair with Marjorie's bandleader husband, Eddy Duchin.

With no great moral imperatives at stake, Kathy decided to stay to be Averell's official hostess, help keep him happy and to offer enough of an alibi that his affair with Pamela could be conducted with at least a minimum of discretion.

The fact that she was having a fabulous time made it easier for Kathy to make up her mind. With more Americans arriving in London by the week, moguls, generals and reporters flocked to the Harrimans and Pamela's apartment and cottage for information, food and drink. Among them: Bill Paley and Edward R. Murrow of CBS, Hollywood producer Darryl Zanuck, Jack Kelly, the head of Pan American Airways in Britain, newspapermen Quentin Reynolds, William Hearst, Joseph Evans; William Walton from *Time* and his colleague Mary Welsh, who later married writer Ernest Hemingway; General Fred Anderson of the Eighth Air Force Bomber Command and Britain's chief of air staff Charles

"Peter" Portal; John Hay Whitney, a cousin of Olive, Lady Baillie, and two old friends of Pamela's from Leeds Castle, David Margesson and Geoffrey Lloyd.

When they were not entertaining themselves, the most powerful American in Britain and his lively daughter were on everyone's A-list. Pamela was already a fixture at the best gatherings and often brought along her housemates. "Life is unbelievably social," Kathy wrote her sister only a month after arriving. "Every night next week is booked up already and the weekend hasn't started. The only thing people seem scared about is being lonely, so they date up way ahead of time to ensure against an evening alone."[47]

The already hectic pace picked up more once the United States joined the war. On Sunday, December 7, 1941, Pamela was at Chequers for dinner with Averell and Kathleen, Gil Winant and General Hastings "Pug" Ismay, Churchill's beloved and trusted chief of staff. Clementine was, as usual, upstairs alone when Churchill's valet, Sawyers, carried in the small fifteen-dollar fliptop radio Harry Hopkins had given the prime minister for his 9 P.M. ritual of listening to the BBC news.

Churchill was lethargic and depressed, holding his head in his hands when the announcer ran through some short items, then announced a bulletin: "The news has just been given that Japanese aircraft have raided Pearl Harbor, the American naval base in Hawaii. The announcement of the attack was made in a brief statement by President Roosevelt. Naval and military targets on the principal Hawaiian island of Oahu have also been attacked."[48]

Churchill slammed his hand down on the top of the radio and, lethargy dissipated, pulled himself out of his chair. "We shall declare war on Japan," he exclaimed. "Good God," Winant declared. "You can't declare war on a radio announcement." Within minutes, the Admiralty confirmed the BBC report. The prime minister immediately called Roosevelt, who greeted him with "We're all in the same boat now." Roosevelt said he would go to Congress the following day to declare war on Japan. Churchill said he would do the same at the House of Commons and added, "This certainly simplifies things."[49]

Conspiracy theorists later suggested that Churchill knew of the impending attack because Britain had cracked Japan's naval code, but deliberately withheld the information from Washington to draw the United States into the war. Pamela calls the inference groundless. Not only were Churchill and Ismay genuinely surprised that night at Chequers, but Churchill had no desire, she said, to see the United States involved in a Pacific war which would distract its attention from the struggle in Europe.

Also, if the British had such information, it would have been difficult to keep the news from the United States. By December 1941, Americans were already working at Bletchley alongside British cryptanalysts, decoding incoming intelligence. "Anything about Pearl Harbor," said Pamela, "would have reached the Americans simultaneously with the British."[50]

There was no dispute, though, about Churchill's reaction to the news. The prime minister was absolutely elated by the implications of Pearl Harbor. For nineteen months, Britain had led a lonely fight against Hitler. Finally, it had a partner who would ensure victory. The night of Pearl Harbor, he wrote later, "I went to bed and slept the sleep of the saved and thankful."[51]

In Cairo, Randolph heard the news of the attack and America's entry into the war just before arriving for dinner at the home of an American woman. "Hurrah, hurrah, they're in it at last," he chortled, to the dismay of his hostess.[52]

On December 8, Pamela was in the House of Commons when her father-in-law announced to the nation that the Cabinet had declared a state of war with Japan. Geoffrey Lloyd whispered to Chips Channon how lucky Winston was: Japan's attack had saved his government if not Britain. The next evening, Channon dined with Pamela, Kathy and Averell and polished off the parliamentarian's last magnum of Krug 1920. "Much talk of a possible Japanese invasion of California," Channon wrote in his diary. "Averell hopes that the American cities will be blitzed so as to wake the people up. He attacked the American isolationists bitterly."[53]

In the spring of 1942, Randolph volunteered to become a paratrooper and took part in a sabotage raid on Benghazi, the German-Italian supply depot hundreds of miles behind enemy lines. The raid was a success, but a road accident on their way home from Alexandria to Cairo seriously injured several passengers, including Randolph, who dislocated a vertebra and was laid up for a month. Returning to England to recuperate, he realized the cracks in his marriage were worse than those in his back.

He and Pamela began fighting almost immediately. Randolph complained about Pamela parking young Winston at Cherkley and rarely seeing him. "I want you," he told her, "to be with my son." When Pamela noted that Winston was also her son, Randolph erupted. "No, my son. I'm a Churchill." Matters were not helped when Randolph heard himself called "Mister Pam."

Pamela had mentally called it all off with Randolph more than a year before. She had her son, her link to Winston and Clemmie. She had Averell and a whole new world. There was no reason even to go through the motions with Randolph. The Cairo fleshpots had taken their toll on his looks. His skin was mottled. In contrast to Averell's flat stomach, Randolph's belly strained against his uniform belt. There was no question of reconciliation. Pamela had already moved on.

Pamela's fascination with all things American had virtually Americanized her. "I was the only English woman living in Grosvenor Square," she said. "It was known as Eisenhowerplatz" [after Supreme Commander Dwight D. Eisenhower arrived in late 1943].[54] Her English friends, other than those in the Churchill circle, had been left far behind. Most of her friends now were American — from the loftiest general, Eisenhower, to the lowliest private — writer Irwin Shaw.

She had "gone over" so far, in the words of former English friends, that she spoke English with a pronounced American accent. She accused Randolph of acting "like a pasha," ordering her around. Pam would have none of it. Randolph's behavior was extreme, but matched a type she could no longer tolerate. Americans were far better to their women than British men, she had discovered. Britons took women for granted — sexually and intellectually — and treated them like pieces of furniture.

The nineteenth-century English explorer and author Sir Richard Burton wrote in *The Book of a Thousand Nights and a Night* that "it is said abroad that the English have the finest women in Europe and least know how to use them." Pamela would say amen to that. She could no longer stand British men. Never again would she get involved with one.

The quarreling was public enough to fascinate the London circuit but surprised no one. "No one blamed her for being unfaithful to Randolph," said Lord Norwich. "He never stopped being unfaithful to her and was anyway the most insufferable man to live with in the world."[55]

Waugh and Cecil Beaton walked straight into the middle of a family fight. "It was very interesting," Waugh wrote his wife after dropping by to see Randolph and Panto, as he called Pamela. "At first Lord Digby was there & he & Panto went into the bedroom for a long conference. Was he attempting to adjust a difference between the young couple? . . . Panto hates him so much that she can't sit in a room with him; she could not look at him." As for Pamela herself, Waugh noted she was "looking very pretty and full of mischief."

Other cronies who used to delight in tormenting Randolph at White's piled it on. "His spotted face and gross figure," said gossip Bruce Lockhart, repelled Pamela, who "can no longer bear the sight of Randolph."[56]

In early 1942, Harold Nicolson noticed Randolph's "little wife squirming" in embarrassment while hearing him speak in the House of Commons.[57]

"Met Clarissa Churchill," Randolph's cousin, James Lees-Milne wrote in his diary on March 18, 1942. "She told me that Randolph's wife had no intention of sticking to him."[58]

The humiliation became too much. In November 1942, saying he was "fed up," Randolph walked out. His move was just what Pamela had hoped would happen, as it would absolve her of blame in a divorce action. Her explanation was that Randolph "seemed to prefer a bachelor's existence."[59]

That was true. Randolph's friends behaved the same way. Evelyn Waugh's behavior toward his wife, Laura, was appalling. He disregarded her feelings, showed up periodically to impregnate her and insisted that marriage should not interfere with his clubs, friends or life as an "independent gentleman."[60]

It was also true that Randolph was angry about Pamela's affair. The relationship itself did not trouble him. No hypocrite,

Randolph was quite devoid of sexual jealousy. What bothered him was that Averell, with an introduction from his father, had betrayed a male friendship.

Pamela went to see Winston and told him in the Cabinet Room at 10 Downing Street that she wanted a divorce but that she hated the thought of hurting him or Clementine. She had tried her best. The prime minister was not surprised. Randolph, he told her, could bring her nothing but unhappiness. She was a kind and good young woman and he and Clemmie genuinely loved her. Earlier that year, in a letter to Randolph, Winston had called Pamela "a great treasure and blessing to us all."[61]

Winston gave her permission to dissolve the marriage, and a divorce was eventually granted on grounds of desertion on December 18, 1945. The decree awarded Pamela custody of their son, Winston, who had just turned five.

"When he came back from the Mideast, we both realized that we'd made a mistake," Pamela said later. "At nineteen, I was not a responsible person, and it was difficult being married and not married. If we'd been together it might have worked." That was graciously said, but there were no circumstances under which this marriage would have worked. Separation of war kept the couple married longer than they ever would have been if they had spent the intervening time together.

Randolph could not have sustained a relationship with anyone, and never did — not with a second wife, not with his son, never his mother, and, after the war, he quarreled to the point of estrangement with his beloved father. Being Winston Churchill's son was too difficult for Randolph. "He needed someone like his own mother, who lived entirely for her husband," was Pamela's diagnosis. "I was young and headstrong and had no ideas of just being an old-fashioned wife. I wanted to get out and do things."[62]

Newly footloose, with a five-hundred-pound annual stipend from the Churchills, whose name she would never relinquish, a minor allowance from her parents and money from Averell, she took the furniture she wanted from Randolph and wasted no time getting out and doing things.

CHAPTER SEVEN

Fred, Bill and Jock

WHEN THE MINISTRY OF SUPPLY BUILDING was bombed in 1943, Pamela's secretarial job lost much of its appeal. From the outset, two years before, she had been bored there. She hated clerical work and its dreaded, endless typing. However much she needed the income in early 1941, she could not stand the restrictions of any kind of office routine.

"She dislikes the job because it limits her social life," *Time-Life* correspondent Mary Welsh cabled her New York headquarters in April 1941, only weeks after Pamela began the job and started seeing Averell Harriman.[1] Two years later, she was even less satisfied with the time she was spending at her small desk in a corner of the bureaucracy.

Fascinated by flyers, she talked for a while about becoming a ferry pilot, delivering new planes to units, but the idea was ludicrous. She was a skilled horsewoman, but she could barely drive. Kathleen Harriman was always nervous when Pamela climbed behind the wheel. As for mathematics, a useful tool for pilots, Pamela's knowledge dropped off fast after rudimentary arithmetic. What really seemed to attract Pamela to flying was the pilots. Clementine Churchill said the whole idea was unthinkable with Randolph, Sarah and Mary Churchill already in uniform and the baby needing attention.[2]

Randolph was then in Yugoslavia, serving as British liaison officer to Marshal Tito's Partisans. However many his faults, lack of physical courage was not among them. Pamela's husband brought with him "an infectious mixture of courage and enthusiasm" and was "an unqualified success" from the moment he parachuted into the Bosnian highlands, according to Sir Fitzroy Maclean, the brigadier in charge of Britain's mission to Tito.

"A man essentially of the same tough calibre as the Partisan soldiers with whom his lot had been cast, he was without fear," said the earl of Birkenhead, his comrade in arms. Randolph's bravery he described as "almost insolent and contemptuous."[3]

Not to mention reckless. A plane crash and a series of forced retreats could not dim the thrill of guerrilla warfare and a fascination with the explosive nature of Balkan politics. Maclean believed the assignment was "one of the happiest periods of Randolph's life."[4]

Randolph was not, however, happy with one bit of news from his father. Winston wrote that he had gone months without seeing his grandchild and namesake.

That report prompted Randolph to begin protesting regularly in letters that Pamela should spend more time with young Winston, a complaint that she could not dispute. So many people were passing through her life by then that Pamela wanted more freedom to come and go as she pleased. There was too much fun and excitement going on to be tied down at a ministry desk. It was not her fault that she was meeting all these high-powered people at Downing Street, but it had been hard balancing those experiences with the numbing routine of her day's work. Finally, a bronchitis attack provided a good excuse to quit the supply ministry and begin part-time work for the Women's Volunteer Services.

To provide a home for The Child and his nanny, she moved out of the apartment with Averell and Kathy in late 1942 and took her own flat a few minutes' walk away on the sixth, or top, floor of 49 Grosvenor Square facing the Connaught Hotel. Young

Winston was two years old and declared later himself that he had been "parked for some considerable time" at Cherkley. At No. 49, he had a room of his own with a single dormer window through which he could see Hyde Park, where anti-aircraft guns put on a nightly fireworks display.[5]

Some old girlfriends of Pam's who visited noted that the baby was rarely in evidence, but the small flat that she was to keep for nearly ten years was thoroughly charming, the drawing room painted in a flattering peach and beautifully furnished with a modest but well-chosen collection of antiques. Much of the charm came from the rooms' casual elegance, the ever-present flower arrangements and the discreet collection of silver-framed photos of Pamela and young Winston with the prime minister and Clementine.

She entertained small groups — generals, diplomats, journalists and socialites — with great flair and frequency. Always eager to be helpful, she was quick to offer advice to them about where to go if they needed anything, from a car to good theater tickets, and expected the same kind of help in return. It was the beginning of a quid pro quo approach to transactions that would serve her well in the fund-raising business four decades later.

Hearing that Lieutenant General Ira Eaker, commander of the Eighth Air Force, was headed for Morocco and Algeria, she was not at all reluctant about asking his aide James Parton to see if he could bring her back fabric for upholstery and curtains. Parton found her some peasant cloth, which was clearly unsuitable, but she could not have been more gracious with her thanks.

Others had greater success in showing up at No. 49 with more-precious goodies. Although there was rationing all over Britain, dinners at Pamela's were always multi-course affairs.[6] Such hard-to-find treats as oysters, salmon, prime steaks and the best whisky, as well as more mundane but equally rare egg dishes, whole milk and chocolate all graced her table.

The treats were provided by her pals in the military or bought on the black market. Pamela refused to use the phrase "black market." She realized that it was politically incorrect for the prime minister's daughter-in-law to be lavishly entertaining rich friends when Winston Churchill was calling for sacrifice and unparalleled austerity. Her solution was to feign ignorance about the origin of the treats.

Her guests all knew as well as she did where the goodies came from. Some — invariably the few women who were invited — were more curious about another aspect of the supply line. "We wondered how *did* she pay for it all?" said one childhood chum.[7] This woman's assumption, and everyone else's, was that the notoriously stingy Averell paid. Beaverbrook also helped out. As far as Max was concerned, the salon Pamela established was a treasure trove, a font of information well worth supporting regardless of cost which, in the overall scheme of things, was minimal.

The question of what Pamela ought to do in daytime was resolved in September 1943 just as Averell and Kathy prepared to leave London. Brendan Bracken, Churchill's creative minister of information, had been pondering what to do about the influx of American and Canadian officers and men pouring into London. Thousands were highly skilled professional men — few other than journalists were women — with advanced degrees in business, law, medicine, education or with professional talents in music, theater or the arts.

Bracken was to Churchill what Harry Hopkins was to Roosevelt, an all-purpose aide whose title was irrelevant. He had a mop of wiry red hair, thick glasses and a memory for people, events and architecture so remarkable, said John Colville, that "when Brendan was available, no books of reference were required."[8]

Like Hopkins, Bracken could get things done quickly. He knew that Ashburnham House, a historic fourteenth-century building inside the Westminster Abbey close which was part of the Westminster boys school, had been evacuated and, like so many central London properties, was available.

In July 1943, the government temporarily took over the building and established the Churchill Club, a high-class recreation hall for all ranks of English-speaking servicemen with "cultural affinities," a place not just to get lunch or dinner, but to read a book, hear a lecture or concert. "Culture is the purpose of the club, a matter that England always seems to find time for even in the midst of war," said the *New York Times* just before Churchill officially opened the club in mid-September.[9]

Culture was the bait to draw a crowd, up to seventy-five or eighty at dinner and as many as two hundred for a special event; the real purpose was to have like-minded people meet, perhaps over a martini made of gin and real vermouth; elsewhere in England, bitter beer replaced the hard-to-find mixer. Membership involved a modest screening process and a word-of-mouth invitation. A wonderful idea, the club was a haven for the cream of the new arrivals, many of whom stayed in the city for months and, in some cases, for the duration of the war.

On musical evenings, a group from the London Symphony Orchestra might play in the drawing room, or Dame Myra Hess, the great pianist, would perform. Foreign secretary Anthony Eden was a club sponsor as well as an occasional speaker along with Hugh Gaitskell, one of the Labour party's leading theorists. Writers Arthur Koestler and Rose Macaulay spoke.

Sir Kenneth Clark, the director of the National Gallery, was a frequent lecturer, often, as he put it, "when a more eminent performer had let us down."[10] His wife, Jane Clark, worked in the library, so the great art historian was usually on the premises. Contemporary poetry readings were a popular attraction and drew writers from T. S. Eliot on down. In the audience might well be actors David Niven, James Stewart or Clark Gable.

One night, by bizarre coincidence, Edith Sitwell was reading "Still Falls the Rain," her poem about the bombing of England, when a doodle-bug, a V-1 flying bomb, approached the club. "It came nearer and nearer and seemed to be over the house," Clark recalled.[11]

John Lehmann said that "the rattle grew to enormous proportions and it was impossible not to think that the monstrous engine of destruction was pointed directly overhead. Edith merely lifted her eyes to the ceiling for a moment and giving her voice a little more volume to counter the racket in the sky, read on: 'Still falls the rain, still falls the blood from the starved man's wounded side, he bears in his heart all wounds.' " The full house appeared to be holding its collective breath. "She held the whole audience in the grip of her discipline, the morale of her unspoken assertion that poetry was more important than all the terror that Hitler could launch against us. Not a soul moved and at the end when the doodle-bug had exploded far away, the applause was deafening."[12]

When the reading was over, Clark commended the poet for her composure. "The great point of wearing long skirts," said the gangly, storklike Sitwell, "is that people can't see when one's knees are knocking together." Bill Walton, the *Time-Life* news correspondent, said at that moment, "You knew the Empire was going to survive."

Bracken thought Pamela would be a natural to work at the Churchill Club and he was right. She did not, however, found the club or direct it as many, including her son, have said and as Pamela herself has claimed. Mrs. Euan Wallace, known as Barbie, the wife of Churchill's minister of agriculture, started and ran it. The club was up and operating well before Pamela joined. Churchill officially opened the premises in September 1943, but Pamela was not a regular for several more months. In fact, she worked there only sporadically. She was there the evening General Dwight D. Eisenhower, back from North Africa, dropped by in his new capacity as the London-based chief of the Allied Expeditionary Force. The club was so jammed that night with what seemed to be most of its six hundred members that the supreme commander ended up in the kitchen helping dish out food.

Pamela made an extraordinary impression on those who frequented the Churchill Club. "She was beautiful and very much admired," said future U.S. Supreme Court justice Lewis Powell, who was then serving with the 319th bomber group.[13]

Some club members simply gawked because, by then, Pamela had a knockout figure: slender waist and legs; full breasts and hips.

"Breathtakingly beautiful," was the description of Elie Abel, the journalist and author, who was then in the Royal Canadian Air Force. "We didn't even dare talk to Pam in those days, but we'd gaze longingly at her red hair halfway down her back."[14]

Her temperament was more important than her looks. She had

energy and exuberance and an optimism that made men far from home gravitate toward her. She also had a certain precocious air. Everyone was aware that Pamela was uniquely plugged in with Britons and Americans. Some had heard she had a fondness for Canadians as well. There was a certain amazed speculation about just how much she knew. The club alone was a gold mine of all-star sources.

"The information you could pick up there!" recalled a still-astonished Bill Walton. "Rank was abandoned at the door and the room would be filled with generals, captains and majors, all of whom were mad for Pamela."[15]

And Pamela for them, if they were of sufficient rank. "You didn't see any corporals or sergeants around Pam," said Larry LeSueur, a CBS correspondent in London in 1943.[16]

Pamela did not have an assigned job other than to represent the family and help Barbie Wallace co-hostess. But she had developed the talent of making men around her simultaneously at ease and yet curious. Club members knew she was better born and better informed. A natural mixer, she was comfortable to be around. The officers laughed with her, watched her glide from man to man, and wondered about her flirtatious, come-hither style that made her appear available even when she was not. Often, though, she was.

"Pam's particular gift for the club was entertaining the generals," said Mary Lutyens, the sister of Barbie Wallace, both of them daughters of Sir Edwin Lutyens, Britain's foremost architect until his death in 1944. "Quite honestly, she didn't do an awful lot of work. She used to come in when she wanted. Then very often she left very early because she said she had a headache." Mary worked at the club, soliciting books and cataloguing them for the library, performing barmaid chores, and was there when Pamela arrived. Just how did Pamela entertain the generals? "She took them home with her, very largely."[17]

Pamela's increasingly refined entertaining began while Averell was still based in London and, when he was in town, often included him. There was nothing secret about their affair and they were widely known as a couple, so widely that word got to New York. Marie Harriman ignored the relationship as long as she could. Her own involvement with Eddy Duchin put her in no position to be hypocritical. "As long as it was discreet," it was all right, said Peter Duchin, who was raised by Marie Harriman. "It was the kind of thing one did in those days."

But when the British press and gossip columnists began talking about the two of them, Averell's wife felt humiliated. She was willing to divorce him if that was what he wanted. Eddy Duchin had asked Marie to marry him, but she had declined. She preferred to stay married to Averell, but not if he were going to be sloppy.

She cabled him: "Keep your affairs clean and out of the papers or you will be facing the most costly divorce in the history of the republic." She was not particularly interested in money, but she knew that any reference to "costly" would get her husband's attention in ways no mere warning would. According to Peter Duchin, the cable "scared the shit out of Averell."[18] He promised Marie that he would stop seeing Pamela. But he did not.

Their affair continued unabated until October 13, 1943, when Franklin Roosevelt solved the Harrimans' problem by naming Averell U.S. ambassador to the USSR in place of the miscast and frustrated former chief of naval operations, William H. Standley. Several of Pamela's contemporaries wondered whether the president's intention was to separate her and Averell to keep their ever more public affair from embarrassing Winston. But no available historical evidence supports such a theory.[19]

There was, however, considerable reason to replace Standley. The former admiral had been cut out of most substantive exchanges with the Soviets and excluded from virtually every meeting with Joseph Stalin. Averell, though, would be America's point man with the dictator, who was directing the USSR's war against Hitler.

For the remainder of the war, Pamela wrote Averell regularly to keep him posted on events in Britain. Sometimes she would awake in the middle of the night and, unable to sleep, pick up her pen and write him page after page, telling what all their friends were doing, with whom she was partying, and describing the latest war damage.

At one point, she remonstrated with him for not keeping in touch with Beaverbrook and told him to contact Max immediately.

At other times, she described the bombing of a train on which she was riding, anti-aircraft activity and the detonations of the more advanced V-2 rocket, which killed nearly three thousand Britons and injured an additional sixty-five hundred between September 1944 and March 1945.[20]

However much she cared for Averell, Pamela was not a one-man girl. He might have been the most important American civilian in Europe, but she had plenty of other boyfriends. Her Randolph experience had taught her never to put her faith completely in one man. It was a lesson she took to heart and one which eased her sense of loss when Averell dropped out of her life.

From the start of her affair with Averell, Pamela never believed it was anything more than a wartime romance with important strategic overtones. She never thought that they would spend the rest of their lives together. She suffered no delusion that the affair would lead to anything else. She took the relationship at face value. It worked for each of them beyond the good sex and companionship.

Years later, U.S. secretary of state Henry Kissinger would say that "power is the greatest aphrodisiac." That's what Pamela felt with Averell. They were a power couple and that realization set her blood racing faster.

To call their 1941–43 relationship more a business arrangement than a love affair might be slightly crass but not inaccurate. The affair involved powerful elements of commerce and self-interest. Averell was getting what he wanted — sleeping with a pretty young woman and enjoying a degree of familiarity in his access to Churchill and Beaverbrook that he could not have dreamed of having otherwise. Pamela was at the center of the most significant action in the world, receiving financial support, up to her eyeballs with her adored Americans and doing important work for her father-in-law, whose relationship with the United States and Roosevelt was always more troubled than he let on at the time.

Fidelity to each other was never an issue. There was no understanding that they would see only each other. Nor did Averell and Pamela ever discuss the possibility of getting married. When Kathy Harriman once mentioned that Averell obviously cared much more for her than Marie and asked if they had thought of getting married, Pamela was shocked. The age difference was far too great. It had never occurred to her. How naive could Kathy be?

Averell was already divorced once. To divorce Marie and marry Pamela would remove any possibility that he could reach any of the great elective or appointive offices that he wanted. As for Pamela, she had tried marriage and saw no benefits in the institution. Averell and Pamela were absolutely cold-blooded in analysing their respective situations. They both knew that Averell would eventually move on and that Pamela would find someone else.

Such certainty gave Pamela a wonderful sense of freedom. Averell could make no demands on her and she felt no obligation to him. She was a bachelor girl answerable solely to herself. Selfish? Certainly. But she never felt her behavior hurt anyone else. To this day she puts on blinders when thinking about how her behavior might affect others. Her attitude is that she is the only one who might be hurt in her relationships, so she watches out for herself and assumes others do the same.

Nor did she ever worry about what people thought about her, an attitude that she attributed to a genetic inheritance from adored ancestor Jane. Pamela knew that her parents and English friends thought she was an oddball who refused to toe the line of convention. She loved being unique.

Many of Pamela's admirers have been publicly identified, but not all. One very important lover, whom she met before Averell moved to Moscow, was Frederick L. Anderson, who by 1943 was in charge of the Eighth Air Force Bomber Command and was one of the most powerful generals in the European theater.

Anderson was "big, hearty, bluff, with a genial face, straightforward with no pretensions," said Lieutenant Colonel James Parton, then top aide to Lieutenant General Ira Eaker, who was Anderson's boss.[21] "Very manly," said Larry LeSueur.[22] The son of a New York State farmer, Fred Anderson graduated from West Point and worked up through the ranks to become a major general.

Fifteen years older than Pamela, Anderson had first come to England in 1941 as director of the Bombardment Tactics Board, a group of U.S. officers sent to observe Royal Air Force bombing methods during the Battle of Britain. In early 1943, he returned as the commander of the Fourth Bombardment Wing of Flying Fortresses. He led his bombers repeatedly on raids into Germany, winning the Air Medal and Silver Star for gallantry and explaining, "I find it much harder to stay on the ground than to fly with my planes."[23]

"He was a bomber pilot who thought like a fighter pilot," said Tex McCrary. "He was combative and he cared about his pilots."[24]

Anderson took over the bomber command later in 1943 and when the U.S. Strategic Air Forces in Europe were established in January 1944, he became deputy commander for operations under General Carl "Tooey" Spaatz, chief of staff of the Army Air Forces, in coordinating the bombing of Germany from England and Italy. Anderson was also much more than a pilot, as he proved after the war when he became a successful investment banker and entrepreneur. More intellectual than many generals, he took part in diplomatic missions to Moscow, where he saw Averell, and was Dwight Eisenhower's military representative to the 1945 Yalta conference of Roosevelt, Churchill and Stalin, which Harriman also attended.

Pamela thought Anderson was a marvelous guy and very, very attractive. Lord Beaverbrook was elated by her latest conquest. There is no record of Anderson visiting Chequers, although he may well have accompanied Eaker from nearby High Wycombe, where the Eighth was headquartered. But Pamela did bring her general to Cherkley for Max to work on.

One weekend in 1944, just Max, Pamela and Fred were in residence when a flying bomb glided toward the estate only to become tangled in one of Beaverbrook's favorite yew trees 150 yards short of the main house. The 4 A.M. blast shattered every window, blew open shutters and doors and brought down a half dozen ceilings in the house, which bombing specialist Anderson thought was about to collapse. In the middle of the night, after Fred taught the chauffeurless Max how to put his car in reverse, Beaverbrook drove the three of them in their pajamas around the property to inspect the damage.

The significance of a special relationship with an Anderson, or a Harriman, was related to the complicated partnership that existed throughout the war between Britain and the United States. Immediately after Pearl Harbor, Churchill spent three weeks in America discussing joint strategy with Roosevelt.

One day, FDR was wheeled into his visitor's room only to discover that Churchill was emerging, dripping wet and completely naked from his bath. The president apologized and began to beat a quick retreat, but Churchill motioned him to stay. "The Prime Minister of Great Britain," he said, "has nothing to conceal from the President of the United States."[25]

A nice Churchillian touch, but for all the intimacy of the alliance, there were vital disagreements between London and Washington on how to conduct the war. Part of the problem stemmed from the experiences of both sides in World War I. America came three years late to that war. Even then, the United States refused to become full partner with Britain and France against Germany, but maintained an independent command structure. During the Churchill visit to Roosevelt, the two sides decided that in this war there would be a unified command in various theaters. Still, basic differences remained.

Both the Americans and Russians wondered whether Churchill's reluctance to invade the Continent quickly meant that he had a special agenda to beat Hitler in such a way that Britain would not lose its Empire and the resources it controlled. The U.S. military brass preferred a major troop buildup in England in early 1943 with the invasion of France that summer. Britain, with the near debacle at Dunkirk seared fresh in memory, doubted that a cross-channel attack could be mounted so quickly, since so many British forces were fighting in Africa and Asia.

Roosevelt wanted to aid the beleaguered British troops in Egypt by helping Churchill invade Algeria and Tunisia. But FDR's own military commanders worried that if the U.S. effort were diverted to the Mediterranean, an early invasion of France would have to be postponed. Churchill wanted to soften up Germany, beating them in North Africa first, then come up from the south through Italy, the soft underbelly of the Axis. That jab would set Germany up for the haymaker coming their way when the Allies stormed into France.

The U.S. command believed that British Strategy was designed to ensure its continued grip on the Suez Canal, which was both its Middle East anchor and a lifeline to imperial points East. "The British," said U.S. secretary of war Henry Stimson, "are straining every nerve to lay a foundation throughout the Mediterranean area for their own empire once the war is over."[26]

Other differences bedeviled relations. Washington worried that Britain's repressive approach to India, the jewel in the crown of Empire, would undermine India's efforts against Japan. There were quarrels about how to deal with Stalin. At the Teheran Conference in late 1943, when the Big Three leaders met for the first time, Roosevelt deliberately baited and taunted Churchill so Stalin would not think the United States and Britain were ganging up against him. Churchill later grumped that the pleasant marriage of 1942 had turned into a difficult triangle by 1943.

More discord developed over efforts to develop an atomic bomb. Britain held an early edge in bomb theory. The United States raced to catch up with greater resources, but each side had suspicions of the other that limited full cooperation. Finally, as the Allies headed toward D-Day on June 6, 1944, Churchill continued to worry that invasion was premature and that tragedy loomed on the other side of the twenty-one-mile English Channel. The psychology of the alliance was also constantly evolving. From late entrant and junior partner, the United States by late 1943 had become the dominant partner and Britain's role had waned.[27]

In such an environment, Pamela's talents and aptitude for keeping Churchill and Beaverbrook informed through back-channel relationships was crucial. She did not participate in all the substantive talks, but did sit in on many and, naturally, spoke to all the participants before and afterwards. When Anderson went to Cherkley to spend the night, he and Beaverbrook closeted themselves alone for hours before Pamela was able to reclaim her general. Information was being exchanged.

It is impossible to know how much was classified and how highly or even to what extent such cooperation mattered between Britain and the United States, who were already sharing enormous amounts of intelligence. Nevertheless, the contacts were intense and came at a time when there were also substantial differences. Pamela not only played an important role in putting them together, but she was privy to enormous amounts of information. In her early twenties, she may have been the most influential intelligence broker among the Western allies. Not a spy as such, but a cat's paw with exceedingly soft fur.

In addition to Anderson, she frequently saw Eaker, Spaatz and Britain's air chief marshal Sholto Douglas, commander of the fighter command, who became Eaker's deputy in 1943 when the American was named commander-in-chief of air forces for the Mediterranean. Her sources were unparalleled. No one else had the ability to move between the two sides at such high level and on such an intensely personal basis.

She has love letters from three separate participants at the 1945 Yalta Conference: Harriman, Anderson, and another great and high-ranking admirer, Sir Charles Portal, or Peter Portal as his friends called Britain's chief of air staff.

Portal shared many of Anderson's qualities. In addition to being a skilled and daring pilot, he was intelligent, courageous, charming, with a strong sense of discipline, yet not at all pompous or stuffy. As marshal of the RAF, he outranked the American, but they knew each other well. Less clear is whether each was aware at the time of the other's relationship with Pamela.

Her physical type too — tall, dark, trim, with sharp facial features, including a great beaked nose and two years younger than Averell — Portal was a clear thinker and solid commander who directed the combined bombing offensive against Germany in which the United States bombed by day and Britain by night. He was not the operational director of the RAF, but in more than two thousand meetings with the British military chiefs of staff and their American counterparts, he ran the air war's strategic planning — and did it brilliantly.

"I would rate him one of the top military leaders of the war," said James Parton, chairman of the commission which produced the Eighth's official history and Eaker's biographer.[28] Portal's British colleagues agreed. "Portal has everything," said Churchill, who called him the "accepted star of the Royal Air Force." Sir Arthur Harris, better known as "Bomber" Harris, said, "Anything you could do, Peter Portal could do better." Dwight Eisenhower, while president, told Lord Plowden that he considered Portal to be Britain's greatest war leader, "greater even than Churchill."[29]

Portal had been the RAF's bombing commander since 1940 and frequently met with Churchill and Beaverbrook when he was minister of aircraft production. That's how he met Pamela and fell head over heels in love with her, another married man who found the young woman irresistible. She is taciturn on the exact nature of her relationship with Portal. Contemporaries, who regularly saw Pamela at the time of her involvement with Portal, are less reluctant. "She had an affair with Portal," claimed one who, late at night, dropped Pamela off on occasion to meet Portal. Smitten, the air force chief poured out his heart to her in a succession of passionate, colorfully descriptive and endearing letters which she still keeps in a locked vault in her Washington, D.C., home.

Pamela's involvements extended beyond the political, military and diplomatic arenas. She cut as big a swath through the lofty ranks of powerful American civilians. One was Bill Paley, whose wife Dorothy had been a friend of both Winston and Randolph Churchill since meeting them in New York in the early 1930s. Paley himself was a friend of Averell's, albeit not a very close one. In 1929, the W. A. Harriman Company had a business relationship with Paley's CBS which developed into a social connection.

In the early 1930s, the Paleys and Harrimans often saw each other at weekend parties at the Sands Point, Long Island, home of Maggie and Herbert Bayard Swope, the former editor of the *New York World*. The Swopes' parties were legendary. Some said they were the model for those F. Scott Fitzgerald described in *The Great Gatsby*. The crowd included many who gathered at Arden for the Harrimans' Thanksgivings. At both places, Harriman and Paley often found themselves in fierce croquet matches.[30]

Paley had been to London many times and in 1937 had had a serious flirtation with Lady Mary Dunn, Pamela's landlady when she met Randolph. In August 1942, just before Pamela moved to 49 Grosvenor Square, Paley flew to London to talk to his CBS bureau chief, Edward R. Murrow, about war coverage.

On the Pan American Clipper with him was John Hay "Jock" Whitney, who in the late 1950s would be named U.S. ambassador to Britain by President Eisenhower but then was enroute to London for a posting as an air force captain. Randolph met Paley at the airport and drove him to town for dinner with Pamela. Later that night, the three of them went to a nightclub, where they ran across Jock, who also happened to be a cousin of Olive, Lady Baillie, whom Paley also knew from prewar and pre-Pamela visits to Leeds Castle.[31]

Paley spent a month in England then, being squired about by newsman Murrow, dining with Winston Churchill and most of his Cabinet, and, naturally, accepting Beaverbrook's invitation to Cherkley. Murrow warned him, Paley said, that Max "took particular pleasure in extracting indiscreet information from his guests by getting them as drunk as possible."[32]

The press lord had a bottle of scotch brought to the table and the two moguls drank and traded stories through dinner and into the night. Max poked and prodded, but Paley did not know anything more than he had read in the papers or heard on radio. Beaverbrook, on the other hand, fascinated his guests — who included writer H. G. Wells and Lady Edwina Mountbatten, whom Paley was pursuing — with tales of wartime diplomacy and the battlefront, all "quite indiscreetly" in Paley's words.[33]

His treatment of Paley was no different from Max's efforts to suck the substantive juices from every fly who was invited into his parlor and became stuck in his spiderweb. In early 1944, Paley returned to London in a colonel's uniform as chief of broadcasting within the Psychological Warfare Division of the Allies planning for Operation Overlord, the cross-channel invasion of France.

There he joined an extraordinary coterie of friends and associates all living within walking distance of one another in Mayfair, all competing for Pamela's attention and favors and all succeeding. In addition to Paley, who was living at Claridge's, there was Grosvenor Square neighbor Jock Whitney. Only Fred Anderson needed to drive to get to Pamela's. On at least one occasion, all three men dined there together.

"Pamela's parties were very, very good," Paley said. "She was extraordinary in the way she took care of her men. She called me up once and said, 'What are you doing about liquor? I know it's hard to get.' I said, 'I don't know where to get any. Could you take care of it.' The same if you needed a car, she would say, 'Call this place or that place. Anything you need or want, please call me.' That made it all very cozy and welcoming."[34] In return, Paley brought her hard-to-get presents, on one occasion four pairs of stockings that he picked up on a quick trip to the United States.[35]

According to Paley biographer Sally Bedell Smith, Paley and Pamela had a short-lived affair about which the CBS chief later bragged. Pamela never did. Some contemporaries wondered if Paley were telling the truth about bedding Pamela or simply engaging in locker-room boasting. What is certain is that his relationship with Pamela did not approach the significance of her other involvements. While he may have been a lover, he fit more in that large category of men whom Pamela liked and admired and thought one day might prove useful, as indeed he would.

When he introduced her to Jock Whitney, Paley told Pamela that they were just made for one another and he was right. Like Pamela, John Hay Whitney was an authentic aristocrat with that extra touch of class that even top breeding cannot guarantee. Both his grandfathers, Williams Collins Whitney and John Hay, were U.S. Cabinet members considered to be presidential material. Like Pamela, in addition to a distinguished pedigree, Whitney had inherited good looks, a princely poise, a warm, generous charm and a social status far above the Digbys', if below the Churchills'.

Like Averell, he was a fine polo player. In 1933, Jock became the only polo player featured on the cover of *Time* magazine; the story inside noted that the then twenty-eight-year-old was worth an estimated hundred million dollars, somewhat more than Averell. In London, his flatmate was Averell's former teammate, the great player Tommy Hitchcock, who had given up his ponies for a wartime job of arranging the fitting of Rolls-Royce engines into

U.S. Mustang fighters, an endeavor that killed him in a 1944 test-flight crash.

Later on, like Averell, Jock put together one of the great private art collections and served with distinction as a diplomat and as a friend and adviser to presidents, Dwight Eisenhower in particular. One of America's most generous philanthropists (unlike Averell), Whitney was dubbed "Aga John" by All-American football player and society maven Shipwreck Kelly.

Whitney also owned the great Greentree Stable, which produced some of the nation's finest thoroughbreds and steeplechasers. He could easily have been a terrible snob, but with a deft common touch — he asked to be dropped from the Social Register because he considered it undemocratic — the altogether humane Jock Whitney was the very epitome of a modern gentleman.[36]

Which did not mean that he did not love a good time. He most definitely did. A prince of New York's café society, Jock was a two-fisted drinker and a popular man about town. Actresses Tallulah Bankhead, Paulette Goddard and Joan Crawford were only a few of the women he escorted. In London, the Whitney-Hitchcock parties at their Grosvenor Square flat were legendary for their collection of titled Englishwomen, stunning actresses and models. "For a fellow with only one yacht," a friend once observed, "he sure has had a lot of girls in a lot of ports."[37]

As Jock's biographer E. J. Kahn Jr. noted, "the wild oats he sowed were strewn from coast to coast and across an ocean."[38] He was married thoughout the thirties to Mary Elizabeth "Liz" Altemus, a Philadelphia debutante who, when they divorced in 1940, married Harry Hopkins. When he arrived in London in August 1942, he had been married only six months to Betsey Cushing, the former wife of James Roosevelt, eldest son of Eleanor and Franklin. The separation, the war, London's ambience, his eye for first-class women, and Pamela's own special charms — all combined to make their pairing inevitable.

He spent Christmas 1942 with Averell, Kathy and Pamela, but the relationship took off after the Harrimans moved to Moscow. Jock had other girlfriends while he was in London, but Pamela was special. Fifty years later, and years after his death, she still considers Jock Whitney her best friend ever.

They could talk about anything, from a shared love of horses to war news. They both knew the social code, but Jock was also one of those rare Americans who did not feel inferior when faced with an aristocratic British accent. Married to the former daughter-in-law of the president, Jock was at ease with the soon-to-be-officially-former-daughter-in-law of the prime minister.

Finally, one of Pamela's great attractions is that for all her femininity, she has many male traits, or at least qualities that from the 1930s to 1970s were considered more masculine than feminine: she was and is competitive, calculating, independent of mind, interested in substance, direct and completely unfazed by locker-room talk. "Goddamn bastards" flows off her tongue just as easily as "That's a Degas." Such links freed them to treat each other as equals.

Because Jock and Pamela understood one another, there was no sexual game playing, no flirtatious courtship. Their relationship was very down-to-earth. She was not jealous and was happy to talk with him about the other girls; she told him about her men. At first he was just a good friend, then the last barriers came down and he became a better friend. "It was a real thing between Jock and Pam," said Jock's lifelong pal Tex McCrary, who arranged to have General Ira Eaker hire Jock as the Eighth Air Force's public relations officer.[39]

Word got back to New York on their relationship too. There was some confusion on the social circuit whether Pamela was having an affair with Averell or Jock, or both. Some of the confusion was deliberate to protect, or keep in the dark, Marie Harriman and Betsey Cushing. Neither was fooled. Each knew her husband was involved with Pamela. In 1944, Sheila Digby wrote Pamela from New York to say that the talk of the town was that her older sister was about to marry Jock Whitney.

Sheila got it wrong. Pamela was never going to marry Jock Whitney, although she would have loved to had he asked her. He didn't. Neither did Averell nor Fred. But Sheila had the verb right. Pamela did want to marry. Her sights were set on another powerful married man, the most famous American of all in wartime Britain, CBS broadcaster Ed Murrow.

CHAPTER EIGHT

Ed

"We AREN'T THE AMBASSADORS and interpreters of American ideas and opinion in England," Gil Winant cabled Harry Hopkins in 1940. "Murrow is the man of the country who is doing the greatest job of all, of interpretation, representation and understanding, of morale building in England and the United States."[1]

Ambassador Winant was not alone in his assessment of the broadcaster's influence. Winston Churchill was one of Murrow's biggest fans, fully aware of the role Britain's Boswell was playing in shifting American public and political opinion away from isolationism and toward intervention. Murrow's talent and influence guaranteed him easy access to 10 Downing Street and to Chequers, where he and the prime minister huddled over matching scotches, splash of water, no ice. "In Britain, Murrow was Mr. U.S.A.," said Bill Paley. "He knew everyone of consequence in Britain's war effort as well as numerous plain Londoners. Everybody who knew him trusted him."[2]

That was true in the United States as well. As the voice of the first war broadcast live, Murrow came daily into millions of American living rooms. At the White House, President Roosevelt's Oval Office door was open to him. On the Sunday evening of the attack on Pearl Harbor, only hours before war was declared on Japan, Roosevelt and Ed Murrow ate sandwiches and drank beer into the night as the president confided to the newsman details of the casualties and numbers of ships and planes destroyed in the bombing raid.

No one outside government matched Murrow's access; no one inside, with the obvious exception of FDR and Churchill, his influence. It was quite a podium for a journalist from the humblest of origins, a background far removed from those of Averell Harriman, Jock Whitney or Pamela Digby Churchill. Born in a small house in a hollow on the bank of Polecat Creek near Greensboro, North Carolina, in 1908, Egbert Roscoe Murrow was the self-assertive runt of a three-boy litter, a scrapper with a foghorn voice who stood up to his older brothers and bore the bruises to prove it.

When he was five, his family sold their furniture, sat up for six nights on a train and moved cross-country to join cousins in Blanchard, Washington, a farming community of three hundred people thirty miles south of the Canadian border. Roscoe Murrow, his father, had trouble making ends meet, trying and losing a succession of jobs. When their money ran out, the family set up a tent on a corner of the cousins' property.

Until Roscoe got a steady job on a logging camp railroad, the children often sat in the chill damp and ate in silence by the light of sputtering candle ends, knowing that their parents were going hungry so they would have food. Even when their financial situation improved, the Murrows remained cautious: leftovers were served first at the next meal. Ethel Murrow was the backbone of the family. A frugal, hard-working and strong-willed Methodist, she had the boys read a Bible chapter aloud every night until they went to college, taught them to be honest, to study hard and to set goals at school and on the job.

Her youngest started working part-time at fifteen in a logging camp, a masculine environment peopled with taciturn, no-nonsense lumberjacks who spoke their mind clearly and directly, as he would. A year later, when his boss began calling him Ed, he happily retired the Egbert. [In 1944, he legally became Edward.]

At Edison High School, Ed was voted most popular and graduated at the head of his class. He took a year off to raise enough money to attend Washington State College, where another woman mentored him, a broadcasting coach and adviser to the college radio station who introduced the logging scholar to classics and poetry, inculcated his love of music and gave him an added appreciation for intelligent and interesting females.

A speech major, he was active in campus politics, debated and acted, honed his speaking style and graduated Phi Beta Kappa. For the next five years, starting at twenty-five dollars a week, Murrow labored in and around academia, first with the National Student Federation of America, then as the assistant to the director of the Institute of International Education. The jobs involved making speeches on hundreds of campuses, meeting university trustees, Wall Street lawyers and financiers in venerable men's clubs and establishing international student exchanges. The country boy's demeanor received an overlay of sophisticated poise.

The NSFA also provided Ed's eventual bridge to CBS. In 1929, in an attempt to fill dead air in the afternoon, the broadcasting company offered the student group free airtime to provide public speakers who would, in return, give prestige and weight to the new and slightly suspect medium. The "University of the Air" was launched in 1930 and Murrow's persuasiveness helped line up such notables as British prime minister Ramsay MacDonald, Mahatma Gandhi and Albert Einstein.[3]

The NSFA job involved travel to Europe and in 1930, he spent eight weeks visiting Britain and the Continent. He was not much impressed by England. "I thought your streets narrow and mean; your tailors overadvertised; your climate unbearable, your class-consciousness offensive," he said years later. "Your young men seemed without vigor or purpose. I admired your history, doubted your future. . . ."[4]

In depression-wracked Berlin, Murrow witnessed Hitler campaigning to build his National Socialist Workers Party from a paramilitary collection of extreme nationalists to a political organization. Ed was both fascinated and horrified. Here was this odd-looking and strange man dressed in brown who completely captivated huge crowds with a frenzied oratory of hate and power. His ranks of followers were swelling, almost before Ed's eyes, on the twin fears of the rise of Communism and the global spread of economic depression.

As soon as Hitler became chancellor in January 1933, Ed joined an emergency committee to help evacuate 288 displaced German scholars, his first step toward becoming a dedicated antifascist. He called it "the most satisfying experience I ever had."

On a train to a New Orleans student conference in late 1932, he met Janet Brewster, president of the Mount Holyoke student body. Superficially, the Anglo-Swedish, serene, five-foot-four wavy-haired elder daughter of a prosperous middle-class Connecticut car salesman had little in common with the tall, saturnine, blue-collar Murrow, whose drive, ambition and fairness helped mitigate the fact that he was also moody, vain and hypersensitive.[5] After a courtship by letter, they were married in 1934, honeymooned in Mexico and settled down to apartment life on Manhattan's East Sixty-eighth Street.

A year later, CBS hired Murrow as "director of talks" to arrange full-time for celebrities to speak on the network. In 1937, he was sent to London as "European director," a one-man foreign staff given the task of organizing cultural programs. As an assistant, the twenty-nine-year-old Murrow signed up a wire-service reporter named William L. Shirer.

When the Nazis marched into Austria in March 1938, Murrow and Shirer dropped the culture beat and switched to hard news. With Vienna-bound commercial flights canceled while he was working in Warsaw, Murrow chartered a plane to the Austrian capital. At 2:30 A.M. on March 13, he delivered a vivid radio report describing the arrival in the streets of young Nazi storm-troopers tossing oranges to residents, and the mounting anticipation that Hitler would arrive within hours.

The impact in the United States of the live broadcast was dramatic. The CBS switchboard lit up and the network immediately asked for more reports from Murrow. His *Anschluss* debut was the first of more than five thousand voicers Ed would make from Europe, bringing the war into American homes and revolutionizing the nascent broadcast industry.

As the Continent moved toward full-scale war, he began hiring the rest of the "Murrow boys" — among them, Eric Sevareid, Larry LeSueur, Charles Collingwood, Richard C. Hottelet, Howard K. Smith and the one woman in the group, Mary Marvin Breckinridge — a team that for decades gave CBS a deserved reputation as the best in the broadcast-news business.

The literate Eric Sevareid was struck by their first meeting: "I was sharply impressed by a young American, a tall man with a boyish grin, extraordinary dark eyes that were alight and intense one moment and somber and lost the next. He seemed to possess the rare thing, an instinctive, intuitive recognition of truth. His name was Edward R. Murrow. He talked about England through half the night and, although he had been there only a year, one went away with the impulse to write down what he had said, to recapture his phrases so that one could recall them and think about them later. I knew I wanted to listen to this man again, and I had a strong feeling that others ought to know him."[6]

When Murrow asked Sevareid to quit his writing job at the Paris *Herald Tribune* and join him, his friends thought he would be crazy to do it, but Sevareid felt that "there was something about him that evoked a feeling of trust." The twenty-six-year-old reporter signed on.

The war made Murrow a legend. Two days after the German army occupied Austria, CBS launched the "World News Roundup," a succession of shortwave radio reports from correspondents in various European capitals. The program was a huge hit with listeners and set a precedent for coverage that televised nightly news still followed more than a half century later.

In London, Murrow eschewed rehashes of wire service reports. He insisted that his staffers, most of whom were former United Press wire service reporters, produce pertinent, original essays, a new kind of broadcast journalism that was heavy on sights, sounds and perspective. Listeners could live events through the correspondents and draw reasoned conclusions.

"He told his men that eight out of ten stories should be

original," said David Halberstam, who chronicled Murrow's role in the rise of CBS in his book *The Powers That Be*. "He wanted thoughts and ideas, a sense of the issues at play and a sense of the texture of the country they were covering."[7]

Ed always sought what he called "the little picture," how individuals fit into the great events that comprised "the big picture."

Murrow's own portraits of the war — the life of Londoners under fire, the metallic taste in the mouth while squatting in the belly of a B-17 Flying Fortress on a bomb run over Germany — were vivid masterpieces, the taut, ominous voice etching indelible images on the minds of his listeners. His sense of timing could make silence as eloquent as the understated prose he delivered in an all-American baritone. His trademark was the lingering pause in his nightly introduction: "This — is London."

Night after night, Ed took his microphone and his transatlantic audience out onto the roof of Broadcasting House, the Portland Place headquarters of the BBC, to capture the sounds of falling bombs and broadcast live the air-raid firestorm around him, never revealing where the explosives were landing. A night bomber's exhaust trail was "a pale ribbon stretched across the sky"; anti-aircraft fire "seemed to splash blobs of daylight down the streets"; bomb detonations "looked like some giant had thrown a huge basket of flaming golden oranges high in the air."[8]

Other times, he prowled the streets in a houndstooth sports jacket and trench coat, placing his microphone on the sidewalk to pick up the clacking and scuffing of heels on pavement as Londoners hurried into air raid shelters. Murrow wouldn't go into air raid shelters himself except to report, say, on a Welsh storyteller entrancing dozens of children too frightened to sleep.

"Once you start going into shelters," he told LeSueur, "you lose your nerve."[9]

At home or in the office, whenever the sirens blared, Ed stuck to what he was doing and ignored the warnings. In restaurants, he seemed to prefer sitting near the window or under a skylight.

His analysis was incisive. On August 18, 1940, he broadcast how, an hour after the all-clear sirens, Britons in one bombed neighborhood were back sitting in deck chairs on their lawns, reading their Sunday papers. "There was no bravado, no loud voices, only a quiet acceptance of the situation. To me, those people were incredibly brave and calm," he said, making clear that the impression he had forged in 1930 had changed.

"They are made of stern stuff. They can take what is coming. . . . Now there is room for many opinions about the diplomatic, economic and military policy of British government. . . . If the people who rule Britain are made of the same stuff as the little people I have seen today, if they understand the stuff of which the people who work with their hands are made, and if they trust them, then the defense of Britain will be something of which men will speak with awe and admiration so long as the English language survives."[10]

The following Sunday, he brought a fresh, clear eye and ear to straight reporting of the facts, "calling them as I'm seeing them," as he once wrote to his parents.[11]

"The damage done by an exploding bomb to windows in a given area is a freakish sort of thing. A bomb may explode at an intersection and the blast will travel down two streets, shattering windows for a considerable distance while big windows within a few yards of the bomb crater remain intact. The glass, incidentally, generally falls out into the street rather than being blown inwards. . . . But the strongest impression one gets of these bombings is a sense of unreality. Often the planes are so high that even in a cloudless sky you can't see them. I stood on a hill watching an airdrome being bombed two miles away. It looked and sounded like farmers blasting stumps in western Washington. You forget entirely that there are men down there on the ground. Even when the dive bombers come down looking like a duck with both wings broken and you hear the hollow grunt of their bombs, it doesn't seem to have much meaning. It's almost impossible to realize that men are killing and being killed, even when you see that ever-thickening streak of smoke pouring down from the sky, which means a plane and perhaps several men going down in flames. On the other hand, when the bombs fall nearby, it's possible to assume the most undignified position in the world without effort and without thinking. The position officially recommended: flat on the ground, face down, mouth slightly open and hands covering ears. Even then the bombs somehow don't seem to make as much noise as they should, but they do seem real."[12]

In the 1950s, Murrow would host a television program called "See It Now," but his voice pictures in the late 1930s and 1940s were so graphic that his radio listeners could see it then.

A workaholic, Ed drove himself to exhaustion. Lean to begin with at six two and 175 pounds, he lost twenty-five pounds during the Blitz. "Have reached point where hands shake so much, can't even read my own writing," he wrote his brother Lacey, then an Army Air Force lieutenant. "Hasten to say that overwork and no sleep is responsible, not fright."[13]

He drank coffee nonstop but ate little, a legacy of childhood. Ed listened to waiters describe restaurant specialties only to order — almost invariably — scrambled eggs. A side order of ham was a splurge.

An omnipresent cigarette charted his fatigue. Starting at a deb-onair angle in the morning, by the end of an eighteen-hour day, it was hanging straight down from his lip. "You could almost call it a drive to self-destruction, but he's never happy unless he's working," said Paley. "When he looks like death, that's when you feel a happy glow."[14]

The CBS chief worried that his star's daredevil propensities concealed — barely — a death wish. Paley could accept the idea that Murrow wanted to witness a bombing run or two. He was furious that the broadcaster ignored orders and went on twenty-five combat missions, but finally decided he could not stop him short of firing him.[15]

When CBS forbade him to take a trip on a minesweeper, Murrow uncharacteristically asked for five days off to relax in the Kent countryside. Permission was granted, but CBS should have known better. Murrow reappeared with a broadcast about life on a minesweeper.

"Ed seemed unable to refrain from putting himself in danger," said Paley. "He did not want to report on danger without having experienced it himself."[16]

"I have a peasant's mind," Ed once explained. "I can't write about anything I haven't seen."[17]

He always pressed the limit, even when driving his small, open roadster around London and out into the countryside. "I had heard of the horrors of war," said Elmer Davis, the broadcaster who headed the Office of War Information, "but I didn't know they included Ed Murrow's driving."

Not many people would drive with Murrow, but they were eager to jam into his and Janet's apartment at 84 Hallam Street, not far from the CBS studios in the basement of Broadcast House near Oxford Circus. The Murrows were not social, but frequently Ed would bring colleagues back for a late supper of bacon sandwiches and arguments into the night about politics and philosophy. Sometimes the tobacco smoke got so thick, guests could scarcely see each other across the tiny living room.

Visitors did observe that there were always several of the latest books on current affairs lying around, but they were puzzled. Ed never read during the war. No intellectual, he was too busy chasing down leads, meeting sources, talking, listening and writing scripts. Still, he always knew what was in the books, as if he had inhaled them the same way he absorbed everyday life, straight through the pores.

The Blitz left Janet and Ed little time for one another. He came home from CBS's B-4 basement studio for a quick dinner and returned to the office — or said that was where he was going — often until 3 A.M., when he came home again to grab a few hours' sleep. Saturdays were their only day together, but they too were frequently interrupted. Ed spent much of Sunday preparing a fifteen-minute feature broadcast.

Janet had her own friends and filled her days with volunteer work. A gifted summer-stock actress during their engagement who switched to teaching high school English early in their marriage, Janet was always busy. In the early months of war, she helped evacuate schoolchildren from London to the countryside, a mission Ed called "misguided." "This business can't be faced by running away," he wrote his brother Lacey.[18]

After the bombing started, Janet set up the London office of Bundles for Britain, working alongside Clementine Churchill and various wives of MPs. The organization was launched shortly before Christmas 1940. By the middle of 1941, women in the

United States had sent to Britain five hundred thousand pieces of clothing, seventy-two mobile feeding units and $2.5 million. Janet worked from the group's headquarters in Dean's Yard next to Ashburnham House, where the Churchill Club opened in 1943. Sometimes, when she heard the bombs and V-1 rockets crumping around Regent's Park, she called Ed's office just to see if anyone would answer and reassure her that they had not been hit.

Accredited as a war correspondent, Janet broadcast home stories about Bundles for Britain for CBS and for the BBC, then broadened her scope to include reports on news events, issues affecting women and Anglo-American relations. Under the sponsorship of Winant's American embassy and Britain's Ministry of Information, she lectured to local audiences about U.S. history, culture and sociology.

Clementine Churchill became very fond of Janet and frequently invited her to Downing Street for lunch. When Ed called to pick her up once, the prime minister heard his voice and strolled from his study. "Good to see you, Mr. Murrow," said the only man in Britain who did not call him Ed. "Have you time for several whiskies?"[19]

Like Harriman, Murrow was a Churchill conduit to the United States. If Averell was the prime minister's link to Washington, Ed brought Winston and the British war effort directly to the American people. "I saw many flags flying from staffs," he reported after one night of heavy bombing. "No one told these people to put out the flag. They simply feel like flying the Union Jack. No flag up there was white."

Broadcasts like that sent goosebumps skittering across the skin of U.S. listeners and intensified visceral reaction to the fighting in Europe and first built, then helped maintain, support for America's involvement in the war.

Ed completely understood and relished his role. When the worst days of the Blitz ended, his parents wrote to ask him when he was coming home. No time soon. "I must stay here and report it if it kills me," he wrote back. "You raised a boy with a big voice. . . . Some people, many of whom I don't know, trust me and they can't be let down.[20]

He adored Churchill, and called him the era's "most remark-able" man. But Ed was no fan of the snooty Conservative party. Nor did he have high regard for Averell, who embodied every-thing the self-made Murrow hated. To the newsman, the diplomat was a stock figure, a pampered patrician born with a silver spoon in his mouth, a man who never had to work hard for anything. A cruel but accurate jibe years later about George Bush said that the president was "born on third base, but thought he hit a triple." Murrow felt much the same about Harriman.

Despite his innate resentment, Ed had to deal with Averell. The Lend-Lease expediter was the other major American player in London and an important source for Murrow. It was through Averell that Ed met Pamela. Pamela's memory is hazy about ex-actly how Ed entered her life. But the record shows that the introduction came on October 10, 1941, a Friday when Ed drove to the weekend house Pamela shared with Averell and Kathleen.

His signature in Pamela's guestbook is a barely legible scrawl, as if he did not want anyone to know he was there. Murrow and Harriman saw each other professionally over the next two years until Averell and Kathy moved to Moscow. But the two men were never close. Ed did not appear again in Pamela's weekend guest-book until September 1944, when he signed in by printing his name in bold block letters, the written equivalent of a bull moose staking out his territory. By then, their relationship had changed as much as Ed's signature.

For all his clarity as a reporter, Murrow was complex as a person. With his brothers, on school squads, with the loggers, he was a team player who believed in male solidarity. But there was a strong loner streak in Ed, who endured powerful mood swings and occasional deep depressions throughout his life. He was com-fortable with others, was a skilled mimic who told hilarious anec-dotes, but he revealed little of himself.

After following him for weeks for a 1938 profile for *Scribner's* magazine, writer Robert Landry said of Murrow, "Despite the easy manner, the fund of funny stories, the man himself remained elusive, noncommittal on all but professional matters, wrapping his privacy around him like a protective covering."[21]

"Murrow's boys" took assignments from Ed, but worked individually and competitively and were no more successful than outsiders like Landry in penetrating their bureau chief's reserve. "He wasn't great pals with anybody," said Richard C. Hottelet.[22] "He wasn't much for small talk," echoed Larry LeSueur.[23]

Eric Sevareid offered the best description of Murrow's knotty personality: "He is a complex of strong, simple faiths and refined, sophisticated intellectual processes — poet and preacher, sensitive artist and hard-bitten, poker-playing diplomat, an engaging boy one moment and an unknowable recluse the next; a man who liked people in general and loved a few whom he held off at arm's length . . . he could absorb and reflect the thought and emotions of day laborers, airplane pilots or cabinet ministers and report with exact truth what they were; yet he never gave an inch of himself away."[24]

Women seemed to understand Ed better. Bill Paley's then wife, Dorothy, found him a kindred spirit. She did not know about his mother or the female college professor he admired, but she could sense that, for all his macho virility, he was more open with women. "Men, of course, were attracted to him; he was such a male man. But I always had the feeling that Ed was more comfortable with women. It's a curious thing: Ed, I think, thought of himself as a rather unsophisticated person. And he felt oftentimes with men that he was competing with a kind of sophistication which he didn't possess . . . I don't think men knew him. I don't think they really knew Ed at all."[25]

Pamela got to know Ed better than anyone but Janet. She had known him socially through Averell and the prime minister, but no sooner had Harriman waved farewell and boarded his plane for Moscow at Heathrow airport than Pamela was crying on Ed's shoulder. She and Averell may not have discussed marriage, but the diplomat had been the best part of her life until then. His departure left a void that she would not hesitate to fill. In no time, Ed was in Pamela's bed.

There were few preliminaries. Almost no wooing beyond a few late dinners. The attraction of two of the brightest stars in the London sky was intensely physical. There were few women who were not attracted to the darkly handsome Murrow and few men in wartime London who would not crawl over broken glass to have Pamela. Neither was an exception. "Ed was crazy about her," said William Shirer.[26]

Ed knew that she was unhappily married, depressed about Averell's departure and available. She could see from the way he responded to her that, wedding band or no, he was just as susceptible a target as the other powerful and married men she had known.

Each represented something entirely different for the other. Their affair was a compelling attraction of polar opposites. Ed was wonderful-looking and knew it, but he was also hypnotized by Pamela's glamour, attentiveness, youthful sexuality and the aura that emanated from her closeness to Prime Minister Churchill. Pam was fascinated by his fame, power and looks, but also his sardonic class consciousness.

He was completely unlike anyone else she had ever met. He was entranced by her but constantly provoked her about being spoiled. She had everything — apparent wealth, luxurious surroundings, incredible connections, a good brain and looks, a terrific personality, superb taste and all sorts of powerful men hurling themselves at her. She was, he teased, too much adored by too many admirers at too tender an age.

He was thirty-five; she was twenty-three. Each was vitally appealing and yet, each was vulnerable and played on the other's insecurities. Despite her admirers and bravado about being a footloose bachelor girl, Pamela had more than a few hangups. She had essentially been left behind by Averell, whom she loved, and she saw no future with Randolph, Jock or Fred. She fretted about her lack of education. She conversed well but with little depth.

She was particulary insecure about her looks, not least the double chin she found difficult to lose. Others raved about what a beauty she was, but she felt more duckling than swan. For his part, Ed had more hangups than any man she had ever known, including Randolph, whose troubles were primarily two-dimensional.

Pam learned quickly that Ed had a tremendous chip on his shoulder. He was forever reminding her how he was the youngest child in a dirt-poor family who had always worn hand-me-down clothes and never had a pair of new shoes. He had hurt his back in a logging camp. The pain endured all his life. He had done everything on his own, including washing dishes to put himself through college. The fact that Averell and she had life handed over on a platter irritated him tremendously.

Ed was a class warrior and it was her class against which he was warring. She and Averell were the haves; he was the have-not. Pamela felt that he despised her aristocratic background and yet was also intrigued by it. Ed planned a day once in the Kent countryside, but insisted they go by train — instead of driving her Jaguar — and eat lunch in a pub. He wanted her to see how "normal" people lived.

There was a bit of hypocrisy involved. Ed loved fine quality and expensive things, especially well-cut Savile Row suits. Hottelet believed that Murrow was trying a good line on a rich girlfriend. "He was not allergic to wealth, never immune to the enjoyment of comfort."[27]

Murrow had great friends in the Conservative party but felt that the non-Churchill wing of the Tories and its appeasement policies had helped bring war on the country. Ed loved the Churchill circle — the Brendan Brackens and Pug Ismays — but overall, he felt contempt for the party. A socialist, Ed was more comfortable politically with the Labour party. He was a great admirer and friend of Harold Laski, the political philosopher and Labour's postwar chairman, and believed that Labour was more realistic, more in tune with modern times and better suited to run Britain after the war.

Because Pamela's political upbringing was all Conservative, they argued often about what would be best for Britain when the fighting ended. She spent hour after hour trying to convince him that being born privileged did not necessarily mean a person was all bad. Some rich people like Averell, for example, worked hard and produced good results.

Amid all the wrangling, combined with a furious passion, Pamela's eyes and mind were opening further. Ed's very different view of politics was a revelation and an education. Highly cynical about the war, he challenged her to reconsider her simplistic view of Americans and Britons. He talked about appeasement, the antiwar movement and about war profiteering from the vantage point of one who understood the extremes of life in Britain, from the plush drawing rooms of the aristocracy to the damp, fetid shelters in London's East End.

He was anguished that U.S., British and Canadian bombers were killing many Allied soldiers as they bombed close to front lines. These were issues that she had never considered until Ed, who could be hypnotic in maintaining her attention. Always demanding, he made her shape up. What do you make of that? he would ask, and wait for a response. He was tough on himself and on everyone around him, from Shirer and Sevareid to her. He provoked Pamela and made her think.

Ed forced her to question preconceived notions about the military and political intentions of Roosevelt and Churchill and strategies formulated by generals they both knew well. Ed, who was out sampling it daily, understood popular British opinion far better than Pamela. She didn't even know any Labour party supporters. He also had examined, in ways she had never contemplated, the conflicting tensions and competing interests at work in Churchill's coalition government.

Although her formal education had been shallow, Pamela had a sharp native intelligence and a considerable number of intellectual building blocks at hand. Her experiences in France, Germany, at Leeds Castle and with the Churchills had given her unparalled firsthand exposure to history in the making.

And now Ed was forcing her to grind all the ingredients against one another to develop perspective, to question convention and superficial assumptions. Instead of merely accepting whatever she was told by powerful authority figures, Pamela was learning to draw her own conclusions. She did not have all the right answers, but she was getting much better at learning the right questions.

Ed infuriated her often because he was tough, but she recognized what was happening and understood that he brought out the best in her. She loved the fact that he took her seriously. As a result, their romance took on a depth that endured well beyond the bedroom.

The hours they each kept fit Ed's life into Pamela's throughout all of 1944. Both were night owls. After dinner at home, Ed returned to the CBS office to work on his script and dictate it to his secretary, Kay Campbell. If Pamela was at the Churchill Club, he picked her up 10 P.M., never stopping to schmooze, and brought her back to CBS. She came over on weekends, too, and occasionally bumped into Shirer, Hottelet or another correspondent. She had a ribald sense of humor and cracked up one day with Murrow and Hottelet over the story of an Englishwoman who described escaping a bombing raid "in virgo intacta."

Ed and Pamela often went together to the tiny BBC studio where — London being five hours ahead of New York — Ed did his live broadcast at 12:45 A.M. She sat alone with him while he smoked and fiddled with notes on a yellow pad, watching the clock face and waiting for the engineer's cue, one twenty-third of a second after being uttered in New York: "Go ahead, London." After the broadcast, she frequently took him home to 49 Grosvenor Square.

Ed did not discuss the affair, but everyone else did. Their relationship was public and especially painful for Janet. Everyone respected her and sympathized with her. "She was a fine wife, very even-tempered, with a lot of guts and a good influence on Ed. She could put a brake on him and deal with his depressions," Bill Shirer recalled. "Janet didn't talk about the Pamela episode, but it disturbed her greatly."[28]

Janet, who was twelve years older than her rival, knew Pamela, more by reputation than personal contact, although she once accompanied Ed to an awkward dinner at No. 49. The flat was filled with men. Janet was the only woman guest and felt very out of place. "Unless you were important in some way, you weren't very welcome there," she said.[29]

Pamela never invited her again, which was fine with Janet. "I didn't admire the kind of person she was," Janet explained.[30] To Ed's down-to-earth, hard-working and pretty but unglamorous wife, Pamela was greedy and self-centered, a calculating and opportunistic user, a self-promoter who lacked morals, whether in dealing with married men or in playing the black market. Others felt the same way.

Janet knew Ed was captivated but hoped her husband would get over this infatuation. The affair, though, proved more than a dalliance. Ed, in fact, was so obsessed that he was subject to jealous rages. Pamela was dating Jock Whitney and Fred Anderson and playing Ed like a trout on a dry fly.

In July 1944, while Pamela was ill in the country with scarlet fever, Ed went by her apartment to leave with housekeeper Marian Martin a gift of two hard-to-get Hershey bars, something to cheer her up. The elevator would not come to the ground floor, so he clambered up the six flights of stairs in the midsummer humidity.

Dripping sweat by the time he reached the top, he discovered Fred Anderson's aide holding open the door of the elevator while he delivered a carton of prime steaks. The broadcaster erupted in rage. Back at his office, he wrote Pam a blistering, abusive letter about the impropriety of an American general paid by U.S. taxpayers delivering steaks meant for U.S. soldiers to a woman who neither needed nor deserved such largesse.

Pamela could barely stop laughing. She found the episode terribly amusing. The letter was so Ed. He was so intense, so insecure. Jock was much more casual about Fred. Whenever she broke a date, Whitney teased her with mock protestations that he had been upstaged because the general was in town.

In September 1944, Janet returned to the United States. She had been traveling almost constantly for the past year as a member of Gil Winant's British-American Liaison Board, investigating complaints about American soldiers. She resigned from the board, telling Winant that her parents were ill and that she might be gone as long as six months. Her parents were not well, but neither was Janet.

She was exhausted, both by her job and the pain of her marriage. Dealing with Ed and his erratic mood swings had become too difficult. After D-Day in June, which Ed had officially announced, he was hardly ever home. When he wasn't in France or in the office, he spent what time he could with Pamela. She did not know if the marriage could survive, but she knew that she needed a change of scene.

No sooner had she left than Ed was wracked by guilt. He was not a religious person, but his mother's Bible lessons had ingrained in him such a puritanical streak that he refused to be photographed without wearing his wedding ring.[31] He never dodged attractive women, but he felt ashamed when he did stray. Pamela was not certain why Janet left but doubted that she was the cause. If she thought that she had been, her behavior would have been no different. Accepting blame was not something Pamela did with much frequency. As far as she was concerned, if there were trouble in the Murrow marriage, it was Janet and Ed's problem, not hers.

Once his wife left, Ed saw even more of Pamela, but he missed Janet terribly. Early in the Blitz, Janet had moved to the countryside for a few days. He wrote her constantly, telling her what a source of strength she was for him. He did it again now, a rapid-fire succession of conscience-driven letters and telegrams that began within days of her departure.

"Dearest Cook. . . . Eating at the Etoile, feeling blue and missing you very much. . . . America to me seems far, far away. . . . You are the only thing over there that I want to see," he wrote on September 26. Three days later, he wrote again: "Dearest Cook. . . . My temper is not improved by your absence. . . . This morning while shaving I was thinking of our last 10 years. . . . think we have missed too much. . . . How long is it since we went walking together . . . or fishing . . . or just loafed. . . . If we have any sense, the best years of our life should be ahead of us."[32]

Ed had not planned on following her to America but decided to join her in November, just after their tenth anniversary. The intensity of his letters picked up. "Darling, I am oh so lonesome. . . . Darling, I long to see you and be with you." On October 26, he wrote her, "Afraid have been a failure at cutting the wide swathe while the wife is away. It might be that I am still in love with you. . . . Tomorrow is our uniwoisity [sic]. . . . Let's renew the contract . . . and I should like an indefinite option."[33]

Ed was playing a double game. He was still seeing Pamela. With Janet gone, he even brought her home to Hallam Street for dinners, once with CBS correspondent Charlie Collingwood and his girlfriend. Pamela loved the evening. She was fascinated by the broadcasters, who were quick, irreverent and powerful, but she also liked the idea of being brought into Janet's space, with witnesses present, and the greater acceptance of her that implied.

The flat, though, she thought was a dump — basic, frumpy,

no class. He would not live that way if she were Mrs. Murrow. While she was intrigued by the chance of seeing Hallam Street firsthand, she much preferred having Ed at her house. He was seeing so much of her that he wrote Janet about going to a dinner party given by "little P." He had left early, he said, but much of the talk had been about Janet. Peter Portal, chief of the air staff, had been "particularly enthusiastic" in his comments about her, Ed wrote Janet, a compliment that "didn't go down well with the hostess."[34]

For all his professions of love to his wife, Ed and Pamela had begun talking about getting married. Janet would never stand in his way if he asked for a divorce, he told Pam. There were no children. He and Janet had gone their separate ways. The break could be clean. He promised Pamela that he would raise the subject on his visit to the States. Later he told her that he had talked with his wife about a divorce, but that Janet absolutely refused.

He would hardly be the first man to concoct such a story, but if that is what he said to Pamela, he did not tell her the truth. According to Janet, there was no mention of divorce when he rejoined her in New York. Quite the contrary. "We vacationed in Florida, played golf and had a lovely time," she recalled.[35]

It was particularly lovely because, after ten years of trying hard and repeated disappointments, Janet became pregnant in February 1945, three weeks before they returned together to London. Both she and Ed were elated. They had all but given up hope of conceiving and had started talking about adopting when the war was over. Janet's condition, though, was not enough to keep her husband faithful once they were back in Britain.

Pamela was pure catnip for Ed. The war was winding down, but he could not stay away from her and discussed endlessly what he was seeing and thinking, an added trove of usable information for Pam. With her letters from Averell in Moscow, her links to everyone of note in London, statesmen and generals on both the British and American sides, Pamela was by then arguably the Allies' single best-informed civilian.

In March, Ed was back flying over Germany. In April, he sent one of the most memorable broadcasts of the war, his first-person account of the liberation of the Nazi death camp at Buchenwald. He was in and out of Paris at the press headquarters in the Hotel Scribe in April but back home in London to report the rejoicing in Europe on V-E Day on May 8. Three months later, atom bombs destroyed Hiroshima and Nagasaki and Japan surrendered. The war was over, Ed broadcast from London, but "the future is obscure."

He meant the uncertainty generated by the loosing on the world of nuclear weapons, but he was also talking about his own future. Ed didn't know what to do next. Paley wanted him back in New York to run CBS news. After more than eight years in Britain, Janet wanted to go home.

But Ed kept delaying. He loved being a reporter. He once told Janet that he'd do it for nothing. He hated the thought of being an executive, cooped up inside and off the air. He shuttled unhappily back and forth to New York, making appearances and negotiating his next assignment.

Pamela's future was up in the air too. Seven weeks after the Allied victory, British voters decided that the man who led them in war was not the leader they wanted for peace. On July 26, 1945, they unceremoniously booted Winston Churchill out of 10 Downing Street in the hope, as Ed had discussed with her, that Labour party leader Clement Attlee would give them a better peacetime life. Churchill was stunned. Clementine tried to ease the shock. "It may well be a blessing in disguise," she told him. "At the moment, it seems quite effectively disguised," he snorted.[36]

His daughter-in-law was soon to be out of the family and out of a job. Her divorce from Randolph would be final in December. Demobilization meant an end to the Churchill Club. The Westminster School moved back into Ashburnham House. Nonplussed and eager to explore the Continent, Pamela pulled on a uniform and went to France to see the war devastation.

Several of her other journalist pals, including Collingwood and *Time*'s Bill Walton, were reporting there and having a ball. When Paris was liberated in 1944, they had driven straight to

Montmartre and Place Pigalle, where a woman jumped on the hood of their jeep and pulled up her skirt to reveal that she had dyed her pubic hair red, white and blue.

They loved Paris and Pamela was happy to be back, share their enthusiasm and follow them to the night club and red light district. Collingwood was a great ladies' man and wanted to add Pamela to his list of conquests but didn't dare as long as she was Ed's girl. Others felt no such compunction. While she was in Paris, one of Pam's generals dispatched a bomber to pick her up and bring her to join him in Frankfurt.

On November 6, 1945, Janet gave birth to Charles Casey Murrow. Ed flew back to London for the birth, then filled in Janet's parents about their new grandchild. "His head was much too big, being in the tradition of Murrow heads," he wrote, and "he has plenty of volume but is lacking in modulation. There are two offers to sign him up as a broadcaster, but I have advised him against any long-term commitments."[37]

Ed remained troubled about his own commitments. He had been seeing Pamela all year. Janet knew it but hoped that Casey's birth, the end of the war and their move back to America would keep the marriage together. But by December 1945, she was in the dark about what Ed was actually going to do. He was not so sure himself.

In mid-December, Ed was in New York to decide once and for all whether to accept or turn down a job as a CBS vice-president. Janet stayed in London with Casey, but Pamela flew over to join Ed for Christmas, hopeful that she could nail down a commitment from him.

Her transatlantic flight with Barbie and Herbert Agar was agony. They spent a day driving to Devon to get on the Pan Am Clipper. Bad weather held them up an extra twenty-four hours. They arrived in Gander, but winter storms in Newfoundland socked them in for three more days. Finally, on Christmas Eve, a frazzled Pamela arrived at the Ambassador Hotel and moved in with Ed.

For all her fatigue, she was ecstatic at being out of England. London was dreary. Churchill was out; rationing was still in. Bomb rubble littered the streets and though the blackout was over, there was little power and light. The elation felt at the end of the war was short-lived, replaced by depression and the widespread realization of how weak Britain had been left. By contrast, not only were American spirits soaring, but New York was aglow. Literally. Park Avenue was festooned with brightly lit Christmas trees. It was as if Pamela had walked from a dungeon into a jewelry story. "I eat all the time here," she sighed to American gossip columnist Cholly Knickerbocker. "You have everything."[38] She felt reborn.

Ed took her to Bill Paley's for Christmas dinner. Bill was divorced by then from Dorothy and dating Jan Rhinelander Stewart, a wealthy and attractive widow. In London, Janet and seven-week-old Casey were alone. For the next ten days, Ed and Pamela were inseparable. He took her to meet a succession of friends, many of whom were shocked that he was with Pamela and not Janet. They dined with playwright Lillian Hellman, whom Pamela loved, with author John Steinbeck, with the socially connected Mary and Harry Warburg, who had relatives in England.

Ed had signed his new contract the day Pamela arrived and, during her visit, he asked her to marry him. She accepted at once, throwing her arms around his neck and squeezing him with all her might. Now that it was finally definite that he would be working from CBS headquarters, they looked at a house to buy on Ninety-second Street on the Upper East Side.

The sense of resolution was exhilarating. An uncertainty about what to do after the war had been building up in Pam, but with a decision made she felt liberated. She felt no remorse, or at least showed no evidence of any, about contributing to the break-up of the Murrow marriage. To those observing the whole painful process, she looked cold and heartless. Pamela, though, had a completely different attitude about the whole affair.

For her, what the Murrows decided was up to the Murrows. Once they chose, and Ed apparently had, then she was involved. But up until that point, she saw the issue as a matter for Ed and Janet to resolve in rational fashion, weighing in such factors as the baby, the move to the United States, his new job and what they all wanted to do with the rest of their life.

Pamela loved Ed, or thought she did. An important part of the equation was that he seemed genuinely to love her. Around her, he was certainly captivated and, unlike the other men she had known in the war, he seemed willing to make the necessary moves to get free to marry her. There was an undercurrent of doubt in her mind, a nagging feeling that they were too different and that she had made the wrong decision, but her reservations were outweighed by the unsettling feeling that she did not know what to do otherwise.

She had a much clearer idea about what she did *not* want to do than what she *did* want. First on the list of "Don't wants" was staying in England. She wanted out, ideally to America, the home since well before the war of all her favorite friends. In cold-blooded terms — and Pamela was fully capable of such icy calculation — Ed was her ticket. Warmer emotions and less selfish motives were also involved, namely that whatever their long-term prospects, at that time Pamela loved Ed as much as she loved anyone.

Ed went back to London to tell Janet that he wanted a divorce. Pamela flew to Palm Beach to stay with the Kennedy clan. Kathleen, better known as Kick, was the deb pal who had come out with Pamela in 1938 when father Joe was ambassador.

In May 1944, to the horror of her Catholic parents, Kick had married Billy Hartington, whose father was the tenth duke of Devonshire, a Freemason and pillar of the Church of England. Four months after her wedding — and only three weeks after her brother Joe Jr. died when his explosive-packed bomber blew up — Billy was killed in action in France. Estranged from her parents after the marriage, the desperately unhappy Kick stayed on in Britain, where she and Pamela saw each other often at parties.

Ed despised the Kennedys, especially Joe Sr. for his anti-British behavior in the months leading up to war and his cowardice during the Blitz. Visiting the Kennedys in Florida, he told Pamela, was like staying with Goering.

The crack was so Ed. She was off to have fun and he had to be such a cynical spoilsport. Her annoyance was mitigated by his promise that he would be back in three weeks with the air cleared about his divorce. He foresaw no problem. Janet was very straightforward and would understand that the move from London and his shift into the executive suite was a natural time for them to split up.

Whether Janet would have agreed to a divorce as readily as Ed predicted — or at all — was moot. Too guilt-ridden at the thought of leaving his wife and newborn son, Murrow did not ask Janet this time either. He wrote Pamela during the three weeks, but when the deadline he had set arrived, Ed cabled her the bad news in Palm Beach: Casey Wins. He hoped the gods would bless her and forgive him.

Pamela collapsed. She was completely shattered. There had been no hint of any doubt in Ed's mind during their time together in New York. He had been so definite. The proposal, the house-hunting, the joy — it had seemed so genuine. She had really expected him to go ahead with it and his decision not to was a total surprise. She was heartbroken, and less angry than deeply sad.

Pamela had told the Kennedys what was up, that she was marrying Murrow, but when the cable arrived, she didn't know what to do. Embarrassed and confused, she wanted to get out of Palm Beach fast.

She called Betsey Whitney at Greenwood, Jock's Georgia plantation, and asked for help finding another place to stay. Betsey knew all about the Ed affair and was saintlike in choosing to ignore Pamela's involvement with Jock. She was also determined to ensure that it would not happen again. That argued for a strategy of helping Pam, not isolating her and giving her cause to run to Jock for help.

Thinking quickly, Betsey said that her sister Babe was nearby in Hobe Sound. She suggested that Pamela get to Babe's as quickly as possible, spend a few days decompressing, then come up to stay with her and Jock at Greenwood. A grateful Pamela did just that. Babe was in the process of divorcing Stanley Mortimer Jr. The following year, she would marry Bill Paley, while Mortimer would marry none other than Kathleen Harriman, Averell's daughter.

Babe was too preoccupied with her own divorce to be of much help. Pamela was not interested in hearing Babe's problems. She has never been good at women's talk and was not close with Babe. But she caught her breath before heading north to Georgia, where Betsey and Jock were wonderful and tried their best to get Pamela back on her feet. They were understanding and consoling, but Pamela was inconsolable.

Averell had never led her on, but he had left her. And now Ed had lied to her and flat dumped her. She sobbed for days. Betsey told her that it was for the best. She never liked Ed anyway. Hadn't Pamela learned from her experience with Randolph that being involved with a journalist was never smart? She should stop crying and be grateful that she had not married him. The marriage never would have worked.

That had been Averell's advice too. She had written him continually in Moscow throughout the war, told him of Murrow's courtship and her plans to marry him. Bad idea, was Averell's reaction. They were too different — different worlds, different beliefs. Ed's guilt would be ruinous. Averell urged her to think again.

Her tears dried, Pamela flew to New York, where, naturally, she ran straight into Ed. Full of apologies about his behavior, he nonetheless resumed his pursuit. He loved her, but his conscience would not let him leave Janet. He could not have lived with himself and that would have poisoned a marriage to Pamela. That was truthful.

Janet called Ed a "thoughtful, caring father who felt great responsibility toward Casey — and me." She was also convinced that there was a greater lesson in her conceiving Casey at thirty-five: "I think the Lord saved our marriage."[39]

Pamela understood Ed's problem. The last thing she wanted was to marry someone who would be wracked by a guilty conscience the rest of his life. She was all too aware that Ed Murrow had one of the world's most active consciences. But if that were the case, would he then please leave her alone.

He could not. He called her. He kept wanting to see her and did. Pamela was torn. She loved him, wanted him and would hang on as long as she had a chance of winning him, but his masochism was driving her crazy.

Pamela contacted Lord Beaverbrook for advice. The press

baron was in Nassau and told her to come down right away. Of course, he would help her. He could use her. He would put her up in a hotel and she could write some stories for the *Evening Standard*. That would help get her mind off Murrow. But Ed kept up the phone chase and called Pamela repeatedly in Nassau. Once he said he would call her between 10 and 11 P.M. She waited in her room, but the phone never rang.

In the morning, she found a note at the front desk saying that Mr. Murrow had called. The hotel operator mistakenly told him she was out. The broadcaster said he assumed she was partying and, with that, his obsession with Pamela snapped. The affair was over.

On April 7, 1946, after nearly four months in America and the Caribbean trying to land or leave Ed Murrow, a desolate Pamela climbed the gangplank of the Queen Mary. She smiled for a photographer, but her heart wasn't in it. The orchid on her lapel and daisies around the brim of her Easter hat could not distract attention from her puffy face and the dark circles under eyes which were bloodshot from tears. She retreated along the deck to her cabin and sailed home to England, her future a complete blank.

CHAPTER NINE

JFK and Aly Khan

FIVE DAYS LATER, Pamela stepped off the Queen Mary and discovered that she had an option after all. Once again a man appeared unexpectedly on the scene to help her out. It was Averell, back in London on his own, at just the right moment to help stabilize her spinning compass while she got her bearings.

Averell was as adrift as Pamela when the war ended. He had stayed on in Moscow as ambassador after the armistices in Europe and Japan, trying to resolve Soviet-American policy differences in Asia. Stalin and his foreign minister, Vyacheslav Molotov, felt that the USSR, though it had fought the Japanese for only two days — compared to the bloody four-year American war in the Far East — deserved to share command of Occupied Japan. Washington rightly refused and eventually got its way, in Asia if not in Europe. In February 1946, Harriman returned via China to the United States and to a very different government from the one which had sent him abroad five years before.

Roosevelt was dead and Harriman, at that moment, had little in common with Harry Truman, the unpolished Missouri politician who succeeded him as president. Harry Hopkins, the friend

Achache-Gamma/Liaison; Time Inc. picture collection

ls Castle in Kent, where Pamela spent
y of her weekends in 1938 and 1939
ting political and entertainment figures
er the tutelage of Olive, Lady Baillie.

hane Boudin, the famed decorator
Paris's Maison Jansen, who intro-
ed Pamela to fine interior design at
ls Castle in the late 1930s and whom
ie Kennedy hired in 1961 to work on
White House.

Jean Marquis, Life magazine © Time Warner Inc.

AP/Wide World

David Margesson (*left*), talking with Ambassador Joseph P. Kennedy in 1940, just
before the U.S. envoy was removed from
his post. Margesson, a Leeds Castle regular,
was Pamela's first political mentor.

Alcohol robbed Randolph Churchill of his looks, wives and friends, but as a youth he w
astonishingly handsome.

Minterne Magna is the Digby family seat, the baronial home in Dorset, southwest England, where Pamela was raised from 1920 to 1938.

Ten-year-old Pamela (*left*), with her father, Lord Digby, and her sister Sheila at a 1930 horse and pony show.

Carnation (*left*) and Pansy (*right*), or Lord and Lady Digby, ready to ride at Minterne Magna with Pamela, 16, and their youngest child, Jacquetta, 8.

George McCullagh (*right*), proprietor of the *Toronto Globe and Mail*, and Lord Beaverbrook, publisher of Britain's *Daily Express* and Minister of Aircraft Production. McCullagh, 32, pursued the 17-year-old Pamela when she visited Toronto; it was the teenager's first experience with an interested older man. Beaverbrook was a Pamela confidant for years.

The TATLER

Vol. CXLVIII No. 1938. London, June 22, 1938.

THE HON. PAMELA DIGBY

A cover girl at 18, Pamela was presented a debutante at court in May 1938, a month before the *Tatler* featured her.

nela and a strutting two-year-old Young Winston, the image of his grandfather, on a
e visit to wartime London from Cherkley, the Beaverbrook country estate where he
nt much of the war.

William S. Paley, president of CBS, en route aboard a Pan American clipper to London, where he became close to Pamela.

Betsey and Jock Whitney in 1942, when the millionaire sportsman began his close friendship with Pamela.

Sir Charles Portal, known as Peter Portal, marshal of the Royal Air Force and one of Britain's greatest war heroes, fell under Pamela's spell.

Gen. Fred Anderson, head of the 8th U.S. Air Force Bomber Command and one of Pamela's high-ranking wartime lovers.

On October 4, 1939, three weeks after meeting one another, Pamela, 19, and Randolph, 28, marry in London so the groom can produce an heir before soldiering off to war.

Wedding day: the bride with Winston and Randolph Churchill.

Pamela in 1941, when she met Lend-Lease expediter Averell Harriman.

Averell Harriman in February 1941, one month before he met Pamela at Emerald Cunard's dinner at the Dorchester Hotel.

AP/Wide World

Averell Harriman with Pamela (*left*) in August 1941, five months into their affair and soon after his daughter Kathleen (*third from left*) arrived to join him in England.

who engineered his original assignment to London, was dead. The new secretary of state was James Byrnes, whom Harriman could not stomach. Byrnes felt similarly about Harriman, which ruled out a job for Averell in the State Department.

There was no good option in the business world. Throughout the war, Averell remained chairman of the board of the Union Pacific, but his younger brother Roland had done a good job of running the company in difficult times and had the respect of the business and financial communities. Averell realized that snatching back the railroad was inappropriate. He also wanted to stay in government if possible.[1]

A week after Averell's return to Washington, George Kennan cabled to the State Department one of the most influential diplomatic analyses in history. Kennan was Harriman's political counselor at the American embassy in Moscow and became chargé d'affaires when Averell departed. His eight-thousand-word cable, which became known as the Long Telegram, warned of the dangers of Soviet expansionism and urged that the United States lead the Western effort to "contain" the spread of Communism.

Kennan argued that the Soviets were "still by far the weaker force," and that they could be contained without a war as long as the United States led the West's response with a policy of "cohesion, firmness and vigor." The USSR had taken every advantage of the flawed February 1945 Yalta agreement and was installing pro-Soviet regimes in Poland, Bulgaria and Romania. Moscow was also reneging on its promise to withdraw Red Army troops from Iran.

At the same time, U.S. troop strength in Europe was dropping as fast as soldiers could be loaded onto transport vessels. In the two years after June 1945, U.S. military forces in Europe plummeted from three and a half million to two hundred thousand. Winston Churchill was worried by the precipitous withdrawal and what appeared to be a growing threat to Europe from Moscow.

On a private trip to the United States in March 1946, he and Harry Truman went by train to Fulton, Missouri. There, at Westminster College, Churchill raised the alarm: "From Stettin in the

Baltic to Trieste in the Adriatic, an iron curtain has descended across the Continent."

In London, the Labour government's new foreign minister, Ernest Bevin, had already warned that "our relations with the Russians about the whole European problem were drifting into the same condition as that in which we had found ourselves with Hitler."[2]

Washington needed someone in London who understood Britain and the Soviets. Gil Winant was still ambassador, but he knew little about Joseph Stalin or Molotov and had already begun his descent into the depression which provoked his suicide the following year. Truman dispatched Averell to replace Winant just as Pamela gave up on Ed Murrow and departed from New York.

It is possible that they coordinated the timing of their arrival. Pamela had maintained a steady correspondence with Averell throughout his Moscow assignment. What is certain is that two and a half years had passed since he left Pamela, but together in England, they picked right up where they had left off.

There were a few problems, though. Unlike his assignment as Lend-Lease expediter, as ambassador, Averell had major social and representational obligations. Pamela could not be his hostess. Families were no longer separated. The freewheeling bed-hopping that had characterized wartime London was over. What was possible then was unacceptable now.

The fact that Pamela was divorced, that Marie Harriman chose still not to accompany her husband and Kathleen was no longer in London with her father was turning the rejuvenated affair into a scandal. Nervous embassy officials urged that Marie join Averell right away. Marie was willing. Her eye problems had improved enough to allow her to travel. She had closed her art gallery and five years of separation had been enough. Plans were made for her to arrive in Britain after the summer holidays.

London may have been the world's second-largest city, with a population of more than 7 million in 1946, but it was still not big enough for Marie and Pamela to coexist in. Pamela had to clear out of town. As usual when she needed help, she went to Lord Beaverbrook, who offered her a job in the New York office of his *Daily Express*. She would leave England just before Marie arrived.

Meanwhile, she and Averell tried to conduct their relationship in a more discreet fashion, meeting at her apartment or at playwright Robert Sherwood's country home in Surrey, which had a croquet court that Averell enjoyed.

On Friday, September 20, the two were together for what they expected would be one of their last weekends when they heard a news announcement on BBC radio. President Truman had fired commerce secretary Henry Wallace for criticizing the administration's tougher policy toward the Soviet Union.

Moscow had pulled its troops back from Iran at the time Averell arrived in Britain, so that crisis had not amounted to much. The Soviets continued to beef up their presence in Eastern Europe, but Averell was no longer in that diplomatic loop. His position in London had been more ceremonial than he had expected or wanted. The news about Wallace discouraged Harriman. If he had been in Washington, he might have had a chance to win the Cabinet job.

Two days later, Averell was at Chartwell lunching with Winston Churchill when a White House operator called Sherwood's house looking for Harriman. Pamela directed the call to Chartwell, where the two men wondered what it was about before the president came on the line.

Harriman predicted that Truman would offer him the Wallace job and asked if he should take it. "Absolutely," Churchill replied. "The center of power is in Washington."[3]

Truman made the offer and Harriman accepted. Back at Sherwood's, Pamela greeted him as Mr. Secretary. Harriman was astonished that she had guessed the substance of the telephone chase.

Averell returned to the United States at the same time Pamela had planned to start working in New York. She went anyway, always happy to be out of England. In no time, however, it was clear that the two of them in such proximity would never work. Because the business of Commerce was business, Averell was often in New York. The gossip started again.

Beaverbrook ordered Pamela to leave and go to his Jamaica estate. She flew down with Lily Ernst, a beautiful, dark-haired, Jewish ballet dancer whom Max had helped escape from Vienna in 1938 and who had become his primary mistress after the 1945 death of Jean Norton.

Pamela drove the three hours from the airport at Kingston to the Montego Bay property and thought she had arrived on the far side of the moon. The road was dreadful. The property was isolated, up on a hillside away from the beach. To keep her busy and justify having her on the payroll, Max had asked her to send back some feature stories for the *Evening Standard*. She did, but it was clear that writing and reporting did not come naturally to the publisher's young friend.

"It was dark. The moon was rising behind the palm trees. The sound of the ocean lapped snugly against the beach" [Pamela began a January 1947 dispatch that the *Standard* billed as an "exclusive" report from St. James's Hospital, a British colonial facility near Montego Bay. In the children's ward], "little iron cots were crammed close together. Inside the harsh black bars, two, three, even four black piccaninnies [*sic*] lay huddled. They lay as puppies do, pushing against one another in their sleep. Seeking comfort and sympathy. Audible whimpers and small cries of pain came from different corners. I have never seen a more pitiful sight."[4]

Nor did she care to experience any more such sights than were necessary. She did not talk to any doctors or nurses, or at least she failed to indicate in her story that she had. Pamela's primary concern was whether she would ever get back to civilization. The month she spent with Lily Ernst felt like six. Pamela was dying of boredom until Max finally told her that the coast was clear and she could come home.

She had no idea what to do once she returned. The immediate postwar time was a confusing time for her. She was nineteen when the war started; twenty-five when it ended; twenty-six when the affair with Ed finally broke up and still that age when the curtain came down on her six-month encore with Averell. The abrupt end of that brief second round did not bother her.

She had not expected to link up with him again after he left for Moscow, so the 1946 interlude was no more than a delicious, lubricious, golden moment which allowed her to postpone any major decisions. Now that he was gone again, the future closed in.

The war had been Pamela's chrysalis, transforming her from caterpillar to butterfly, from giddy young woman to extraordinary sophisticate. A country girl aching for more friends as it got underway, Pamela had amassed an incomparable collection of chums, patrons and admirers by the time the fighting stopped, not to mention a mainlining addiction to power. But what to do next?

All her experiences, friends, lovers, former husband and in-laws, jobs, knowledge — everything had been war related. V-E Day was like the last day of a championship sports season when teammates cleaned out their lockers, packed bags and went their own way. Except that after this season, this team would not reassemble. Pamela was the groupie left behind in the parking lot, waving good-bye to the team bus.

The war had been intense and exhilarating. It was nothing to stay up most of the night, night after night, running on adrenaline. The Ed experience and Averell's return were starbursts which, until they burned out, prolonged that sensation another year.

The postwar, though, was exhausting. A sense of fatigue and apathy took root early each day and weighed heavily. Her experience with Ed compounded Pamela's depression. It took her a long time to get over him. Unlike the romance with Averell, she had hoped, wanted and expected to marry Ed.

She felt a terrible emptiness in London. Her American pals had all returned home and she was back in her apartment with The Child. Few Britons had any sympathy for Pamela. She had lived high on the hog during the war. Many felt that she had sold out and gone over to the occupiers. "If she'd behaved that way in France," sputtered a contemporary, "they would have shaved her head as a collaborator."

The criticism was misguided. Her collaboration had been with an ally, not an enemy, and with her own government. The information Pamela provided, certainly in the estimation of her father-in-law, was a significant benefit to Britain. If her love life had not been so flagrant, she might have been given a hero's medal. She was a femme fatale, a seductress who channeled information, but she was no Mata Hari, the World War I boudoir queen who betrayed French military secrets to Germany.

Still, given the always mixed feelings of Britons toward Americans and the fact that the wartime alliance had been wracked by arguments and jealousy, Pamela faced plenty of residual resentment. To her countrymen, she had at the very least become over-Americanized.

She knew she had. She had loved Americans since she first met the Higginsons in Dorset. She was dying to go to the United States. They had won the war. Just as Winston had advised Averell, Pamela understood that the United States was where the power lay. But she could not get there. She could visit, as she did every year, but she could not move to America because that was where her lovers worked and now lived reunited with their wives.

She had no offers, no place to go, nothing to do, no protector and was desperately unhappy. Part of her believed that she worked as hard as anyone in the war and had earned the right to enjoy life, to play a while. Another part of her was frightened, not only baffled about her next step, but incapable of making an independent decision.

Divorced and with a five-year-old child whom she had ignored almost from birth, Pamela had not been raised with the idea that she might ever actually have to support herself. She had choices but little talent for introspection and was unable to winnow out a preference. She had no particular agenda nor interests beyond maintaining her high standard of living and staying involved, somewhere and somehow, at high level. Uncomfortable on her own, she was someone to whom things happened, not one who caused them to happen.

Years later, a New York friend named Leonora Hornblow, wife of producer Arthur Hornblow, captured Pamela's chameleon-like quality with great accuracy. "When Pamela met a man she adored, she just unconsciously assumed his identity, as if she were putting on a glove."[5]

Mrs. Hornblow was referring to the whole Pamela — from what she wore, ate and how she furnished her homes to her interests and what she thought. And there would come a time when she would become her own person, but this was not it.

Until late in life she would have no well-conceived objective beyond seeking excitement, proximity to power and living with, through and for rich and influential men. Her time at the side of Churchill, Harriman and Murrow fanned those interests into passions. Without them, or any other strong character, she felt lost.

Intellectually, she was a chalice that needed filling. Emotionally too, she was wrung out, left high and dry by the end of the war and her abandonment by Ed and, for a second time, by Averell.

At this moment, it was not obvious to Pamela what to do next or even where to look. Whatever, wherever and whoever — the next phase was bound to offer a pale imitation of the highs she had experienced in the previous half dozen years. When in doubt, she always went to Max, the only man she could count on.

Back full-time at the helm of his newspaper empire, Beaverbrook put her to work on the "Londoners' Diary" column in the *Evening Standard*. She had already demonstrated that she was no writer, but back in her own milieu in London, she did not have to be. No one could match her political, diplomatic, military and social contacts. Because she was one of eight reporters and editors working on the popular, long-running gossip column, someone else always wrote for her.

Robert Lutyens, son of the architect and brother of Barbie Wallace Agar, who started the Churchill Club, did much of Pamela's writing. His wife and son had been in Canada during the war and Robert had fallen in love with Pamela. "Now she became rather dependent on him," said Mary Lutyens, Robert's sister. But Robert was small, mousey and, while quite endearing, was not colorful or powerful and was thus not destined to have Pamela reciprocate his affections. Later when she began to hate her job at the *Evening Standard* and made plans to leave, she gave Robert Lutyens the brush-off. She no longer needed him.

Journalism intrigued her. Reporters and writers, including Quentin Reynolds and Irwin Shaw, had been among her best wartime friends and frequent visitors to Grosvenor Square. The only writer that she met during the war whom she disliked was Ernest Hemingway. She hated his crude, macho posturing. He was a troublemaker who showed her no respect. After the war, while sitting in the bar of the Ritz Hotel in Paris, he wrote a poem titled "Black Ass Poem after Talking to Pamela Churchill." The opening line — "We leave them all quite early when dislike overcomes our love" — suggested that she was no favorite of his either. Pamela, though, was secretly thrilled that he had written about her, especially a work, or at least a title, that she considered semipornographic.[6]

However much she liked journalists, she was not cut out for journalism. "Writing stories didn't seem to be her great forte," said Charles Wintour, the distinguished editor of the *Evening Standard* from 1959 to 1980, who was a reporter on the paper at the same time as Pamela. "She seemed to use the phone mostly to arrange her social life."[7]

Nor was she suited temperamentally for the rough-and-tumble bullpen of Fleet Street reporters, few of whom were awed by her relationship with their owner. She had gone in with her eyes open, but the way Max used her bothered her and made her feel uncomfortable. She was a unique source. She knew everyone and listened eloquently. Men gave Pamela Churchill information constantly. Max wanted to be told everything she heard.

Top-drawer news and gossip was what he was after. He sent her to Paris to report on Aly Khan's racing parties and to the south of France, where the "Golden Greeks," Aristotle Onassis and Stavros Niarchos, berthed their yachts, gambled at high stakes baccarat in the casino at Monte Carlo and gamboled with young, hard-bodied beauties on their afterdecks and below. Few senior reporters had such glittery datelines on their stories. London's East End or the industrial Midlands were not places to find Pamela.

From Max's vantage point, it was a sensible use of her connections, but not from Pamela's. She did know a lot, but she felt awkward when asked to dish it out for print. The whole practice was too much like spying on her friends, then publishing exclusive, inside information. Max and his editors dismissed her protestations, but Pamela was squeamish. She loved Max, but this was not for her.

She sought the advice of David Margesson, who had been elevated with a viscountcy to the House of Lords, but who remained a powerful member of the out-of-office Conservative party. He urged her to quit. Journalism was not right for her. Margesson agreed with former prime minister Lloyd George that "no man in any party trusts Max," and advised her to put some distance between herself and the press baron.

Pamela did not quit, because she had nothing else to do and no other immediate source of easy income, but she did consider other options. For a moment, she thought about going into politics. There was a crucial drawback: she did not know whether she supported the Conservatives or the Labour party, although their differences are far greater than those which separate America's Republicans and Democrats or any number of social or liberal democratic parties in Europe.

She had grown up a Conservative by association and Randolph, whose Preston constituency she helped serve while he was at war, had been a Conservative member of Parliament. But Pamela had no core beliefs. Ed Murrow had spun around her political axis. He convinced her that Clement Attlee's Labour party would be better for postwar Britain than the Conservatives despite the fact that both of them adored Winston, who happened to be the leader of the Conservatives.

Since Ed said so, Pamela concurred that the Socialists were the kind of government that Britain needed. Even after Ed dumped her, she continued to believe it and went so far as to consider joining the Labour party. But as Ed faded in influence, Pamela began attending Conservative seminars.

Then she was whipped around again. Beaverbrook had been tarred with some of the blame for Churchill's defeat in the 1945 elections. Mainline Conservatives continued to hate, mistrust and fear the Beaver. They could never forget that he was Canadian, and thus, by their definition, a carpetbagger once and forever. He was all for Churchill, but Max was not a team player. Beaverbrook's influence was enormous, every bit as potent as that of his American counterpart press barons William Randolph Hearst, Henry Luce and Colonel Robert McCormick, but the Conservatives' anti-Max line confused her more.

Henry Kissinger told her in the 1980s that had she not married Averell, she would have been a Republican. He was absolutely correct. Pamela is far more conservative politically than most people believe. But what mattered was that at this moment, she had no man and without one, she had lost her identity. While she may not have known what she was, she had enough sense to back away from politics.

She also still knew how to have fun. She socialized a lot in 1947 with Kick Kennedy, who had emerged from mourning Billy Hartington and was seeing Peter Fitzwilliam, a wealthy, handsome and married peer. Nicknamed "Blood," the dashing Fitzwilliam traced his ancestry to William the Conqueror and was one of Randolph Churchill's roguish friends from his club, White's.

Kick had tried living in the States after her husband died, but she was not able to patch up relations with her parents, Rose and Joe Kennedy. Instead of being happy to have her home, they had forced her to stay out of sight during Jack's run for Congress in 1946 out of fear that her brief marriage to Hartington might cost her brother Catholic votes. Hartington's parents, the duke and duchess of Devonshire, were much more empathetic and were pleased to have her back in England with their family.

In September 1947, Pamela joined Kick and Peter in Ireland at Lismore Castle in County Waterford. The castle had been built by Prince John in the late twelfth century, was later owned by Sir Walter Raleigh and was then the property of Kick's in-laws, the Devonshires.

Jack Kennedy arrived for a reunion with his favorite sibling and several other of her friends, including Hugh Fraser, who was a childhood friend of Pamela's; Sean Leslie, an Irish writer; Anthony Eden, later prime minister and husband of Clarissa Churchill; and Charles Johnson, later British high commissioner to Australia.

Pamela had met Jack several times before on visits to the Kennedys' but did not get to know him until that visit. "Though he was three years older, he always seemed so very young to all of us," Pamela said. "In England we dated very much older men and Jack seemed, well, boyish. Skinny and scrawny, actually. Kathleen's kid brother. Not eligible, so to speak."[8]

Jack did not feel well. His back bothered him and he was unable to join the others riding and playing golf. Pamela loved to ride, but her feelings about golf had not changed, so she had spare time during the day, which she spent with Kennedy.

One morning he asked — quietly and apologetically, she recalled — if she would accompany him on an expedition to find "the original Kennedys," who he believed lived near Dunganstown near New Ross, about fifty miles from Lismore. They drove for hours over terrible country roads in Kick's massive American station wagon, the likes of which had never been seen in that part of Ireland or, for that matter, anywhere in Europe. Arriving finally at New Ross, Jack asked a resident where the Kennedys lived.

His question prompted great confusion. Did he want the Jim Kennedys or the David Kennedys? Jack had no idea, but was directed to a small house with a thatch roof with pigs, ducks and chickens running in and out of the front door. A suspicious woman emerged and sent what Pamela thought were about a dozen Kennedy look-alike children scampering to find their father.

When he arrived, they all had tea while Jack tried to figure out which of the New Ross Kennedys had gone to America. He could not make a direct connection but believed they were probably third cousins. As thanks, he drove the excited gang of children all around the village in the station wagon, then returned to Lismore.[9]

As they pulled out of the village, Pamela looked at Jack and sighed. "Just like *Tobacco Road*," she said.

Jack glared at her in fury. "I felt like kicking her out of the car," Kennedy recalled during a 1963 return visit to Ireland while president. "For me, the visit to that cottage was filled with magic sentiment."[10]

Pamela's description, though, was apt. When they arrived back at Lismore, Kick had only one question about the Kennedy ancestors. Did they have a bathroom? Told that they did not, she broke up in laughter.[11]

Jack was not so upset with Pamela that he avoided her when he left Lismore with Kick for London. He was ill much of the time in Ireland and had sent a coded message to Washington asking for medicine, a precaution so that his condition would not be known to the House of Representatives, where he was serving his first term.

Kennedy was in miserable health most of his life, but he, his family and such friends as Ted Sorensen covered up his maladies to keep him eligible to run for the presidency. One of Kennedy's most serious problems was Addison's disease, a failure of the adrenal glands which, in earlier years, was generally fatal. During his 1960 presidential campaign, which he won by fewer than 115,000 votes, Kennedy told a news conference that he "never" had Addison's disease.

Arriving in London, though, he was so sick that Pamela had her doctor, Sir Daniel Davies, see him on September 21, 1947. Davies immediately hospitalized Kennedy in the London Clinic. "That young American friend of yours hasn't got a year to live," he told her. Addison's disease was his diagnosis. Joe Kennedy hired a registered nurse to sail home with Jack on the Queen Mary. When the ship arrived in New York, a priest boarded and gave him extreme unction, or last rites, before Jack was flown on a stretcher to Boston, where the London diagnosis was confirmed.[12]

Although Jack was never a Pamela boyfriend, Kick was involved when her friend took up around that same time with the world's leading playboy, Aly Khan. Pamela got to know Aly when she, Kick and their circle of London friends went to Paris to attend the racing season. Aly was the son of the Aga Khan, then the fabulously wealthy Imam, or spiritual leader, of the world's Shia Imami Ismaili Moslems, whose fifteen million followers in some two dozen countries in Asia, Africa and the Middle East presented him with his weight in gold — 220 pounds — on his fiftieth birthday and in platinum for his seventieth.

For a direct descendant of the prophet Mohammed, Aly's interests were more corporeal than spiritual. His passions were women and horses, hobbies that would ultimately keep him from succeeding his father as Imam. Aly's annual fixture was the ball he hosted each June at the Pré Catelan restaurant in the Bois de Boulogne following the Grand Prix de Paris at Longchamp race-course.[13]

Decorated with flowers colored hot pink and shamrock green (his racing colors), cases of magnums of pink champagne, two orchestras and party favors of perfume for the women and Cuban cigars for the men, the ball took months of preparation and drew a broad spectrum of the glitterati: French politicians, Indian maharajahs, European business magnates and financiers, the English horsey set, stars like Edith Piaf, tennis champions and tarts of all descriptions. More than two hundred people, including Pamela and Kick, attended in 1947 when Aly's 33 to 1 longshot, Avenger, won the Prix.[14]

In the course of the party, an exuberant Aly asked Pamela to dance. Aly loved dancing, an interest he inherited from his Italian mother, Theresa Magliano, a ballet dancer with the Monte Carlo casino ballet.[15]

As soon as he took a woman in his arms, there was no pre-amble nor any room for error about Aly's intentions: cheek to cheek, he pressed her in toward his groin, then traced languid circles on her back until she could feel his erection rising. All the time, he paid her total attention, asking her what she wanted to do, where she wanted to go.[16]

Aly was not particularly striking physically, only five feet eight inches tall, with a sallow complexion. He was unpretentious, but so self-conscious about losing his hair that he often wore a bat-tered slouch hat pulled down at a cocky angle. His conversational ability was limited to small talk, joke telling, and themes that involved such pranks as whoopee cushions, hand-buzzers and, once, hiding a ripe Limburger cheese under the Ritz Hotel bed of a friend who was trying to seduce a young woman — unsuc-cessfully, as a result of the odor.[17]

What made him special was his unlimited interest in and ca-pacity for pleasing women. In their presence, he concentrated on them to the exclusion of almost all else, quite a different approach from that of misogynist British clubmen and Italian stallions. He preferred bottoms to breasts, but in Pamela he had both. He told her that he would be in London the following week.

Although his marriage had collapsed during the war, Aly had been wed since 1936 to Joan Yarde-Buller, the eldest child of Lord Churston, who was a former aide-de-camp to the viceroy of India. Joan was an unstuffy aristocrat who had provided Aly with the requisite credentials beyond money to make it into English society. Joan had been married to Thomas Loel E. B. Guinness, a busy Tory MP and member of the merchant banking family, when Aly met her at a Deauville party in 1934 and, during a lull in the dinner conversation, loudly asked her to marry him.[18]

Aly's plans for Pamela were not as serious, but, while holding her tight against him, he did ask whether she would join him for dinner in London. Pamela would love to.

On their postball, predawn drive back to the Plaza Athénée hotel, Pamela told Kick about Aly's invitation. The American's eyes widened.

Oh no. Out of the question. That would be a biiiig mistake, Kick squawked, her broad Bostonian accent filling the car.

Pamela could not understand why. He was wonderfully attractive and very sexy.

Precisely, said Kick. He was danger with a capital D. There was no bigger Lothario in Europe, probably not anywhere in the world.

Singer Juliette Greco once said, "I don't know who didn't have an affair with Aly."[19]

Kick had heard the stories and insisted to Pamela that no matter how interesting Aly was, he was not suitable. She didn't mention why, but others in Britain would, mostly men: Aly was dark-skinned.

The best-known South Asian of the day after Gandhi, Aly's father was unwittingly celebrated on posters plastered on London buses which exhorted sweets-loving Britons to buy chocolate, "rich and dark, like the Aga Khan."[20]

Aly, too, was a frequent butt of prejudice. An accomplished jockey, he was once blocked during a race and when he shouted to the front-runner to move over, that rider responded by yelling,

"Shut your bloody mouth, you goddamned nigger." Aly rarely got mad, but he did get even.

"They called me a bloody nigger and I paid them out by winning all their women," he explained later with insouciant nonchalance.[21]

Race, creed or national origin was no impediment for Pamela. She was never racist, never anti-Semitic, prejudiced only against boors and bores. If a man interested her, that was sufficient. Christians, Moslems, Jews, atheists and agnostics: she was an equal-opportunity playgirl and eventually sampled them all.

She had not the slightest hesitation about Aly, who, more important than looks, was a take-charge man of breathtaking charm, vitality and warmth. As usual, once told she could not do something, Pamela was more determined than ever to flout the rule. When Kick put Aly out of bounds, she inadvertently set up a challenge to see who — Aly or Pamela — could seduce the other first. In short order, each won.

They went out as planned the following week. Then he took her to the Newmarket races. Then he began flying her aboard his private DeHavilland, also named Avenger, to the Riviera and his home near Cannes, the Château de L'Horizon, where Winston Churchill painted before the war, which Aly had purchased for eighty-seven thousand dollars.

Designed by an American architect, the house was not grand with presumptuous eighteenth-century French decor, but intimate, charming and comfortable. Floor-to-ceiling arched windows sucked the Mediterranean light into the ten-bedroom, seven-bath house. A broad terrace stretched between gardens of twisted evergreens and lush, cropped lawn. A lower-level patio enclosed a large swimming pool and a broad staircase provided easy access to the sea and the villa's motorboats.

Aly loved to strip to the waist and lunch on the sun-washed terrace. Pamela, whose freckled white skin was not made for sun, once made the mistake of dozing off on the terrace. Sunburn put her in bed for the rest of her visit and set a frustrated Aly to sulking.[22]

He didn't sulk with her often. He was an enthusiastic romantic and as Elsa Maxwell pointed out, "When he fell in love with a woman, it was madly and deeply. The only thing, it might last only one night."

Neither took the relationship seriously; no woman could with Aly and Pamela did not make the mistake of getting overly involved. For him, Pamela was an attractive young woman of impeccable taste, a skillful rider as he was, a girl who loved to play.

Playing with Aly required an exceptional constitution. "That meeting with Aly Khan set me back ten years," said screen actress Irene Papas. "I once left Aly at four in the morning at Deauville," explained Jean Fayard. "When I got back to his house late that same day, he had ridden a horse in the morning, played tennis, flown to England to watch one of his horses run, flown back, and then we played bridge until three the next morning. Meanwhile, he had a few girls around to relax with. At three in the morning, he took his car and drove off to the Casino. He came back at seven and slept until nine."[23]

Pamela had the right stuff to keep up with her latest friend. She loved staying up late and could change direction in an instant. She also had the perfect pedigree to attract Aly. Given his rakish reputation in England, it gave no small pleasure to bed his first Churchill.

For Pamela, Aly was simply great fun. After a succession of troubled, serious relationships, he was the perfect diversion: nothing tangled, pure sport sex and enchantment, the man who hosted the liveliest parties with the prettiest people, most of them exceedingly rich.

She was thrilled to know that their pairing caused eyebrows to be raised in disapproval. Kick had been right. There was a charged sense of danger about Aly which she loved.

It went beyond his utter recklessness, such as reclaiming his family's horses at gunpoint from the Nazis or changing into a dinner jacket while driving his sports car a hundred miles an hour along the Riviera's perilous Corniche.[24] He had been a brave intelligence officer during the war, serving the Free French, the United States' Sixth Army, and Britain, for whom, while serving in Jerusalem, he organized a network of Ismaili spies throughout the Middle East. Aly was nothing less than a character straight out of her Jane Digby past.

Aly also had a deserved reputation as a fabulous lover, which was a first for Pamela. His secret was controlled restraint, or Imsak, taught him in adolescence in a six-week course by an Arab doctor in Cairo. Leonard Slater, his biographer, said that no matter how many women Aly had, "He seldom reached a climax himself. He could make love by the hour, but he went the whole way himself not oftener than twice a week. He liked the effect it had on women. He liked to get them out of control, while he stayed in control."[25]

Pamela appreciated controlling men, but just as her natural flirtatiousness had begun evolving into a more mature sensuousness around Aly, she found another of the playboy's techniques had special appeal. He was promiscuous, but when Aly was with a woman, he focused on her entirely, never taking his eye off her even if another beautiful woman, or anyone at all, even a head of state, entered the room or his field of vision. Pamela adopted the technique.

Focus became more than a key ingredient of her relationships. Whenever anyone wondered How Did Pamela Do It? How Did She Seduce All Those Powerful Men? The answer was in no small part the way she concentrated all her attention totally on the man.

When she was with a man — socially or professionally, not merely sexually — she concentrated on him with laserlike intensity. Years later at receptions or dinner parties, Pamela would take a man who interested her out of a group the way a cowboy and fine horse could cut a steer from a herd for branding. She would approach the man, bring him alone out of the traffic pattern to a sofa, sit down and talk to him for five to ten minutes.

She focused on his strengths: what he was doing, what had happened since they last met, his plans, all in a low, throaty, conspiratorial whisper, and in the process learned his weaknesses or what troubled him. She was glad to answer his questions if he had any, but she was extremely careful never to babble and never to burden the fellow with anything that might be troubling her. She wanted him to shine even as she learned what was on his mind.

Careful never to keep anyone long, especially if his wife was with him, she would then return the man to the group, pick out another and repeat the process, perhaps a half dozen times or more. Rarely did she attempt to talk to a man in a group, rarely did she talk to women, although she tried not to alienate them unnecessarily. For those moments, those men sensed that no one else in the world existed for Pamela. As her reputation grew, receiving the full frontal Pamela treatment, being Pamelized, was a heady experience for most men.

Pamela was in the south of France the following May when Kick arrived with Peter Fitzwilliam for a Whitsun weekend holiday. Kick had recently returned from a family gathering at the Greenbriar resort in West Virginia, where she informed her parents that she intended to marry Fitzwilliam. Rose Kennedy was outraged, quite apoplectic. She threatened to disown and never see her daughter again if Kick wed the married Protestant.

Kick was passionately in love with Fitzwilliam and just as adamant. She did not mind being disowned — she had plenty of money as Billy Hartington's widow — but she did not want to be banished from the family. She hoped to win over her father, who planned to stop in Paris enroute to the Vatican to see if he could arrange a dispensation for his daughter to marry without being excommunicated. "If religion is the problem, I'll build him a bloody church if he wants," Fitzwilliam told friends.[26]

After their weekend in Cannes, Kick asked Pamela to come with them to Paris for support. Pamela wavered but at the last moment decided against making the trip. She drove the two lovers to the airport and wished them luck with old Joe as they boarded their DeHavilland Dove. Flying up the Rhone Valley, the small eight-seater ran into a storm and crashed into a mountainside near the town of Privas. All on board were killed.

Pamela went to the funeral and to Chatsworth, the Devonshires' ancestral home, where Kick was buried. In between bouts of crying, she thought about her close call. Dwelling on it, though, was not her style. She put the accident out of her mind along with Kick. Pamela was getting used to losing friends, though not since the war any with such tragic finality. She had been hurt and been made unhappy too many times not to be developing a thicker skin.

She was also used to leaving family and intimates behind and moving into newer circles, rarely glancing back. She would do the same this time. Pamela missed Kick's hearty ebullience, but she had no reason to maintain ties with the senior Kennedys. Jack she would link up with again when he became president.

Planning ahead was not a strength of Pamela's then, at twenty-eight, but Kick's death did give her pause to reconsider her uncharted future. Randolph Churchill saw her at Fitzwilliam's funeral and barged back into her life. They had been divorced for two years, but for all his bachelor tendencies, Randolph was unhappy living alone and had been busy seeking a mate ever since he and Pamela had broken up. Now he was clobbering her with his prodigious argumentative skills, the same ones he used first to woo her.

She thought life would be a picnic after him, but she was wrong, he told her. Averell had rejected her; Ed had rejected her. She was in thrall to Beaverbrook. Max had seized control of her, the one thing Randolph had always insisted that she avoid. She was leading a silly, idiotic and purposeless life. She was misguided in replacing her British values with those of Americans, continental society types, and wastrels like Aly Khan. She didn't need those foreigners. How could she possibly prefer them to good English men like himself and his friends? Her basic interests lay in Britain.

His sermon was peppered with mea culpas and apologies about how much he was to blame for their breakup, how the war intervened and she had been a child whom he mistakenly tried to fashion into God knows what kind of image he had in mind. The long and short of it was that to judge their suitability for one another honestly and fairly — and, after all, there was The Child to think of — she should give him another chance. Just a weekend to see if their relationship could be salvaged.

To her own amazement, Pamela agreed. Randolph borrowed a friend's castle and they drove there in his scruffy, rusting sedan. Randolph was a horrible driver and got lost. The two-hour trip took four hours. The castle was dark and gloomy. The only indication they were expected was a semichilled bottle of champagne on the sideboard. Randolph was trying very hard, but the whole experience was a total disaster as far as Pamela was concerned. She wanted to get as far away from Randolph as quickly as she could.

Young Winston was out of school, so the next week she took him with her to Aly Khan's. The house was full. In addition to the regular summer crowd always at L'Horizon, Aly was putting up a polo team from Argentina. Aly and Pamela were in a good-friends-but-not-lovers mode. Romantically, Aly was otherwise involved. Rita Hayworth had just entered his life.

It happened after the actress separated from director Orson Welles. Hayworth, the bombshell star of *Blood and Sand* and *Cover Girl*, was salving her pain in the Riviera's Sea and Sun when professional hostess Elsa Maxwell asked her to a party.

"Don't speak to me about a dinner," Hayworth replied. "My heart is rather broken. I can't think of parties."

Maxwell persisted. "The Aly" would be there, she promised, a wonderful prince who would cheer her up. Elsa, then sixty-five, bragged often that she had never had a sexual experience, but if she had ever been given an opportunity to choose just one man, once, Aly, the seducer, her pet, would have been the one.

Hayworth was unconvinced and lamented that, anyway, "I haven't a thing to wear."

Buy a dress, Maxwell instructed. There was a wonderful gown at the shop at her hotel, the Hotel du Cap in Cap d'Antibes. "Come in white and come in late. Make an entrance."

The hostess and her guests were all waiting in the Cannes summer casino when Rita arrived.

"My God," gasped Aly when he looked up and saw Rita enter the room. "Who is that?"

"She is sitting next to you at dinner," Maxwell replied. "And that is all I had time to say," she explained later, for Aly had sprinted from the table to introduce himself to the movie star.[27]

Once Aly beat back challenges for her favors from the shah of Iran and Aristotle Onassis, he and Rita were inseparable that summer of 1948. The movie star later described how Aly "had such an overwhelming effervescence that he sort of devoured you. The world was magic when you were with him."[28]

Two or three days after Pamela arrived, Aly and Rita took off on a trip to Spain, but the running house party at L'Horizon continued without missing a beat. People swam, boated and took care of themselves, sometimes swooshing down the twenty-five-foot slide from the pool deck into the Mediterranean.

Generally, most guests came together to socialize at a daily buffet lunch which featured Aly's favorite, a dessert selection of as many as ten different ice creams and fresh fruit sorbets. Pamela and Winston were having a wonderful time until a telegram arrived one morning from Randolph. He was arriving in the south of France in a few days and would come over to visit.

The news horrified Pamela. She could not deal with Randolph at Aly's. He would mortify her. But what to do? She did not reply to the cable. Maybe she could think of something after lunch. Glum and pouty, she walked out to the terrace buffet. At the foot of the stairs, a motor launch was pulling up with two young men she had never seen before. One was absolutely gorgeous. His head belonged on a Roman coin. She stood transfixed. "*Buon giorno, cara*," he smiled. "My name is Gianni Agnelli."

CHAPTER TEN

Gianni

UNTIL SHE MET HIM on Aly Khan's terrace, Pamela Churchill had never heard of Gianni Agnelli. She had no idea that the twenty-seven-year-old who arrived for lunch was the heir to the Fiat auto empire, Italy's largest private enterprise, although she quickly found out. All she knew at that moment was what she could see: young Mister Agnelli looked so luscious that her knees trembled. He was sun-bronzed, had thick, dark, wavy hair, a brilliant smile and, thanks to his British governess, spoke exquisite English with a slight Oxbridge lilt.

Gianni liked what he saw too. In addition to her auburn hair which glowed in the Mediterranean sun, Mrs. Churchill had milky skin unlike that of any woman he had known, a smattering of freckles, a voluptuous figure, looked him straight in the eye and flirted easily and confidently with him throughout lunch.

She was also new. Angelli became bored at hyper speed. "The most restless man in the world," Bill Paley called him.[1]

He has always been hungry for new experiences and, for much of his life, new women. Pamela was perfect. The fact that she was Winston Churchill's daughter-in-law was an important bonus.

Would she like to come along with him the next night to the weekly gala at Monte Carlo, he asked later that lazy afternoon, twirling the stem of a glass of fresh orange juice. She could think of nothing more appealing. He was not just handsome, but also nice, fun and easy-going. There was not a hint of pomposity about him. He picked her up and they had a delightful evening, chatting, laughing and dancing close.

On Friday, he was leaving with his best friend, Raimundo Lanza, a decadent Sicilian aristocrat who had arrived with him at Aly's, to sail to Capri. Would she like to accompany them? She hated sailboats and was not very good on water in anything less than a good-sized yacht, but Capri? This invitation sounded like too wonderful an adventure to pass up. She had never been to Italy. The prospect of going with two gorgeous men had a marvelous allure. Of course, she would love to go.

Then she caught herself. She was a footloose divorcée, but perhaps she should not go off on her own with two strangers to a new country which had recently been a wartime enemy and where she did not speak the language. She thought she ought to bring, if not precisely a chaperone, at least a girlfriend. Having a second woman aboard posed no problem to two of Europe's biggest playboys.

Agnelli said of course, as she wished. Pamela asked Gloria von Furstenberg if she wanted to go to Italy. A great beauty, then on her second marriage but soon to make the wealthy British banker Loel Guinness, Aly Khan's old rival, her third husband, trophy wife Gloria knew precisely who Agnelli was.

"Sounds like fun," Gloria told Pamela. "Count me in."

There was one slight complication: Pamela had been invited to dinner Friday with the duke and duchess of Windsor. No problem, said Gianni. They would wait for her and leave at midnight from the pier at Beaulieu.

At 4 P.M. Friday, Gloria had to back out. One of her children had come down with measles. At almost the same time, Pamela received a second cable from Randolph. He was arriving the next afternoon. That did it. Forget the "chaperone." Gloria or no Gloria, Pamela was out of there.

She dumped seven-year-old Winston with the family of Prince

Jean-Louis de Faucigny-Lucinge, whose daughter Ysabel, known as Zozo, was a good friend. Zozo had a much younger brother close to Winston's age and the two boys often played together when Pamela brought her son to the south of France.

Prince Faucigny-Lucinge, a distinguished aristocrat and a very close friend of the British royal family's, was scandalized that Winston Churchill's daughter-in-law was staying at Aly Khan's with the grandson of the great prime minister. To correct what he considered a shocking impropriety, he had invited Pamela and Winston to move into his house at Cap d'Ail. Given the invitation, Pamela didn't think twice about calling Zozo and asking her to please take The Child. She would be back in a week or so.

Zozo's father was incensed. It was completely inappropriate that Pamela abandon her son and flit off alone on a sailboat with two Italians she had just met. Pamela didn't care what the old man thought. Events were happening too fast. Besides, it was no big deal. The trip was just a lark, a frothy summer interlude. At midnight, she clambered aboard the *Tomahawk*, Gianni's twelve-meter sailboat, for the voyage to Capri.

In the middle of the night, the sea turned rough. At 4 A.M., a glass of water that Pamela had placed on the ledge above her bed crashed on her head and cut her while she slept. It was hard to tell how badly she was injured, but there was blood all over the cabin. Gianni put in at Portofino and went ashore to call a cousin who had an apartment in the picturesque tourist town.

Along the quay, escorted by Gianni and Raimundo on either arm, the bloodstained Pamela looked like a victim of a Red Brigade kidnapping when she ran into a woman she knew from the Churchill Club. The woman was horrified.

"What are you doing to my friend?" she screamed.

Pamela assured her that she was all right, but she was mortified. And discovered. Word would spread fast.

From the apartment, Gianni called Turin, where Fiat is headquartered, and asked that a car be sent the two hundred kilometers (120 miles) to Portofino and that a plastic surgeon be alerted. In Turin, Pamela begged Gianni to stay with her at the hospital. She had no idea what the doctor or nurses were saying. She did not understand what they wanted to do to her, how they wanted to medicate or repair her. The ever-charming and calming Agnelli, who is rarely rattled, was reassuring. He had no intention of leaving her. Just relax. She would be fine.

The surgeon did his work and told Pamela to return in five days for removal of the stitches. That ruled out leaving Turin. Gianni's family house in the city was closed for the summer, so he took her to the home of another woman, an occasional girl-friend, whom he asked to put up Pamela. The woman seemed used to such requests and agreed amiably. But as soon as Gianni left the room, she asked if Pamela was marrying him. Already dazed, Pamela turned near hysterical. What had she gotten herself into? She wasn't marrying anyone. Who was this woman? What was she doing there anyway? Gianni rushed back to calm her.

At the cousin's apartment, the phone rang. Randolph had ar-rived on the Riviera to learn that Pamela had sailed off with Gianni and Raimundo. In white fury, he called a principessa friend in Rome who also knew Gianni. Like a sheepdog in search of an errant ewe, Randolph was frantically trying to track his former wife down. The princess said that Randolph was charging around the south of France bellowing about his wife. Where was she? Was she in hospital? Was she whoring? Why had she abandoned his son?

Pamela was frightened and not about to say anything. She told Gianni that she was no longer Randolph's wife and would neither accept a call nor phone him. She waited out the five days in Turin, had her stitches removed, linked her arm through Gianni's and went on to Capri for another week as if nothing had happened.

At Capri, they stopped over at the house of Count Rudy Crespi, an old friend of Gianni's. Agnelli had told Crespi that he was bringing a new girlfriend. Crespi said wonderful. He and his wife would be at dinner when they arrived, but Gianni should take his regular room, put Mrs. Churchill in the adjoining guest quar-ters and they would talk in the morning. As arranged, the count came in the morning for coffee with Gianni who, as was his frequent habit in private in hot weather, wore nothing.

"I want you to meet Pam. I'm crazy about her," he told Crespi. "Pamela, come in and meet your host," he yelled into the next room.

Pamela entered, naked as well, walked straight over to Crespi and, without batting an eye, shook his hand, sat on the bed and demurely crossed her legs. Crespi later told friends that he was amazed. She was the first real redhead he had ever seen.[2]

At another time and place, a British duke registered a similar reaction. "I'd never been to bed with a natural redhead."[3]

For Gianni, the Capri scene was perfectly natural. No one was embarrassed. If he had wanted to shock, said a friend, he would have done it the way he once introduced Anita Ekberg to the businessman Coca Cicogna. When he arrived at Gianni's office one day, Cicogna found the Swedish blonde bombshell, a star of Fellini's masterpiece, *La Dolce Vita,* standing naked on his desk.

Capri more than made up for the hospital detour. The holiday was pure bliss. Pamela's luck had come through once more. She was in love again. Exactly a year younger than Pamela, her first boyfriend who was not an older man, Gianni was a golden boy in every sense.

He would later become known throughout Europe as "the uncrowned king." A German magazine once ran a frontal photo of Gianni, standing naked on the deck of his sailboat, captioned "the man who has everything."

In Italy, where governments topple annually on average, he would be the one constant. By 1993, the Fiat conglomerate controlled Fiat, Alfa Romeo, Ferrari, Lancia, the newspaper *La Stampa,* the Juventus soccer team, Château Margaux vineyards, retail department stores, insurance and food companies: the equivalent of Ford, Chrysler, General Motors, the *New York Times,* Nordstrom's, State Farm — businesses worth fifty billion and which employed three hundred thousand people.

With a personal fortune of more than $3 billion, he was the richest man in Italy.[4]

His opulent apartment in Rome is part of a seventeenth-century palace which sits atop the Quirinale hill, across the piazza from the residence of the president of Italy.[5]

On the grounds of the forty-five-room family home, Villar Perosa, thirty miles from Turin in the foothills of the Italian Alps, are buried seven generations of Agnellis, including his parents, who died in separate accidents. His popular sportsman father was nearly decapitated by a seaplane propeller when Gianni was fourteen. His sexy and spirited half-American mother, Virginia, died in a car crash a decade later, in November 1945.

Gianni's grandfather Giovanni began Fiat in 1899, four years before Henry Ford founded Ford. A tough patriarch in an austere city, Giovanni took a special interest in his first grandson, especially after the 1935 death of his son Edoardo, Gianni's father.

The basis of the family fortune came in World War I, when Fiat manufactured trucks, tanks and cars for the military. Communist activism, strikes, social disorder and a breakdown of the parliamentary process in Italy after that war led to the 1920s ascent of Fascist leader Benito Mussolini, whom Giovanni Agnelli supported early. When Il Duce visited a Fiat factory, Edoardo pulled on a black shirt, the Fascist emblem, before welcoming him, while Giovanni led the assembled workers in cheers of "Long live Mussolini."[6]

When his namesake was eighteen, Giovanni sent Gianni on a two-month tour of U.S. auto plants. "We always wanted to know what was going on in Detroit," said Gianni. After a stint at the stark Pinerolo cavalry academy, a family tradition, and studying law at the University of Turin — hence his nickname, l'Avvocato, the lawyer, though he never practiced law — Gianni joined a tank regiment in June 1940 when Italy entered World War II.

He was sent to the Russian front, where he was wounded twice and nearly lost a finger to frostbite on the retreat home. He was then sent in a Fiat-built armored-car unit to North Africa, where he was wounded again, shot in the arm by a German officer during a bar fight over a woman.[7]

When Italy surrendered in September 1943, Lieutenant Agnelli took his cross for military valor and switched sides. He joined the Legnano Group, an outfit that fought alongside General Mark Clark's Fifth Army and ended the war as a liaison officer with the Americans. Grandfather Giovanni, who had continued to manufacture vehicles for the Axis throughout the war, was forced to retire from the company he had founded, but allowed to name as his successor his right-hand man, the canny Vittorio Valletta.

In late 1945, three weeks after Gianni's mother died, Giovanni Agnelli died, leaving Gianni, at the age of twenty-four, the head of the family. Shortly before he died, Giovanni advised his grandson not to settle down right away, but to let Valletta run Fiat as regent. "He told me to have a fling for a few years, to sow my wild oats and get it out of my system, and then maybe I would become a serious man," Agnelli recalled.[8]

With Mussolini dead, Valletta discovered that Italian consumers were better customers than the state. With help from the Marshall Plan, Fiat soon started cranking out the 500 model, Italy's first cheap mass-produced car. Buyers called the car, which sold for less than a thousand dollars, the "Mickey Mouse" and snapped them up by the millions, making the 500 the Italian equivalent of the Tin Lizzie produced by Ford after the First World War and guaranteeing Fiat's success. Gianni, in the meantime, took his grandfather's advice to heart and made a beeline for the fast lane.

Aly Khan, Porfirio Rubirosa, Errol Flynn, Darryl Zanuck, Spain's auto-racing Marquis Alfonso de Portago, Baby Pignatari — society's playboy princes — were all part of Gianni's crowd on the Riviera. "We partied like crazy people," he admitted.[9]

Yachts, pretty young women, nightclub carousing and huge casino wagers churned the action. One 1948 night, an English textile manufacturer named "Lucky Mickie" Hyman took eighty thousand dollars from Gianni, Egypt's King Farouk, Hollywood studio chief Jack Warner and an Indian prince in a single game of chemin de fer.[10]

Well before Gianni became chairman of Fiat in 1966 and his business skills made him a fixture on the financial pages, he was a gossip column Hall of Famer, known for the effortless grace of his pursuits and conquests.

But as much as Gianni partied, he always showed up for work — sometimes with no sleep and his heavy, hooded eyes latticed crimson. Countless times he left Nice airport Mondays at dawn on Fiat's DC-3 for the forty-five-minute flight to Turin. Gianni's friends called the all-nighters *les nuits blanches*, the white nights, a wordplay on the cocaine consumed under the party lights, where darkness never fell. No one played harder, but Gianni always made it back to Turin, anxious not to be labeled a shirker at the family firm.

At the time, for a salary reputed to have been $1 million annually, he held the largely ceremonial post of president of RIV, a ball-bearing company his grandfather founded early in the century. He had a unique notion of just what he was manufacturing. Ball bearings, he once explained, were "these tiny rolling things, which are the most expensive thing in a motorcar, sort of the truffles in a motorcar."[11]

Pamela fell for Gianni the same way that actresses Anita Ekberg, Linda Christian, Danielle Darrieux and countless other beauties had tumbled. Most were more attractive than Pamela, whose looks fluctuated dramatically: pretty during the war; rather dumpy in the trauma of its immediate aftermath; quite striking during the 1950s and the most stunning of all in her seventies. But looks were not what attracted Gianni to Pamela.

She was free-spirited and easy to be with, which is what first drew him and many other men, but she was not frivolous like so many of his usual playmates. She was more than a party girl, although she did love a good party. She was more than ornamentation. There was a nascent soberness to Pamela that set her apart, a worldly-wiseness and depth that she had picked up from David Margesson, Averell, Ed Murrow and old Winston. Both qualities enchanted Gianni. While she had a great "sense of fun," he said, "she considered life very seriously."[12]

Beyond that, her status fascinated him. Models and actresses and showgirls were jumping into bed left and right, but not many English aristocrats were so free with their favors, certainly none named Churchill. It was one thing for playboy Agnelli to carouse around the Riviera, quite another for a former Fascist and Axis officer to find ready postwar acceptance in the top political, diplomatic, business and social circles in Paris, London and New York. Pamela's connections, however, were impeccable. Gianni was delighted when she took him to Blenheim one weekend and introduced him to the duke of Marlborough.

As the much-loved daughter-in-law of the much-loved, victorious war hero, she offered Gianni a postwar seal of approval, an imprimatur of status beyond Italy and instant entrée to the winners' circle. She by then knew Gianni's worth, but she also understood her own. She was fully aware how useful it was for

Gianni Agnelli to be the lover of Pamela Churchill. Italians had been the enemy, but she could change that for her Italian, and perhaps ameliorate the wartime role played by Fiat and speed its reacceptance.

If that were not enough, she had learned her lesson from her experiences with Randolph, Averell, Ed, General Fred, Aly — men for whom she was enjoyable but peripheral. Men on whom she could not rely. Men who left her. Pamela would not make the same mistake with Gianni. She would make herself a central part of his life.

The prospect was no chore. They were both in their late twenties and in marvelous physical condition. Gianni was a wonderful lover, as enchanting in bed as he was in every other aspect of his life. He was younger, needier and less formed than Aly Khan. There was a better chance they could grow together. What was less obvious at the moment was a fascination Gianni shared with Aly for serious womanizing. Years later, his wife, Marella Agnelli, blurted it out in a moment of exceptional candor to Italian journalist Enzo Biagi: "For Gianni, a woman is to be conquered. Not to be loved."[13]

Pamela had no immediate objection to being conquered, but she also wanted to be loved. In love herself, as well as in sexual thrall, she did what many women do with such a partner: knowing firsthand his reputation as a ladies' man and fearing she would lose him, she set about making a honey pot, a nest which he would not leave.

She could not take over his life. Gianni would not let her. He was too male, too Italian, too attracted to others and had too many interests that did not involve her. But she could try to make him value her and perhaps even rely on her. He was learning a new postwar role as well and she could help with everything from introductions to her friends to instructions on how to run a great house: from which house to be in to the decoration of each room; from the hiring and proper training of servants to the right crystal, china and floral centerpieces to grace a dinner table.

Who should dine with them? Who should stay over? Gianni had to go somewhere? There was a leak in the roof or a visitor who needed a doctor? A chef seeking a pay raise? No problem.

Not for Gianni. Gianni loved the finest comforts, but he did not want to make the arrangements himself. Such intricate details took time and required follow-up. They were a pain in the neck. Pamela understood and took everything out of his hands and cared for every need. Gianni was rich, but Pamela had class and used everything she had learned.

Employing all her chameleon qualities, she took on a Gianni persona, down to mimicking his Italian baritone. "She becomes what the man is," said Agnelli's great friend the writer Taki Theodoracopulos, echoing Leonora Hornblow. "She is the greatest housekeeper of all time. She ran Gianni's life perfectly." He knew it, appreciated it — and used Pamela skillfully in return.

They complemented one another. Pamela loves a good time but by nature is not relaxed. Despite the kittenish qualities ascribed to her by Evelyn Waugh, she lacks wit and almost any sense of humor. Gianni exudes ease and humor. When she met him, there was little about him that was serious except his determination to experience everything before settling down. He had no political connections; most of her connections were political. He moved so quickly, was such a social and sexual butterfly, had no mother, no father, no role models, that there was little or no order in his life.

Pamela infused order in him through utter devotion to every aspect of his life. She is not innately bright, but she has a steely intelligence about process. She is also a fast learner, street smart and has uncanny savoir faire. If there was one thing at which she was superbly skilled, it was spotting what a man lacked and filling the gap before he even knew what he was missing.

Following the trip to Capri, Pamela made a conscious decision to go for the gold ring, in every sense of the expression. She was less interested than ever in England. Eight days after the war ended, President Truman canceled Lend-Lease, thereby cutting off the provision of all food and weapons on credit.

The winter of 1947–48 had been the worst to hit England since 1881. Blizzards and subfreezing temperatures ravaged the country. There was such a shortage of coal that electricity was cut back. Industry nearly ground to a halt. Food rationing was more stringent in 1948 than in the depths of the war. Under

Attlee's Labour government, per capita food consumption in Britain was lower than a decade earlier. A few months later, the bottom fell out of the pound. A 30 percent devaluation made Britain's lifestyle teeter.[14]

Given the choice, who wanted to live like that? Certainly not Pamela, who decided that Ed Murrow had erred badly in gilding the Socialist rose. Not after a glorious summer on the Riviera, which had escaped the war almost unscathed. Not after finding herself surrounded by some of the world's fattest wallets on the sleekest yachts.

Britain was miserable enough even without all the characters she was determined to avoid. She did not want to be anywhere near Randolph, English men in general, or her family. If her parents and siblings were not cluck-clucking disapproval over her unchecked, fast-track and distinctly non-English life, her society friends were criticizing her behavior before, during and after the war. Everything argued for her to clear out for good.

Except the Churchills. To appease Clemmie and Winston, who were upset that she was abandoning her English roots and taking away their grandson, she kept 49 Grosvenor Square. Randolph had made threatening noises about suing for custody of young Winston, and Pamela's lawyers told her that if she did not retain the flat as an English base, he might have a case. That would have cost Pam her Churchill link and would have been disastrous.

The Churchill name was her laissez-passer to every drawing room and dining table in Europe and the United States and could never be jeopardized. The flat had been purchased with financial help from Gianni and what was widely rumored to be a twenty-thousand-dollar annual stipend from Averell. She made a tidy profit renting it to Lewis Douglas, who succeeded Averell as ambassador in Britain and who returned every summer for years after relinquishing the post, and later to actor Cary Grant.

At the end of summer 1948, she moved to Paris, just as Jane Digby had a century earlier. The French capital was the obvious place to construct her nest. Turin was a company town. There would have been little for Pamela to do but wait on Gianni, too restrictive a prospect for each of them. The south of France was for summer idylls. As a Fascist capital, Rome was inappropriate for a Churchill.

Paris was perfect. The City of Light was re-lit after the war. Pamela could speak the language, had friends, knew her way around, and would have plenty of opportunity to enjoy life and expand her horizons when Gianni was not present. Paris was politically acceptable: Charles de Gaulle had organized the Free French forces while living in London during the war, occasionally dining at Downing Street with the Churchills, including their daughter-in-law.

In January, she extricated eight-year-old Winston from England and installed him in LeRosey, an exclusive Swiss boarding school which Aly Khan's sons attended.

In Paris, another rich man did her a favor. Paul-Louis Weiller gave her a place to live, a pretty flat on rue Delabordère in Neuilly. A wealthy industrialist with huge property holdings in and around Paris and Versailles — at one point he owned ninety-seven homes — Weiller was known for providing houses for defunct royals and others with gold-plated names who, in his debt, attended his parties. Otherwise, few would have come.

Diana Cooper, wife of Duff Cooper, Britain's ambassador to France from 1944 to 1947, called him "the frog who people can't endure," and habitually referred to him as "poor Louis" in her correspondence to Evelyn Waugh.[15]

Weiller bought friends by providing food, drink, the loan of his Rolls-Royces, the gift in 1951 of a ten-thousand-dollar Dior mink coat to Diana, who called it her "coat of shame," for accepting it. He gave the Windsors a house in Neuilly and Winston Churchill's daughter-in-law two places, the second in Versailles. That was before Gianni bought her a spectacular third-floor apartment near the place d'Alma at 4 avenue de New York whose floor-to-ceiling windows overlooked the Seine and the Eiffel Tower.

The five years beginning in 1948 were the happiest of Pamela's life. They were play years, fun years, a reward for having done what she considered her bit in the war. Everything was new and glorious. The future, at least on the Continent, appeared filled with opportunities.

Pamela's whole outlook changed. She had felt frustrated and suffocated in England, but living in France and loving Gianni Agnelli was an effervescent experience, an infusion of pure oxygen and ambrosia, imbibed at dinner parties in Paris, at balls in silk gowns in Rome, in furs at snowbound villas in Saint Moritz, and in bathing suits under gaily striped deck awnings and at most of the great estates in the south of France. "When Gianni was with Pamela Churchill," said Princess Irene Galitzine, "the parties went on and on and we all ran from villa to villa."

Before one such party in Beaulieu, an emergency call went out from a worried hostess to the British embassy in Paris. Did the Aga Khan outrank the duke of Windsor? "His Highness the Aga Khan is regarded as God on earth by his many million followers," came the reply, "but an English Duke, of course, takes precedence."[16]

Pamela forgot about politics because she had no stake in French affairs of state at that time. Instead, she picked up where she had left off during her schoolgirl year in Paris and began to learn more about art, especially the fine decorative pieces she had been introduced to at Leeds Castle by Stephane Boudin. Weekends in warm weather, she and Gianni sometimes met in the south of France. On occasion, he joined her in Paris; more often, she flew to Turin. It was known to be her second home. Mary Welsh, Ernest Hemingway's fourth wife, came to visit Pam and Gianni there in November 1948.

In midwinter, Susan Mary Patten (who later married columnist Joseph Alsop) was sitting at home in Paris writing placecards for a dinner party when her telephone rang. Pamela, who was an acquaintance but not a friend, was on the line from Turin. She had a terrible problem and could Susan Mary help. Clementine and Winston Churchill were coming through Paris by train and would stop for a few minutes at the Gare du Nord to drop off young Winston. She was supposed to meet them, but it was snowing in the Alps. No planes were leaving Turin for Paris and she was unable to make the rendezvous. Would Susan Mary please collect her son? Pamela would get to Paris one way or another and pick him up as soon as she could. Susan Mary was surprised but said, of course she would.

"A nightmare," said her husband, Bill, an attaché at the American embassy. "Rush hour. It will take you forever and once you get there, how will you get through security and convince Winston Churchill, who has no idea who you are, to hand over his grandson?"

They decided that she should take the chauffeur, a diplomatic passport and their nanny, an Englishwoman who wore respectable tweeds and a round felt hat and looked quintessentially nannyish. Susan Mary got through security by pushing the nanny ahead of her.

"There was half the French government. The train was already in and Mr. Churchill was pacing up and down the platform looking furious," she recalled. She raced up to Mrs. Churchill and told her what happened to Pamela. Clementine looked uncertain. Susan Mary introduced the nanny. Clementine's furrowed brow cleared. She consulted with old Winston and turned over young Winston. They were grateful, reboarded the train and chugged off.

Young Winston adapted immediately, with the confidence of a child used to being left by his mother with perfect strangers, including a houseful of Patten guests. Within days, a handwritten letter of thanks drafted on the train arrived from Clementine Churchill. There was no word from Pamela, who never called to inquire about her son or even whether the transfer had been made. Three days later, without warning, she appeared at the house in a gorgeous full-length fur coat and ran up the stairs. Winston flung himself into her arms. Thanks a lot, Pamela told Susan Mary as she dashed out of the house, her last words on the matter.[17]

For the four summer months in both 1949 and 1950, Gianni rented a large house at Cap d'Antibes called Château de la Garoupe. It was situated on a promontory with a beach on one side and rock bathing on the other. Pamela moved in from June through September and young Winston came with his nanny. A diving instructor arrived mornings to pick up the boy and give him lessons at the nearby Eden Roc pool. At other times Winston swam, snorkeled or ran around in a small motorboat given him by Gianni, whom he liked very much.

From England, Randolph had been screaming at Pamela that Gianni was spoiling Winston with gifts that his father could not afford. But he did not press the matter. Instead, to Pamela's relief, Randolph gave up. After a three-month courtship sparked by endless fights and a mid-engagement suicide attempt by his fiancée, Randolph married June Osborne, a beautiful but neurotic colonel's daughter who had been a schoolmate of Pamela's at Downham.[18]

At La Garoupe, guests came and went constantly in a Gatsbyesque parade of swimming, boating, waterskiing, parties and balls. Gianni hosted; Pamela handled all the arangements — guest list, staff, fresh flowers, menus, wine, linen — and hostessed brilliantly. No guest who had visited once and ordered Campari ever had to request his favorite again. If one smoked Gauloises, one was never offered Gitanes. Butlers trained on the model of Elsie Woodward's major domo Arthur Putz recorded such details. If an overnight guest were allergic to feather pillows, she would find they had been replaced by foam rubber.

Extra bathing suits, lounging robes, sandals, suntan creams, fluffy towels — all were provided. Lunch for a guest at Cannes' Carlton Hotel, whose twin cupolas were reportedly modeled on the breasts of Caroline Otero, mistress of Edward VII and Kaiser Wilhelm II? The chauffeur was poised for the trip and would wait to return the diners to the house.

Everything Pamela had learned about hospitality — at Minterne Magna, Leeds Castle, Downing Street and Chequers, from hosts as disparate as Emerald Cunard and Aly Khan — was practiced and honed. Pamela missed nothing. Squint into the sun on the terrace and instantly an umbrella was adjusted. Squirm on a sofa and, in no time, Pamela or a servant was proferring an extra pillow.

Gianni loved it. Very traditional in his habits, he liked a woman to fix him things. Very neat and precise, he always preferred his surroundings just so. Pamela ensured that his environment was perfect. She was an artist at providing service. No geisha ever performed with greater anticipation, thoroughness or expertise.

"She was very important for Gianni," said Princess Galitzine. "He became more international in her company, not so local. She taught him a lot, in entertaining, in taste, in things like selecting furniture."[19]

In 1951, Gianni bought La Léopolda, the fabled and enormous property overlooking Cap Ferrat. The house and grounds had once belonged to King Leopold II, who amassed his fortune when Belgium owned the Congo. Halfway between Nice and Monte Carlo, La Léopolda was both more accessible and more secluded than La Garoupe, as well as much bigger. There were wildflower gardens, sculpted cedars, lawns to rival the carpeted fairways of Augusta, a gigantic pool with statuary and fountain and a villa with views up and down the coast. All combined to make La Léopolda the most spectacular estate on the Riviera, or did once Pamela supervised its redecoration.

Life changed once they moved into La Léopolda. Pamela was not positive what was different. She either felt, was advised, or was instructed as a result of child custodial legalities — it is not clear which — that it was inappropriate for young Winston to stay at the owned property, although it had been all right when Pamela and Gianni were renting. Winston was a more impressionable eleven by then, so his age may have been a factor.

Winston spent most of the summer with Randolph and his new wife, June, in England and joined his mother for August. Instead of La Léopolda, Pamela had him bring a friend for the month to Deauville, where Aly Khan loaned her a house. Deauville is lovely, with a beautiful beach, a great racetrack and a renowned casino, but for Pamela it might as well have been Outer Mongolia. She hated every moment she was stuck in Normandy with the children and sat under her beach umbrella in agony, all too aware of what she was missing in the south of France. Not much imagination was required. Friends called daily from Cap Ferrat and Monte Carlo to tell her which girls Gianni had gone off with and on whose yacht.

Gianni was incapable of fidelity. Pamela knew that and understood it in theory. But comprehension did not make it easier to accept. By 1952, the fourth year of their affair, relations had become strained. They spent the summer together at La Léopolda, but for Gianni, the affair was winding down. Pamela, then thirty-two, was still consumed by him, but the long evenings of partying were becoming tiresome, especially with him flitting about, distracted by younger beauties.

Bored one evening when Gianni disappeared at a party in Beaulieu given by Hungarian businessman Arpad Plesch, Pamela was driven home by another guest. At 1 A.M., she walked into La Léopolda to find Gianni in bed with ravishing seventeen-year-old Anne-Marie d'Estainville. Pamela exploded. She screamed curses and flailed away at them with her fists and nails. You bitch, you bastard. Get the hell out, both of you.

They did. Pamela was furious, then distraught. Gianni had often gone off with other women, an embarrassment she simply endured. Some of his friends humiliated her unmercifully. Peter Zervoudachi was a Greek friend who could not stand Pamela. "Peter was outrageous. He didn't like her because he found her oppressive, always trying to control Gianni, to make him like an English gentleman," said Taki Theodoracopulos, laughing. "Peter would take a hooker and make sure he went to bed with her in Pamela's bed and leave traces behind. She loathed him with a passion. Whenever she would say, 'Did you use my bed?' he would say, 'Yes, the girl was wonderful.' "[20]

Gianni had never hidden the fact that he ran around. With Latin braggadocio, he told her of the beauties he had bedded. She rationalized his confessions as evidence that he really loved her, that he would never tell her such things if she were just another one of his girls. And she was not.

She was the only woman living with him in the south of France and this made the confrontation with Anne-Marie horrible for her. He had never humiliated her so flagrantly before, not to her face, not in the house they shared. She loved this man, but he had hurt her deeply.

Pamela tried to sleep, but could not. Her heart hammered. She took a sleeping pill and finally drifted off. She had no idea what time it was when the phone rang. A friend was insistent: Come quickly. There has been a terrible accident. Gianni was in the emergency room at Nice hospital. Six people were involved; one was dead. Who, they didn't know. Pamela woke Angelo, the chauffeur, crying "*Uno è morto*," and together they raced to the hospital.

In a fury after being slapped by Pamela, Gianni had raced off to drive Anne-Marie home to Cap Martin. A reckless driver at any time but further destabilized that night by cocaine and liquor, he sped along the Lower Corniche and missed the left turn before the entrance to the Cap Roux tunnel. At 4:10 A.M., his car smashed into a delivery truck carrying four butchers to morning market in Nice and crushed their Lancia into the mountain rocks. One of the butchers screamed that his friend was dead.

A dazed Anne-Marie climbed out of the wreckage and stopped the first car to come along. Three friends from the Beaulieu party were inside. Driver Carlo Stagni got out to help, coolly ordering the other two to take Anne-Marie home. En route, they stopped to wash out her cuts with vodka. She tiptoed into her house, woke up at 11 A.M. and told no one she had been in the wreck.

The butchers were extricated and all survived. Agnelli representatives dealt with them generously. A quickly fabricated cover story proved acceptable to the police. Everyone's discretion obviated the need for an embarrassing inquiry.

This left only Gianni, who had been grievously injured. Pamela almost fainted when she arrived at the hospital and saw his injuries. His jaw was shattered. Blood streamed from facial cuts. Those injuries were minor compared with his crushed right leg, which was broken in seven places, the same leg which had been badly fractured in a previous car accident. Pamela recovered her composure immediately and began to demonstrate that she not only rose to the occasion in a crisis but was a superb nurse — as Leland Hayward and Averell Harriman later learned — whenever her man, her provider, faced medical distress.

Pamela, Gianni and most of their friends on the Riviera had for years used a Doctor Pascal in Cannes. She called and briefed him. He told her to put Gianni in an ambulance right away and bring him to the Clinique Lutetia in Cannes. There the leg was encased in plaster, but the cast was too tight when the leg swelled. Gianni was in agony. Too many of his friends were swarming into the clinic when he needed rest and his pain seemed too severe.

Swamped and out of her depth, Pamela called Italy and asked his sister Susanna for help. Suni, as she is known, was an operating theater nurse during the war and worked on hospital ships tending the wounds of young Italian, German and English men. A tall, no-nonsense and commanding woman who looks like Gianni and was later successful in Italian politics and in running the Italian Red Cross, Suni arrived quickly. She arranged a charter plane to take her brother to the Instituto Ortopedico in Florence. Seats were removed and Gianni's stretcher placed on the floor, where Pamela sat, his head in her lap, for the journey.

The institute's top surgeon, Professor Dogliotti, opened the cast and discovered that gangrene had set in. Amputation was recommended, but Gianni adamantly refused. Another operation was required immediately. The clinic would not give Gianni a general anesthetic because Pamela informed Dogliotti, as she had told Pascal when he asked at Cannes, that Gianni had been taking cocaine. He would have to get by with a local anesthetic.

The doctor asked Pamela to come to the operating room, sit by Gianni's head and cover his eyes while they cut. Forty years later, she can still see the knife opening up his leg, smell the toxic excretion and feel his tears oozing down her hand as Dogliotti began to cut away the gangrenous flesh.

Gianni's recovery took months. Pamela stayed with him in Florence, slept by his bed, went to a nearby hotel for two hours in the morning and showered, then returned to the institute. From Florence, they went to Forte dei Marmi, the Agnelli family home on the coast near Lucca for another six weeks. It was nearly four months, almost Christmas, before Gianni returned to Turin.

He thought a great deal about their relationship during convalescence. He was approaching thirty-two and had begun to consider the inevitability of marriage. Pamela had started thinking about marriage soon after she met Gianni.

He had tried repeatedly to discourage her, told her straight out he did not want to marry. When that did not work, he warned her gently, realistically and repeatedly that he had no intention of remaining faithful to her or anyone else. He considered monogamy, or any restrictions, unacceptable. An Italian wife would stay with him no matter how he behaved. But if he married her, he told Pamela, she would eventually find his behavior intolerable and leave.

It was a gracious construct, used perhaps with lesser skill by other men for generations, but it did not work. Pamela could not argue with the rationale, but she did not want to hear what he was saying because she was determined not to relinquish her latest great love.

Suni Agnelli had also given her fair warning. In 1948, very early in the affair, but as soon as she noticed the seriousness of Pamela's intent, Suni cautioned her that Gianni would never marry a non-Catholic. Pamela was undeterred by what some might consider a substantial obstacle. To the contrary, she immediately began the complicated and expensive process of converting to Roman Catholicism and transforming her divorce from Randolph into an annulment.

Ever since Everard almost derailed the family fortunes in the Gunpowder Plot, the Digbys have been fiercely anti-Catholic. Not that religion was very important for the contemporary family. As a child, Pamela had been christened and confirmed and attended Sunday services at the Anglican Church of St. Andrew at the entrance to Minterne Magna. A few friends were Catholic, as were such ancestors as her father's namesake, Kenelm, but she thought little about the faith until she faced the self-imposed choice of converting or losing Gianni for certain.

She began the process with the help of Father Joseph Christie at the Farm Street Church, lovely and Roman Catholic, in Mayfair, not fifty meters from her Grosvenor Square apartment. She would have to become a Catholic to secure a church annulment, so she hired a lawyer and also read about the conversion of Clare Boothe Luce, wife of the publisher of *Time* magazine

Young Winston was upset by her decision. He liked Gianni but was opposed to his mother's leaving the Anglican Church, which was, after all, the nation's religion. She tried to get him to accompany her to Farm Street, but he refused. On the religious front, endless depositions were required of such friends as Olive, Lady Baillie, and David Margesson, who had been involved in her decision a decade earlier to marry Randolph.

(Lady Baillie was not at all surprised that the marriage had collapsed. She was more startled at hearing out of the blue from Pamela. Although she was Pamela's virtual foster mother, raising the Digby girl at Leeds Castle with her own daughters, Pamela had completely dropped out of their lives. She did not write or visit the family, nor did she have any substantial contact with them after Olive provided the necessary depositions. When Pauline, the daughter who introduced Pam to Leeds, died, there was no word from Pamela. The Baillie family concluded that Pamela must have decided she did not need them anymore. Such behavior would be repeated throughout her life. Pamela revels in her historic link to the Churchills, but otherwise, she does not look back. She makes new friends to fit new needs.)

Meanwhile, Pamela formulated another excuse. As long as she was not free to marry Gianni in the Catholic Church, she rationalized that living with him was all right. They would put off any real decision about marriage until the annulment issue was resolved. The arrangement was not all right with the Catholic Church — which considered such behavior a mortal sin — but that did not concern Pamela. That was not the kind of church discipline she had in mind. She made her own rules.

At the same time that she began the process of converting to a religion adamantly opposed to birth control, Pamela had an abortion.

She could not have one in England or Catholic Italy or France, so she flew to Switzerland, then the abortion capital of Western Europe. Pamela went to Lausanne, home of a variety of gynecological clinics, including the famous Montchoisi maternity hospital, where Aly Khan arranged to have Rita Hayworth give birth to their daughter, Yasmin.

Once Gianni made the plans, they checked in the night before at the Beau Rivage Hotel. The next morning, they stopped in a small café, had coffee, croissants and a good cry, an extraordinary display of emotion from Gianni. There was no debate about having the child. Gianni had no intention of marrying Pamela then, which might have given her some hint about what was to happen later.

Gianni did not remain in Lausanne with Pamela, but, ever restless, left her alone and proceeded on to the luxurious Villa d'Este Hotel on Lake Como. Disappointed that he did not stay but determined not to complain about what she could not change, Pamela had the abortion.

The following day, still nauseated and wobbly, she joined him at the Villa d'Este, where he told her about a gorgeous model he had picked up the previous evening and with whom he had spent the night. The confession hurt her, but deep into what psychiatrists call denial, she chose to consider the admission one more strange example of how much he loved her.

Their relationship remained intense for most of the next four years, with Pamela ordering Gianni's life and widening his social circle while her annulment proceedings bumped along toward final disposition by the Vatican. If the summer of 1952 and the Anne-Marie episode indicated to some that strain between them had increased, Pamela's extraordinary efforts at nursing Gianni back to health that autumn suggested to others that her stock had rallied. Pamela knew better. She had a strong feeling that she would come up short with Gianni and began to hedge her bets. Most others, however, thought she might be closing in on the prize.

In England and Italy, the campaign to prevent a marriage picked up. The Digbys and the Churchills were both distressed by the relationship. Her parents knew they had little influence over her decision, but Pansy and Ken both made clear anyway that they were opposed to her marrying Gianni.

The only one whose opinion did carry weight with Pamela was old Winston, who, by 1951, was back in 10 Downing Street as prime minister for the second time. He asked her whether she intended to marry her Italian beau. On hearing that she hoped to, he said that he would be very unhappy if she did. Marriage to one of Britain's former enemies, so soon after the war, was not at all suitable.

In Italy, Gianni's three sisters saw Pamela as a gold digger and were unalterably opposed.

Gianni's brother, Giorgio, who had been mentally unstable since the death of their mother, Virginia, in 1945, tried radical measures: he once tried to kill Pamela, shooting bullets through the door of the bedroom she shared with Gianni. He missed but nearly succeeded in frightening her to death.

Gianni took the incident in stride. In their parentless family, he had little time for coddling his vulnerable brother, who was eight years younger. Giorgio was twenty-two when he opened fire — he was thirty-five when he died in a Swiss clinic — and Gianni sensed he was not fully aware of what he was doing. Gianni, though, knew what he was doing, and it was not getting married.

The only one who wanted to see Gianni married to Pamela was Pamela.

She flew to England at Christmas to be with young Winston, whom she had not seen since Gianni's accident. After the holidays, she returned to Turin, but the equation changed when her annulment came through in January 1953.

The basis for the annulment was shaky, the result of a bit of semantic legerdemain. Pamela formulated the strategy from her initial reaction to the widespread advice she had received not to marry Randolph. At nineteen, she had dismissed friends' warnings by saying if the marriage failed, she would get a divorce on the grounds that it had been a wartime marriage and she had been too young. At the time she said it, her attitude was more blasé than calculating, but the excuse constructed in advance suggested that she had prior reservations and was at least considering an escape clause.

Such friends as Olive, Lady Baillie, and David Margesson gave depositions about her premarriage comments which gave the Vatican grounds for ruling that she had invalidly entered the marriage; ergo, it was invalid. She received her annulment and was free to marry in the Catholic Church.

Gianni, who had plenty of time in his sickbed to consider his future, had other ideas. A private man with his thoughts, he denied to friends that he had dwelled on all the predictable intimations of mortality, but the accident had jolted him psychologically. He realized that he had to make a decision: he could either keep being a playboy or he could be a good Fiat man. The way to do the latter was to marry and have children, but he was not about to marry Pamela.

"Of course she wanted to get married. She tried like hell," said Taki Theodoracopulos, saying on the record what many of Pamela's friends acknowledged privately was true. "But he wasn't going to do that. Gianni was not going to marry a woman who had screwed other rich men around Europe and have children with her. Marry someone who had been giving it away? It was not going to happen. He and his family are too bourgeois, too concerned with respectability."[21]

In the final highly Italian and completely double-standard analysis, Pamela was well bred and well named but otherwise was little more than a high-class courtesan who had been kept by a succession of rich, powerful men. She was not even Italian. He liked her, showered her with gifts and would remain friends with her, but it was time to move on.

Pamela didn't fool herself. She knew the annulment meant that if Gianni would not marry her once she was free, their affair had no future. That realization hurt even though, by then, it was not a big surprise. She sought consolation in her Catholicism, and sat in church for hours in Turin and wept, hoping for some other solution. After several days of discussion, they decided it was over.

Gianni drove with her from Turin to the French border. They had loved each other and the emotional pain of parting was agonizing. At the checkpoint, he got out and limped over to the car that his chauffeur had been driving behind them. He stood in the road and waved sadly as Pamela drove away.

He called Pamela frequently in Paris and they continued to meet. But Gianni had already had another quarry in mind, even before the "formal" break with Pamela. She was an Italian beauty named Laudomia Herculani, who was married to a prince. Friends maintain that it was Gianni's attraction to Laudomia that did more to break up his relationship with Pamela than the annulment. But because she was married and divorce was out of the question in Italy in the early 1950s, Laudomia could not become Mrs. Agnelli either.

In October, Gianni phoned Pamela in Paris and asked to come see her. Princess Marella Caracciolo di Castagneto, who had been in love with him for years and who was a great friend of his sisters, was pregnant. That was no surprise to Pamela, who had long believed that the Agnelli women pushed their friend Marella into Gianni's bed every chance they could in the precise hope that this would happen.

Pamela laughed bitterly at published stories that Marella canceled a trip to be by Gianni's side and help nurse him back to health after the accident. It was untrue. Pamela did the nursing; Marella's role had been irrelevant.

Nonetheless, the outcome was clear and Pamela had no intention of being obstructionist or causing a scene. Gianni said that Marella refused to terminate the pregnancy. Pamela advised that he must then marry her. He did not want to marry anyone for all the reasons he had already explained. This was different, Pamela told him, playing out the drama whereby the object of her affections succeeded in extracting not bile from her, but an actual blessing.

He had to marry sometime and Marella was the perfect candidate. He should go ahead and do it. Good luck and stay in touch. Privately, she took solace in the fact that Marella was pregnant. If she had not been pregnant and still Gianni wanted to marry her, then Pamela would have felt more hurt. This way, Gianni was hurt as well, which helped ease her pain.

The following month, in a quickly arranged ceremony at Osthofen Castle near Strasbourg attended by only one hundred guests, an uncharacteristically sullen-looking Gianni married the swan-necked princess, who later became known as one of the world's most glamorous women. As New York society columnist Cholly Knickerbocker wrote, "It was truly a marriage made in heaven."[22]

In Paris, Pamela took pleasure in her conviction that the marriage was hell. Whenever Gianni called or saw her, which was often, he told her how trapped he felt. Marella was incapable of running a house in anything like the manner of Pamela. It was nice to hear that she was missed, but the satisfaction was limited. She had spent five years trying to land Gianni. A big part of her life had ended and not at all the way she wanted. Thank heaven, she had a backup.

CHAPTER ELEVEN

🄡 🄡

Elie

WHILE GIANNI WAS RUNNING around late in their affair and most cognoscenti were predicting that he would never marry her, Pamela knew enough to take out insurance. Her circle since childhood had been peopled almost exclusively with the wealthy, so lowering her living standard was out of the question. She had already experienced being broke with Randolph, a torment she would do anything to avoid reliving.

Gianni was famous for his generosity to girlfriends — five, ten years after a breakup some still received jewels, boats or cars — but Pamela realized that his charity would not extend to supporting her indefinitely in the style to which she had become accustomed.

The senior Churchills were helping provide for young Winston and she had a tiny alimony from Randolph, but currency exchange rules in the 1950s prevented British citizens from taking anything but a minuscule amount of sterling out of the country. Returning to England would be an admission of defeat that she refused to make.

Absence from home had not made her heart grow fonder. She

missed her Digby family about as much as she missed the entire populace of Englishmen — not one bit. And there was still no one beckoning her to move to the United States. So she would stay in France, but to continue operating at high level, Pamela needed a new patron.

She made the calculation without illusion. The experience with Gianni created a carapace over her emotions. She had been dropped once more by a rich, powerful man, this time by a single man she truly loved, one to whom she had devoted herself utterly. If she relived the five years they had together, she would not have done anything differently. She had loved him as hard and as best she could. She tried to do everything for him without encroaching on his freedom. Still her efforts had not worked.

So now it was time to be tougher and less emotional. Love, fascination with, and focus on, a single man became secondary considerations behind taking care of her own needs. There was nothing happenstance about the selection process. She targeted and chose carefully. "The rest of us were giving it away," said a woman friend. "Pamela parlayed it into good stuff." The situation called for a man to support her, so she looked around for another rich lover, passion desirable, but not a requirement.

Elie de Rothschild was the all-too-willing candidate. She met the banker and proprietor of the Château Lafite vineyard at the Deauville racetrack he frequented with their mutual friend Aly Khan and his polo-playing companion Porfirio Rubirosa, the Dominican-born gigolo.

In the hunt for a benefactor, once again Pamela's timing was impeccable. Elie's wife, Liliane, was pregnant with her third child in 1952 when Pamela met Elie, scion of one of Europe's most distinguished and wealthiest families. That he was Jewish made no more difference to Pamela than the fact that Aly Khan was Moslem.

Elie was actually a distant relative by marriage: in 1878, the earl of Rosebery married Hannah Rothschild, the mother-in-law of Pansy Digby's sister Eva, Lady Rosebery. Sixteen years later, the earl became prime minister of Britain.

Liliane had not yet recovered from giving birth to her daughter Gustava when, early in 1953, her sister Therese died in the

Rothschilds' Paris mansion on the avenue de Marigny across the street from the Elysée Palace. Liliane had adored Therese and was so shattered by the loss, which was followed by the death of her stepfather and collapse of her mother, that she went into seclusion for a year.

"She wouldn't see anyone or do anything. She went into a kind of eclipse," said Alan Pryce-Jones, Randolph Churchill's old friend and the husband of Therese Fould-Springer. "I remember saying to Liliane, 'You're insane. If anyone is going to go into an eclipse, it is me. You've got to deal with your husband. You know your husband. Don't be surprised if he goes off with somebody else if you don't take care of him.' And, of course, he went straight off with Pam. She rather took him over. "[1]

Another source close to the Rothschild family corroborated the circumstances: "Liliane was out of circulation and off with her sister when Pam moved in. She always seems to move in on people when wives are off duty."[2]

Elie was no runaround in the Gianni Agnelli mode, but he was tall — five eleven — and good-looking, with a winsome smile, piercing eyes, a neatly trimmed mustache, wiry build, chiseled features, and he liked interesting, pleasing women. Liliane's seclusion made him ripe for plucking. Their marriage had survived a difficult start which included a proxy wedding while he was in a German prison camp. A superb rider, Elie went to the Second World War on horseback and was captured along with much of his regiment, the Anciens Cuirassiers, near the Belgian border.

He was sent to Nienberg, near Hamburg, where he immediately began plotting an escape. Found out, he was sent to Colditz, then to Lubeck, one of the toughest POW camps. There he was reunited with his brother Alain and both served out the war. Fortunately for the two of them, they were treated as captured officers and thus avoided the extermination camps.

While in Colditz, Elie had written his childhood sweetheart, Liliane Fould-Springer, and asked her to marry him. They had been engaged before he was captured. His mother had hoped he would marry and, at the time he wrote, Elie doubted he would survive the war. Liliane's parents thought it foolish that their

daughter take on the Rothschild surname with the Nazis in control
of France, but Liliane was charmed by the proposal and accepted.

Elie made his vows in April 1941; Liliane, six months later.
The marriage had a poignancy that went beyond its ceremony:
Liliane's great-uncle was Achille Fould, whose Crédit Mobilier
had tried and failed a century before to drive the Rothschild
financial empire out of business.[3]

After the war, Elie, Alain and their wives shared the avenue
de Marigny property where the brothers had grown up. Very
close, the men were, nonetheless, very different in temperament.
Alain was serious and conservative, later the head of the Jewish
community in France and a man who took his free-time pleasure
in the solitude of sailing. Elie was more dashing, a would-be
playboy whose best friends were Aly and Ruby, the biggest
swordsmen since Don Juan, if not before.

He also knew Gianni Agnelli quite well in early years, less so
later. Elie was a polo fanatic, had his own team and hosted a
great shoot. Compared with the others, however, Elie was a "serious" playboy, a Jewish playboy. His love was medicine and he
might have been a doctor if he had had his choice of occupations.
But he was channeled into the family banking business, where
he worked hard, and to Château Lafite, which wine experts have
long considered one of the greatest vineyards.

Elie also ran his houses. To complement the best wines, he
hired the finest chefs. In Rothschildian tradition, he was also
a great art connoisseur and a major collector. Rembrandt's *The
Standard Bearer*, believed to be a self-portrait, is in Elie's collection,
as is *The Marsham Children*, which Gainsborough painted in 1787.
He has a strong interest in contemporary art, which he purchased
in great quality and quantity in the 1950s and 1960s. One of the
foremost collectors of Dubuffet, he also numbered works by Picasso, Klimt, Nevelson and Spain's Antoni Tapies among his
favorites.

Liliane is a charming hostess — "I do hope you enjoy the
wine," she told a recent guest. "It's homemade." But friends
doubt that she has ever seen a kitchen. She is the family intellectual, very bright, a voracious reader, an exceptional designer
and decorator with a brilliant eye for eighteenth-century art,

which she has studied and collected for decades. Among her prizes is an Elizabeth Vigée-Lebrun portrait of Comtesse du Barry, who succeeded Madame de Pompadour as mistress to Louis XV.

In the later 1950s, Liliane and Elie moved to their own home, a spectacular residence on the rue Masseran, built by Brongniart in 1785, which Liliane filled with Rothschild portraits and such historic pieces as a pair of seventeenth-century Louis XIV cabinets decorated with tortoiseshell and inlaid with mother-of-pearl and ivory, and a cabinet-bibliotèque decorated in gilt-bronze by André Boulle, cabinetmaker to the Sun King.

For all her many talents, however, Liliane was not pretty. Pamela thought she looked like an old toad and was not the least bit surprised how easy it was to attract Elie. Nor was Liliane attentive to her husband, certainly not in her horrible 1953, and even in a good year, nothing like Pamela. "Liliane certainly wasn't going to worry about bringing Elie his slippers," her brother-in-law explained. "Pam was. She's so good about paying attention to all the small things."

Small details matter to ex-cavalryman Elie. When the Rothschilds opened a hotel in Paris, his explanation of how he wanted it run revealed more about him than the establishment. "I want my bath to run hot in two minutes flat. I don't want to hear plumbing noises. I want a good bed and pillows. I want my breakfast right away. I want good croissants. I want people to be polite to me and I don't want to hear their side of the story."[4]

Pamela provided all that and more. She rode horses with Elie and explored art galleries, accompanied him on weekends to Rothschild properties in Morocco, on business trips to Zurich and Geneva and to the caves at Château Lafite. Discretion was required. Unlike her open relationship with the unmarried Gianni Agnelli, her affair with the married Elie de Rothschild was clandestine. They never went out together in public, though everyone in France's café society knew that Pamela had become *la regulière* for Elie.

Those who didn't have all the details understood the gist, sometimes with awkward results. The duke of Windsor once asked Liliane which of the Rothschilds was involved with Pamela. "My husband," she replied.

The affair filled a need for Pamela that was more than financial. She hates being alone, yet despite the glamour, all her relationships essentially had failed. She was forever being abandoned. Ed Murrow had told her that she had been too much adored at too early an age. Well, she had not felt too much adored in too long a time. It was imperative that she be supported, but she was just as desperate to be adored.

Elie, who has both a passionate and a sentimental streak, did adore her. "I've heard him say that he genuinely loved her," said one who knows him well. "It was much more than a flirtation." In 1991, journalist Henry Brandon returned from Europe to tell Pamela that Elie had told him that in spite of all the intervening years, she was still the love of his life.

She was flattered to hear that but doubted the report was true. She had a very clear and unemotional idea from the outset of her value to Elie, who she believed had more hangups, worries and insecurities than any man she had ever known, more even than Ed Murrow.

As a prisoner of war, Elie felt the gut-wrenching vulnerability of being a Rothschild in the hands of Nazis who forced him to wear a yellow star pinned to his prison garb.

He was married to a physically unattractive woman who, for all her intelligence and charm, he had little pride in showing off to male friends with their higher premium on tactile beauty. As a result, Pamela found that Elie had surprisingly little sense of self-value. His arrogance and a style that could fairly be called peremptory concealed a startling lack of confidence. Her worth came from his believing that an attractive woman who was not a transient tart treasured him.

Liliane was unaware of the relationship for some time, but when she did find out, she was devastated. She was under no illusions about Frenchmen and their mistresses. A regular nooner meant nothing. What mattered was care and devotion, whether that meant putting one's husband or one's lover first. After a dozen years of marriage and other family distractions, Liliane was lacking in the devotion department. She recognized the seriousness of the threat from Pamela, who was by then already well known in Europe as a femme fatale.

Pamela's secret was not that she was gorgeous. She had a good body and a thinner, more sculpted and elegant face in the 1950s than in the 1940s. As she moved into her midthirties, her face was also taking on character.

Nor was her talent merely in paying attention, but that she paid attention to those special vulnerabilities of men, those needs that powerful men know they have but which are sometimes hard to identify when disguised by wealth, prestige and authority.

Pamela, who had been used to the company of such men from her late teens and had witnessed their foibles firsthand — drinking, gambling, drug habits, intellectual insecurities, squirrelly little butterflies dipping and weaving inside their psyches. She was not overawed by rank and, by paying careful attention, could identify such frailties and apply her own medicine with accuracy and sensitivity. She sneered at psychiatry as borderline fraudulent. But, in a way, she almost qualified for a license in the manner in which she listened and gave succor, couch occasionally included.

She flitted and fluttered over every aspect of a man's life, boosting his ego, anticipating his every interest, convincing him that her time with him was the greatest thing that had happened since the juxtaposition of the planets. Certain men succumb to this line all the time. Elie, no particular charmer with the ladies, certainly not in comparison with Gianni, was one of them.

Thomas Mann was once asked to explain the appeal of Alma Mahler-Werfel, who was married to the composer Gustav Mahler, the Bauhaus architect Walter Gropius, the poet and writer Franz Werfel, was mistress to the painter Oskar Kokoschka, was pursued by Gustav Klimt, and enjoyed dalliances as well with a virtual generation of dimmer cultural stars. Before her death in 1964, Alma was to Vienna's cultural milieu what Pamela was and would become to political circles. Mann thought about Alma's irresistibility for a few minutes, then, with a smile, summed it up as, "She gives me partridges to eat, and I like them."[5]

Elie felt much the same about Pamela. She learned fast what he wanted, and soon, much as he described what he wanted from a good hotel, he boasted to friends that "she brings me my drink and keeps quiet." She did not press him to share his thoughts or

ponder the meaning of life or challenge him intellectually, recognizing quickly that he was no more intellectual than she.
Pamela did what he wanted, made no demands on him and never
insisted that he hear her side of the story. She was a discreet
mistress who made him feel good.

She made him feel so good that Liliane feared she might lose
her husband. "She was scared to death by Pam," said Susan Mary
Alsop, one of Liliane's best friends. "The sense of threat went
very deep."[6]

So deep that Liliane became very antagonistic to anyone she
knew to be a friend of Pamela's.

So deep that she took her youngest daughter in her baby carriage and patrolled the sidewalk outside Pamela's apartment on
avenue de New York, waiting to see if Elie would show up — or
depart.

So deep that forty years later Liliane still cannot bring herself
to mention Pamela's name, but calls her "that woman."

Sex was not the key to "that woman's" relationship with Elie,
or Gianni or Aly. Sex was easily available in remarkable profusion
and variety for such men. Indeed, sex was not that important to
Pamela. She once confided to Marina Sulzberger, wife of the *New
York Times* diplomatic correspondent, that she did not particularly
enjoy going to bed with men. Writer Peter Viertel said that Pamela
told him the same, that bed was not all that important to her.[7]

A European man who spent many nights with her during the
1950s confirmed that, saying that "her amorous temperament
was not very big."[8]

She did it as best she could and had no particular reservations,
but what was enjoyable and important to Pamela was to please
her partners so they would adore her and need her. Romance
mattered greatly for her.[9]

Nor was sex the crux of Elie's attraction. Sex was important,
as was Pamela's solicitous attention, but what mattered above all
to Elie was that Pamela was an attractive English aristocrat who
sought to please him. Class did not matter for a fling, but it was
an important factor in an affair.

"He could have had a million tarts. What mattered sexually
was that she was an English aristocratic tart," said a close observer

of the relationship. "Elie and his friends could go to Madame Claude's all the time. But with Pam you had something different. She was a high-class English rose named Churchill. Elie wasn't coming home to a woman who he knew was a totally different class."[10]

According to a French banker who has known Elie for years: "He will not bother with people he does not consider his equals."[11] Pamela was *du même village,* "from an equivalent milieu."

It was important to Elie that Pamela was a strong and independent woman. Liliane was like that. Weak, submissive, servile women bore men like Elie or Gianni. Pamela's talent was to do a lot for Elie but also to keep him interested, not an easy task when a man has so many other options. Her strength was that she did her homework. "To keep her husband," wrote Frederic Morton, author of *The Rothschilds,* "a Rothschild wife must often keep half a dozen households and be at home in ten different fields."[12] Pamela understood such implicit requirements.

She labored hard to upgrade her knowledge of furniture and art, but she also studied the history and techniques of wine making so she could converse more intelligently about Elie's major passions. She went back on her own to art galleries that they visited together to inquire about specific paintings which had sparked Elie's interest. She knew horses firsthand. To keep up with Elie, she built up her knowledge, read increasingly about bloodstock and followed the French and English press during the racing season.

It was an added attraction for Elie that rich friends had already kept or slept with Pamela. Some men find such worldliness offputting, but for Elie de Rothschild, an experienced collector, it was reassuring that his trophy girlfriend had passed inspection by his peers.

"If you think someone is a great artist, and everyone has bought his work as great art, you look at the artist with renewed interest," said one who has tracked Elie's thinking on such matters. "If you knew that all these other men were after her and wanted to go to bed with her, your desire was enhanced."[13]

*   *   *

Because Elie was a part-time lover, Pamela had the rest of her Paris life to herself, at that time a more than suitable arrangement. She did not pine to attend dinner parties or spend summer holidays with Elie. Her days and nights in France were as full as those of Jane Digby, whose affair with Prince Felix Schwarzenberg was also plagued in its Paris days by obstacles and exclusions.

She had established an independent lifestyle soon after moving to France in 1948 because, even when her affair with Gianni Agnelli was in full flower, he spent the majority of his time without her in Turin. Her routine changed little when she took up with Elie.

She had moved to France eager to try a new life, anxious to broaden her horizons, to discover and sample everything she could. Her knowledge of theater and dance was limited. For all her wartime friendships with writers, she was not much of a reader. She had a good, basic grounding in the decorative and fine arts thanks to the schoolgirl stint in France and, more important, her experience at Leeds Castle with Stephane Boudin. She reestablished contact with him and Jansen as soon as she arrived in Paris.

She also came into contact with the interior decorator Georges Geffroy, who all but adopted her. Boudin created spectacular looks. It didn't matter to him if a piece were legitimate as long as the effect was right. "Votre altesse royale," he would say to the duchess of Windsor with a delighted clap of his hands, "I believe that by great good fortune, I have *precisely* the piece to fill out your so *charming* scheme." The price, of course, was always high.[14]

Geffroy, though, was a font of pure decorating knowledge who knew the pedigree of every piece he inspected. Pamela was an eager apostle.

Nearly every afternoon, they made the rounds of the *antiquaires*, the antiques dealers, on the Left Bank while Geffroy conducted a one-student tutorial. Pamela grew to love eighteenth-century pieces, the same period that fascinated Liliane de Rothschild. This was more coincidental than purposeful. It was true that Pamela's two primary patrons in the 1950s were interested in fine arts and not politics, which argued for a shift in focus. But she was living for herself as well. She was hungry for this education, wanted to develop her own taste and style and was fascinated by what Geffroy taught her.

He helped her develop an eye for only the best. Initially with hesitation, and later with ease, she could turn over a Chinese bowl or check the back of a vermeil clock and determine whether it was a reproduction or a legitimate antique. She loved Louis XVI mirrors and delicate escritoires and soon discovered that she preferred the entire period to the more rococoish Louis XV pieces which the Rothschilds enjoyed.

What Pamela liked was less significant than how she learned to determine what she liked. That education all took place in dealer backrooms and established an approach that she drew on later in politics, where she took pride in calling herself a "backroom" girl. The frontroom was show, the backroom reserved for those in the know. Pamela and Geffroy spent no time in the frontrooms. On their regular circuit visiting dozens of dealers, they blew right through the curtains to the back to see the latest new objects, pieces that in many cases had yet to be priced. The appeal to Pamela was learning the tricks of the trade from the inside looking out. The reverse was for neophytes and rubes.

Gerald Van Der Kemp, the distinguished curator of Versailles, the palace built by Louis XIV in the mid-seventeenth century, became one of her best friends. He had met the Churchill family before the war, had known Randolph and repeatedly joined Pamela for dinner at avenue de New York, where they talked so late that he often slept over on, not in, her bed. "She was *très raffinée*, with very sophisticated taste," said Van Der Kemp. "Everything in her house was perfect."[15]

From bibelots to cut-flower arrangements to clothes closets for evening gowns to the ever-present silver-framed photos of Pamela with the Churchills, the apartment was in perfect order and looked elegant but was also welcoming and comfortable.

Zozo de Ravenel believed that her friend's taste was innate. "Pamela was born with it. You cannot get it," she said. "She has an eye for the very beautiful and very special. She knows how to pick out the very best."[16]

Van Der Kemp introduced her to Versailles' artisans and preservationists, who taught her about constructing and repairing fine pieces. Pamela hired Madame Brocard, who created embroideries for Versailles and for Queen Elizabeth II, to embroider her eighteenth-century furniture and to hand-make tableclothes and bed hangings.

Pamela takes pains to avoid any discussion about how she paid for all this, especially since Lord Digby said he gave her an allowance of four hundred pounds sterling a year and was, as was his wife, Pansy, terribly impressed that their daughter was able to economize so well that she could drive him around Paris in a pale blue Rolls-Royce.

When the subject is raised, Pamela dodges. Times were so different then; exchange rates were more favorable; she got good deals because she was known. All of which is true, but none of which explains how she amassed such a high-quality collection on an income of less than fifteen hundred dollars a year. Everyone who knew her at the time was fully aware that on her own she did not have two francs to rub together, but Pamela hates to acknowledge that rich men kept her and gave her money.

Instead, she resorts to petty deceit, not unlike her explaining that Gianni told her about his other girlfriends because he loved her so much. Her financially less well off French admirers were not fooled. "She was liking money very much," said one, "but happily not the little that was mine."

Another great friend through much of the fifties was André de Staercke, Belgium's ambassador to the NATO Council. He was both dean of Council diplomats in terms of service and, at thirty-six in 1952, its youngest member in age. De Staercke saw Pamela constantly at dinner parties but took to dropping by her apartment in the evening for a dollop of caviar, a whisky and some comfort. They had the closest of friendships and could talk, as Pamela did with Van Der Kemp, about anything: gossip, art, men and politics.

De Staercke introduced Pam to his mentor Paul-Henri Spaak, the great Belgian statesman who played a major role in helping draft the United Nations Charter and in establishing the European Economic Community and NATO, the North Atlantic Treaty Organization. In later life, Pamela boasted how well she knew Spaak, to enhance the myth that her political roots were always tended. But she exaggerated. She indeed knew Spaak, but politics were not of much interest during this incarnation in France.

As Odette Pol Roger explained, "Pam wanted to know interesting people, but she was not mad for politics" in the 1950s.[17] Zozo de Ravenel rarely heard Pamela discussing politics then either. "Now she has become more political, but then it wasn't political."[18]

Because Ambassador de Staercke was a bachelor and was seen at Pam's so often, the diplomatic circuit had them linked, but they loved each other without being lovers. Nonetheless, said de Staercke, "the essence of Pam is that she never stopped being seductive."[19]

Pamela spent the summer of 1955 in the south of France visiting friends and cruising on Stavros Niarchos's yacht in Greece. Charles Wrightsman, the Texas millionaire and donor to New York's Metropolitan Museum, was in France as usual, badgering her to have a medical checkup. Pamela always ignored him. She figured Wrightsman for a hypochondriac, said there was nothing wrong with her and that if she ever asked her English doctor for a checkup, she would be laughed out of his office.

English doctors were good if you were sick, but they had very little patience with patients who wanted anything as banal as a checkup, considering it an unnecessary American indulgence. After being hectored daily, though, Pamela finally gave in to humor Wrightsman. There was nothing wrong with her, but she'd do it anyway, just to indulge him. She came to the States every November or so and would have a medical check. Wrightsman beamed. He would take care of all the arrangements.

That fall, a letter arrived from Dr. Dana Atchley, a prominent physician at New York's Columbia-Presbyterian Medical Center, whose patients included Madame Chiang Kai-shek, Spencer Tracy, Katharine Hepburn and Elizabeth Taylor. He had booked her in for a week, which seemed like a long time for a mere checkup, since nothing was known to be medically amiss.

Pamela wrote back, saying that she planned to be in New York for only two and a half weeks and had no intention of spending nearly half her visit in hospital when she was perfectly healthy. She would come for two days. She checked into Harkness Pavilion, grew achingly bored during the tests and, armed with instructions to call later for a few outstanding results, returned to the St. Regis Hotel the day before Thanksgiving.

She called the hospital at 4 P.M. and was told brusquely that tests revealed she had cancer in her pelvis. Pamela almost panicked, but the calculating and analytical part of her nature quickly assumed control. If she appeared shocked, she assumed, the nurse would tell her nothing. She took a quiet breath and, as calmly as she could, asked the nurse to explain more precisely what the tests had turned up.

Her Pap smear was positive, the nurse said, but added that it could be an error. Pamela asked how often Pap results were wrong. Never, the nurse replied. Still, they'd do another test to be certain. But the next day was Thanksgiving and the test could not be given until Monday.

Pamela couldn't wait. The uncertainty would drive her mad. She asked how late they were open that day. Until 5 P.M. If she arrived at the hospital before then, they would do another smear right away. Pamela slammed down the phone, raced out of the St. Regis and ran frantically into the street, past the doorman and gaping pedestrians, hollering and waving for a cab.

She composed herself on the ride, arrived with two minutes to spare, chatted lightly with the attendants about how a mistake must have been made, was retested and sent off with instructions to call again in two days.

On Thanksgiving Day, she drove to the Whitney estate on Long Island for the holiday meal. Betsey Whitney instantly spotted that Pamela was distraught and asked what was wrong. Pamela dissolved in tears and explained. She must immediately call her doctor at their hospital, Betsey insisted. Pamela thought she meant "their" hospital as if it were the closest one they frequented. Only later did she discover that a substantial part of New York Hospital had been funded by Jock Whitney's father. It really was their hospital.

She went in the Monday after Thanksgiving in 1955, had exploratory surgery and a biopsy the following morning. The doctor confirmed she had cancer and needed a hysterectomy within the next few months. She could return to England and have it done there if she preferred. Pamela snorted. Her English doctors would never believe she had a problem. Sir Daniel Davies might have discovered Jack Kennedy's Addison's disease and he was personal physician to Queen Elizabeth II, but she did not trust British medicine. She preferred that the operation take place in New York.

The hospital experience frightened her badly. Not one who thrives on her own, Pamela felt particularly lonely sitting in New York looking at x rays and wondering how long she had to live. Two aspects of dying were especially difficult.

One was her feeling that everything she had experienced in her life until then had been a preamble to more significant experiences, including requited love. She didn't want to die in the middle of the introduction. Secondly, she discovered that she was less frightened of dying than she was of dying alone.

She needed someone and cabled Randolph to see if young Winston could join her in New York for the Christmas holiday.

The original Churchill family plan was for Randolph, his wife, June, their six-year-old daughter, Arabella, and fifteen-year-old young Winston to congregate at Chartwell for Christmas with Clementine and old Winston, who had just retired from his second term as prime minister. Young Winston was scheduled to join Pamela after the holiday.

Pamela pleaded with Randolph to allow him to come earlier. AM SO LONELY AND ALONE WOULD MAKE ALL DIFFERENCE IF WINSTON COULD ARRIVE 20TH DECEMBER. PLEASE REPEAT PLEASE CABLE YOUR AGREEMENT. LOVE, PAMELA.[20]

Randolph relented. Winston arrived and he and his still-recuperating mother spent Christmas with the Whitneys.

Pamela returned to Europe in January but came back to New York in June for the hysterectomy and a two-week hospital stay. Discharged on June 30, she went straight to the Whitney's Greentree estate on Long Island for ten days, followed by another month on her own at their mansion on Fisher's Island. On August 11, having recovered most of her strength, she flew to Bermuda to spend a week with the Paleys, finally returning to Paris in September.

Thanks to generous friends, Pamela's convalescence was every bit as first class as her life when she was healthy.

Most of her friends checked in with her while she was ill, including Elie and Gianni, who called constantly. Averell was the major exception. They had seen each other once in the late 1940s in Paris, where he had successfully administered the Marshall Plan of postwar aid to Europe, but the encounter was not a memory to cherish. Averell criticized the way she was running around Europe with playboys. He advised her to straighten up and demonstrate some purpose in life, as he had.

He had returned from Paris to the United States in 1950 to run for president. *"Merde,"* said Marie Harriman when he told her his intentions. She had told him before that she would "jump off a bridge" if he ran for elective office, but once Averell made up his mind, his wife was a good sport and went along.

He ran for the Democratic nomination in 1952 but was disparaged by the political pros, who considered him haughty, imperious and boring and called him "Honest Ave the Hairsplitter."

He was trounced by the eventual nominee, Adlai Stevenson, but he was running again in 1956 and this was his excuse for going nowhere near his former girlfriend while she recuperated in New York Hospital. Kathleen Harriman visited. So did Ed Murrow, although his drop-by took a specific request from Clementine Churchill, who phoned Ed at CBS and asked him to stop by and try to cheer her up.

Pamela was pretty glum. Losing her child-bearing capability at the age of thirty-six did not bother her. She wanted no more children. No worries about birth control or another abortion were also plusses. Nor was she concerned about the unmarried life. All manner of serious people, including Averell, advised her to stop being frivolous, to marry and settle down, but she wasn't ready. She was put off by the constant admonitions. But she was disheartened that there was no real romantic involvement in her life.

Elie filled a void and was convenient, but there was no real sizzle with him as there had been with Ed and Gianni. With either of them, there had also been the possibility of a future. Not with Elie. However much he later proclaimed his love, their relationship was more a calculated partnership and business proposition than real romance. His support enabled her to continue her education because she was still looking, although precisely for what, she did not know. So much of her life had been guided by men that she was certain it would take another man before she discovered her niche.

Meanwhile, there was plenty to do. When not on call for Elie, she was wide open for other adventures, primarily in three distinct areas: decoration education with such men as Geffroy, Van Der Kemp and Boudin; the diplomats and writers circuit, including a variety of French intellectuals; and the glamour, glitz and gowns of café society.

All her experiences took place in a 1950s France that was bursting with newborn life after war and Occupation, reaching out with renewed optimism and hospitality. "It was a marvelous period, especially for Americans," said Susan Mary Alsop, who arrived from the United States in 1945 and stayed sixteen years. "The French had been locked up for four or five years and were bored stiff with one another's company. For once, they were extremely curious about Americans, very eager and very hospitable, which is not always the case."[21]

Journalist and author Theodore White came to Paris in 1948 to cover the Marshall Plan and found the city "still in its green and leafy heart, blessedly French. The old lavender and pewter buildings rose in the familiar fin de siècle shades and shapes of gray, the mansard skyline of the Impressionists still unspiked and unspoiled by new skyscrapers."

But if the city appeared unchanged physically, there had been an emotional transformation that White also spotted: "that Spring was something more than a season of the year: it was the beginning of a spring that lasted several years, a romance of politics between France and America, whose common purpose bloomed in Paris. Frenchmen were beginning to feel French again, but with a returning pride that still embraced Americans."[22]

Janet Flanner, whose wonderful "Paris Journal" dispatches described the rebirth of France to *New Yorker* magazine readers, wrote that same spring that "France is like someone who has unexpectedly climbed a very high hill and stands breathless and poised on the crest."[23]

Washington Post editor Ben Bradlee arrived in 1951 as the press attaché for the American embassy, switched to become a *Newsweek* correspondent in 1953 and remained based in Paris until 1957: "All expatriates think that their time in the foreign land is the best, but this seemed awfully good to all of us. We worked hard as hell and we played hard as hell."[24]

Pamela linked up with some of her old wartime London gang, including Irwin Shaw and photographer Bob Capa. Shaw and his wife, Marian, were living at 24 rue du Boccador, a handsome old apartment building with a wrought-iron elevator on a quiet street around the corner from the Hotel George V, not far from the Champs Elysée. Shaw's novel *The Young Lions* had been published in 1949 to great acclaim, and when he moved to Paris the following year, he instantly became one of the most prominent Americans in France. "He was rich, famous and the one handsome celebrity every hostess in Paris wanted to capture," Ann Buchwald said later.[25]

She would have known. Named Ann McGarry at the time, she and her then boyfriend, Art Buchwald, a twenty-five-year-old columnist for the Paris *Herald Tribune*, lived next door to each other in studios on the top floor. Art paid forty-five dollars a month for his; Ann, thirty-two dollars for hers. Teddy White and his wife, Nancy, had much more space in their third-floor apartment, one level up from the Shaws, which was why they paid a comparatively princely hundred dollars. Across from the Whites lived French film producer Raoul Levy, who, while they were all living there, discovered a young beauty named Brigitte Bardot, the symbol of the lush sensuality of France in the 1950s.

Irwin Shaw was a great favorite of Pamela's from the days when she first met him at the Churchill Club and went on to see more of him and his writing pals at the White Tower, a Soho hangout for journalists. She loved his looks. Shaw looked like a young lion or, at the very least, a young boxer. He had a head of tight dark curls, a great beaked nose, strong chin and powerful shoulders, oversize for the 175 pounds he carried on his nearly five-foot-ten frame.

Shaw walked like an athlete, with a hitch swagger up on the balls of his feet, and his languorous half-closed eyes could not disguise a wellspring of vitality and virility. The writer had a magnetic charm that made him irresistible to women and a warm sense of humor that smoothed the edges of banty-cock machismo. He had a swarm of girls eager to be with him. It was common in Paris to have a wonderful lunch, a great bottle of wine and retire to an apartment for a pleasant no-commitments finale. Shaw loved the routine.

Mary Welsh told her *Time* colleague Bill Walton that "Irwin was the best lay in Europe," while Carol Saroyan and Oona Chaplin said they had heard that he was also the best lay in Hollywood.[26]

Pamela knew that only secondhand. She never slept with Irwin, but he used to joke with her that if he hung around long enough, he might get lucky. She was not a regular at the Shaws', but she went by for dinner from time to time, in Paris and at their home in Klosters and a house they rented next to La Garoupe.

"When I first met her, I thought she was quite forthright and had opinions and was very upfront with them," said Marian Shaw, a former actress who was bright, funny, gorgeous, and a fabled hostess in her own right. "One dinner at our house when Gianni was not there, she kind of held the floor. But later she seemed to change her style and listen a great deal more."

At her own apartment, Pamela introduced guests individually by taking them by the arm, escorting them quickly around the room, whispering the name of each guest in their ear. "She was an extremely deft and gracious hostess," said Marian Shaw. "She was very discreet and very considerate of the men she was with."[27]

Bob Capa was almost inseparable from Shaw, so frequently at their house that Marian once told Irwin to throw him out, she was so sick of girls calling him day and night. Hungarian-born, Capa earned a reputation as the world's finest war photographer for his daring action images during the Spanish civil war, a renown he burnished during World War II. In addition to pure talent, he was bright, witty and irreverent and spoke an endearing fractured English friends called Capanese. Shaw had first met him in a New York bar and wrote later: "I recognized him immediately: the thick-lashed dark eyes, poetic and streetwise, like the eyes of a Neapolitan urchin, the curled, sardonic mouth with the eternal cigarette plastered to the lower lip."[28]

Like Shaw, Pamela knew Capa from London, where he too lived in the Dorchester until management tired of the endless parade of young women he brought up to his room and asked him to leave. She had nothing to do with a photo session he had with Lord Beaverbrook, who agreed to the sitting only because he thought Capa was Frank Capra, the Hollywood director, a misunderstanding the photographer did not dispel.[29] Indeed, Capa had changed his name from Andrei Friedmann, both to avoid anti-Semitism and in the hope that it might serve him better in precisely such situations.

She saw more of Capa in Paris, once meeting him and writer John Steinbeck at the Lancaster Hotel. Just back from Russia, where they had not had a hot bath for three weeks, one lay in the tub and the other sat naked waiting his turn, both regaling Pamela with stories of the horrors of their trip in between calls down to room service for more champagne.

Capa captivated Pamela the way he enchanted every woman. "All women adored Capa," said Ben Bradlee. "They mothered him. Then he fucked their brains out. His laissez-passer was that he was this little lost child."[30]

At a New York party, Capa announced that because U.S. immigration authorities refused to grant him a visa extension, he was being forced to leave the country. Toni Sorel, a lovely model who had met him that evening, said she would marry him the next day so he could stay.

Pamela did not tumble that far, but she did fall for Capa, who she thought was absolutely wonderful, not least for the day when he chased her laughing all the way down the steps of Sacre Coeur in Montmartre. "Everyone always talks about the rich men I have slept with, no one ever talks about the poor men I have slept with," Pamela once lamented to a woman friend in Paris.[31]

She did not specify anyone in particular, but the irrepressible Capa was a better candidate than most. He had champagne tastes — he bought his shirts and ties at Sulka — but a beer budget, and was called on the carpet in Paris for too many expense-account lunches, including one with Pamela.[32]

Her entrée to the circle of French intellectuals was provided by France's answer to Emerald Cunard and Olive, Lady Baillie — the poetess Louise de Vilmorin, who convened a salon at the family estate in Verrières-le-Buisson, forty minutes south of Paris, where she occupied one wing and her three brothers another. An extraordinary character who collected people — including a Texas Hunt and a string of European counts as husbands, and British ambassador Duff Cooper and man of letters and politician André Malraux as lovers — Louise fascinated Pamela.

Tall, lame and frail, she was famed for her wit and dazzling conversation. Every Sunday, Louise put a pot au feu on the dining room table and drew a crowd that included film director René Clair; dancer and choreographer Roland Petit, later director of the Paris Opera Ballet; playwright Marcel Achard, a longtime friend of Irwin Shaw; and author Maurice Druon.

Pamela found the bachelor Druon especially attractive. He fit all her criteria — handsome, smart, adroit, convivial, discreet, and beautifully mannered. He was a frequent guest at her lunches and dinner parties, but their relationship became more serious.

She introduced her father to the writer, who laughed at the recollection of how the "charming, portly, red-faced" baron would arrive in Paris with a suitcase filled with carnations from his garden at Minterne Magna, enough stems protected in water tubes so he would have a fresh flower for his lapel for each day of his visit. Pamela and Druon traveled together, visiting young Winston at Eton, and on several occasions went to Sussex in southern England to stay with Herbert Agar, the American essayist who married the Churchill Club's Barbie Wallace.

Going to Louise's and becoming involved with intellectuals like Druon gave Pamela a better postgraduate education than whatever she received at the Sorbonne or Louvre. She marveled at the intellectual byplay, often sitting for hours, knowing when to keep quiet about substance and absorbing everything she could from conversations which touched on politics but more often involved theater, dance, writers, art and music — the creative spectrum. She rarely delved deeper into the subjects under discussion through research on her own, but she was growing in knowledge every day if only by osmosis.

"She was no Simone de Beauvoir, but she was cultivated, and capable of reacting intuitively and sensibly," said a participant at many of Louise's soirees where Pamela was present.[33]

She was not so cultivated that the doors to France's most respectable drawing rooms were open to her. Her more scandalous escapades, especially betraying the respected Liliane de Rothschild, kept her from penetrating *le gratin,* France's upper crust.

Le gratin would come to her when she returned in triumph in 1993, but she did not need the true upper crust then, with one notable exception. In April 1957, when Queen Elizabeth II made her first state visit to France as queen, Pamela launched an all-out campaign to be included at the British embassy's reception for the monarch. When no invitation was forthcoming, a bevy of Pamela's friends called to ensure that she was invited, but to no avail. So intense was the pressure that Cynthia Jebb, wife of the then British ambassador, Sir Gladwyn Jebb, exploded, declaring that Pamela would not be invited because, "I will not have that tart in this embassy."[34]

Otherwise uninterested in France's shortlived Fourth Republic coalition governments, underwhelmed by the blueness of anyone's blood and footloose enough to disregard convention, Pamela had more than enough to keep her busy in the crowd at Louise's and the other local set, *la bande,* of writers, artists and actors organized by Diana Cooper and supplemented by such visiting Britons as Waugh, Stephen Spender, Cecil Beaton, Chips Channon and Harold Nicolson.

As ambassador and glamorous lady, the Coopers operated at the very center of Parisian society from the liberation of France in 1944 until Duff left the job and returned briefly to England in 1947. Food, drink and political and physical warmth were available in abundance during the critical years they occupied Britain's glorious embassy on the rue Faubourg St.-Honoré — library designed by Georges Geffroy — and where their *salon vert* was thronged daily.

Pamela knew them slightly then but saw more of them after she moved to France in 1948, as the Coopers had returned immediately on Duff's retirement from the Foreign Office. They took up residence outside Paris in the great park of the Château de Chantilly in the smaller, serene Château de St. Firmin, the broad lawn of which featured chestnuts and elms and ran down to a lake with fountains, a perfect country retreat for a gentleman ambassador.[35]

Diana Cooper, a former actress, perennial socialite, pen pal of Evelyn Waugh and perpetual center of whatever orb in which she circulated, was another role model for Pamela. Married to Duff in 1919, the year before Pamela was born, Diana was born Lady Diana Manners, an aristocrat who, by going on stage at a time when actresses were equated with whores, took the kind of risk that the descendant of Jane Digby could appreciate.

Like Olive, Emerald and Louise, Diana was intelligent and charming and could draw the most interesting people to her gatherings; unlike them, she was ravishingly beautiful. Her "flawless, awe-inspiring beauty," said Violet Trefusis, could light up a room.[36] "She looks and moves like Helen of Troy," was Chips Channon's assessment.[37]

Diana adored her husband, Duff, and everyone whom he loved, which was no small number. There seemed to be not a jealous bone in her body. Despite Duff's affair with Louise, Diana thought Louise was marvelous. "Louise opened all her petals as suddenly and as gloriously as a night-flowering cereus," she described their first dinner together. Louise was "the hub and heart" of *la bande*. "It was Louise who let in the light to an Embassy that might have been as drab as embassies often are," Diana said.[38]

The American journalist Joseph Alsop said the same and more about Diana: "England's most golden brilliant young men were half, three-quarters or altogether in love with her." So was Pamela. To her, Diana's combination of traits was unbeatable and so she adopted several.

One was Diana's intimidating stare. In Diana's case, the blind stare was primarily caused by bad eyesight. Rather than acknowledge the disability, the former actress turned it to queenly advantage. Pamela assumed the look for protection, an invisible seal to hold off unwanted approaches.

Diana's parties always had to have a special touch, perhaps a theme or a decoration that would sear them into the memories of the guests. A Christmas party for 150 included a present with a name on every package, individually selected for each guest. For a dinner for Field Marshal Montgomery, she imported a thousand red roses and a young woman who had fought with the French Resistance. The woman sang ballads about the underground effort and brought the guests to tears and cheers.[39]

The size of the group did not matter. "Every meal, even lunch with two guests," said Susan Mary Alsop, "was a piece of theater for Diana; one never glimpsed the effort or machinery behind the scenes." And one would not with Pamela's seamless productions either.

Pamela shared some less attractive qualities of Diana's as well. Both were covetous and always ready to accept cash or presents from men, a fairly common trait among people who circulate with others far wealthier. Diana was twenty-eight years older than Pamela, but she too took money from Lord Beaverbrook, whom she called "this strange attractive gnome with an odour of genius about him."[40]

Both also shared a reluctance to pay out money to settle debts. Diana was once sued by a plastic surgeon when she tore up his bill for a thousand dollars and said that instead she would recommend him to her friend the queen of Romania.[41] Pamela's unwillingness to settle her own prewar gambling debts was merely a hint of things to come when faced with resolving estate and various monetary disputes in later years.

On the other hand, Pamela could not tolerate Duff. He was infamous for his "veiners," raging tantrums when the veins on his forehead popped out and throbbed and his face turned purple. Pamela had no interest in argumentative Englishmen who could not hold their temper or liquor. Randolph's screaming fits had given her sufficient experience with that brand of irascibility. (The two infamous tempers clashed directly one evening in the Paris embassy after he and Pamela had separated. Randolph engaged in a screaming battle over the Nuremberg war trials with Duff, who slapped him on both sides of the head and, forehead vein thumping, excoriated his guest's rudeness, drunkenness and immorality until Randolph ran off into the darkness while guests stared, mouths agape.)[42]

One night Pamela would be with the intellectuals at Louise's, another with a bunch of Americans who wanted to go out and eat well or drink late at a place like the elegant Chez Carrère, at 45 rue Pierre-Charon, which was a favorite hangout for Shaw, Capa, Viertel, the Buchwalds, director John Huston, the model Bettina, who dated Aly Khan, and where Edith Piaf and Yves Montand sang.[43]

Or she was in a gown at a costume ball given by Arturo Lopez, a Chilean billionaire with a Louis XIV complex, whose yacht, the *Gaviana IV*, his Neuilly house and grottoed garden and his collection of fifteenth-century art were legendary.

Carlos de Beistegui, or Charlie, as he was known to his friends, was a very wealthy Mexican-Spaniard renowned for his eye for beautiful women and for his decorating skills. He threw garish parties at Groussay, his eighteenth-century château on the outskirts of Paris. Pamela was a regular guest at Charlie's parties, but they were not to everyone's taste. "A despised little worm" was how Diana Cooper once characterized Beistegui.[44]

Cecil Beaton found Groussay ostentatious: "a re-creation created against, and to spite, the present times. Here, inside a Russian facade, is a long-discarded Victorian England peopled with Beistegui's French, Spanish-Mexican and South American weekend guests. They wear English tweeds, English cashmere jerseys, English brogues. They skim through the *Illustrated London News* and walk on lawns until it is nearly lunchtime when tasselled footmen serve marrow or drippings on toast with a glass of Madeira. Conversation is mainly about those who do, or do not, possess great taste — or great furniture. The host does not encourage political argument or controversial or inflammatory subjects. Unfashionable pursuits or unpopular personalities are distasteful. Here is one place where, at whatever cost — and the cost must be astronomical — the outside is determinedly kept at bay."

Beaton had nothing good to say about his host, either. "Beistegui is utterly ruthless: such qualities as sympathy, pity or even gratitude are completely lacking. He is without a doubt the most self-engrossed and pleasure-seeking person I have met," and in the lofty circles in which Beaton traveled, he had met many.[45]

Pamela was hardly one to criticize a materialistic pleasure seeker, not if he followed such pursuits tastefully. She was enchanted by Groussay and by Charlie's Palazzo Labia in Venice, which boasted a Tiepolo fresco — *The Banquet of Cleopatra* — and where she spent a summer with him. The provocatively named Labia was the site of the most spectacular ball of 1951, when fifty gondolas filled with gowned, jeweled and bewigged guests costumed as eighteenth-century pashas, princesses and pages paraded regatta-style up the Grand Canal past thousands of applauding spectators to a gala which ended the next morning with guests still dancing on the piazza.[46] Photographs which immortalized the event were taken by none other than the disapproving Beaton.

Pamela was generally about in Paris, sometimes escorted by homosexual walkers, at other times by distinctly hetero escorts, or entertaining at home most nights. How did she keep coming up with things to wear? Christian Dior, who taught her that her red hair meant she should wear the right red and not avoid the color as she had all her life, dined with her, gave her some clothes and sold her others at reduced prices. But she also was fitted by and bought couture from Balenciaga and Chanel. Did Elie pay for lavish gowns when he was never able to escort her to a ball? Pamela does not say.

But such glamour did not come cheap and designers' largesse rarely extended to gowns. At a ball given by Marie-Laure de Noailles at her huge house on the place des Etats-Unis, Diana Cooper came in character as Lady Blessington, the novelist and famous English beauty; Pamela came in pale blue as Titania, the glamorous and powerful Queen of the Fairies from Shakespeare's *Midsummer Night's Dream*.[47] Pamela hosted one of the preball dinners at her apartment and, ever thoughtful to provide extra enhancement, brought in a hairdresser, Monsieur Guillaume, and two assistants for last-minute touch-ups.[48]

Many Christmases throughout the 1950s Pamela spent at the Palace Hotel in Saint Moritz. With custody of her son shared with

Randolph, young Winston came on school breaks from Eton and Oxford, but his skiing fanaticism meant that she saw little of him. Winston was usually among the first on the mountain shortly after dawn and the last to leave at dusk when he moved on to his own party circuit.

Pamela spent more of her time socializing with the crowd that included the shipping tycoons Onassis and Niarchos. Ari Onassis loved old Winston Churchill, invited him on Mediterranean cruises aboard his opulent 325-foot seagoing mansion, the *Christina*, and, in return, was invited for lunches at Chartwell.

But Pamela never liked Ari. He was too earthy, vulgar and ugly for her tastes. She was not amused by his smashing crockery in a restaurant, then leaping to his feet to join a bunch of Greek sailors dancing the *syrtaki* shoulder to shoulder.[49] His volatile temper, especially when drunk, made her uncomfortable. Such lack of dignity and control are anathema to Pamela, who still has a handwritten note of abject apology from Onassis for an unexplained, embarrassing transgression one evening in the south of France.

Stavros Niarchos, the great business rival and estranged brother-in-law of Onassis, was more Pamela's type. She considers him a great and enduring friend. Cultured, educated, private, with an aristocratic face and a supple, smooth skin that women gushed over, and exuding power as well as wealth, Niarchos was a friend of the Windsors' and Gianni Agnelli's. Like Gianni, he had a mischievous sense of humor and had a Cap d'Antibes estate, Château de la Croë, the ceiling of which opened to the sky and stars.

Like Elie, he was an aesthete who had cordon bleu chefs, elegant furnishings and a priceless art collection, many of the best pieces of which he kept on the *Creole*, his 190-foot three-masted yacht on which Pamela cruised with him. Like both, he played hard — with a succession of wives, two of whom died in questionable circumstances, and a long series of mistresses — and worked hard. He was so absorbed with business that on safari he had chartered planes drop him information packets into the bush. Aboard the *Creole*, deck stewards in starched whites attended to guests while Niarchos pored over telexes and huddled with assistants. He could not tolerate being cut off from information.

Pamela absorbed the lesson. In later years, even in such relatively out-of-the-way places as Barbados and Sun Valley, she made certain that her important visitors always had newspapers or news summaries available and made arrangements that they be provided by special packet or fax when necessary.

Niarchos was very generous to friends and hard-working employees. He had a habit of putting aristocrats on his payroll, including Prince Alexander of Yugoslavia and the Marquess of Milford Haven, a nephew of Lord Mountbatten, and handing out diamond bracelets and fur coats to women he fancied.[50]

Just what he may have given to the daughter-in-law of Ari's yachting guest is not a topic they discuss, but it would have been completely in character for Stavros to have treated Pamela generously. Jan Cushing Amory, a pretty, blonde, well-born former girlfriend both of Niarchos and of young Winston, said that Pamela's son was well aware of his mother's relationship with Niarchos.

Amory was Niarchos's date at a St. Moritz New Year's party given by the Aga Khan in the late 1960s, when she first met young Winston. Niarchos told the young man, "Be a good boy, Winston, and bring me a vodka tonic, the way you used to bring me an orange juice with Mummy." The implication, of course, was that he brought the juice to them at breakfast. "I brought juice to Gianni," Winston retorted, "but I don't remember you." The shipping magnate roared with laughter at the comeback.[51]

Ever the eager student throughout her years in France, Pamela picked up an infinite number of pointers from the duchess of Windsor, whom admirers called "the best wife in the world" for the unending attention she lavished on her duke. Pamela is a seductress, but Wallis Warfield Simpson pulled off the seduction of the century. On the other hand, Wallis ended up in exile with one of society's shallowest men, so the advantage may ultimately still go to Pamela.

Most intelligent people found the former king a dimwit. "I think him stupid as well as a prejudiced man," said Marietta Tree after dining with the duke.[52] Diana Cooper called both Windsors "pathetic" and him "much duller and sillier."[53] But to Pamela, the duke was a charming conversationalist who was eager to natter on about the old days in England or various races and shoots he had attended.

The duchess was much sharper. Pamela appreciated her shrewdness and power of calculation. She was mesmerized by her impeccable taste and the treasures they had removed from Buckingham Palace and displayed to perfection. Beyond mere presentation of the pieces was the aura of history emanating from their ties to royalty.

Other hostesses might also be able to set their table with a quartet of eighteenth-century George II saltcellars, but no one else could say, as did the duchess, "These belonged to my husband's great, great-something, granduncle, the Duke of Cumberland, the one the Scots call The Butcher of Culloden. *We* prefer to think of him as the sportsman who bred Eclipse, the greatest racehorse in the history of the turf. You know, 'Eclipse first, the rest nowhere.' "[54]

The added impact of historical association was not lost on Pamela, who dined with the Windsors several times a month and studied every move the duchess made.

She noted how the duchess watched her husband constantly. If he were cold, she got him a wrap or promptly summoned a doctor. If he were stuck in an unpleasant conversation or too long with a dance partner, she rescued him. She monitored his diet. Before a dinner party, she briefed him on all the guests, what subjects he should address and avoid. Her biographer Ralph Martin said that "she was not only his wife and sweetheart, but his sister and mother."[55]

No detail of their home was too small to ignore. The duchess searched endlessly for just the right piece of furniture, which was eighteenth-century French. The tables were covered with a collection of gold, porcelain and enameled bibelots, each sitting on a piece of felt cut to its exact shape so as not to scratch the antique. If one were particularly delicate, she placed it on a wax impression so the piece would not shake. She took original boiserie and panels of faded chinoiserie wallpaper and had them restored, copied exactly where necessary and reinstalled. Historic paintings and photos in polished silver frames were scattered about the drawing room and library, giving the house a personal touch.[56]

In a successful attempt to remove some of the museum-quality feel of the house, its private rooms exuded coziness, with soft chairs designed for comfort and pillows in profusion. "However palatial," wrote Martin, "there was still a classic simplicity about most of the furnishings. Flowers were everywhere in giant arrangements with a vivid use of color. They gave the home a warmth and intimacy."[57]

Days before any entertaining, the chef sent sample menus and wine lists. Tables were rarely larger than for eight. Once seated, the duchess kept a small gold book in which she wrote notes about the guests, the meal, something she had heard or wanted to pursue. A small bell sat by the duke to summon service instantly, which was how he liked it. The women adjourned to the drawing room after the meal, but the separation lasted only moments before the duchess was back summoning the men to rejoin the ladies. Later, she would list in another book the menu, wines, seating plan and any parlor games they might have played, so no guest would ever be forced to endure a repeat of too similar an evening.

All these touches Pamela later adopted and adapted. She even improved upon the one aspect of the Windsors' entertaining that was singularly unimpressive — the guests, who tended to be boring social climbers. "The café society the duchess took up with in Paris was downright trashy," said Cecil Beaton. Cyrus Sulzberger agreed, describing the guests at one Windsor dinner in the 1950s as "a weird collection of social derelicts."[58]

By 1958, Pamela had had a very good run in France, but she was approaching forty, an age at which — however unfairly — rich European men look for younger mistresses. Her string was running out. Elie de Rothschild had kept her well for nearly six years, but, like Gianni Agnelli, he was not going to marry her. He did discuss the possibility of divorcing Liliane. But as was the case with Gianni, discussion did not lead anywhere.

Pamela was not surprised. Years later, Pamela told herself that she could not marry Elie just as she could not marry Gianni because he, too, was a European — although in his case a POW, not a former Axis officer — and old Winston did not want her to marry such a man. But that was another rationalization.

Pamela was not as anxious to marry Elie as she had been Gianni. She liked him, but he was a colder man and she did not love him. The relationship had fulfilled its purpose for her, but it had a studied quality to it and lacked zest. There was also a problem about young Winston: her son liked Gianni, who was kind and generous to him, but hated Elie, for whom The Child was simply baggage and who could not stand him either. Elie turned a perpetual cold shoulder on Winston and literally closed the boy out when he wanted time with his mother.

Ultimately, the choice was not Pamela's. Elie decided on his own after speaking with several friends. When he consulted Loel Guinness, by then married to Pamela's friend Gloria, Elie was told that if he were contemplating leaving Liliane to make an honest woman of Pamela, not to bother. The issue was whether he loved Pamela enough to break up the marriage with Liliane. He did not.

Several other factors were involved. One was that rich French men, like rich Italian men, rarely — very rarely in the 1950s — left their wives to marry their mistresses. The journalist Taki Theodoracopulos, a polo teammate of Elie's, was adamant on the point: "Elie is a man who never, ever, ever would divorce his wife to marry his mistress. European Jews, like Catholics, don't trade in their wives for a new model."

Some do, but Elie never has. After Pamela, he had a long affair with the late Françoise de Langlade, editor-in-chief of French *Vogue*, who later married couturier Oscar de la Renta; in the 1980s and 1990s, he was involved with a French gallery owner by whom, friends say, he had a child. By those later stages in their marriage, Liliane de Rothschild was less worried about losing her husband.

Even if he had been inclined to marry Pamela, the late 1950s were a difficult time for Elie to contemplate divorce because his cousin Guy de Rothschild had recently taken the step and wreaked havoc within the family. In 1957, Guy ended his twenty-year marriage to Alix, whom the family loved, to marry Marie-

Hélène Van Zuylen, a twenty-six-year-old Catholic divorcée with a Vatican annulment.

The divorce and remarriage of the forty-eight-year-old Baron Guy — to a glamorous and controversial woman whose grandmother was herself a Rothschild who married a Catholic — created a family scandal and a sensation throughout Europe. For the first time in French Rothschild history, the head of a family branch married a woman outside the faith. Guy resigned the presidency of the Jewish community in France, passing the position to his cousin Alain, Elie's older brother.[59] No one in the family was eager to see the then forty-one-year-old Elie leave the most popular Rothschild woman to marry *his* Catholic divorcée with her annulment.

One of the most oft-told anecdotes about Pamela is how she learned that the affair with Elie was over. The story — uncorroborated by either Pamela or Elie, but repeated as fact with almost lip-smacking glee by several of their friends — involves Pamela returning to her apartment on the avenue de New York for a staff meeting and not finding her regular butler, who was due to assist with a dinner party. She called Elie's office to find out what had held him up. The butler would no longer be assisting Madame, she was told. She was on her own.

CHAPTER TWELVE

Leland

PAMELA IS NOT A SULKER. She cries when she is hurt or upset, but she does not wallow in self-pity. When she is angry, her mouth stretches taut and flattens across her teeth; her blue eyes turn the color of pond ice, steely opaque. When discouraged, she picks herself up, turns aggressive and seizes the next available opportunity.

Her decade in France was fun, profitable and offered a spectacular education. Being there fit an important criterion: from the long hemline and full skirt of Christian Dior's "New Look" to the Marshall Plan, NATO and Jean-Paul Sartre, France was the place to be, the center of the postwar social, political and intellectual action in the late 1940s and 1950s. Sociological Zelig that she is, naturally, that's where Pamela was.

By the end of the fifties, events had shifted to the U.S. and she was becoming itchy. She had tried to move to the States with Murrow after the war but failed and settled for France. A dozen years later, she would have stayed in France had her relationship with Elie worked out, but the longer it lasted, the more she realized it too would fail.

She saw friends like Gloria Guinness bag rich husbands, but Pamela's aim was higher than Gloria's and her shots missed. Part of her problem was that her targets were too prominent and she was too visible and too obvious an adventurer. She had too big a reputation as a geisha to too many rich and powerful men. The well-known ones comprised a virtual fraternity. Women talked about "Pammy's club" and wondered whether this one or that was the newest member.

Myths enhanced her reputation. Was it true that a German industrialist asked her to pick out any car she wanted as a gift, that she specified a certain top-of-the-line model with special upholstery but asked that he give her the money so she could order and pick it up herself? And how excited the man was when she showed off the precise car she had described, unaware that another man had already given it to her? They could not corroborate the story, but it sounded so Pammy and they loved laughing about it. One of Pamela's less well off admirers said that he was living proof that wealth was not her sole interest, but he did concede with a certain understatement that "she had a reputation for liking money."[1]

Writer Peter Viertel knew her in the Tout Paris crowd and determined that she was addicted to the good life. "Virginia Hill, the girlfriend of Bugsy Siegel, once said that when she was seventeen, one of the gangsters bought her a fur coat. The next year she got a lesser gift, went back and said, 'You son of a bitch, you spoiled me. Now keep it up.' I think that sort of applies to Pamela."[2]

Draping herself and home in finery, hosting parties or simply cashing checks was important, but that was not Pamela's primary goal. She had been pathological about money ever since the Randolph experience and would remain so the rest of her life. Still, she was no mere gold digger. She liked interesting, powerful men and would settle for no less. She wanted a good two-way relationship: a man whom she could indulge as much as he indulged her. If she married, the duchess of Windsor could count on losing another title: Pamela would be the best wife in the world. But it was not going to happen in Europe, where too many men agreed with Sir James Goldsmith's axiom that when a man marries his mistress, he creates a job vacancy.

Elie was final proof that while rich European men housed her, gave her servants, decked her in jewels and gowns, bought her cars and airplane tickets, took her on yachts, or sometimes just to the movies, and remained friends years after they stopped sleeping with her, they would never marry her.

In sales terms, Pamela could not close. That was not so important in her early thirties, when it was enough to enjoy life without stopping to think about tomorrow, but those days were slipping away. In seeking the right someone who would commit, she needed an American.

From what she had learned about Americans during the war, Pamela tended to agree with Nancy Mitford's depiction in *The Blessing,* a wonderful period novel about a beautiful, aristocratic, but somewhat less than brilliant English country girl living in France in midcentury, that "in America, if you hold a woman's hand you are expected to go round the next day with the divorce papers."[3] She had charmed and been charmed by Americans since childhood. Babe and Bill Paley helped her find one of her own in New York.

Entertaining Pamela was expected when she crossed the Atlantic. After all, no one was a more hospitable host than she when American friends visited Paris. But Babe Paley did not like Pamela, whom she called "that bitch," and was not enthusiastic about this visit.

Barbara Cushing Paley was Betsey Cushing Whitney's sister. Both Cushing girls were wary of a Pamela Churchill on the prowl, given her history with their husbands, Bill Paley and Jock Whitney, and their fears that she was coming around for another try. Pamela was well aware of their concern. She knew that Betsey feared that she was after Jock and that Babe did not trust her at all. That did not mean that they avoided each other, simply that everyone was careful.

The Whitneys would have hosted Pam at Greentree, but in 1956, Dwight Eisenhower had named Jock U.S. ambassador to Britain. He and Betsey were living in London, so the assignment went to Babe. She asked Nancy "Slim" Hayward, who was going to Europe that week, if she could borrow her husband, Broadway producer Leland Hayward, one night as Pamela's escort to the theater. Slim did not think twice about the request. If she had, Leonora Hornblow later pointed out, Slim might have realized that "here, into their midst, was the vixen."[4]

The two women hardly knew each other, but Pamela had given Slim a lunch once in Paris and had been delightful. Slim said fine to Babe's request and flew to Madrid to party with Lauren "Betty" Bacall. According to a close friend of the late Babe, there was a larger purpose to the date: "This was a plot by the Cushing girls to get Pam off their backs by linking her up with Leland. These were smart ladies who knew the game and were going to deal with this problem. They weren't really doing the dirty to Slim because Slim was the worst wife in the world."[5]

Slim was three years older than Pamela, a California girl who had been married to movie mogul Howard Hawks before she married agent-producer Leland Hayward in 1949. By 1958, their marriage was in deep trouble. A vivacious sophisticate, but also a moody character known for her caustic bitchiness — or as she put it, "my tendency to go for the sarcastic conversation stopper" — Slim was the first to admit that "I wasn't always adorable."[6]

In a marriage of peaks and valleys, the recent years had been all troughs. "More often than not I felt I was an underpaid nanny saddled with troubled children. Every time the phone rang, it seemed, it would be the Menninger Clinic calling to say that Billy Hayward had run away or Stockbridge [the Austen Riggs Foundation] announcing that Bridget had had a seizure or a tearful Brooke recounting the usual troubles in a young marriage."[7]

Slim was flagrantly adulterous and running away from Leland so often that most of her friends thought she was trying to get rid of him anyway. She certainly was unconcerned about Leland taking Pamela to see *A Raisin in the Sun*.

Pamela had met Leland once before, on producer Alexander Korda's yacht when she was living with Gianni. Leland remembered when they gathered for drinks at the Paleys'. She knew who he was: after a long career as an agent and producer, Leland

Hayward was a big, powerful name. They hit it off immediately. She looked fabulous in brown taffeta with her red hair and blue eyes. "Ravishing," said Leonora Hornblow, who saw her at the theater.[8]

From the first moment, Pamela thought Leland was fascinating. He was creative, trenchantly funny, foulmouthed in an engaging way and kept her laughing most of the way to the theater. They were having such a good time together that the action on stage became a distraction. At intermission, he and Pamela thanked the Paleys and left.

Later that night, Pamela called their hosts at home.

"Bill, you're not going to believe where I am."

"No, I'm not, Pam. Where are you?"

"I'm right here in bed with Leland."[9]

Both she and Leland laughed. Telling Paley guaranteed that word would spread. Soon after, Leland told Random House founder Bennett Cerf that "she's absolutely great in bed" and could do sensational tricks with ice cubes.[10] Leland's assessment differed in tone, but not necessarily in substance, from the Paris reports that sex was not of paramount importance to Pamela. It was not, but she reacted to the particular situation. Her response to Leland, who was new, excitable and enthralled, was heartfelt and fervent.

The affair took off like a shot. They went out several more times and Leland told her that his marriage was a mess, that Slim was bored and irritated with him and was running around on him in the Hemingway crowd and elsewhere. All he wanted to do was theater work. At the end of the week, Pamela returned to Paris, where Slim and Betty Bacall had arrived from Madrid to meet Leland.

At the Ritz Hotel, Slim was handed a number of phone messages. Mrs. Churchill's car was outside and at her disposal. Mrs. Churchill had planned a dinner for Mrs. Hayward. Slim could not figure out Pamela's sudden interest. Pamela invited the two women for supper, which involved comfortable gossip and chatter until Pam asked, "Are you happy in your marriage?" "I stupidly said something like 'No marriage is perfect,' " Slim admitted.

A phone call interrupted the cozy dinner. Slim did not realize it until later, but Leland was calling from New York to report on his arrival the next day. Pamela waited for Slim to tell her that Leland was coming, then invited her to another dinner party for twenty with him to be followed by the theater.

In the car en route to the play, Pamela sat next to him, also at the theater, where Slim sat several rows ahead. Finally, Pamela took them to the Lido nightclub, where she danced with Leland. All Slim wondered was who was picking up the tab. "It didn't occur to me to wonder why Pam was providing all this for us."[11]

The next day, Slim and Leland flew to Munich, where he was negotiating with Baroness Von Trapp over rights to the family's story, which would become *The Sound of Music*. Slim forgot about Pam, but in the course of eleven bargaining sessions with the baroness in the first half of 1959, including some that may have been superfluous but offered a good excuse to stop in Paris, Leland continued to see Pamela.

In February, Slim — who was no longer so slim — went to the Main Chance spa in Arizona to diet for a week. Pamela sped to New York. When Slim returned, she was surprised that Leland had accepted a dinner for them both at Pam's the following night, a Sunday, when they never drove from Long Island into Manhattan.

The surprise turned to anger when she arrived at Pamela's suite to find it filled with the Sterling Silver hybrid roses that Leland had always sent to her. Still, Slim was too myopic or too uncaring to take the threat to her already wobbly marriage seriously. In fact, the inroads had been made. After Pamela's thirty-ninth birthday that spring, the fifty-seven-year-old Leland proposed, telling her that he would ask Slim for a divorce after *Gypsy* opened on May 21.

Pamela was elated. She liked Leland a great deal. For all his surface toughness, he had an air of vulnerability about him that she found very appealing. It was obvious that he was captivated. But she had heard these divorce promises before, especially the part about how the wife would not stand in the way.

She knew better from Ed Murrow. What happened in real life, she found, was that once the man confronted the decision, he almost invariably backed down. Leland did seem different and she had faith that he meant what he said, but she was not taken in by the sweet talk. If he were to go through with it, she had to force the action. It would never happen otherwise.

Her friends in Paris told her not to be silly. If Leland really loved her and wanted to marry her, she should tell him to go to New York, get divorced and come back to Paris with a wedding ring. Until he did, she should stay put in her sumptuous apartment and not disrupt her life. That was a nice, romantic concept, but Pamela knew that waiting was the path to disaster.

If this was what it appeared — real love — then she did not want to lose her opportunity. In his enthusiasm and directness, Leland encapsulated so many American characteristics that she liked and had missed. She could not afford to stay torn because, while it was a gamble to pull up stakes and move to New York, it was a bigger gamble not to act.

On the other hand, she argued to herself, how much of a gamble? If she stayed in Paris, she could be trapped and end up with no one. Elie was not a marriage candidate; Leland could not move to Paris. She had been there eleven years. Long enough. Like Jane Digby, it was time to reinvent herself.

She had been warned that Leland had a difficult family situation, but she was willing to take the chance. In New York on the arm of a theatrical legend, she would have entrée to all of America, from Broadway to Hollywood. As always, she knew that ultimately she had to rely on herself, but this was her best option. If she got her foot in the door, she could deal with whatever obstacles lay behind it.

Pamela cleared out of Paris as fast as she could — within a matter of weeks in the summer of 1959. Marina Sulzberger went by the avenue de New York apartment while Pamela was packing and was astonished, she told Susan Mary Patten, to find both Gianni Agnelli and Elie de Rothschild in the living room.

"Marina expected these two men would be perfectly nice but not on speaking terms and there they were as friendly as you can imagine, saying 'Oh, Rothschild, you're going to miss Pam terribly; so am I.' 'By the way, Pam, that pretty chair there [which had been a present from one or the other], you'll take that with you to New York, of course.' No question of giving it back. No question of giving anything back. 'That necklace,' oh, forget it.

Marina said it was the most comical scene. Absolute farce. Pam saying, 'Oh, come on, Elie, come on, Gianni: you know I shouldn't have that.' She eventually got everything. Pretty nifty things too."[12]

One nifty thing was that Gianni did not ask her to give back the apartment. Pamela turned it over to a broker, who sold it for five hundred thousand dollars, which she pocketed. Elie had given her a maisonette on Hyde Park Gardens in London which she decorated in ice-blue satin and kept as a legal base for Winston. In the meantime, she moved lock, stock and barrel to the Drake Hotel in New York City.

Winston, then an almost-nineteen-year-old Oxford student, arrived to join her for the summer, relieved that the affair with the despised Elie was over and eager to learn about the American he expected was his stepfather-to-be.[13]

Leland Hayward was producing *Gypsy,* starring Ethel Merman, on Broadway at the time, as well as closing the deal for *Sound of Music,* which turned out to be the apex of one of the theater world's most dazzling careers. A thin, fidgety and intense man with an infectious grin and beseeching blue eyes, Hayward wore a crew cut, casual clothes and loafers which gave him the look, said a contemporary, of an aging Ivy League freshman: "His tanned face wears a look of tense enthusiasm when he is with friends, and a blank, washed-out expression when confronting a movie executive."[14]

His face was craggy but debonair. Women didn't find him handsome; they thought he was adorable. He exuded vitality and attentiveness. "He was a sharpie and a tough guy," said James Michener with affection.[15]

Such a sharpie that in 1948 he had tried in vain to purchase from Michener for five hundred dollars all theatrical rights to *Tales of the South Pacific* behind the back of his own Broadway partners, Richard Rodgers and Oscar Hammerstein.[16] But not such a tough guy. "He pretended to be tough, but he was the warmest friend I ever had," said Josh Logan, a frequent producing partner.[17]

Unlike any Englishman or European Pamela had known, Leland was quintessentially American. Born in 1902 in Nebraska City, Nebraska, he grew up playing along the banks of the Missouri River, the only son of Colonel William Hayward and the former Sarah Ireland and the grandson of Monroe Leland Hayward, U.S. senator from Nebraska.

Will Hayward became Nebraska's youngest county judge, but when he lost an election for state legislature, he moved the family to New York, where he became a successful lawyer and a U.S. attorney. When the United States entered World War I, he trained the army's first black regiment, the 369th Infantry Regiment of Harlem. He led the unit to France, where he commanded the regiment at the front under fire for more than six months, winning it citations for valor and himself the croix de guerre and membership in the Légion d'Honneur.

Leland went to a succession of boarding schools, finally graduated from Hotchkiss and in 1920 went on to Princeton, where he promptly flunked out. His father stopped his allowance and got him a job as a twenty-five-dollar-a-week reporter on the *New York Sun*, which fired him so quickly that Will Hayward had to talk Princeton into readmitting his son.

Two months later, Leland quit to marry Lola Gibbs, a beautiful Texas socialite and pilot who taught him to fly. His passion for flight lasted all Leland's life but not his passion for Lola. The marriage barely made it past a year. In 1930, they remarried but soon hit the rocks again and broke up for good in 1934.

Along the way, Leland held a series of jobs which eventually brought him to Hollywood as a producer of twenty silent pictures for First National. "They stunk," he said later. "I had Claudette Colbert in one picture with Frank Capra directing and it was so foul that neither of them could get another job in pictures for three years."[18]

His career as a talent agent began by chance in 1926 when he was drinking at the Trocadero nightclub. The proprietor, lamenting his paltry business, said, "I'd pay three or four thousand dollars a week to get an attraction to pull the crowds in here. Somebody like the Astaires, for instance."

Hayward stood up, went straight to the theater where Fred and his sister, Adele Astair, were playing in *Lady, Be Good!* and passed on the offer. They signed up for four thousand dollars and Leland collected his four hundred dollars every week of their twelve-week run at the Trocadero. "The pickings were so easy," he said. "I decided this was my line of work."

Next, he went to John Rumsey, president of the American Play Company, a well-established literary agency, and talked him into giving him office space and half the commission on any plays or books Leland might sell. As soon as he moved in, Leland removed the fusty theatrical photos from the walls of his office. He painted the walls vivid reds and oranges, put down a bright blue-and-yellow carpet and, to avoid the sound of ringing, installed a light to bathe his room in magenta to alert him to incoming phone calls. When Rumsey complained about the cost of the renovations, Hayward responded with his life's guiding principle: "Put up an impressive front, Jack, if you want to make money."

The paint was barely dry when he began making money fast. By 1927, Hollywood was turning out talkies. The motion picture industry had become an insatiable maw for properties and talent, actors and writers. Leland signed up some of the brightest stars because he held out for high salaries and would do almost anything to keep his clients happy. With Hollywood agent Myron Selznick, he launched the first talent raids on studios, which broke the producers' collusionary control over pay scales. Stars like Myrna Loy and Fredric March found that Hayward could get them up to five times what they had been earning.

Once, Hayward introduced writer Charles MacArthur to producer Irving Thalberg as "the greatest writer in America today." Thalberg offered him a thousand dollars a week and MacArthur, who was unemployed and broke, reached for his pen. Hayward knocked his arm aside and coolly informed Thalberg that MacArthur's fee was twenty-five hundred a week. The writer blanched. Thalberg laughed and said the highest he would go was twelve-fifty. Hayward told him to forget it and hustled out the door the horrified MacArthur, who was ready to hit his agent. As they were leaving the lot, a Thalberg flunky stopped them. If they would return to the office, the producer was ready to sign for twenty-five hundred dollars.

Service mattered as much as money. Ernest Hemingway signed up with Leland after hearing what the agent did for a client, writer Donald Ogden Stewart. Stewart told Hemingway that when he had to make an unexpected trip to Europe when the banks were closed, Leland raced around town cashing small checks at restaurants and bars, loaned him a thousand dollars and made all the passport and travel arrangements for the Stewarts' child and nanny to follow. When a troubled client was ordered by a doctor to chop wood for therapy, Hayward sent him three tree trunks.[19]

By 1932, Hayward gave back the one-third share he had purchased in the American Play Company in return for clear title on all his clients. He and Selznick opened their own office on Madison Avenue, where Leland installed a roof garden, a twenty-two-foot-long desk that had once been an Italian monastery dining table, a set of sunlamps, a glass-enclosed shower and, gadget-freak that he always was, a phonograph that played two dozen records in succession.

Later, when he began wearing fine-cut flannel suits, a Calder mobile dangled from the ceiling, and a Klee, a Picasso, a Grant Wood and two Braques graced the walls. His favorite position was supine on one of several sofas or in deep, cushioned arm chairs. Dubbed "the Toscanini of the telephone" by writer George Axelrod, he would stretch out and conduct business, juggling up to six calls at a time on phones sitting on his thighs, stomach and chest.

He flew his own plane seventeen hours each way three times a month between New York and Hollywood and had a thousand-dollar standing bet with Selznick that Myron would kill himself by overwork before Leland killed himself flying. Hayward signed up so many clients that he never met most of them. When he walked into a Los Angeles party given by his librettist team of Russel Crouse and Howard Lindsay, he looked around and asked, "Who are all these strangers?" They were all his West Coast clients.

The East Coast was always Leland's coast and not just because of his New York and school roots. "As far as a producer is concerned, the theater is the best place for intellectual ideas," he said, explaining why he did not like to stray far from Broadway.[20]

A custom evolved whereby he spoke to no client who earned less than thirty-five hundred dollars a week. That left plenty to talk to, including movie stars Clark Gable, Ginger Rogers, Helen Hayes, Katharine Hepburn, Gregory Peck, Cary Grant, Henry Fonda, James Stewart, Greta Garbo and Judy Garland. In addition to Hemingway and MacArthur, his stable of writers included Dashiel Hammett, Edna Ferber, Irwin Shaw, Ben Hecht and Billy Wilder. His client list read like a literary and theatrical *Who's Who*. Hemingway called him "the greatest agent in the world."

Just before the start of World War II, he bought a small flying school near Phoenix, won a government contract to train army pilots and in ninety days turned the premises into Thunderbird Field. Movie starlets helped hand out diplomas at the first graduation ceremony while Hoagy Carmichael, a stockholder in Hayward's enterprise, thumped out piano tunes.

Soon he set up a training center for British pilots; then, to haul high-priority military freight, he established an airline to fly a secret Pacific Coast route to twenty-two army bases.

By war's end, thousands of pilots from twenty-seven different nations had earned their wings at four Hayward flight centers. He joined the board of Trans World Airlines and hired the Hollywood restaurateur David Chasen to supply better meals on the planes.

Later, he cofounded Southwest Airways, which became one of the country's most profitable airlines, a result in part of such Hayward innovations as folding cabin doors which became stairways and enabled planes to land, drop passengers, reboard and taxi away all in ninety seconds.

In the mid-1940s, in what was until then the biggest entertainment deal ever, Leland merged his agency with its three hundred writing and acting clients into the mammoth Music Corporation of America and began to produce plays.

His first, in 1944, was *A Bell for Adano*, the dramatization of John Hersey's novel about reviving democracy in a Sicilian town occupied by Allied forces. A tremendous hit, it was followed by *State of the Union*, which won writers Lindsay and Crouse the Pulitzer prize; *Mister Roberts*, with Henry Fonda, which Hayward later also produced as a movie; *Anne of the Thousand Days;* Rodgers and Hammerstein's *South Pacific*, another Pulitzer winner, starring Mary Martin; Lindsay and Crouse's *Call Me Madam*, with Ethel

Merman, and *Peter Pan,* a streak that made him a Broadway wunderkind.

He also produced the movie versions of Hemingway's *The Old Man and the Sea,* with Spencer Tracy and *The Spirit of St. Louis,* the saga of pilot Charles A. Lindbergh, which starred his client, friend and fellow flyer Jimmy Stewart. Leland's terms were never complicated: "I want to be able to do anything I want to do and spend as much as I want to. I want to knock a home run or strike out."[21]

Married five times to four women, Leland had more strikeouts than home runs in his personal life. Before divorcing Lola for the second time, he romanced Greta Garbo and King Kong's Fay Wray, then settled into a serious affair with Katharine Hepburn.

"He was fun. He wasn't complicated. He was easygoing. Not too set in his ways. Loved the ladies and sailed from one island to another with joy and ease," Hepburn said. "I suited Leland perfectly. I liked to eat at home and go to bed early. He liked to eat out and go to bed late. So he had a drink when I had dinner and then off he'd go. Back at midnight. Perfect friendship . . . an extremely easy relationship. . . . Joy was the constant mood." Leland asked Kate to marry him, but she refused.[22]

She loved him, but she was separated from Ludlow Ogden Smith, did not want to marry again and never did, not even Spencer Tracy, with whom she had a twenty-seven-year love affair. Hepburn kept living with Leland through 1933, when she starred in *Little Women,* 1934, when she won the Academy Award for *Morning Glory* and the 1936 *Mary of Scotland.*

That year, Leland's client Edna Ferber opened her hit play *Stage Door* with Margaret Sullavan, one of the most talented actresses of the 1930s and 1940s. Discovered on Broadway in *Dinner at Eight* in 1932, she became a film star the next year in *Only Yesterday* and scored her greatest success back on Broadway in 1943 in the John van Druten drama *The Voice of the Turtle.* Poet Ogden Nash rhapsodized: "The fairest of sights / in twinkling lights / is Sullavan with an A."

Stunning as well as gifted, Sullavan had straight gold bangs, an irresistible crooked grin and a bewitching husky voice that suggested it spoke for a breaking heart.[23] Leland had been Maggie

Sullavan's agent for several years — just as he had represented her first husband, Henry Fonda — before they became lovers in 1936 as her second marriage, to director William Wyler, was breaking up. Leland lived with Sullavan when he was in New York and with Hepburn in Los Angeles.

When Maggie became pregnant late that year, Leland married her at Clarendon Court in Newport, Rhode Island, his father's home and later the ill-fated home of Sunny and Claus von Bulow. He did not tell Kate. He flew to Los Angeles intending to inform her, drove to her house and sat in the driveway trying to work up his courage. Chickening out, he turned around without entering the house, drove back to the airport and flew himself home to New York.[24] Hepburn heard about the wedding when Walter Winchell broadcast the news on his Sunday radio show. Dining with George Cukor at the time, she broke out crying.

The Haywards were married for twelve of Maggie and Leland's most productive years, but it was a surprise to many that the union lasted that long. The two were a magnetic couple but polar opposites, miscast in pretend-adult roles. He was an absentee father who kept dashing from coast to coast; she was a homebody. He loved Hollywood; she so hated it that she insisted on moving from California to rural Connecticut to guard her privacy. He was easygoing and indulgent with their children; she was strict, forbidding them to listen to radio or read comic books, and insistent that they conform to her celluloid notion of what constituted family life.

The children were picture-book kids — golden, gorgeous, talented, but not easy. Stepmother Slim Hayward, who married Leland in 1949 and whom the children adored, described them in her autobiography: "Brooke, the eldest, was most like her father, very sure of herself and capable of charming anything and anyone. She was enormously talented. She could paint, draw and she could write extremely well — as we found out when her autobiography, *Haywire*, was published; . . . Bridget was Brooke's antithesis: quiet, shy and ethereal. It was as if she had drawn a circle around herself which you felt you wouldn't dare invade. . . . Billy, the youngest, was so adorable . . . terrifically funny, with a real knack for pranks and enough charm to make you overlook them. He, too, had dark places you didn't want to touch."[25]

Maggie tried to manage everyone. She loved Leland but hated relinquishing so much of him to his career. To keep him in line, she forbade him to take business calls during family hours, a restriction which nearly drove him mad. He regularly sneaked out of the house and walked a half mile to a country store to call his office to find out what was going on.

"Your mother is a remarkable woman," Leland once told Brooke, "but she can't tolerate what she can't understand." He hated the solitude so much that he developed a violent allergy to flowers and everything about the country, eventually including his wife. "Like any Eden," said John Leonard, "it came with a built-in curse, a trapdoor. Daddy left."[26]

Once out the door, Leland married Slim. Maggie married Kenneth Wagg, an English manufacturer of powdered malt drinks. Brooke ran away and married, the first time after her freshman year at Vassar. Bridget and Bill left their mother at sixteen and fourteen to live with their father, who could not handle them. Bridget withdrew into long, private silences, suffered epileptic seizures and depression and was institutionalized at Austen Riggs. Bill, who spread toothpaste on his bedroom walls, Vaseline on the floor and set fires around the house when younger, was sixteen and threatening to run away from prep school to work in the Oklahoma oilfields when his father sent him to the Menninger Clinic in Kansas.

Slim coped as best she could during her ten years with Leland, but the strain wore heavily. By the time Pamela arrived on the scene, the couple was at drawn daggers. For all his charming bravura, the producer felt the stress of a relentless work pace, two disturbed children, a medical condition resembling bleeding ulcers which caused three life-threatening bouts with prolonged internal hemorrhaging, and a wife transformed into an overbearing virago.

Slim understood the pressure he was under and articulated a key part of the problem. "Leland was not a man who was very good on his own. What he lacked — and clearly wanted — was a woman who could have an identity and still be his constant companion."[27]

Maggie Sullavan, coping with her own demons that led her to commit suicide on New Year's Day 1960, did not understand that. Her move to Connecticut had thus automatically doomed her marriage. Once Slim's wanderlust got the perhaps understandable best of her — she would slip off to Russia with Cary Grant or to Cuba with Hemingway — she forgot her own insight and made the same mistake. Leland ate creamed chicken, mashed potatoes, pureed peas — nursery food, for God's sake. He wanted a nanny. If Slim wouldn't nanny him, Leland knew someone who would. The best a man could get: an English nanny who would care for the house, garden, staff and his every need. Pamela.

In the spring of 1959, *Gypsy* was such a mammoth hit that Slim thought the worst of their marital troubles were behind them. Unaware of the divorce master plan that began ticking away once the opening day curtain rose on the musical, she suggested a long summer holiday in Europe capped by a month in Venice to mark their tenth anniversary and a fresh start.

Rather than tell her the truth, Leland agreed to the trip. A week before they were scheduled to leave, he hedged. Business commitments meant that he had to postpone his departure. Slim was to go ahead. He would meet her in Madrid, where Hemingway was chronicling the mano a mano competition of the two great matadors Antonio Ordonez and Luis Miguel Dominguin, the basis of his final book, *The Dangerous Summer*. The trip suited Leland's purpose. He needed Slim out of town.

On July 5, he asked Brooke to dinner at Le Pavillon in New York to celebrate her twenty-second birthday. It was clear he was in an ecstatic mood and after his third Wild Turkey on the rocks, he told her that he had some exciting news. He had met the most wonderful woman and was going to marry her. "But you're already married," Brooke sputtered. "True," he conceded, "I've got to get a divorce."

He was telling her then because Slim was out of town for six weeks and Pamela was arriving the next day and moving into an apartment at the Drake Hotel. He usually wasn't a great fan of Englishwomen. "They all have bad teeth and talk through their noses; they're also all amoral, as opposed to immoral — big difference — all without exception. Don't know why that is. They all lead restricted lives until they get to be about sixteen and then they start screwing anything."

Brooke asked what she was like, this wonderful creature who had him feeling so incredibly boyish. "In an old-fashioned, good, ol' boy way, he said, 'I'll tell you, this is the greatest courtesan of the twentieth century.' " [When Brooke wrote *Haywire* in 1977, lawyers made her change "courtesan" to "charmer," a concession to Pamela's then being a private citizen. "But courtesan is what father called her," Brooke said.] Leland gave her a résumé of Pamela's past, naming names of as many of her lovers as came to him, including that of his great friend Bill Paley.

"Father loved the idea that he and all these very rich, powerful and talented men were all sharing her. He loved the idea that they all had something in common," Brooke said. "It energized him. He was part of a club. The Pamela club."[28]

He explained that she had the most gorgeous apartment in Paris, filled with "priceless" furniture and "unbelievable" jewelry, was currently supported by Elie de Rothschild and marveled that "it cost ten thousand dollars a year just to keep her apartment in fresh flowers." Pamela could keep seeing Elie, according to Leland, but she wanted to get married and so did he. She was the ultimate trophy wife.

Brooke was flattered and appalled. Her father had never confided anything personal and here he was telling her about jumping into bed with this extraordinary woman on their first evening together. By the time he finished describing her Titian tresses, silken complexion and days as an interlocutor for Churchill and reporter for Beaverbrook, Brooke was quivering with anticipation. Pamela sounded like a combination of Mata Hari and Brenda Starr. Leland asked her to be discreet. He first had to break the news to Slim.

Brooke promptly drove home to Connecticut and told her mother. "Leland can't be serious," Maggie said. She told her husband, Kenneth, who knew Pamela well from Europe. "That's preposterous," Wagg said. "Leland must be going berserk. She's the ultimate gold digger."[29]

Leland flew to Europe two weeks later to inform Slim. Faced with losing a husband she had made little effort to keep, Slim reversed course and fought back. She could not stop Leland from having an affair with Pamela, "but whatever you do, for your own protection, for your own dignity, don't marry her," she told him. "You don't have to. Nobody *marries* Pam Churchill. Gianni Agnelli didn't do it. Elie de Rothschild didn't do it. Ed Murrow didn't do it. Why should you?"

But the endgame had already moved toward checkmate. "Like a brilliant chess player, Pam knew her moves far in advance," Slim explained later. "Pam understood what Maggie Sullavan and I hadn't: Leland was a man who liked being taken care of. If you did that, you could get anything from him."[30]

In Leland's case, "anything" was not necessarily limited to his resources. He was ebulliently extravagant even when he could not afford it. The impressive front mattered. "Leland's always had a compulsion to live beyond his means," Maggie Sullavan once remarked. "If his income were a million dollars a year, he'd spend a million and a half."[31] The habit held true for his films, where he was notorious for running over budget.

Leland's generosity and free-spending ways were on full display during his enthusiastic courtship and he gave Pamela the undeniable impression that he was far wealthier than he was. Not that she put his bankroll in the Agnelli or Rothschild league. She knew better than that. Diana Vreeland, then editor of *Harper's Bazaar*, and a friend separately of Pamela's and Leland's, warned her about what she was getting into. The Hayward children were difficult; theater life was rough and miserable on the road. Marriage to Leland would be nothing like the lush, controlled existence she was used to. Pamela was not dissuaded in the slightest. "I'm going to marry him because I've had everything in my life, but I've never really had a husband. Leland is going to be my husband."[32] Once she began taking care of him, he'd be in clover. She was right.

Pamela spent six weeks in the Drake. The day after she arrived, the dreary hotel wall decorations were removed and replaced by glorious Impressionist paintings loaned her by philanthropist Mary Lasker, a collector and dealer of old and modern French masters whom Pamela knew through the Whitneys, the Paleys and Gerald Van Der Kemp in Paris. At the end of summer, she moved into an apartment at the Carlyle Hotel arranged for her by another longtime admirer, New York lawyer and investment banker Walter Thayer, who had met her in London as a member of Averell Harriman's Lend-Lease team and who was then an executive in Jock Whitney's newspaper and communications empire.

It was Thayer who provided young Winston with a job that summer as a *Wall Street Journal* intern. In early autumn, Thayer arranged a two-thousand-dollar-a-month two-year sweetheart lease on a spacious suite in the Carlyle Hotel. The hotel furniture was taken away and the apartment refurnished with the classically delicate Louis XVI chairs, tables and sideboards Pamela had shipped from Paris. Designer Charles Eames saw the elegant collection of museum-quality late eighteenth-century pieces and told intimates, "I could see her whole stable of 'special friends' was represented."[33]

"Like a tortoise bringing her house on her back" was how Pamela depicted the process, the psychological and proprietary purpose of which was as great as its decorative intent. "This furniture was very special to me and around it I built my nest. Certain objects meant a particular way of life and I tried to put them in their new settings in ways that did not look like just French rooms that had been transported across the Atlantic," Pamela explained. In rental properties especially, "always the first move has been to get rid of other people's clutter and install my own. There has to be a certain amount of clutter to enforce your ownership of a room. Flowers or pillows or photographs — these can make a room suddenly spring to life."[34]

Leland had been living in an apartment borrowed from screenwriter and playwright Harry Kurnitz. When the Carlyle suite was ready, he moved to an adjoining apartment with a connecting door. While Slim was still in Europe, Pamela and Leland spent weekends at Slim and Leland's Manhasset, Long Island, home. It had been a long time since young Winston had seen his mother "so radiant and happy."[35]

When Slim finally returned to New York, she was annoyed to find that Pamela had been living in her house, and livid when she discovered red stickers on certain furniture and paintings identifying pieces that Pamela wanted in the divorce. Adding insult to injury, Leland asked her to sit in Nevada for six weeks so they could divorce and he could marry Pam. He was too busy to go himself. Slim laughed in his face, told him to go fuck himself, and put the brakes on the divorce.

Pamela wasn't surprised. She knew the routine. Slim did not want Leland, but the moment someone else did, especially someone as well known as Pamela, suddenly Slim was up in arms to keep him. Pamela was glad she had not heeded the advice to stay in France. If she had, and Slim had taken the offensive, she might have lost out. Pressing her advantage, Pamela virtually grafted herself to Leland. In September, she accompanied him to New Haven, where *Sound of Music* began rehearsals.

They checked into the Taft Hotel with Howard Lindsay and Russel Crouse and their wives; Dorothy and Richard Rodgers; Mary Martin and her husband, Richard Halliday, who was producing the show along with Leland and Rodgers and Oscar Hammerstein. Oscar was not there, too sick after undergoing an ulcer operation which revealed he was suffering from incurable cancer. He made it in mid-October to Boston, the second tryout stop, where Pamela was astonished to see him write the lyrics for "Edelweiss" overnight. It proved to be the last song on which he and Richard Rodgers collaborated.

They stayed on the road until mid-December. *Sound of Music* was opening on November 16 at the Lunt-Fontanne, while the curtain for George Axelrod's *Goodbye Charlie*, which Leland was also producing and which starred Slim's pal Betty Bacall, went up at the Lyceum exactly a month later. One show would have been hard, but two simultaneously was brutal, particularly with the troubled *Goodbye Charlie* trying out in Pittsburgh, Detroit, Cleveland, Baltimore and Philadelphia. They'd catch a matinee in one city and fly to another for an evening show. Pamela was fascinated. Her knowledge of America until then had extended little past the pleasure domes of New York, Washington and Palm Beach. Touring opened up a whole new world of places, close contact with creative people and nonstop action. She loved every minute.

Always a quick study, she was learning an offstage role as much as Mary Martin was becoming Maria Rainer onstage. "She went from knowing nothing about Broadway to being able to quote box-office grosses in about two weeks," said Brooke. In Paris, with decorator Georges Geffroy, she had perfected the art of the backroom. Backstage was no different in concept, only in detail. "I look on myself as a backstage person, really," she said. "But backstage people are very important. They're the ones who get the show on the road."[36]

There were also links between the stage and parliamentary politics. "An opening night is like an election," Pamela noted in 1965. "The tensions, rewards and disappointments are very much the same."[37]

To the offstage work, she brought special touches, including a trunk of pots, pans, dishes, silverware and a hot plate. Room service rarely operated past 10 P.M. in the 1950s and early 1960s, but Leland and his merry crew needed TLC and she, by God, intended to provide it. At midnight, while the men talked out fixes and rewrites, the former drawing room darling rolled up her sleeves and stood over her hot plate stirring up Leland's favorite frozen potato soup and chicken hash, which he washed down with enough Wild Turkey to leave a drinker with less alcohol tolerance babbling or senseless.

Leland rarely went to bed before 3 A.M., when his nightly battle with insomnia began, and he started gobbling barbiturates — downers — to which he was addicted. Terrified of being without his pills, which he carried in a satchel, he ordered huge quantities of drugs from Dr. Saul Fox, who gave him up to six months' supply at a time. On New Year's Eve 1958, he wrote Fox asking for three-quarters-of-a-grain and grain-and-a-half capsules of Seconal, carbonal, Tuinal and Nembutal ("lots of these — they work the best") and also "some red seconal rockets and any new ones you've got that are great."[38] In June 1963, he wrote Harry Kurnitz: "Please bring me a lot of seconals."[39]

Pamela did not see that the drugs, heavy drinking and heavy smoking affected Leland's work or slowed him down. On the contrary, he had his hands in everything. He invested little if any of his own money in his shows, but he raised cash from backers, settled contracts and spent much of his time negotiating between directors, writers and actors, many basically insecure but with big egos. Often, he had to work around oddball idiosyncrasies, such as George Axelrod's refusal to walk on the right side of the street.

Pamela took it all in.

When Rex Harrison was being impossible during rehearsals for a television show, Leland hired two marshals, stationed them on either side of the stage, and told his star that if he tried to walk off, the marshals would physically return him. He was under contract and would perform the way he was ordered.

In Philadelphia, she watched Leland dump an actress in such a way that he would not have to pay her. Forced to repeat a scene again and again, the woman finally blew up and said "No more." A lawyer instantly stepped from the wings and cited her for breaking her contract.

Pamela learned about the critical importance of cast chemistry and the tricks stars used to hold center stage and audience attention. When Ethel Merman, a master at putting other actors off stride, felt a backup actor was getting too much attention, she would start a song early to cut short the other's ovation or move off a stage position to draw audience attention. There were stars who hated rehearsing, just like politicians. Blowups between principals needed smoothing over.

For *Sound of Music*, it was not easy with star Martin married to producer Halliday, whom composer Rodgers could not stand. One day Rodgers exploded and yelled at Mary Martin to get her "fag" husband offstage. Martin, who had possibly the cleanest mouth in the history of show business, was shocked, walked off and demanded an apology. Rodgers refused. With opening night two weeks off, the resultant uproar took the diplomatic talents of both Pamela and Leland to resolve. Twenty years later in her

Georgetown living room, Pamela would apply some of the same hardball/soft-glove techniques to resolve differences between warring camps of politicians, policy wonks and money men.

In February 1960, Leland produced one of his great television specials, *The Fabulous Fifties,* for Bill Paley's CBS network. A two-hour retrospective hosted by Henry Fonda and with appearances by Rex Harrison and Julie Andrews, Jackie Gleason, Mike Nichols, Elaine May and a host of others, the show was a smash. "Hayward was called on to compress five million minutes into 120 and, by golly, he almost did it," said *Variety.*[40] "A literate joy," said *New York Times* television critic Jack Gould.[41]

By the time the show aired on the heels of two Broadway shows, Leland was exhausted. He and Pamela also realized that Slim was doing nothing about a divorce. Her strategy was to ignore the situation until Pamela got tired of waiting and returned to Paris.

But Pam, who had been a remarkable support personally and professionally at a tough time for Leland, was there to stay. "I'm here and I will not be dislodged," she told Brooke and Bridget Hayward. "This is going to be a very nasty divorce. Your father is going to be taken for everything he has. He will be broke at the end of it. Slim has declared war."[42]

The only way to get Leland divorced was to live for six weeks in Nevada, so in mid-March the tired but happy lovers flew to Las Vegas and moved into the Churchill Downs wing of the Sands Hotel.

The Vegas scene astonished Pamela. No windows in the casinos; no meals at anything like normal times. But they had fun. They made friends with the bellboys, who told them which slot machines paid quick jackpots. Pamela, who was used to ten-thousand franc chips clacking at Monte Carlo, broke up in hysterical giggles when dimes poured out of the one-armed bandits and slid through her fingers onto the floor. Scooping them up, she'd run to the blackjack table and immediately lose everything.

Weekdays they had to stay in Las Vegas to meet residency requirements and the wait was excruciating for Pam. Other than gambling, or a drive to Lake Meade and Boulder Dam, the only tourist attraction, and waiting for Leland to get off the phone, there was nothing for her to do. Weekends were better. They often drove to Palm Springs, where they rented the home of singer and song writer Johnny Mercer, whose hits included "Jeepers Creepers" and "You Must Have Been a Beautiful Baby." Frank Sinatra often dropped by, sometimes with Rosalind Russell and her producer husband, Freddie Brisson. Edie and Bill Goetz were frequent visitors. She was the daughter of Louis B. Mayer; he, the film producer of *Call of the Wild, Sayonara,* and, appropriately, *The House of Rothschild,* although there's no evidence anyone spent much time discussing the last one.

The six weeks out west had one striking effect: as Pamela had transformed herself effortlessly from Englishwoman to European, she had passed through the looking glass again and was now distinctly Americanized. She became more direct, spoke up louder, changed her more delicate eating habits of fish, pasta and salads to more red meat and potatoes. It showed.

As she switched from Château Lafite to Wild Turkey Manhattans and whiskey sours, she put on fifteen pounds, went up a full dress size and began to look far more matronly than she had in Europe. Her regular topics of conversation changed from furniture and horses to entertainers and production schedules. The neon of Las Vegas and bleached sand heat of Palm Springs made the tree-lined boulevards of Paris and the yachts moored at Monte Carlo seem very distant.

When the waiting period neared an end, Slim sent out a boyfriend with her paperwork instead of a lawyer. Leland knew and liked the fellow. He loved to gamble, was keen for a weekend in Las Vegas and the three had a wonderful time playing away the final two days of exile. The settlement had involved a long dispute over money, in which Leland offered to assign Slim his quartershare producing royalties from *Sound of Music.* She turned them down, saying she did not think the play was any good. Thirty years later, until 1992 when her rights ran out, Pamela was still receiving up to fifty thousand dollars yearly in stage, film and music royalties from the cash-cow production.

On May 4, Leland was granted the divorce and he and Pamela flew straight to Carson City, where they were married by Chief

Justice Frank McNamee of the Nevada Supreme Court. Pamela had wanted to marry in the Catholic Church, but that meant Leland needed to have Rome annul his two marriages to Lola Gibbs, who had been institutionalized. His two more recent wives did not count. Maggie Sullavan had killed herself in January 1960 and the Church never recognized his marriage to Slim. The procedure seemed endless, but Pamela was adamant. She had gone through the whole rigamarole herself in the abortive attempt to marry Gianni. She was damned if all that effort was going to waste.

There was another reason for her insistence. At the time, Pamela took her Catholicism seriously. The faith in general, if not all its precepts, had captivated her and proved to be more than a mere obstacle to be overcome in her pursuit of Gianni, only to be discarded when the strategy failed to work. She felt a fervor not uncommon in converts.

One of the most famous converts in the 1940s was Clare Boothe Luce, the editor of *Vogue* magazine turned playwright who was serving as congresswoman from Connecticut in 1944 when, amid enormous publicity, she converted to Catholicism after the death of her daughter, Ann, in a car crash. Pamela had met her husband, Henry Luce, during the war in London and had also once been assigned by Lord Beaverbrook to interview the *Time* publisher.

Pamela was quite taken by Luce, who later admitted to his longtime confidante Mary Bancroft that "Pamela Churchill practically tore her clothes off" to get at him in one of their early meetings.

But if Pam and Luce had a fling, as Bancroft suggested, it was Clare, the epitome of Modern Woman, who fascinated her over the longer term. She was intrigued reading the stories of Clare's conversion in search of solace, guided by the dynamic Bishop Fulton J. Sheen, the voice of Catholicism on radio and later television.

Mrs. Luce's zeal was well known but best related in a perhaps apocryphal anecdote about her making an insistent religious point to Pope Pius XII in 1953 while she was U.S. ambassador to Italy. The story had His Holiness responding in beleaguered fashion,

"Mrs. Luce, you must understand that I too am a Catholic. . . ."

The conversion of Pamela's sister Jacquetta to Catholicism in preparation for her 1950 marriage to future member of Parliament David James made the idea of converting more real than theoretical. Until then, Pamela's knowledge about the religion came primarily from three Catholic friends, Clarissa Churchill, old Winston's niece, with whom she attended Downham School, Hugh Fraser, a childhood chum who was later an MP and the husband of author Lady Antonia Fraser; and Kick Kennedy.

Pamela noted how Clarissa and Hugh gave up meat on Fridays and went to mass regularly on Sundays, a practice she followed on occasion with Gianni in Italy. As a woman for whom a sense of order is important, she grew to appreciate the discipline of the religion. She also had witnessed how such Catholics as Rose Kennedy could push the obligations to extremes, as the matriarch did in cutting off her daughter Kick when the young woman married the Protestant son of the duke of Devonshire.

During difficult periods with Gianni, the back-and-forth over the future and their ultimate breakup, Pamela discovered, as Clare Boothe Luce had, that her new Catholicism offered a tremendous solace and a sense of strength. So she had no intention of jettisoning her religion when it came time to marry Leland.

After two years of securing affidavits about Lola from relatives and mental clinics and asking old Joe Kennedy for help in soliciting the support of Francis Cardinal Spellman, head of the New York Archdiocese, Leland gained his annulment in early spring 1962. Soon after, Pamela and Leland remarried in church in Harrison, New York. Nedda and Josh Logan gave the reception.

She did not wait for the second ceremony to start transforming Leland's life. That process had begun as soon as she became Mrs. Hayward in the civil ceremony in Nevada. With her proceeds from the Paris flat, she paid $220,000 for an apartment at 1020 Fifth Avenue which had been owned by Alfred Vanderbilt's mother and was just down the avenue from the Woodward home where she had first stayed in New York in 1937.

The two-story flat was lovely, with a paneled library and dining room that overlooked the Metropolitan Museum of Art. When she left Paris, Boudin of Maison Jansen had written his New York representative, Paul Manno, to say that Mrs. Churchill was arriving, that she had been a "very, very cherished client" for many years — he had done La Léopolda and her Paris apartment — and to take care of her.

When Pamela first met him at Leeds Castle in the late 1930s, Boudin was a top decorator. By the early 1960s, the pale, abstemious little man with the dapper mustache was widely considered the world's best. If your White House or apartment had not been done by Boudin, you simply were not first class.

Manno met her at the Carlyle and helped decorate the suite. When Pamela bought 1020 Fifth, Boudin came over and with Manno planned a lavish redecoration, from preliminary sketches and the construction of scale-model maquettes in Paris to the final installation of hand-carved wooden cornices and every stick of furniture and adornment.

The major pieces were all Louis XVI, some with flower-embroidered silk upholstery originally made for the wedding of Marie Antoinette to the future king. Pamela did not have enough to furnish the entire apartment, nor did she want a completely French one, which she knew would have looked out of place in New York.

She supplemented the French pieces with American antiques, including work by the cabinetmaker Duncan Phyfe and a unique, circular mahogany dining room table. Comfortable American sofas and occasional chairs were upholstered in fabrics which complemented the walls. The most striking were those in the dining room, covered by canvas hand-painted in Paris with a trompe l'oeil trellis.

Pamela supervised everything, down to the installation of every lamp. Except for providing a fine Vuillard and a glowing Soutine portrait, "Leland had nothing to do with the decoration at all," said Manno. "She has perfect taste and paid attention to every detail. You'd think you were in Buckingham Palace."[43]

The overall look was nonintimidating elegance which stopped short of flamboyance, artificiality or overdecoration. The cost was high enough to surprise Leland, but not so high that he could not handle it following the success of *Gypsy* and *Sound of Music*.

Because Pamela had paid for the apartment itself and because it was their main home, he withheld criticism. He had good taste himself and recognized that the apartment was lovely, a masterful job by his talented new wife.

Once the apartment was finished, Pamela pouted and began complaining that no Englishwoman could live seven days a week in the city even if her front lawn was Central Park. Leland had been forced to give Slim the Manhasset home in their divorce settlement. Another place on Long Island would not work, not with Slim out there and Babe Paley, who was too much competition for Pamela socially.

Westchester County was the logical alternative, but Leland was not keen on the idea. He had a legion of allergies and gulped antihistamines to ease battles with hay fever that left him slumped in an armchair, eyes throbbing, nose red and holding a soggy handkerchief in each fist. Physical problems were not the only drawback. He had an obsessive fear of snakes and a belief that anything north of Yankee Stadium was uninhabitable wilderness.

At the same time, Pamela was browbeating him, her habit when she wants something. Yet, he did adore her and wanted her to be happy. He agreed grudgingly as long as she met certain stipulations: she had to find the house; it could not be too far from the city; and the decorating budget would be strictly limited, nothing like what she had spent on the apartment.

On her forty-second birthday, Pamela stayed with Irene Selznick in Bedford Village in Westchester County. She went to church by herself in nearby Mount Kisco and later, stopping for gas, asked the attendant if he knew of any houses in the area for sale. He mentioned one on a hill overlooking Croton Reservoir. She drove straight over to look, spoke to the owners and a week later bought the Yorktown Heights property for ninety thousand dollars. The Catholic Church had come through once more.

The house was hideous, too modern for Pamela. But she loved the property's fifty-seven wooded acres and gorgeous view of forest and water, which Diana Cooper said reminded her of Lapland.[44] Boudin and Manno rushed up to Pamelize the house, country style.

A two-story bank of high, wide windows flooded the house with light and created a natural airy sensation. Outside, a heated circular swimming pool was situated under hillside trees. Inside, a modern kitchen and water softener were installed, staff quarters appointed and extensive clothes closets constructed. Slate-black floor-to-ceiling shelves were installed in the library and filled with books, more for appearance than for reading pleasure.

An all-black-and-white sitting room with a Picasso drawing over the sofa was created for Leland's television watching. Stained and painted bamboo furniture, some English Regency style, came from Hawaii and Hong Kong along with several Charles Eames pieces from California. From France came Louise de Vilmorin's favorite floral pattern wallpaper named "Verrières" after her home and blue-and-white toile de Jouy–patterned towels. Cozy sofas, silver-framed family photos and vases of fresh flowers were reminders of England and made it homey.[45]

Because Pamela loved the place, Leland liked it too, more so after he bought a three-seater Bell helicopter that allowed him to commute to New York City in eighteen minutes. Pamela purchased a yellow-and-black lawn tractor to keep the landing strip trimmed. She spent hours riding it and cutting paths for walks through acres of ragweed, poison ivy and brush.[46]

In keeping with Jane Digby's practice of creating English gardens wherever she lived, Pamela planted an English garden of wildflowers and filled the house with them, careful to avoid those that made Leland sneeze. They named the house Haywire, after Leland's cable address, and went up most weekends when Leland was not on the road.

Their two nests completed, once again Pamela became bored. "It was intolerable to sit at home with a very busy man and do nothing," she said.[47] In 1962 she became a student at Helen Worth's cooking school in New York. Pamela was never a cook, although for years she had directed kitchen staffs and at that time had a Finnish chef who prepared fine French food. As she had learned from the duchess of Windsor, that was not enough. She did not want to cook herself, but the duchess had told her that she should understand the process. Ms. Worth held a similar belief. "You can't say to a cook, no matter how much you are paying them, that you don't like something. You must be able to say, 'I want it done this way.' "[48]

The cooking course gave her the grounding she sought, but it occupied only occasional hours and Pamela needed something more substantive to keep busy. She asked Paul Manno if he'd like to go into business with her and open a New York branch of Jansen. He was interested but did not have enough money. She advanced him his third share on a handshake. Jansen Paris held the other third. The baron's daughter from the nation of shopkeepers knew a great deal about decorating but knew little more about retail than how to round up rationed and black market supplies in war. But as with everything else to which she set her mind, she learned quickly.

As she had in Paris with Geffroy, Pamela prowled antiques warehouses and estate sales. The shop provided the chance to write off regular travel to Europe. Careful not to be gone long and upset Leland, she went on buying trips with Manno searching for antiques, small furniture and decorative accessories, items that started as low as three dollars, but quickly soared for pieces like a silver centerpiece of a swan with flexible wings that she found in Portugal.

In the time-honored practice of social ladies who open shops, she recycled some of her own pieces and house gifts through the boutique at 42 East Fifty-seventh Street and demonstrated that she did not have just a good eye and great taste. Friends and critics alike had known for some time that she had a wonderful talent for money and figures. Jansen proved them correct.

"She's a brilliant businesswoman," said Manno. "Perhaps the finest business acumen I've ever seen. Pamela understood sales. She had an innate sense of value and knew how to price, how to buy, how to deal with important customers, how to mesmerize a truck driver or delivery boy into doing exactly what had to be done. On top of that, she could read a balance sheet, so we made money. Not enough to retire on, but we made some money."[49]

The ladies-that-lunch crowd applauded her industry. Some who continued to fear her reputation as a femme fatale were delighted that Pamela had found an acceptable outlet for her energy that did not involve their husbands. She was keeping a relatively low profile at the time, but the venture also earned good publicity. BARON'S DAUGHTER FINDS SHOPKEEPING TO HER TASTE was the headline of a 1965 *New York Times* article on her Jansen experience.

She helped run the shop until 1967, when Leland became ill with pancreatitis and she quit to take care of him full-time. He was forced to stop smoking and drinking and to adhere to a rigid diet that he hated. When he switched to milk, a lot of the fun went out of the daily lunches at the Colony, where his name was engraved on his table's silver champagne bucket. Instead of sleeping in mornings, he often jolted awake just after dawn in terrible pain and had to inject himself with morphine.

Leland's career rose steadily through the thirties, forties and fifties, but it had peaked by the time he met Pamela. Slim took consolation in pointing out that after he left her for Pamela at the time of *Sound of Music,* he never had another big hit. She was right. "By the time Pamela gets there it's a busted flush," noted Jones Harris, son of producer Jed Harris and actress Ruth Gordon, and a one-time boyfriend of Brooke Hayward's.[50]

Leland never slowed down until he became sick. He simply did not have any hits. His most ambitious stage effort in the 1960s was *Mr. President,* a political musical written by the usually reliable Lindsay and Crouse, with songs by Irving Berlin and directed by Josh Logan. With the Kennedys in full swing in the White House, a play with a presidential theme by these creators looked on paper like a sure-fire hit. High expectations prompted a near-record advance ticket sale of $3 million, but the show had a disastrous opening in Washington, D.C., and turned out to be one of Broadway's biggest disappointments.

The critics were merciless. "The most solemn musical comedy ever," said the *Washington Post.* Director Josh Logan saw no reason to disagree: "Some shows at first sight seem to be dogs and turn out to be great. Others at first sight, seem to be great and . . . *Mr. President* was one of the latter."[51]

John Kennedy broke away from the White House situation room, where he was monitoring the Cuban missile crisis, to attend the second act on opening night in October 1962, but the show's prospects were no better than those of the retreating Soviets. Pamela, however, was magnificent. She never left Leland's side that night at a huge postperformance supper at the British embassy, where the "Cream Chicken Hash" main course, his favorite, was one of the few bright spots for the producer. Nor did she roam very far for weeks thereafter.

After *Mr. President*, Leland's creative team fell apart. Oscar Hammerstein had died in 1960. Lindsay and Crouse were both ill during production and never wrote another show. The loss of such monumental talent, as well as the *Mr. President* fallout, left Leland in a rut from which he was never able to emerge. If losing his stars was not problem enough, neither could he adapt to the fact that theater was changing. The golden era of the American musical was slipping away.

Roosevelt, Truman and Eisenhower were history. Kennedy's New Frontier thrived until that dreadful moment in Dallas. Then there was Lyndon Johnson and the confrontational politics of the 1960s. The free-speech movement took hold in Berkeley, California. Theater began moving off-Broadway, became more avant-garde and headed into the Age of Aquarius. Not one of the changes augured well for Leland.

In September 1964, *New York Daily News* columnist Robert Sylvester asked: "Whatever became of Leland Hayward?"[52] He did not answer the question. If he had and had been frank, he might have said that Leland's run was over. With hindsight, it is clear that Leland's career went into a spiral after *Mr. President* in 1962, with the rest of the decade one prolonged death rattle. He optioned some properties in 1963 and 1964, but they went nowhere. For the first time, he had difficulty attracting backers. In 1965, he coproduced *Hot September* with David Merrick, but it closed in Boston after three weeks and never made Broadway.

There was not enough activity to keep Pamela occupied. Her enthusiasm for *Sound of Music* was easy to understand: it was not only her first Broadway experience, but a huge hit. She was interested in the modestly successful 1961 play *A Shot in the Dark* because it was a Harry Kurnitz adaptation of a farce by Marcel Achard, her good and great friend from Louise de Vilmorin's drawing room.

But afterward, as Leland's Broadway action waned, so did her interest and involvement. A socially prominent Washingtonian who had dated Pamela in the 1950s and who frequently visited the Haywards in the 1960s said that "after the initial flush of excitement, Pamela was not interested at all in the entertainment business while married to Leland."

She turned her full attention to the Jansen shop, saying that she would have been more connected to the theater world if she had not been pushed away. "I was told that as a producer's wife, I must never offer an opinion. . . . I am permitted to read scripts, but that's really rough because if I don't like one I'm told I know nothing about the theater."[53]

Leland returned to television in 1964 and 1965, producing American versions of the British satirical hit "This Was the Week That Was," or TW3 as it was known. Despite separate tries over two TV seasons, the show failed to take off. Repeated preemptions during the political conventions and 1964 Johnson-Goldwater campaign hurt. A more basic problem was that the program never reconciled the different visions and styles of Leland, its sixty-three-year-old establishment producer, and David Frost, the then twenty-three-year-old irreverent star.

Frost thought Leland was wonderful, but the critics did not. "The show is neither witty nor funny, only embarrassing in its persistent clumsiness and poor taste," wrote Jack Gould in the *New York Times*.[54] "Humdrum and pedestrian" was *Variety*'s verdict.[55] Frost met Pamela and could tell that the theater had lost whatever appeal it had held for her. "I don't think she had any great love for the smell of the greasepaint and the roar of the crowd."[56]

The remainder of the sixties was a bust for Leland. By the time *The Mother Lover* opened and closed on one February night in 1969, he had hit bottom. Almost no money was coming in, 1020 Fifth Avenue was sold, and he and Pamela were living off capital banked from triumphs long past. Pamela was an angel of mercy, nursing him mentally and physically. On weekends she ceaselessly invited neighbors and small groups of friends to Haywire to keep him company at mealtime. When she had to go out, she made certain he was never alone.

In February 1971, weakened by illness but irrepressible, the promilitary, Republican Leland was trying his best to adapt to the new political environment. He was producing what for him was an unlikely venture, *The Trial of the Catonsville Nine*, by antiwar activist Daniel Berrigan, when he suffered a ministroke and was admitted to New York hospital.

Treatment continued for weeks, including an operation on a blocked neck artery which was bungled and for too long cut off oxygen to his brain. The entire time Pamela reprised her hospital stay with Gianni Agnelli and spent most of her waking hours by Leland's bedside. Pamela finally took him home to Haywire, where he died on March 18, 1971, two days before her fifty-first birthday. She was exhausted and so traumatized that never again would she celebrate her birthday. Then her stepchildren Brooke and Bill showed up and Pamela's worst nightmare began.

CHAPTER THIRTEEN

⚐ ⚐

Brooke and Bill

THE RELATIONSHIP BETWEEN BROOKE and Pamela was star-crossed from the outset, a classic case of a talented and head-strong daughter clashing with a determined, self-centered step-mother in a battle of wills for father-husband's love and favor. This struggle turned ugly fast, outlasted Leland, scarred each woman and left a legacy of enduring mutual contempt.

Brooke channeled her anger into getting even in *Haywire*, her 1977 bestseller, in which she cast Pamela with unerring accuracy in a supporting role as the Wicked Stepwitch of the West. Pamela pushed along the track of her agenda like a bulldozer in overdrive, her blade parrying lobbed caricatures, her goal a successful mar-riage, a stimulating and financially secure life and full entry onto the much sought-after American circuit.

The two women met for the first time on a hot July night two days after Leland told his daughter of his intention to dump Slim and marry Pamela. Brooke was living in Greenwich, Connecticut, with two small children and a nanny, exiting from her first mar-riage and commuting to New York daily to model and take acting lessons. Beautiful and precocious, she had been a *Life* magazine cover girl at fifteen and that year, at twenty-two, was on the cover of *Vogue*.

When Brooke arrived at the Drake Hotel with Leland, Pamela had been in residence a scant forty-eight hours, but already the suite bore her special touches: the loaned Laskers on the walls, a small Rodin bust on a table, fresh flowers everywhere, including an orchid plant in a blue and white Chinese cachepot, the white light bulbs replaced by pink and the scent of Rigaud candles. Pamela came down a long hallway, bussed Leland on the cheek and launched herself at Brooke.

"How nice to meet you," she said, simultaneously pinning on Brooke's lapel a large carved ebony blackamoor encrusted with diamonds and sapphires and clothed in a gold vest and turban with diamond-dusted feathers. "Now this is very valuable, so don't ever give it away or sell it."

Brooke was so astonished her mouth fell open. What an overdone entrance. The pin was valuable, but it was also too exotic, too weird, too wrong. One did not hand over on first meeting something so opulent. It was inappropriate. And besides, a blackamoor. Brooke was not politically conscious then, but her own personal Negro lapel pin? Maybe in the thirties, maybe in Europe, but not in New York City on the cusp of the sixties, not after the National Guard had integrated Little Rock's Central High and the southern civil rights sit-ins were about to begin.

Brooke felt it was distasteful to walk up to someone for the first time and pin on such an extravagant gift, especially since it appeared to be a hand-me-down that Pamela no longer wanted. When Brooke told her mother the next morning what had happened, Maggie Sullavan rolled her eyes: "Oh my God, poor Leland. I've never felt sorry for Slim until now."

Neither daughter nor mother was aware then that gift giving in advance is a regular Pamela practice to guarantee obligation. When she met a man she fancied in France, Pamela often went straight to Cartier the next day and bought him, to be sent around, a present — gold cuff links or a silver cigarette box engraved in her handwriting with "Thank you for the most wonderful evening. Love, Pamela." The object of her attention would then feel obliged to respond with a larger gift.

Dinner, at Pavillon again, of course, was pleasant enough, but Brooke was baffled. This woman was totally unlike what she had expected. She was no dashing Brenda Starr, lively girl reporter; no alluringly seductive Mata Hari. Pamela was only thirty-nine, but matronly, and somehow managed to look dowdy in a Dior.

Conversation at dinner was banal. Pamela knew nothing about the theater, nothing about politics and, for someone who had known so many Americans during the war and had visited so often, very little about the United States. She did not appear anywhere near as high caliber as Slim or Maggie, whose presence could dominate a room. This woman was completely the reverse: plain and undemanding. And yet, there was Brooke's father, tough, snappy Leland, so adoring and puppyish that he could barely get through his vichyssoise. Which, of course, was the point. Because Pamela displayed no overwhelming star qualities, Leland was the star.

About four weeks later, the two met again and Pamela was a different woman, having already begun to adapt to her new environment. She was vivacious and exhilarated at reacquainting herself with everything going on in New York. She'd been to the stores and knew what and where all the newest things were. "You have the best shopping in the world," Pamela told her. "You have Hammacher Schlemmer," a store which then specialized in exotic hardware.

She had met Diana Vreeland, had been to the theater and seen Leland's friends, eaten at the Colony, met Brooke's sister Bridget and brought her presents, seen Bill Paley and begun to scan the *New York Times* so she could join in conversations. The gossip columnists were on to the fact that she and Leland were an item, that he had holed up in Harry Kurnitz's "love nest," and what was Slim going to do when she got home? PAMELA AND HAYWARD MAKING BIG PLANS, was the headline on a Cholly Knickerbocker column.[1]

"Pamela loved that it broke in the papers," because it gave her legitimacy, Brooke said. "Father wasn't that thrilled because it meant that he was going to lose a lot of money in a divorce. And he did."[2]

On January 1, 1960, Maggie Sullavan died in New Haven

while trying out a new play. Brooke heard the news when she called her stepfather, Kenneth Wagg, to wish her mother good luck. Wagg said Maggie had just died; her heart had given out. Soon after, swaddled in sable, Pamela picked up Brooke from the Gate Theater, where she was appearing off-Broadway in *Marching Song*, to take her home. En route, she told Brooke that her mother had killed herself. Brooke was irate.

"How do you know it's suicide?" Brooke asked.

"Sleeping pills," Pamela responded.

"I don't believe you. I seriously doubt if it was sleeping pills."

"Yes, she did; it was sleeping pills. She was a very, very disturbed woman."

"Which was undoubtedly true," Brooke said. "But I didn't want her critique at that moment. I wanted her to say, 'I know you loved your mother very much.' But there was never anything cuddly about Pamela. She was rather reptilian."[3]

"She had never even met Mother," Brooke wrote in *Haywire*. "There was something obscene about her telling me that Mother was dead; that she had killed herself, that she was unhappy; that one should be philosophical about these things. No aspect of this was any of Pamela's business."[4]

When Bill Hayward was told of his mother's death and asked to fly home from Kansas, he went to a Topeka men's store to buy an inexpensive dark suit for the funeral. Measured and fitted, he put the suit on the charge account Leland had set up when Bill was first institutionalized at Menninger's. When the store called the Hayward number at the Carlyle to verify the charge, Pamela answered the phone and turned it down. Bill came east in jeans. More confident now that Slim was back and Leland had formally asked for a divorce, Pamela had begun to exert control.[5]

In October that same year, Bridget Hayward committed suicide in her New York apartment. She had been back and forth to the Austen Riggs Clinic in Stockbridge, Massachusetts, and was fighting her own private battle with depression and epilepsy, of which Pamela and Leland were unaware.

Leland called her at the apartment occasionally and when there was no reply assumed she had checked herself back in to Riggs. In fact, when she felt an attack coming on, she would lock herself in her room and take Dilantin, a prescription drug, to reduce convulsions. Writing in her diaries, which Pamela has kept but has never shown Brooke or Bill, Bridget cursed the Dilantin, her handwriting reduced to a scrawl as the pills and seizures wrestled for control of her body and mind.

When Pamela broke the news of Bridget's death to Brooke, she admonished her: Brooke was in no way, shape or form to cry in front of her father. "I don't want your father to become emotionally upset. I don't want him to start one of those bleeding attacks," she said. "I expect you to behave in very mature fashion. I don't want any tears."[6] There were none.

Before the funeral, Brooke and Pamela went to Bridget's apartment to pick out clothes for her burial, a blue silk dress and turquoise earrings. In Bridget's jewelry box, Brooke came across an emerald ring and two pearl necklaces that her mother had assembled, purchasing them pearl by pearl with her winning proceeds of a weekly hearts game she played with movie moguls Sam Goldwyn and David O. Selznick. When the girls were toddlers, Maggie Sullavan had occasionally threatened to sell the pearls, noting that they were "the only valuable things I've got." Over the years, the necklaces had taken on legendary status, in part because neither Brooke nor Bridget had even seen them until their mother had died that previous January. Since then, Bridget had kept the necklaces together, but neither girl had ever worn them.

Pamela picked them up. "These are valuable."

"You bet," Brooke replied, putting them back in the jewelry box and taking it with her.

Going down in the elevator, Pamela smiled at Brooke. "We have just read the will and your darling sister, sooo adorable, has left your father her entire trust fund. She must have known how much we could use it."

"How interesting, Pamela. How interesting and ironic, since it was Mother who set up that trust fund with the proceeds from *Voice of the Turtle* [in 1943, some $150,000]."

"And not only that," Pamela continued, "but she left him her entire savings account, which seems to have about twenty-five thousand dollars in it. Amazing, isn't it?"

"Yes, indeed, but, of course that was mother's life insurance," Brooke replied.

The exchange troubled Brooke: the smile, the statement. "She was trying to get across that the money which otherwise might have gone to [Bridget's] brother or sister was instead going to Father and her. It was a gloat. A little teeny gloat. It was the first time I thought, this money thing is odd."[7]

Bill Hayward never should have been in the Menninger Clinic, the psychiatric center in Topeka, Kansas. He is a bright, charming man with a wonderful sense of humor who is now a successful Los Angeles lawyer. His father slammed him in the mental institution because he didn't know what to do when Bill left Maggie and moved in with him. Bill and Bridget had walked away together from their difficult mother and were crying out for attention from their father.

Leland was too preoccupied in 1956 filming *The Spirit of St. Louis* to give it to them. Bridget needed help, but Menninger's was little more than a thirty-thousand-dollar-a-year jail/babysitting service for Bill, who tried to escape at every opportunity. He wed another inmate as a ploy to get out and joined the army to ensure that Topeka was behind him.

The marriage didn't work, but Bill was sent to Germany, where Leland called him in early 1962. He and Pamela would be in Switzerland in March. Bill should meet them there and they would celebrate his twenty-first birthday, his coming-of-age, an important celebration. Winston was coming. The boys could ski together.

"That sounds great," said Bill. "I'm seeing a girl named Gerda, though. I'd like to bring her along."

"Fine," Leland replied.

Until Pamela heard about the girl. Suddenly Gerda was going to be awkward. Bill convinced his father otherwise and the matter was forgotten. After several calls in which Gerda was mentioned and dropped, the plans changed.

The new venue was London and Bill was expected to meet Pamela's parents. At the same time, Bill was summoned by his commanding officer, a Major Forbes. The criminal investigation division had advised the major he had Winston Churchill's grandson in his unit — which stunned Forbes as well as Bill, who had never considered himself related to Churchill. Bill's family, Forbes was told, was very influential and had asked for an investigation of Bill and Gerda's relationship.

"I was incredibly pissed off, seriously, seriously angry," said Bill. He immediately called his father. "I was just raging and he kept saying, 'I don't know what you're talking about.' He denied any knowledge of it."[8]

Leland soon called back, all apologies. Pamela thought Gerda was a prostitute seeking an American visa through her relationship with Bill. Bill declined to note any irony. Pamela launched the investigation by calling Kay Summersby, Dwight Eisenhower's wartime aide and alleged lover. The report had been forwarded to a London psychiatrist. Bill felt every shred of his privacy had been violated. He was more determined than ever to bring Gerda to London for the family reunion and did. At Heathrow airport, they were met by Pamela and Winston in two cars.

"Bill, you ride with me," Pamela said. "Gerda can go with Winston." Once in the car, Pamela tore into him immediately; "Don't you have any idea how wrong it is to travel across an international border with someone you're not married or engaged to?"

Bill was indignant. "Isn't that the pot calling the kettle black, Pamela? When I met you, you were traveling across international borders with my father. You weren't engaged. He was married to someone else. To hear this from you is unbelievable."

Bill was amazed that Pamela was oblivious to her meddling. She kept telling him how she was only acting in his best interests. He decided then and there that Pamela would not last. "I made an instant decision that Leland was going to figure her out and she'd be out of here." He laughed. "I was completely wrong."[9]

After the abortive reunion, Pamela and Leland returned to New York and had dinner with Brooke and her new husband, actor Dennis Hopper. Over drinks at 1020 Fifth Avenue, Brooke asked whether they'd seen Bill in Europe. "That unleashed the dogs of war," she recalled.

"Your brother is the most reprehensible human being I have

ever known," Pamela said, downing the remains of a scotch sour.

"Wait a minute. He's not at all reprehensible. What did he do?" Brooke asked.

"Slow down," Leland interjected. "Stop. Whoa."

Pamela would not be headed off. "Bill deliberately set out to torture your father to such an extent that he would drop dead. He brought this hooker to England."

"Now Pam, now Pam," Leland tried again. Pamela grew angrier. Her face turned the color of her hair. Until then, Brooke had never seen her lose control. Nor had she ever witnessed such a display of the maxim that redheads are tempestuous by nature.

Leland finally calmed Pamela down and the foursome proceeded by limo to dinner. Not to Pavillon, where they usually ate, but to Frankie and Johnnie's, a Broadway steakhouse, which Leland never frequented.

In the restaurant they discussed art. Leland was knowledgeable and Dennis had recently begun buying paintings. A painter himself who later collected Frank Stella and Roy Lichtenstein, Dennis said that his favorite painters were Willem de Kooning and Jackson Pollack.

"Oh, I knew that beatnik," Pamela said, using her favorite word for any man who did not wear a suit.

"You knew Jackson Pollack?" Leland asked. "I never knew that."

"Oh yes."

"How did that happen?"

"I met him one summer. He was the biggest slob I've ever met. Just dreadful. Smoked cigarettes. Drank beer. Thoroughly unattractive. Awful man. Awful painter. Horrible. Horrible."

Dennis was riveted. He had long wanted to meet Jackson Pollack, but he was also shy and did not want to confront Pamela on Pollack. Instead, he asked Leland the background on his Vuillard. Leland perked up. Pamela cut in.

"Leland, now that we've brought this up, don't you think we should leave those paintings to the Met?"

"What?"

"Yes," she went on, "we could have them in a living trust and keep them on the walls while we're alive and then they could revert to the museum."

"Well, I've never thought of that."

"I think it's a very, very good idea," she said, ending the conversation.

The men adjourned to the rest room. Pamela patted the chair next to her for Brooke to move over.

"Are you shopping here?" Pamela asked.

"God no," said Brooke, who lived in Los Angeles. "I'm so pregnant that all I could buy are maternity clothes and I've got plenty of those."

"No, no, no. I meant for Dennis."

"For Dennis? What am I going to buy Dennis?"

"Well, you know why we're eating here."

"No. I have no idea. It quite astonished me."

"Because I knew Dennis wouldn't be presentable," she whispered. "That tatty old raincoat . . ."

"That's a brand-new raincoat, Pamela. Bought this very day at Brooks Brothers." Silence. Pamela did not speak again. Brooke was baffled. She could not understand why Pamela hated her brother and her husband.

Outside the restaurant, they said their farewells and went their separate ways.

"Boy, that is one evil woman," Dennis told Brooke in their cab.

"I beg your pardon?"

"You know why she said that thing about the Met?"

"No. I don't understand why she said most of what she said."

"Because she is worried now that the paintings might fall into your hands. Because I had noticed them, admired them, discussed them. She doesn't want you to have them. Furthermore, I don't think she wants you or Bill to inherit anything from your father. What do you think that whole thing with Bill was about? That girl wasn't a hooker. She said that to set you and Bill up and I am now one of the instruments. She's going to use me to turn your father against you. It's already underway."

"Dennis, that's the most ridiculous, paranoid thing I've ever heard."

"I know these kinds of women," he said. "I know I'm right."

Brooke and Dennis returned to California after the dinner at Frankie and Johnnie's. They had met in New York in 1961 when both appeared in the play *Mandingo,* but Dennis had varied interests and was never quite certain what he wanted to do. "Photographers always thought of me as an actor, painters thought of me as a photographer and actors . . . well, Paul Newman said, 'You should really concentrate on your painting.' "[10]

After their daughter Marin was born in 1962, Dennis was mostly a druggie. The next six years, until she left him in 1968, were awful for Brooke. During those years, Leland came to California regularly. He invited Brooke to join him for lunch on occasion, but he never went to her house, saw Dennis or his own grandchildren. "It was all very formal and cold," said Brooke. "Pamela would be there, of course. I never saw Father again without Pamela." Whenever Brooke spoke to Leland by phone at home, Pamela picked up and monitored the call.

As far as Pamela was concerned, Leland's family was crazy. Despite his five marriages and barbiturate addiction, she refused to acknowledge that Leland himself was anything but stable. But the rest? First wife Lola and son Bill were institutionalized; Maggie and Bridget had killed themselves; Brooke was still in her twenties, had three children and was twice divorced.

"I don't think she's had a very happy life," Pamela said of Brooke years later. "One of Brooke's problems is that she and Jane Fonda were brought up together. And Jane became a very successful actress. And Brooke wanted desperately to be a good actress and it didn't work out for her. She also wanted to become a very good mother and I don't think that really worked out. So I think there were a lot of frustrations within her about her own life."[11]

This degree of dysfunctional life was a completely new experience for Pamela. So far as she was aware, no one in her family had ever been to a psychiatrist or ever gone to a doctor unless physically sick. Depression or other mental illnesses were not, by her reckoning, illnesses, an attitude many Britons share. She had never even known anyone who had had mental problems. She was not certain that psychiatric disorders really existed. To her, young people were not disturbed. They were immature and could be straightened out with discipline.

In Brooke and Bill's case, the discipline was to ignore them. When either came to New York, the guest rooms at 1020 Fifth Avenue were not available. In late 1962, his army duty completed, Bill left Germany on a troopship for the United States. He had informed his father that he wanted to stop over for Christmas, but when he arrived in New York and was discharged on December 21, the Hayward apartment was shut. A message instructed him to move into the River Club. Pamela and Leland had flown to Palm Beach for Christmas and a New Year's Eve party with Jack Kennedy, the Agnellis and other friends. Bill called and was told not to come to Florida. Leland suggested that a visit to Brooke in California was a better idea.

In the mid-1960s, with the Hayward children gone, Pamela broke into the Manhattan social circuit. It had taken her a while to crack and for a long time she was frozen out of the top coterie. After her assault on Slim Hayward, few of the ladies who lunched at the Colony, La Grenouille and La Caravelle trusted Pamela, "the famous international siren," as gossip columnist Knickerbocker called her.[12]

"Tout New York is divided into warring camps," the Slim or Pamela contingents, Truman Capote had written in August 1959 as the battle was joined. "Babe and Minnie [the third Cushing sister] have vowed undying enmity to 'that bitch,' while sister Betsey is Mrs. C's greatest partisan, so grateful is she that the threat to her own happy home has been removed."[13]

Proclaiming himself "a Slimite to the death," Capote received a telegram from Slim soon after Pamela and Leland were married: "I wonder if she tied a ribbon on it," Slim cabled.

A year later, Capote called Slim to insist she help him. "What possible trouble or disaster could befall Pamela?" he asked.

"I don't know. Why?" Slim asked.

"Well, I sent a cable to Gloria Guinness saying, 'Isn't it a shame about Pam.' Now I know I'm going to get a cable back, saying, 'What do you mean?' And I've got to invent something quickly. But what can it be? She can't be pregnant."

"No. We know she can't be pregnant. I don't know what it could be, but I'll try to think of something." Slim thought quickly and fired off a cable to Capote: HOW ABOUT CLAP — AS IN APPLAUSE?

By the middle 1960s, it was obvious that the Haywards were a happy couple and, more important, that Pamela was a devoted wife who had stopped looking over other wives' shoulders for the main chance. Capote had relented and considered Pamela one of his "swans," ten or a dozen women — including Babe, Gloria Guinness, Marella Agnelli and Slim — who to him symbolized all that was classy and beautiful.[14]

It was perfectly natural that the Haywards be included at his "party of the century," the Black and White masked ball he gave at the Plaza Hotel in November 1966 for *Washington Post* publisher Katharine Graham and 539 other of his best friends.

He asked Pamela and Leland to host a preball dinner party with a show-biz crowd that included Claudette Colbert and Frank Sinatra and his new wife, Mia Farrow. Other ball guests included some key figures from Pamela's past: Marella and Gianni; Laudomia Herculani, Pamela's successor in Gianni's affections; Marie and Averell Harriman, who ignored Pamela when he saw her socially; Betsey and Jock Whitney; Babe and Bill Paley; three Rothschilds, but not Elie; Mrs. Stavros Niarchos; Count Rudolfo Crespi, her old Capri host; Mrs. William Woodward, who housed the Digbys on her first trip to the U.S., and Slim.

Capote wrote Pamela into *Answered Prayers*, his unfinished novel that caused a sensation when one twelve-thousand-word chapter — "La Côte Basque 1965" — was published in the November 1975 issue of *Esquire*. The title came from Henri Soule's prestigious restaurant on East Fifty-fifth Street, which the swans patronized.

The characters included P. B. Jones, a Capote clone if not his imaginary evil twin, and the fictional Lady Ina Coolbirth, a "tall, big, breezy peppy broad," who together over many glasses of Roederer Cristal told a series of scandalous, gossipy stories that the writer had been collecting for years while lunching, cruising and partying with his Black and White Ball guests.

Around the room and through the story, giving it extra cred-

ibility, Capote scattered the names of real characters: Carol Mat-
thau asks Gloria Vanderbilt if she'd been to a party at the Josh
Logans'. She had, but only for an hour. It was "marvelous," said
Capote's Vanderbilt, "if you've never been to a party before."
Jackie Kennedy and her sister, Lee Radziwill, were there, "in
whispering Bouvier conspiracy . . . a pair of Western geisha girls."
Diana Vreeland, "the pomaded, peacock-iridescent editor" of
Vogue; and sisters Babe and Betsey.[15]

"Outwardly Lady Ina was Slim; inwardly, she was Pamela,"
said Gerald Clarke, Capote's biographer. Truman told Clarke that
Pamela had actually experienced everything that happened to
Lady Ina in his story, including being raped by clan patriarch Joe
Kennedy. "Whether it happened or not, I have no way of knowing," said Clarke. "The book was fiction and Truman sometimes
made things up, so he may just have elaborated a good story. But
I did find out that while Truman occasionally exaggerated, and
although he had a reputation as a tremendous liar, really most
of the things were true."[16]

As Capote's Jones listens in rapt fascination, Ina describes how
"the old bugger slipped into my bedroom, about 6 o'clock in the
morning, the ideal hour if you want to catch someone really
slugged out." When she awoke, "he was already between the
sheets with one hand over my mouth and the other all over the
place. The sheer ballsy gall of it — right there in his own house
with the whole family sleeping all around us. But all those Kennedy men are the same: they're like dogs, they have to pee on
every fire hydrant."

Afterward, Ina continued, "Can you imagine? He pretended
nothing had happened. There was never a wink or a nod, just
the good old daddy of my schoolgirl chum. It was uncanny and
rather cruel; after all, he'd had me and I'd even pretended to
enjoy it; there should have been some sentimental acknowl-
edgement, a bauble, a cigarette box. . . ."[17]

Ina, it turned out, was fortyish and "on the rebound from an
affair with a Rothschild who had been satisfied with her as a
mistress but hadn't thought her grand enough to wed." Her
friends were pleased when she turned up with a new husband:

"true the man was humorless, dull, sour as port decanted too long — but, all said and done, a lucrative catch." Leland? Of course not. Averell? Certainly possibilities there.

"My kind of woman needs a man," Lady Ina explained. "Not for sex. Oh, I like a good screw. But I've had my share. I can do without it. But I can't live without a man. Women like me have no other focus, no other way of scheduling our lives; even if we hate him, even if he's an iron head with a cotton heart, it's better than this footloose routine."

Slim was furious with the story, especially with another anecdote that involved a Bill Paley–type character having horrific sex with a woman who shared some similarities with Marie Harriman, who left menstrual bloodstains "the size of Brazil" on the sheets at his pied-à-terre in the Pierre Hotel.

She and the Paleys cut the writer off after the excerpt was published. Capote told Slim, in vain, that Lady Ina was not she. In fact, he told other friends, he was describing Slim's worse enemy.[18] That could have been none other than Pamela, who, unlike the others, was not troubled by Truman's piece. She liked being considered outrageous — Jane Digby again — and she loved publicity. A little distance made the scandal buzz easier for her to take. By the time "La Côte Basque" was published, Pamela had left New York for Washington and taken on a completely new persona.

Nonetheless, Capote turned to Pamela again for inspiration for another character featured in "Unspoiled Monsters" and "Kate McCloud," two more chapters from *Answered Prayers* which Esquire published in December 1976.

Calling the woman Rose Grantwell, the writer described her in one of his notebooks: "There are certain women, and a few men too, who, though perhaps not born rich, are born to BE rich. By and large, these persons are artists of an odd variety; money, in astronomical amounts, is their instrument — they require it as a violinist requires a violin; a painter, paint. Without it they are creatively impotent; with it, they fuse elements — from food to fine motors — into fantasies that are both visible and tactile. In other words, they know how to spend dough; but in a manner that, while morally arguable, is at least aesthetically valid."[19]

Capote has been accused of and damned for innumerable transgressions but never for lousy insight or a weak eye for detail. His Rose notes fit Pamela to a tee, as did his Ina characterization. There was no reason why he should not have captured her. She loves gossip almost as much as he did and she saw more and more of Truboy, as Bill Paley called Truman, as the 1960s progressed.

"We spent a lot of time on yachts together," Capote told biographer Clarke. "Anybody becomes a confidante on a yacht cruise and I think I've lived through every screw she ever had in her life. Believe me, that's an Arabian nights tale of a thousand and twelve! She's interesting because she has fantastic taste and she knows everything about everything, but she has no intellectual capacities at all. She's some sort of marvelous primitive. I don't think she's ever read a book, or even a newspaper, except for the gossip column. . . . Pamela's a geisha girl who made every man happy. They just didn't want to marry her."[20]

By 1970, Leland's health and career were failing, but Bill Hayward was in good shape. He had taken Leland's advice and gone west to see Brooke. There he met Dennis and teamed up with him, childhood friend Peter Fonda, who had also been in love with Bridget, and Jack Nicholson and coproduced *Easy Rider*, a watershed film which made them wealthy and famous just as Leland's career hit the end of the road. "He was having serious financial problems by then," said Bill, who loaned his father money to produce *The Catonsville Nine*, an unlikely project for Leland but right up Bill's alley.

Brooke was back in the family fold, reinstated after her 1969 divorce from Dennis. "As if nothing had happened," she said. "It was back to the old days. Everything was very cozy." Pamela invited Brooke to stay with them at Haywire. At the time, Brooke was involved with actor and screenwriter Buck Henry, a writer of the 1967 hit *The Graduate*, who had written and acted in the just-released *Catch 22*. Pamela liked Buck because he was a star. Leland approved because he had hired him to write and act in "This Was the Week That Was."

Leland had a stroke that summer and was limping and having

difficulty getting around. Because of his infirmity, Brooke felt it would be sensible to tie up some loose ends. In front of Pamela one day, she asked her father, "Now that you've sold 1020 Fifth Avenue, I wonder if you two could tell me where my mother's pearls are and also that big square-cut emerald ring that you gave Mother."

"Good question," Leland responded. "Pamela, where are the pearls?"

"They must be in a safety deposit box," she said.

"I'd like to get them back," Brooke said. "My daughter is now ten years old and I'd like to have them for her. And I've never worn them myself." They were too valuable for Brooke and Bridget to wear, but when they were old enough and responsible, Maggie Sullavan told her daughters, they could have them. When she died, her husband, Kenneth Wagg, turned them over. Bridget held them until she died because she had a locking jewelry box given her by Slim, and Brooke was worried about the security of her West Side apartment. After Bridget's funeral in October 1960, Pamela had brought up the subject of the jewelry.

"Leland, do you know that Brooke had these pearls and this big emerald of her mother's?"

"Yeah. So?"

"Well, I think she should put them in my safe."

Brooke broke in. "I absolutely do not wish to do that because I will never wear them."

"But you don't have the slightest concept of how valuable they are," Pamela said.

"I actually do since they've been in a safe deposit box all my life and I've never worn them. I could put them in a safe deposit box right next to my apartment, take them out and wear them whenever I want."

"That is insanity," Leland said. "You live right across the park from us, literally ten minutes. You could just take a taxi if you want to wear them. Pamela, show Brooke your safe."

Pamela took her down the hall and into a closet where the safe had been custom designed to fill an entire twelve-foot-tall wall. The safe comprised fifteen to twenty drawers, each with its

CBS broadcaster Edward R. Murrow, the most famous American in wartime Britain, became obsessed with Pamela.

Pamela leaving New York for England on the *Queen Mary* in April 1946 after learning that Ed Murrow had decided not to leave his wife and child to marry her.

International News Photo/Bettmann News Photo

Marie Harriman stayed in New York during the war, but when Pamela and her husband briefly resumed their affair in 1946, Averell's wife decided to join the statesman in Europe.

A svelte Pamela and Young Winston in the south of France at the outset of her romance with Gianni Agnelli.

Gianni Agnelli and his sister Suni in 1948 when Pamela met the heir to Fiat and began their five-year romance.

Gianni Agnelli, 32, marries the pregnant Princess Marella Caracciolo di Castagneto, 26, in November 1953 after breaking off his affair with Pamela.

Pamela and Young Winston leaving New York for Paris after her 1956 hospitalization for cancer surgery.

Old friends Elie de Rothschild (*left*), and Aly Khan at the racetrack in Chantilly, France. Pamela had a fling with Aly; a five-year clandestine affair with Elie.

Broadway producer Leland Hayward and his wife Slim in 1949. Ten years later, Pamela moved on Leland while Slim was playing around in Europe with Ernest Hemingway.

Pamela picked up countless tips on how to run a home and care for demanding men from the duchess of Windsor, whom she accompanied to the 1957 funeral of couturier Christian Dior.

Pamela and Leland in New York during their 1959 courtship. Pamela, who changes her appearance like a chameleon, has taken on a more matronly look en route to her second marriage.

AP/Wide V

After an early fascination with Broadway, Pamela became bored and, in 1963, opened the Jansen Boutique in Manhattan.

Clementine and Winston Churchill at the 1964 wedding of their grandson Winston to Minnie d'Erlanger. Old Winston would be dead in less than a year. Pamela is third from right, rear.

Cheray and Peter Duchin. Peter was raised by Marie Harriman; both helped Averell through his bereavement after Marie's death in 1970.

Brooke Hayward and Peter Duchin, happily married after each separately endured unpleasant experiences with Pamela.

In September 1971, thirty years after beginning their wartime affair and six months after the death of Leland Hayward, Averell married a delighted Pamela.

After ten years of marriage, Pamela and Averell celebrate his ninetieth birthday with a $220,000 political fund-raiser.

Pamela and National Gallery director J. Carter Brown, the man in her life following Averell's death, after what friends called "the best face-lift in the world."

Bill Clinton arrives with Hillary at Pam[ ]
Georgetown home for dinner in Noven[ ]
1992, two weeks after he was elected [ ]
ident of the United States.

Pamela in May 1993 at her U.S. Senate
confirmation hearings to become U.S. a[ ]
bassador to France.

own combination and each lined in dark, plush, gray velvet-like moleskin. There was a drawer for the diamond sets, another for pearl sets, yet another for emeralds. Indian jewelry filled a drawer. Each drawer was about a meter wide and nearly six inches deep. Some were double layered with special places for rings, earrings and bracelets.

"There was nothing haphazard," Brooke recalled. "It was as organized as Harry Winston's, just unbelievable. I don't wear a lot of jewelry and don't appreciate it much, but I appreciated this." Brooke said the hell with it. Refusing to keep her few pieces there was not worth a big argument. She never thought what she would do if she wanted the jewels and Pamela was not there. She gave her stepmother the necklaces and emerald ring.

Ten years later at Haywire, Brooke was relieved that her father remembered the exchange and recalled even that he had helped instigate the storage arrangement. Pamela said she would check the next time she was in the city. The subject came up several more times. Pamela's response was the same. The safe was built-in. When the apartment was sold, the jewels went to a bank. She had not had a chance to check at the bank. "Then Father died, and I just knew that my worst fears were about to come true."

Brooke had a taste of impending trouble the previous summer. Pamela took her for a drive one day, stopped at the foot of Haywire's long, winding driveway and burst into tears. Given the family's theatrical background, Brooke was certain that Pamela was acting for some reason or another.

"I'm so worried, Brooke, so worried," she said. "I don't know anything about Leland's finances."

Brooke did not care about her father's finances. She knew he had spent most everything he had. "I'm using my capital to live," Leland told a friend in the late 1960s. "I know what I'm doing and I'm doing it on purpose."[21]

Brooke was also certain that whatever Leland had left would not be going to her or Bill. They had been getting along recently, but Leland's icy, standoffish behavior during her marriage to Dennis made it obvious to her that she had been written out of his will. Bill assumed that he had been cut out too. He and his father had a terrible fight after Bill ran off with a woman, leaving his then wife Rita and their two children. But if the will didn't matter to either of Leland's children, it did to Pamela.

"I can't find his will," she told Brooke. "Nobody knows where his will is. He won't tell me where his will is. I've asked him a million times."

"So what?" Brooke asked. "Who cares where it is?" She did not know herself, although she assumed Pamela was asking to see if she did.

"Well, there's no indication how much money there is, what kind of shape he's in financially . . ." Pamela's voice trailed off. There was little question that she was frightened.

The will appeared at the reading, held at Haywire three days after Leland died. Brooke believed one or more of the three executors, all friends of her father's, had been holding the document. The family adjourned to the downstairs sitting room for the reading conducted by Pamela's brother, Eddy, who had become Lord Digby. The procedure took only a few moments because the will was simple.

It was dated 1948. Leland had not updated the document since his divorce from Maggie Sullavan. Under its terms, half of everything he had went to his three children, of whom two survived. The rest went to his wife, although there was little left beyond two properties, Haywire and a small Manhattan apartment at the Beekman. That was not the point. The point was that he had not left any cash and had thus not taken special care of Pamela.

Brooke, Bill and Pamela were astonished when Lord Digby finished reading. Brooke can only guess why he never updated the will. Part of her believed that her father never got around to it. Another part believed that the terms of his divorce from Sullavan prevented any meaningful alterations, but also that he could not bring himself to cut off his children. She also wondered whether her father had figured out Pamela's acquisitive nature. "My hunch is that, as utterly besotted as he was with her, he saw something of what she was doing. He was not a stupid man. He was an agent. He knew something about money even if he wasn't into estate planning."

Other friends of Leland agree. "He knew what was going on,"

said a woman who had known Leland for years. "Pamela was wonderful to him in one way, but he was so smart. He'd been around beautiful women his whole life long. I don't think he was unaware of what she was doing."[22]

Pamela had paled. "I want to be executrix," she announced.

"Fine," said Bill. "Of course, I'll have to get in touch with my lawyers." Brooke was with Bill. She declared that she still expected her pearls and emerald ring to be returned.

The meeting broke up hastily. A star-studded roster of show-biz guests was arriving upstairs for the wake and lunch. Frank Sinatra was escorted to the casket for a private viewing. So was Jacqueline Onassis. On this freezing March day, everyone was bundled up in dark, warm clothing except Jackie, who wore all white — suit, shoes, purse, gloves, even white-rimmed dark glasses.

That evening, after the guests departed, Pamela summoned Brooke to her bedroom. As her stepdaughter sat, Pamela erupted. "She lost it. She had a fit, a tantrum. Redheads do have tantrums. She stomped. She screamed. She threw herself around the room," Brooke recalled. "I don't think any of it was rehearsed. It was just a pure breakdown."

"He's left me penniless," Pamela screamed.

"She could not believe that she had been married for eleven years to a man who had left her nothing. So I say, 'You can't say he's left you penniless. God knows this house is worth a pretty penny and everything in it is yours, so you're not penniless.' Well, that didn't seem to help. I didn't want to say what about the numbered bank account in Switzerland filled with guilt-money from your European boyfriends. I didn't say any of that."

Pamela was seething. "I just can't believe it," she whined.

"The implication," Brooke said later, "was that Bill and I were stealing from her by having any of it. She was the one who spent it all" on gardeners, maids, a cook and driver.

Pamela had treated Leland wonderfully, wonderfully well. He was the only man who had ever left another woman for her and she adored him. Her focus never dimmed and she waited on him hand and foot. When he was well, he began coming home for lunch rather than eat at the Colony because Pamela had a manicurist waiting — he never had a manicure until he met her — and a masseuse. "What an amazing way to live," Leland used to say in wonderment and joy. Also expensive. Pamela cut back toward the end and reduced staff, but their overhead remained high.

Brooke and Bill moved from Haywire to New York and spent part of the next month working out the terms whereby Pamela would become executrix. They posed three conditions: there would be three appraisals made of Leland's possessions before he married Pamela, and Brooke and Bill could buy them back at the middle appraisal; Leland's photographic equipment would go to Bill; the pearls and ring would be returned to Brooke.

Pamela agreed to the conditions, said both Brooke and Bill, and was named executrix. But none of the stipulations was met, which prompted Bill to sue Pamela.

Bill wanted to purchase his father's office desk, chair and some books on the theater; Brooke wanted nothing. The middle appraisal was $750. Bill wrote a check for the amount. Pamela returned it torn in half, saying it was not enough. She produced another, much higher appraisal which Bill was unwilling to pay. "She wanted to give the books to the Lincoln Center," said Bill. "I don't think she had it reappraised to annoy me as much as she used it to get a higher tax credit."

Leland and Bill were camera fanatics who often took pictures together and swapped equipment. When 1020 Fifth Avenue was sold, Leland consolidated his gear at Haywire. When on the day before the wake Pamela asked Bill to take pictures of the casket, which was covered in an extravagant blanket of carnations, she opened Leland's storage cabinet. This held a wide assortment of Hasselblad, Nikon and Leica camera bodies, lenses, motor drives, lighting and darkroom equipment.

When Bill returned after their agreement was reached, the majority of the valuable pieces of photographic gear were gone. A neighbor of the Haywards dropped by Fox and Sutherland, a Mount Kisco photography store, a day after the funeral. The neighbor and Mr. Fox commiserated about the death of Leland, who had given the neighbor photographic advice and who had spent hours in the store. Mr. Fox told his customer that he was doubly stunned. Just that morning, Mrs. Hayward had delivered some of Leland's best cameras to be sold.

And while it was not part of the agreement, Bill never saw again his father's collection of scores of men's watches. Two were given him. There was no word on the fate of the others. (Once, Bill's son Leland came to visit, carrying a leather attaché case that Bill recognized as having belonged to his father. "Where'd you get that?" he asked his son, who replied: "I got it from Winston.")

The pearls and emerald ring were never seen again. A month after the funeral, Pamela asked Brooke to come to Leland's city office, which was being dismantled. Sitting with her feet up on his desk, Pamela told her: "I think your father must have sold those pearls, because I can't find them. It's so interesting. I gave him a beautiful Cartier watch and I can't find that either. I just wonder if he could have sold it." Blind with rage, and believing that Pamela had often sold jewelry in the past, Brooke stalked from the room to seek out Kathleen Malley, her father's longtime secretary.

"Malley, do you think Father could have *sold* my pearls?" she asked.

"Dear girl, your father never threw away or sold *anything*. You'll find in his safe deposit box the first pair of cuff links he ever bought."

"Do you suppose Mrs. Hayward could have misplaced them?"

"Mrs. Hayward has never misplaced a safety pin."

"Then where do you suppose they are, Malley?"

"I don't know."

Brooke left and called her friend Jean Stein. Together they went to a jeweler, where they sold for five hundred dollars the blackamoor Pamela had given Brooke on their first meeting, which she had never worn. The cash was little consolation. "What am I going to do?" Brooke lamented. "She was the caretaker of the one thing I had from my mother and she betrayed me." Jean replied: "Someday you'll write a book about it."

Five years later, Brooke was sitting in the Château Marmont in Hollywood when Pamela telephoned: "I hear you're doing a book."

"You're right," Brooke said. "I have and I've finished it. Thank God, it's in and it's getting edited now and it's going to be out next year."

Silence.

"What is it called?" Pamela asked.

"It's called Haywire."

Longer silence.

"Why?"

"Basically it's because my family is crazy and it was father's cable address and it's also the house he died in."

A really long silence. Then, Pamela said, "I see," and hung up.

Pamela immediately destroyed the stationery, address cards, napkins, matchbooks and everything else embossed HAYWIRE. That same day, she renamed the house Birchgrove, which was what Britain's Conservative prime minister Harold Macmillan called his country home.

🔁 🔁

CHAPTER FOURTEEN

Frank

LELAND'S DEATH TERRIFIED PAMELA. By and large, she had been completely happy during their twelve years together. She had finally had a faithful man who adored her. The only difficult times had come at the very end, when Leland became increasingly frustrated by his health, but Pamela had never slacked in her efforts to care for him. That was all the more reason why the business with the will shocked her. She was frightened by what she considered to be her precarious financial situation and incensed that Leland, a theatrical legend on both coasts, had not provided better for her.

The day of the funeral, Walter Thayer told Pamela she did not have enough money to keep Haywire and would have to sell the house, an alarming possibility for anyone with Pamela's financial neuroses. There was such a short-term cash flow problem that, according to friends, Gianni Agnelli stepped in to help out with immediate needs, including paying for some funeral expenses.

If money was vitally important, it was not her sole concern. For a woman who had spent most of her life living through men, the prospect of having to cope as a single again was devastating.

It had been twenty-five years since Ed Murrow dropped her, the last time she had felt so alone. That rejection was horrible, not least because she had no one in the wings, a problem bound to be more difficult to resolve at fifty-one than at twenty-six.

She was not entirely lacking for male companionship. While Leland lay ill, Pamela saw a great deal of Dr. William Cahan, a distinguished surgeon at New York's Memorial Sloan-Kettering Cancer Center, whose patients included Leonard Bernstein, Yul Brynner and Babe Paley in addition to Leland. Cahan had once been married to a Pamela, the daughter of stage star Gertrude Lawrence. That marriage collapsed in part because of the handsome surgeon's wartime affair with a Danish journalist named Inga Arvad, who was simultaneously involved with a young U.S. naval lieutenant named John F. Kennedy.

At the time Cahan was seeing Pamela Hayward, he was married at Mary Arnold Sykes "Sisi" Cahan. Certain of Leland's friends maintained that Pamela broke up the Cahans' marriage, but the claim is exaggerated. Pamela may have been the final straw, but the Cahan union had been under severe strain for years, as friends confirmed and as Dr. Cahan detailed in his 1992 autobiography *No Stranger to Tears*.

Brooke Hayward was upset that Pamela was out and around with Cahan while her father lay dying. Nor was Sisi Cahan pleased that her husband escorted Pamela to the opening night of *The Trial of the Catonsville Nine* while a hospitalized Leland was trying vainly to recuperate from emergency surgery to repair a neck artery which carried blood to his brain.

"Bed-bound in New York Hospital and convalescing, he asked if I would take Pamela to the opening night. *The Catonsville Nine* was an artistic and dramatic success and Pam and I returned to Leland's room that night to tell him. He was elated," wrote Dr. Cahan. "However, what with the cumulative tensions between Sisi and me, the fact that I had escorted Pamela became another bone of contention, particularly as there had been some attendant gossip about us, all of which was untrue."[1]

The Cahans' bickering intensified and Sisi told friends that Pamela and her husband were having an affair. Leland died six weeks after their opening-night date. The Cahans separated less than a month later.

Some Hayward friends believed Pamela and Dr. Cahan would marry. "He was always at Haywire," said a neighbor who knew the Haywards well and visited the Westchester property frequently. Perhaps just conscientiously making house calls? "Oh God, no. He was always there. They were terribly close. Everybody expected them to get married."

Not everybody. Cahan was a fine surgeon and highly respected, but other friends of both doubted that he was wealthy enough for Pamela. "She didn't love just for money, but after Randolph she didn't fall in love with any poor people," said a New Yorker who had known her since the war. "The meter was always running."[2] Whether or not money had anything to do with what happened or did not happen, their friendship went no further.

Three years after Leland died, Dr. Cahan married Grace Mirabella, the talented editor-in-chief of *Vogue*, who later launched the magazine bearing her name.

The morning after Leland died, Pamela placed a call to Cheray and Peter Duchin. Attractive, gregarious and well plugged in to the New York social scene, the Duchins were weekend neighbors whom Pam occasionally invited to Haywire for Sunday lunches to help cheer up Leland when his health began to fail.

On March 19, the Duchins were not at their Bedford Village home, but in Hobe Sound, Florida, where they were taking care of Averell Harriman. After forty years of marriage to Averell, Marie Harriman had passed away the previous September. "Pamela called to tell us that Leland had died and please could we make sure that Averell knew that Leland had died," said Cheray Duchin Hodges. "His obituary was in the *New York Times* that morning and please, would we in some way point it out at breakfast time."[3]

Cheray was surprised by the call. The Duchins had not seen the Haywards for some time and were unaware that Leland had been close to death. Nor had Pamela ever had any extended discussion of Averell with Peter, who had been raised by Marie as an unofficial Harriman ward. During an after-meal walk one day, she asked him how Averell was and to say hi, but that was it.

Both Cheray and Peter deliberately ignored Pamela's request. Averell was seventy-nine and hated talking about or being reminded of death. He made a point of not reading obituaries. Later in the day, Cheray mentioned casually that Leland had died. Averell made no response at all. "I looked back on that call later and thought, how stupid we both were," said Cheray. "God, is she ever calculating."[4]

Calling Leland's death "an overwhelming shock," Pamela admitted that "I kind of was stymied" in trying to decide what to do next.[5] There was no question that she wanted to remarry as quickly as possible. Having spent her twenties and thirties maintaining how wonderful it was being a bachelor girl, she knew the lonely fate of single women in their fifties. She was not going to dawdle. But first she had some chores to complete.

Leland's mother, Sarah, lived in Van Nuys, California. She was in good health for eighty-five but had difficulty hearing on the telephone. Pamela wanted to go west and console her, discuss Leland's death and estate and try to reassure her that she would be taken care of, as indeed she was.

Grandsarah, as her grandchildren called her, was worried that she might lose her house in the fractious maneuvering between Brooke, Bill and Pamela over the will. "We took an obligation to pay her, support her, but it didn't give my grandmother any peace of mind," said Bill Hayward. "I didn't feel comfortable about Pamela being her landlady. But in fact, Pamela was great to my grandmother after Leland died."

Pamela had been fond of her mother-in-law ever since Leland introduced them early in their courtship. It would have been hard not to like and respect the older woman, who was warm, direct and who also shared a surprising number of traits with Pamela. Chief among them was that both were crazy about Leland or "the most wonderful person in the world," as she called her son. Like Pamela, she had grown up in a tiny, isolated farm community, Nebraska in her case, which she was anxious to leave. She too was high-spirited and had little proper education, dropping out of boarding school in her teens when she fell in love with Leland's father, "the best-looking man I ever saw."

Shades of early Averell! It was more like shades of early Randolph, though, when the marriage broke up, which was quite unusual in 1911. "I just got bored with him and he was probably as bored with me" was her no-nonsense explanation. She turned around and married a very wealthy businessman, moved to Park Avenue and, sharing custody of her only child, parked Leland in a succession of boarding schools.[6]

Pamela knew the story well from long talks with Grandsarah. The echoes of their common experiences helped forge a bond that made it natural for her to ease the older woman's concerns after Leland died.

Gloria and Jimmy Stewart, the latter a flying buddy as well as a longtime Leland client, invited Pamela to come stay and use their West Los Angeles house as a jumping-off place for Van Nuys, a half hour away by car. Pamela had spent a week at the Stewarts', visiting Grandsarah and the Fondas, when Frank Sinatra invited her to his home in Palm Springs. She eagerly accepted and Frank sent his plane to pick her up. That is one version of the story.

A variation is that Pamela called Frank, said she was in the neighborhood and asked if she could come by. Whichever is correct, it was entirely in character for Sinatra to be a gracious host for Pamela, especially at that moment. He is famous for lavishing care and generous attention on the wives of dying men or their widows, as Betty Bacall, Phyllis Cerf, Leonora Hornblow and Edie Mayer Goetz have all attested.

He was charming to Pamela too because he was a good friend of Leland's. He had not been a Leland client, but he had appeared in two of the producer's television spectaculars and the men shared many mutual friends. In the sixties, the Haywards were among the regulars invited for Christmas and Easter holidays to Sinatra's Palm Springs home, along with Roz Russell and Freddie Brisson, Edie and Bill Goetz, Leonora and Arthur Hornblow, Ruth Gordon and Garson Kanin and Phyllis and Bennett Cerf, whose Mount Kisco home Frank used as a summer retreat in his bachelor days before he married Mia Farrow in 1966.[7]

Sinatra's Palm Springs estate is actually a compound of various houses and cottages, perfect for large groups of pals, whom he loved to collect. Pamela thought it was the Italian in him which fostered a need to have lots of "family" around. He made certain that his guests had every comfort and convenience. Each bedroom had a fully stocked bar with snacks, his-and-her closets and bathrooms with toothpaste, shampoos, slippers, bathrobes all provided. The main kitchen was open twenty-four hours a day, partly for the convenience of guests and partly for Frank, a committed night owl, whom they sometimes found sitting up at 5 A.M. watching television. A guest could have anything from omelettes to steaks to calamari delivered within minutes by picking up the phone.[8]

Pamela loved the company but hated the compound, which she found in appalling taste. There was no rhyme, reason or grand design to the collection of cottages which sprawled higgledy-piggledy across the property. Most visitors found the informality charming, but Pamela considered the hodgepodge an assault on her eye.

One year when the group gathered for Christmas, Frank had added a cottage and Pamela and the others trooped into downtown Palm Springs to buy paintings to decorate the place. Frank ordered by wall in the dealer's studio. He'd take all those modern ones on the left wall, another dozen from a wall in the next room. Pamela thought the pictures were terrible, but the expedition was fun and the cocktail-fueled hanging procedure hilarious.

Pamela was around for various stages of his short-lived marriage to Mia Farrow. She adored Mia and found her a wonderful child-woman. While the gang of regulars, sometimes augmented by the visiting Lucille Ball, laughed through anecdote-laden meals, Mia retreated to her bedroom, where she played with dolls or drew pictures of her horse, oblivious to all else going on. Pamela thought the marriage was doomed from the start by differences of age, temperament and interests.

What really surprised her was Mia's insistence on resuming her acting career rather than devoting herself 100 percent to the marriage, as Frank wished. The concept of a woman pursuing a profession instead of servicing her husband was totally alien to Pamela. When the marriage collapsed, Mia asked Pamela to speak to Frank to see if he would reconsider. Pamela did, but with little expectation that it would do much good, especially since she thought Mia's position was untenable. No feminist, then or ever, Pamela agreed with Frank that a wife's place was in the home.

Pamela was no different from the untold numbers of women — and men — who loved being around Sinatra, partaking of the glitter, glamour and adrenaline rush that came from being with a gigantic but potentially dangerous star. Sinatra was a Jekyll and Hyde celebrity of fabulous talent, wealth and fame who could be transformed in a flash from Mr. Wonderful, donating a hospital wing or anonymously picking up all the expenses of an ailing friend, into a mobbed-up Mr. Terrible who, usually when drunk, was prone to threats and violence. Leland and Pamela used to talk about Tough Frank, but they never witnessed his dark side. They only saw Compassionate Frank, who would sit all night by the hospital bedside of the dying Lennie Hayton, husband of singer Lena Horne, hold his hand and urge him to rally and never to give up.

Pamela had a particular fondness for flying anywhere on Frank's jet. (Or for that matter, on anyone else's, including that of her Mount Kisco neighbor Edgar Bronfman, the Seagrams distillery boss.) In 1970 when Leland was ill, he urged her to go along with the Hornblows to a Sinatra concert in London. When it ended, they joined Frank for dinner at Winfield House, the official residence of then U.S. ambassador to Britain Walter Annenberg and his wife, Leonore.

Frank was flying directly back after the dinner-dance and Pamela thought nothing of swanning out of the residence on his arm into the limousine that took them to his plane. By the time they landed in Westchester, where he dropped her off before flying home, gossip columnists had an affair well underway if not consummated at thirty thousand feet above the Atlantic.

The rumors intensified after Leland died and Pamela turned all dewy-eyed and clinging when Frank turned up at the wake at Haywire. They reached fever pitch when Pamela moved into the Sinatra compound in May 1971 for what Rosalind Russell called "sunshine, fresh air and friendship."

In early June, Fleet Street picked up the story. "There is speculation in California that Frank Sinatra is thinking of marrying again. His bride-to-be? Pamela Hayward," trumpeted the *Sunday*

Express.[9] Later that summer, the *Daily Mirror* predicted that Pamela and Frank would marry in September.[10] In her best-selling biography of Sinatra, Kitty Kelley claimed that Frank wanted to marry Pamela but that she rejected his proposal.

None of these stories was true.

Was there a fling? Almost certainly, according to friends of both Pamela's and Frank's. Sport sex was of no consequence to either of them. But there was no affair and no proposal and no realistic prospect of marriage because, while Frank respected Leland and was more than willing to be kind and sympathetic to Pamela, he didn't much like her.

She was not his kind of woman. It had nothing to do with her looks, which she had allowed to become somewhat dumpy in Leland's final years. Frank liked any number of women who were less than physical beauties. It was Pamela's personality that grated on him. The singer found her boring, arrogant, pompous, pretentious and generally phony. She is more than that, but it was an accurate assessment as far as it went. She is fully capable of displaying all those attributes.

"Pamela sure tried, but Frank had no interest at all," said a woman who has been a Sinatra friend for decades. "He likes someone who can fuck, fight or hold the light with that Vegas showgirl glamour. That's why Barbara [Sinatra] has been so fabulous for him."[11]

"Frank had great contempt for Pam," said another woman who knows both parties well. "She asked to come by and he expected it to be for two days. But she stayed and stayed and stayed and finally he had to throw her out." He even asked the Annenbergs for advice about what to do with her. Sinatra told one friend that Pamela thought that he was crazy about her and wanted her, but that was the farthest thing from his mind. "As far as he was concerned, she was a woman whose husband he greatly respected and he wanted her out of the house and he finally threw her out."[12]

"She went absolutely gaga over Frank Sinatra, was very turned on and used to flirt with him," said a fourth source who knew both principals well. Later, Pamela's obvious interest in Sinatra would annoy Averell, who was jealous. When it got into the papers that Pamela was close to marrying the singer, Bill Hayward called Sinatra, whom he knew through his father, to ask if the reports were true. "Frank said, 'Nah, she's too old for me, and besides, she's got no sense of humor about anything.' "[13]

When young Winston once said at a dinner at Orsini's restaurant in New York, "Thank God, Mummy didn't marry Frank," one guest cracked up laughing. "I wanted to say, 'As though she had a chance.' I don't know what she was telling the rest of the world about Frank Sinatra, but I sure know what he was talking about."

In fact, Pamela was truthful in what she said publicly, namely that Sinatra was a friend who had been very kind to her. She did not claim then or since that there was an affair or that he proposed. If he had offered, her situation would have eased. She was at the end of her rope by mid-June, frantic about what to do and how to avoid having to sell her house.

When Walter Thayer urged her to put the Westchester house on the market to reduce expenses and gain some capital, she half-joked that for all he or anyone else knew she might marry Onassis or Niarchos in a few months and all her financial troubles would be behind her. They were not candidates. Onassis was married to Jackie Kennedy and Niarchos to Tina Livanos at the time and, like Sinatra, neither had asked her.

Nonetheless, citing them in the abstract was an indication of what Pamela had in mind. She had no intention of lowering her sights nor did she believe she might have to. One of her better qualities is an absolute refusal to give in to pessimism or despair. When she wants something — a house, a car, a trip — nothing is allowed to stand in the way. She goes all out to get it, beating down every obstacle.

If something does not work out the way she wants — not marrying Ed, for instance — she moves on with her head held high. No spirits are allowed to flag, an approach honed under Winston Churchill's roof during the darkest days of war. As a result, she is not one to brood, torture herself or even turn introspective about setbacks. Whether it be the failure of a love affair or cracked ribs in a fall from her horse, Pamela dismisses pain and nails a smile in place.

The smile can light up a room, but it is frequently artificial. Pamela is a natural optimist — she was certain the United States would join the war and Europe would be saved from Hitler — but she is not by nature a happy person. She correctly disputes claims that she always gets her own way. In her mind, she has been frequently disappointed: by family — her own and Leland's — by fickle friends, irresolute lovers and husbands who left her in precarious financial straits. Every bad experience made her tougher internally even as her own ambition and behavior — more controlled and compassionate during her marriage to Leland — made her appear outwardly more vulnerable.

Her determination to get back on her feet after Leland's death took on a certain sense of urgency. She was so worried about resolving her future that in July she left New York for London, where she began to think the unthinkable: moving back to England. She was not there two weeks before all the bad old feelings came rushing back and she realized that whatever connection she had to her homeland had been irrevocably severed.

She was still being held to account for her wartime behavior. To many of her fellow Britons, she was an aging courtesan who had given it away a few too many times, starting when her husband was overseas defending his country. She felt no better about Britain. The men there still depressed her. Her Digby family ties had not improved. Seven years later, she would not even return for her mother's funeral.

Like a dervish, she rushed on. The next stop was a return to her old haunts in the south of France, but that too was an experience she could not repeat. Not only was she off that circuit but every well-married woman in Europe knew precisely what Pamela was up to: she was back prospecting and trolling. The "Widow of Opportunity," as she was then known, was on the prowl. They took special precautions to inspect and upgrade their defenses. Some all but dug moats and installed electrified fences.

Gloria Guinness had known Pamela too well and too long to be afraid of her. Unthreatened in her own marriage and quintessentially chic, she had plenty of confidence and knew every trick in Pam's book anyway. She and her husband, Loel, invited their old friend aboard their yacht for a Mediterranean cruise.

Pamela intended to spend the summer in France and as much time as possible on the boat. But suddenly she decided she could not stand the futility of life aboard ship any more, broke off the cruise and bolted home to Birchgrove. Whether there was a specific reason for her leaving abruptly is not clear. Some sources maintain that she fathomed that she had no future in Europe and decided to press on. Others say she learned that *Washington Post* board chairman Katharine Graham was hosting a party that she did not want to miss.

She may or may not have known about the party when she scampered off the Guinness boat, but what is clear is that she was despondent when she arrived home in Westchester. "You know the sort of awful August days when there's no sun and everything is sort of dark and raining and it's hot summer? And I came home to an empty house — and the *depression* of coming back," she remembered.[14]

There was a message waiting asking Pamela to call Mrs. Graham. Truman Capote claimed to Brooke Hayward that he arranged to have Pamela invited by his old friend and Black and White Ball guest of honor. "Truman claimed that she came off the [Guinness] boat very depressed and they talked one morning and he said, 'Well, listen, Pamela. What about Averell Harriman? Let's remember, Marie died a year ago. Kay Graham is giving a big dinner. He's going to be there. Call her. She's an old pal of yours, and go. Forget this European stuff.' He claimed it was all his idea."[15] Katharine Graham maintained it was all a coincidence.

Pamela jumped on the shuttle to Washington and went to Graham's Georgetown home, where the arrangement had been made to seat Averell next to Pamela. No, no, Pamela protested. Not side by side. Back to back was better. Less obvious, but at the same time more tantalizing and provocative. Averell would be forced to twist in his seat slightly and lean to face her. To respond to the tease properly, he would have to work a little. If he went for the lure, everyone who knew their history, which meant everyone at the party, would notice. The seating cards laid out, Pamela went upstairs to change for dinner.

CHAPTER FIFTEEN

Averell II

AT DINNER, Pamela and Averell twisted in their seats and talked and talked, ignoring most of the sixty guests, who instantly noticed what was going on and began talking about them. Pamela focused totally on the older man. Sensitive to his hearing problem, which was always worse in a crowd, she looked him straight in the eye and took care to enunciate clearly and avoid rolling her r's in the Churchillian cadence she often affects.

The two were so engrossed that when Liz Stevens, wife of the American Film Institute director, George Stevens, approached, Averell could not conceal his irritation. Why, he snapped, in a manner which years before earned him the nickname "the Crocodile," was she interrupting them when they were so obviously engaged? Stevens backed off fast.

They had a lot to discuss. They had spoken only twice in the twenty-five years since Averell relinquished the job of U.S. ambassador in London in 1946 and returned to the States to become Harry Truman's secretary of commerce.

The first was in Paris in 1949, when he was Marshall Plan

administrator and remonstrated with her for ruining her life by running around with European playboys.

The second time came in January 1965, when they flew home together from Winston Churchill's funeral aboard an Air Force jet provided by President Lyndon Johnson. Dwight Eisenhower led the U.S. delegation and he and Averell used the flight to end a bitter feud that had separated them since 1952, when Harriman sought the Democratic nomination for the presidency that the Republican Eisenhower won.

During that campaign, Averell attacked Ike bitterly: "He gets a briefing on economics from Herbert Hoover and a lesson on labor from Robert Taft," Harriman told a Democractic rally in Madison Square Garden. "When it comes to political decency, he clasps the hand of Joseph McCarthy." The former Supreme Commander knew Averell well from their days together in wartime London, when they were close enough to share great gobs of caviar that Averell brought Ike from Moscow, where he was seeing Stalin. A decade later, they were on opposite sides and Ike responded in kind, calling Harriman a "complete nincompoop. He's nothing but a Park Avenue Truman."[1]

Averell was pleased to have the quarrel resolved and, except for the time that he spent in the forward cabin talking to Ike, he and Pamela spent the rest of the eight-hour flight reminiscing. It was an emotional time for Pamela, who was then forty-four and back in England for the first time in a year, when she had returned home for her own father's funeral. Two days before old Winston died on January 24, her first grandchild was born, young Winston's elder son, Randolph. A great Churchill had died; a new Churchill had entered the family.

Harriman enjoyed talking to her in the relative privacy of the government plane, but he was always too embarrassed to acknowledge her presence when they crossed paths in public. He would not, for example, recognize her at Capote's Black and White Ball in 1966, although the Harriman and Hayward names followed one another on the guest list.

The snub had nothing to do with Pamela, who was always charming to her former lovers, or for that matter with Marie, who, with the passage of a quarter century, had by then dismissed the affair as wartime diversion. Stodgy Averell, however, may still have been smarting from a New York nightclub incident after the war when a guest at the table with him and Marie recognized Pamela across the room and, unaware of their history, began to gossip about her past. Averell sat stiffly, staring at the table and pretending not to hear. Good sport Marie stood up, pulled off her dark glasses and feigned an exaggerated stare toward Pamela, who was oblivious to the activity across the room.[2]

The Paris years had given the Harrimans a chance to repair what had been a rocky marriage. "They were very different types and the marriage did not work very well," said Ellen Barry, a longtime friend of Marie's. "She talked about leaving Averell but decided not to."[3]

A grandchild said that the real love of Marie's life remained Cornelius Vanderbilt "Sonny" Whitney, whom she had divorced to marry Averell. Sonny had been a run-around — he had cheated on her on their honeymoon — and was generally a difficult man, which was why she left, but he always had a big piece of her heart.

Marie drank scotch and talked frankly about her personal life to friends. Averell drank, but sharing confidences was never his style. He had pursued Marie passionately when she was married to Sonny Whitney, she confided. During their affair, sex with Averell was great, but his ardor cooled quickly after she left Whitney and they married.

He complained that Marie was too small for him sexually, although he could not explain why she had not been too small before they exchanged vows. Marie's conclusion was that he either had a Madonna complex about her or had simply lost interest. Averell also seemed upset that, although she had been only twenty-seven when they married, she never gave him children, especially a son to carry on the Harriman name.

Kept at arm's length by her husband, Marie went her own way with a succession of men, although one she lamented missing was James Forrestal, the secretary of the navy, who had been considered, at least in Washington circles, the Warren Beatty of his day. She rejected his advances once, saying they knew each other far too well even for a tumble, but later had second thoughts. "I wish I'd had an affair with Jim Forrestal," she mused to Luke Battle, a Washington friend, after Forrestal's suicide. "I'd like to have known what all the fuss was about."[4]

Averell also had second thoughts. After telling Marie that he did not want a divorce over Pamela, he later considered leaving her for a vivacious Washington journalist. When he was secretary of commerce and living in the capital while Marie remained in New York, Averell had become involved with Kay Halle, a delightful blonde whom he had known since the 1920s and whose wealthy father owned a department store in Cleveland.

Kay, or Katie as she was known to some friends, worked in the Office of Strategic Services (OSS) before turning to writing and counted the Roosevelts among her many influential friends in the Democratic party. Ironically, one of her closest confidants was none other than Randolph Churchill, who had proposed marriage to her in 1931, eight years before he met Pamela. She adored Randolph as an older sister might, but never slept with him and never had any intention of marrying him. Nonetheless, they remained dear friends until Randolph's death in 1968.

Kay's relationship with Averell was different: a full-blown affair during which he too asked her to marry him. She loved Averell and considered the offer seriously but finally turned him down, preferring to keep her prized independence.

"She knew if she married Averell she would be bullied beyond belief," said Timothy Dickinson, a friend of thirty years.[5] With no regrets but considerable bemusement, Kay fascinated friends with the story of how Pamela had captured her two closest male suitors. It did not bother her and she never had a bad word to say about Pamela in public. But in private, said a friend, she called her a "high-class prostitute."[6] Pamela just ignored her.

The Paris assignment put an end to the long periods of separation between Marie and Averell. After twelve years of operation, she had closed her Fifty-seventh Street gallery soon after Pearl Harbor, but she still had a rich collection of French Impressionists and contemporary American painters she had featured at the gallery, including Walt Kuhn, Isamu Noguchi, John Kane and Patsy Santo. She shipped them and some Cézanne, Matisse and

Picasso favorites to Paris, where she and Averell entertained informally, preferably low-key evenings with bridge or canasta the main attraction. The cozy pattern continued when they moved back to New York and Averell ran unsuccessfully for president in 1952 and 1956 and successfully for governor in 1954.

Averell was a good Marshall Plan administrator, but he was a weak politician and a stammering, leaden campaigner who managed to blow a huge Democratic lead in the New York gubernatorial race. He eked out an eleven-thousand-vote win of the more than five million cast.

"He accomplished nothing as a one-term Governor, for, unfamiliar with state issues, there was nothing that he wished to accomplish," Georgetown University fellow Jacob Heilbrunn wrote in the *New Republic*. "Like George Bush, he sought power as an end in itself."[7] When Averell ran for a second term in 1958, he was humiliated by another megamillionaire, the more personable and politically deft Nelson Rockefeller.

An assessment of Harriman's state record by Daniel Patrick Moynihan, New York's senior senator, who had been a young aide to Averell in Albany and once wrote an unpublished biography of his boss, shocked a November 1991 audience gathered to mark the centenary of the statesman's birth. "Averell never understood our party in New York," said Moynihan. "He ruined the party, rendered it incapable of governing."[8]

Pamela was so infuriated that she stalked out of the hall in the middle of Moynihan's remarks. He had committed more than a social faux pas. The ceremony, after all, had been organized by Pamela to help canonize Averell. Moynihan, an invited panelist, was mouthing sacrilege. Averell had so prided himself on his 1954 victory, his only popular election victory, that the rest of his life he insisted on being addressed as "Governor."

Nonetheless, Pamela is convinced that had she been married to Averell at the time, the 1958 result might well have been different. There is not an iota of doubt in her mind that she would have made Averell a better politician and possibly president.

The second notion is ludicrous. The dour Averell never had the popular touch a president needs. The first, though, is surely true. Even the statesman's best friends and supporters admit that

Averell was a lousy politician. Pamela would have been more directly involved, more organized and better attuned to campaign finance than Marie Harriman, who hated the nuts and bolts of politics. But there was nothing wrong with Marie's political instincts.

Out of office in 1959, Averell was supporting Missouri senator Stuart Symington for president in 1960 until Marie persuaded him to wake up, get with it and back John Kennedy. Harriman had an aversion to Kennedy because of his long-standing antipathy toward JFK's father, whose wartime behavior he considered despicable. Another difficulty was that Kennedy had not sought him out. Campaigning on a platform of youth and vitality, the Kennedy clan saw little reason in the early stages of their drive to solicit the help of a tight-fisted sixty-nine-year-old who had not been an early supporter.[9]

He finally came aboard and when Kennedy won, the president was persuaded by such thoughtful New Frontier types as Arthur Schlesinger Jr. to give him a chance. "I thought Harriman had one or two missions left under his belt," the historian told Bobby Kennedy.[10]

The president agreed on the condition that Harriman start wearing a hearing aid. Averell got fitted, took a modest State Department job, worked eighteen-hour days and soon enjoyed his finest hour of government service. He spent fourteen months from 1961 to 1962 laboriously negotiating the Laos neutrality accords and, a year later, produced the Limited Test Ban Treaty, which was the first major arms control agreement between the United States and the Soviet Union and Averell's greatest triumph of statesmanship.

Always in search of any post that would keep him somewhere close to the center of power, Harriman swallowed his personal dislike of Lyndon Johnson and pleaded to be included in LBJ's new administration. "One of the most self-absorbed and coldly ambitious men I have seen in government," said syndicated columnist Joseph Alsop, Harriman "rarely took a direct stand and was well capable of covering his tracks with a careful re-ordering or reassessment of the facts when his reputation was threatened."[11]

When Johnson left office, Averell immediately tried to ingratiate himself with the incoming Republican administration by offering his Eighty-first Street house in New York City to Harvard professor Henry Kissinger to use during the transition. It was a blatant attempt to avoid isolation during the Nixon years.[12]

Averell had little influence on Johnson, who understood Harriman's cold ambition, but he never stopped trying to be a player. Averell's legendary persistence, combined with a willingness to ingratiate himself — and adapt his political convictions to those of whatever master he sought to serve — paid off. In 1968, the president named the then seventy-six-year-old to be U.S. envoy to the Vietnam peace talks in Paris and gave him a strong number two in Cyrus Vance, the skillful troubleshooter who a decade later became President Jimmy Carter's secretary of state.

Working for Johnson made it impossible for Harriman to support the presidential challenge that year of Robert Kennedy, who had become a close ally six years earlier during the Cuban missile crisis. Averell had courted Bobby, originally to insinuate himself into his brother's inner circle, but the political relationship evolved into a genuinely warm friendship. Marie and Ethel Kennedy became the best of friends and the two families often entertained each other at their houses in Georgetown, Hickory Hill, Hyannis and Sun Valley. In 1967, the Kennedys named their newborn son Douglas Harriman Kennedy for Averell.

At home, Averell and Marie were closer than they had ever been. Instead of growing apart, they had grown together. They moved to Washington during the Kennedy years and Averell discovered that the president, like Franklin Roosevelt, thought that the wisecracking, ribald Marie was wonderful. She became a grande dame of the Georgetown set, loved having friends over for all-night bridge games, and entertained in casual elegance in the Impressionist-filled drawing room or out by the pool in one of the chic neighborhood's deepest tree-shaded gardens.

When John Kennedy was assassinated, the Harrimans generously turned the house over to Jacqueline Kennedy and her children while she planned her future. Marie and Averell moved to a nearby hotel. "I hate it here," Marie cracked two days after they moved out. "Room service is awful and the fucking tub is so small I can't take a bath. But poor Jackie. She needs the house more than we do."

By the time Averell returned from the Paris peace talks and Richard Nixon took over the White House, Marie's health was fading. Her eyes had never been good and angina, respiratory ailments, high blood pressure and a weight problem were all taking a toll. Averell was twelve years older but in remarkable shape except for his hearing. He skied expert runs at Sun Valley well into his seventies and swam vigorously at the Hobe Sound house he had bought as a peace offering to Marie after his affair with Pamela. He took such pride in his flat-bellied looks and energy that Marie could not resist scoffing to anyone who remarked on his fitness. " 'Christ,' " she'd say. " 'You'd look good too if you did nothing but play polo until you were 50.' "[13]

She told some of her women friends that he would easily outlive her and would have to remarry because he was hopeless on his own. She had two candidates in mind: Luvie Pearson, the handsome and clever widow of columnist Drew Pearson, and Mary Russell, a widowed neighbor whose parents were Russian aristocrats and who had served as a translator for Averell on trips to the Soviet Union. Either would be fine, she told a bridge partner, just so long as he did not marry "that bitch Pamela."

Marie's death in September 1970, after a massive heart attack, devastated Averell. Normally stoic in the extreme, he virtually collapsed. At midnight, two days after her death, he asked to be driven to Joseph Gawlor's funeral home so he could see Marie. Allowed entry despite the hour, he insisted that the coffin be unlocked and opened. "I want her wedding ring," he told a startled companion, who wet Marie's finger and managed to pry off the band and hand it to Averell.

At a postfuneral reception at the house the next day, he asked that Ethel Kennedy meet him privately in the library. He wanted her to have Marie's ring, he told her, because Marie so loved Ethel that she would have wanted her to have her most treasured possession. Ethel was dumbstruck. "My God, what am I going to do?" she asked a friend a few minutes later. "I can't take this." The friend responded: "You've got to do this because that's what he wants."[14] Ethel put the ring on and, more than twenty years later, said, "I wear Marie's wedding ring proudly to this day."[15]

The friend concluded that Averell so respected and loved Ethel and Bobby, who had been assassinated two years before, that he was determined to maintain the relationship. After the Washington service, Marie was buried in the Harriman plot at Arden, alongside Averell's parents and sister Mary on a pinetree-shaded knoll overlooking the lovely family chapel of St. John's. Next to her was a space for Averell and, if he did remarry, plenty of room for another wife as well.

Averell was so despondent after Marie's death that his family feared for his health. Marie's granddaughter, Alida Morgan, came by the Washington house almost daily and found him disoriented, sitting in Marie's room, holding objects that had belonged to her and weeping. "He felt his life was over," said Peter Duchin, who had been raised by the Harrimans. "He was crushed beyond belief."[16]

Peter and his wife, Cheray, took their children out of school in New York and moved to Hobe Sound for the winter to keep Averell company, play croquet and bridge with him and arrange for visits by such old friends as Douglas Dillon, the former secretary of the treasury, and Eugene Black, the longtime director of the World Bank. Peter, who had followed in his father Eddy's footsteps as a society bandleader, left his band up north and flew out from Florida to join them for bookings around the country. Averell talked about Marie incessantly and considered commissioning a book about her. When he realized it would unavoidably involve their personal lives, he dropped the idea.

When his godmother Marie's will was reviewed, Peter learned that he was not in Averell's will. Marie had planned to leave Peter a Degas statue of a dancer in a tutu but was unable to because the figure was not hers to give. It was part of the Marie and W. Averell Harriman Collection, which Averell was negotiating to give to Washington's National Gallery in Marie's memory.

Peter, instead, was given some money and a Daumier bronze. (Later, after Averell died, Pamela sold the Degas dancer to raise cash to make good on Averell's $10 million pledge to Columbia University. According to one friend, Pamela lamented "Columbia wants the money and I haven't got it." After selling the statue, however, and resolving at least a portion of her obligations, she had enough left over to purchase John Singer Sargent's *Stairway in Capri*.)

In the course of discussions with Marie's New York lawyer, Sol Rosenblatt — whose son was married to the daughter of the trustee named for Peter by Eddy Duchin — Peter was told that Averell had made no provision for him. Peter was disappointed, not so much because he was not to get any money but because of what the decision meant about his relationship with Averell: namely that he was Marie's boy and should suffer no delusion about being Averell's too. After all, he called Marie "Mom," but Averell was always Averell.

Peter never expected to inherit much money, but he did think he would get something, possibly fifty thousand dollars. To learn otherwise made him more sad than angry, but later that winter Averell eased the jolt when he promised Peter that he would give him an acre of land on one side of the Hobe Sound property.

He and Cheray had an architect friend draw preliminary sketches. They reviewed them with Averell, who thought it was a great idea that they should build as soon as they saved up some money. They checked with the exclusive Jupiter Island Club to determine whether there would be any problem joining because the club had once barred a guest of Marie's on the grounds — she believed and thereafter boycotted the place — that he was Jewish.[17] No problem at all, the Duchins were told. They could join as soon as they began to build.

At the end of April 1971 — a month after Leland Hayward's death across the Hudson River from Arden — Averell left Hobe Sound to return to Washington. The Duchins were scarcely back in their New York house when Averell called and asked if they could join him that summer at Sands Point, his Long Island Sound estate: "You bring your nanny, I'll bring the cook and maid. I'll come up every weekend from Washington and we'll share it." Which they did.

Averell came up regularly on the Eastern Airline shuttle, carrying his own bag, except for the weekend when he stayed in Washington to attend Kay Graham's party. The following weekend he flew up and reported that he had seen Pamela at Kay's.

"Nothing more," said Peter, "but you could sense a little frisson."

Pamela called Sands Point immediately. She explained how she had seen Averell and how it was such a wonderful and warm reunion. They had spent the whole evening talking. She would love to come and spend a weekend. Would the Duchins arrange it with Averell? It was fine with them. They were happy to try anything to help Averell out of his depression. Peter asked, " 'How about Pam for the weekend?' and before '. . . end' is out of my mouth, 'Yes' is out of his."

She arrived the following Friday. She and Averell and the Duchins plus Michael Forrestal, son of the navy secretary and a Harriman protégé went next door for dinner at the home of Evie and George Backer, old friends from Averell's days in Albany, with Marie and Ed Goodman, who also lived nearby.

The next day Pamela was given a tour of the local estates before dinner at the Goodmans. Neither Cheray nor Peter could make the Saturday dinner. Cheray had a long-standing invitation elsewhere and Peter had a band job.

When Peter returned after midnight and went onto the porch for a nightcap, he flipped on the lights to find Pamela and Averell on a bedlike couch, her blouse undone and her skirt bunched up around her waist. Averell's shirt was open, his pants down around his ankles and his face was covered in lipstick. "Averell's expression was wonderful," Peter recalled. "He looked so happy."

Pamela whipped down her skirt and gathered her blouse. Averell yanked up his pants but could not pull up his zipper because it was stuck on his shirttail. By the time he did, Peter had apologized for intruding and had run out of the room to wake Cheray and tell her what was happening.

As he regaled his wife with the story, Pamela stomped deliberately down the corridor past their room, saying, "Goodnight, children," to her guestroom, where she slammed the door to indicate that Averell was not with her.

"Half an hour later, we heard this crash," said Peter. "I ran down the corridor and asked Pam, 'You all right?' "

"Oh fine, couldn't be better. The lamp fell down."

"The next morning at nine," Peter continued, "she burst open our door and sat on our bed with her negligee on, absolutely radiant and filled with energy. She had this blushing little-girl look which was very beguiling and could have nailed a few guys and said, 'My God, you won't believe what happened. It was the most wonderful night. Averell was so romantic. He was wearing silk pajamas and tapped on my window and climbed through.' " The noise had been Averell crashing through the screen.

Pamela was ecstatic. Averell was enchanted. Sex had always been important to him. Five years before, Lyndon Johnson had asked Averell to fly to Chile to roll back the price of copper. Joe Califano, one of the president's top aides, protested. The trip was too strenuous for a seventy-four-year-old. Nonsense, said Johnson. "You just call him up and get a car over to his Georgetown house. Ol' Averell likes women. You just tell him . . . we'll put a couple of pretty nurses on the plane and they'll start working on him as soon as the wheels are up and by the time he gets to Santiago, he'll have it up."[18]

He had not only rediscovered sex, but with a familiar partner who was eager to relive his glory days and play "Remember When" — as in "Remember when Max [Beaverbrook] wanted to . . ." or "Remember when Stalin told you . . ." He soared out of his slump and from that moment on, they were inseparable.

At the end of August 1971, he asked Pamela to come to Washington with him when he closed Sands Point after Labor Day. "I have told him that I will never go back to Washington unless I am his wife," Pamela told Cheray Duchin. To paraphrase a lyric from *South Pacific,* one of Leland's old shows, Pamela sensed that once he had found her, he would never let her go. "She played this brilliantly," said Cheray. "The next thing I know, they're engaged."

In mid-Sepember, Averell confirmed publicly that they would marry, "before the end of the year, probably next month."[19] They were actually married within ten days — a year and a day after Marie's death and six months after Leland's — in a ceremony conducted so quickly that young Winston was not able to get to New York in time. In London, he broke the news to Clementine Churchill. "My, my," she said with a chuckle, "an old flame rekindled."[20]

When 150 friends arrived at Harriman's New York townhouse

for 5:30 P.M. cocktails on September 27, 1971, they had no idea that ninety minutes earlier a wedding had taken place at St. Thomas More Catholic Church. Pamela wore a simple white V-neck dress with a brooch and a heavy gold necklace with pearls and gems, but there was no announcement, no cake, no toasts, no best man or matron of honor. Guests only began to catch on when Pamela greeted Kitty Carlisle Hart by squealing, "We did it. We did it."[21]

They acted so fast, said one source, because Pamela did not want it said or written that she married an eighty-year-old, which Averell would become on November 15. "Forget eighty," said a relative. "She wanted him before he keeled over. That could have happened at any moment and she would have lost everything."

In fact, the two merely moved up their plans to meet Pamela's condition that she would not go to Washington without a wedding band on her left hand. A rejuvenated Averell wanted her with him and was happy to oblige. Five days later, the newlyweds moved into the Georgetown house, only five blocks from Kay Graham's. "You know," Pamela told the publisher, "it was always Averell."

Pamela immediately began taking over his life. She summoned decorator Billy Baldwin to redo the N Street property. One of the first changes was the noticeably public hoisting through a second-floor opening of a large, thirty-thousand-dollar enameled wood four-poster double bed for the new master bedroom. No longer would Averell and his wife sleep in separate rooms on separate floors.

Averell had never shown any interest in fancy living. "He had that curious contempt for elegance that only the wealthy can normally afford," said George F. Kennan, his number two at the Moscow Embassy.[22]

Pamela had other ideas. Out went Marie's funky, casual furniture; in came elegant French and American antiques. Sailcloth throw cushions were replaced by fine needlepoint pillows with the Digby crest of an ostrich with a horseshoe in its beak supported by two chained monkeys and the family motto: *Deo Non Fortuna,* "From God Not Fortune," which more than a few visitors found wryly amusing.

The crest was stamped everywhere, on stationery and match-books; a silver ostrich later replaced the standard hood ornament on Pamela's Mercedes. The house was repainted in fresh garden hues: dark and lettuce greens, soft rose, vivid delphinium blues.[23]

Pamela flooded the house daily with freesias and armloads of other fresh flowers. Averell was euphoric.

"Pamela's so wonderful," he told Peter. "On my bed every morning is my favorite flower."

"That's great, Ave," Duchin responded. "By the way, what is your favorite flower?"

"I don't know, but it's on my bed every morning."

Washington's finest architect, Hugh Newell Jacobsen, designed removable glass panels for the sun porch so it could be used year-round for dinners or receptions without closing it in and losing the view of the terraced garden. "Don't tell Averell what it's going to cost," she instructed him in a mock conspiratorial whisper. "He's a bit mean with money, so just tell me and I'll take care of it."[24]

Averell was so upset by the size of the interior-decoration bills that Baldwin's assignment was cut back. "The finest business acumen" that decorator Paul Manno ever encountered had been applied to finessing the expenses. A close friend came over one day and was struck by the subtlety of the decorating changes.

"It looks marvelous. What have you done?"

"Ssshhh," Pamela responded. "Don't say anything. I've sent one piece out at a time to be redone. He senses something is different, but he doesn't know what it is."

"That was the first inkling I had that she was getting Averell to spend some money. Before then he wouldn't part with a cent."[25]

Pamela proceeded with care. Leland too had been stunned by the magnitude of the decorating bills she had run up and, if she had overplayed her hand then, she was not about to repeat the mistake. In Hobe Sound, soon after the marrige, she asked Dan Caulkins, a friend and regular visitor, not to point out to Averell some changes she was about to make to the garden and around the pool. Averell had refused to let her spend the money, so she had ordered gardeners to reseed and replant the areas in secret overnight, in the hours between his afternoon and morning swims.

"Won't he notice?"

"No, he won't," she replied.[26]

As he aged, her control grew, especially after she helped select a new manager of the Harriman office in New York which oversaw the family's finances and settled the bills.

For all her early caution, she eventually got what she wanted, with a license to spend that would have been inconceivable during the Marie era. When married to Marie, Averell had been so tight he squeaked. His sisters, brother and he had inherited $100 million from their father, E.H., but Averell never picked up a check and for years had no credit card.

Anyone who rode in a cab with him was asked to split the fare if not to pick it up entirely. Flights longer than the shuttle were booked to include lunch or dinner so he would not have to pay for a separate meal. He always brought a brown bag lunch to the office. If he worked late, he ordered in food for himself but not for subordinates helping him. He sat at his desk and ate in front of them.

One year, friends came to Hobe Sound for Marie's birthday and asked Averell what he had bought for his wife. Nothing, he said. She had everything she needed. Get in the car, two of them insisted. They'd drive to the store and help him pick out something. Averell went grudgingly and demanded they circle the block until they found a meter with time left on it. Once parked, he strode into the local drugstore and bought her a bottle of Nuit de Paris perfume, the cheapest scent they stocked, borrowed the money for the purchase and, over the protests of his fellow shoppers, took it home for Marie.

He had once asked Bill Walton to come to Florida from New York to help on a project but refused to give him a plane ticket. Walton made the round-trip by bus.

It was not a matter of Averell's denying others perks he had himself, because, for most of his life, other than money and property, he had few toys. He had no limousine, no chauffeur, no private jet when he and Pamela married. It was Pamela who convinced him that he needed all three, salesmanship that ultimately added years to his life. Averell eventually agreed. The plane was the toughest sell. It took her years of wheedling before he finally broke down in 1984, barely compos mentis at the age of ninety-two, and allowed her to buy a $3 million Westwind.

There was, however, a dark underside to Pamela's makeover of Averell's life. She sharply reduced contact with almost everyone who had known Averell through Marie, which covered the previous four decades. According to one former pal: "My husband and I knew Averell and Marie from the forties and were included at lots of things, but once he married Pamela, we were never invited again. I was part of Marie's circle and therefore ostracized. She wiped out Marie's circle."[27]

Pamela began the purification process with Marie's family. "She was determined to exclude everyone from Mummy's family," said Marie's daughter Nancy Lutz.[28] Averell's reserve melted in the presence of his grandchildren and step-grandchildren. When Marie's granddaughter Alida came to visit, she often brought along college pals. They thought Averell was wonderful, always curious and never condescending to students.

On the contrary, he was eager to learn what they thought about events and the rationale behind their analysis. But when Alida dropped by the Georgetown house in mid-November 1971 to wish him a happy eightieth, new staff had been hired. A butler she had never seen before directed her away from the front door to the kitchen entrance, where she was told that she needed an appointment to visit the house. A Tiffany calling card would be sent her if she left a forwarding address. Did she ever discuss it with Averell? "I never saw him alone again. I never talked to him alone on the phone again."[29]

Nancy Whitney, another Marie granddaughter, said that "it used to be that you could call and, if Averell knew you were on the phone, he would say, 'Oh, come over immediately.' But Pamela would say, 'Averell is very tired. He cannot see you.' I'd say that I'm going to be here for a week. Do you think possibly later? And she'd say, 'No, he's much too exhausted. He needs to rest and can't possibly see you.' "

Nancy's father, Harry Payne Whitney, Marie Harriman's son, was hospitalized once at the same time as Averell. Harry asked a nurse to wheel him to his step-father's room. "Pamela pulled the door closed, stood in front of it and said, 'You may not come into this room under any circumstances.' "

The same thing once happened to Nancy Whitney at Birchgrove. She had taken care to arrange a visit to see Averell in such a way that Pamela could scarcely say no. When she arrived, Pamela emerged and led her on a three-mile walk. When they arrived back at the house, Pamela stepped inside and closed the screen door.

"Good-bye, Nancy. It was very nice to see you."

"Excuse me, Pam. I came to see Averell and I'm not leaving until I do see him. That's why I've come here." She almost shouted it out, hoping that he had his hearing aid turned on and would hear her. "Which he did, and he charged out, pulled me inside and was absolutely thrilled and delighted to have a visitor," she said. "But the family was the old regime and we all had to go. She was very blunt about it and made it perfectly clear that we were not welcome in her sphere."[30]

Why did she behave in such a manner? Pamela would argue, and did, that she was trying to preserve Averell's health and strength to prolong his life. She would succeed in that goal, but there was more to the rationale. Lack of formal education was not the only deficiency which made Pamela feel insecure. In this instance, Pamela lacked confidence because she had had a miserable history with the families of her men. Ed Murrow's wife and son had stymied her. Gianni Agnelli's sisters had obstructed her every effort. She still bore the scars of dealing with Leland Hayward's children. She was fifty-one years old and Averell was her last chance. She had no intention of letting his family prevent her from controlling her marriage to her third and, ideally her final, husband. Pamela could best do that by seeing to it that Averell was thoroughly dependent on her.

Cheray Duchin learned that her family's time with Averell had run out when a package arrived at their home. There was no note accompanying the box, which was filled with a jumble of every framed picture of the Duchins and their children, photos with and without Averell, that had been in the Harriman houses. "I found it really tacky, but the message could not have been clearer.

There was not one picture of any of us in a Harriman house ever again."[31]

Some of the pictures that stayed, changed. Marie Harriman had a Walt Kuhn still life with green apples and shovels at Hobe Sound that was beginning to deteriorate in the sea air. She decided to send it back to New York for safekeeping but so loved the painting that she asked Bill Walton, the war correspondent, who was also a fine painter, to make her a copy. He agreed, painted a witty copy on a piece of brown paper, made a frame of driftwood and signed it "Homage à Marie, Bill Walton." When Pamela took over, she had Walton paint out the "Homage à Marie."

The Harriman houses themselves changed. Pamela did not like Averell's Manhattan home. She said it was too depressing, but it also had been Marie's. Too many memories, so it was sold.

Next, Pamela persuaded Averell to dump the Hobe Sound property. Averell had loved the home, with its professional croquet court, ocean views and a neighborhood of conservative friends whom he had known for decades. Pamela's rationale was that as Averell got older, he needed a warmer winter climate than Florida. It was not an unreasonable explanation, but old Averell friends and family members were cynical, and with reason. They believed that Pamela wanted to leave because she was never accepted at Hobe Sound.

"She couldn't stand Hobe Sound, hated it," said a close friend. "Averell couldn't understand why she didn't like Hobe Sound, but he went along with it."[32] Pamela's reaction should not have reflected poorly on her. There is much to dislike about Hobe Sound, which is one of the snootiest, most prejudiced communities anywhere, filled with the kind of patricians who looked down their thin noses at Pamela's past escapades.

Mrs. Joseph Reed — Permelia Reed — the powerful local doyenne and arbiter, was singularly unimpressed by Pamela's résumé. Even Marie Harriman, who was quite a populist, never much liked the place and imported most of her own friends, but she put up with it because Averell liked it. Because of Averell, Pamela was not frozen out, but neither was she ever made to feel comfortable.

She preferred Barbados, a more temperate island with ties to

England and a few good Broadway friends like actress Claudette Colbert. It meant a much longer flight for Averell, who was suffering from bone cancer and was becoming increasingly infirm by the early 1980s. His health and the difficulty of changing commercial flights en route to the island made a more compelling argument for the private jet.

Peter Duchin was sitting next to Pamela at the annual Al Smith Democratic dinner in New York City when she told him she was planning to sell the Hobe Sound house.

"Oh my God, really?" he asked, a sense of dread settling into his craw.

"Yes, I think we've got a very good buyer."

"Well, I hope you're not going to sell that acre that Averell gave me."

"Why shouldn't I?" she asked. "You don't have it in writing."

She bought a gorgeous estate named Mango Bay in Barbados, which the British set designer and architect Oliver Messel built in 1968 on a beachfront near Alleynes Bay on the Caribbean side of the island. The two-level, four-bedroom house, with an adjacent two-bedroom cottage, is constructed of pale coral stone and furnished in large part with pieces constructed from cane and coral by island artisans.

Wonderfully airy, with giant archways opening onto broad views of the sea and gardens overflowing with orchids, bougainvillea, limes, papayas and, naturally, mangos, it was used by the Harrimans for Christmas and winter retreats for themselves and friends like Cynthia and Richard Helms, the former CIA director, or Russian specialists Colette and Marshall Shulman from Columbia University, whom they flew in on the jet.[33]

After Walter Thayer's warning that she would have to sell it, Pamela took special pleasure in keeping Birchgrove, the former Haywire, where they spent part of each summer when the Washington weather became too hot and humid. Averell loved its cheery coziness, but the fifty-seven-acre hilltop property also allowed him to maintain a New York residence. It was the only one he had left in the Empire State after giving up the Manhattan property and having turned over the one-hundred-room baronial Arden estate to Columbia University years earlier.

But Birchgrove was too far from Washington to get to on weekends before the arrival of the Westwind, which Averell thought should be used only for business anyway. Which meant that after decorating the Georgetown house, Pamela was in the same position with Averell that she had been in a decade before with Leland: she had no readily available country place.

She fixed that in 1977 when Averell bought Willow Oaks, a sixty-eight-acre country home near Middleburg, Virginia, the heart of East Coast horse country and only an hour's drive from the White House. The picture-book estate sat on a hill overlooking Goose Creek and offered views to the foothills of the Blue Ridge Mountains. The fieldstone house was lovely and the grounds offered something for everyone: a cottage and tennis court for guests, a swimming pool for Averell, and stables and a holly-enclosed jumping ring for Pamela, who never lost her passion and talent for riding.

(William Rich III, who handled the Harriman financial affairs, realized that the house offered something else, a substantial tax break if it became their official residence. Not only were Virginia's property taxes much lower than those in the District of Columbia, but the estate could save up to $7 million in inheritance taxes when Averell died. There was a small problem. The Harrimans realized that the financially strapped local government in Washington, D.C., might look unkindly on the change because it stood to lose so much revenue. If it wanted to be difficult and challenge the amount of time they spent in Virginia or the District, where they still maintained offices as well as the N Street house, the District could make the issue awkward. The Harrimans seized on a practical solution: a fund-raiser at the Georgetown house for District of Columbia mayor Marion Barry. The residence change went through without a hitch.)

"It was the setting that really won us," said Pamela, who later bought three hundred more neighboring acres for protection from developers. "That and the fact that you can ride in any direction for as long and as far as you wish."[34]

Always a gutsy horsewoman, Pamela could ride with extra confidence in Virginia because Averell bought her only the finest horses. In this area, he needed little convincing to spend the extra tens of thousands of dollars that separate an average mount from a quality jumper.

It was more than his experience as a nationally ranked polo player that made him more knowledgeable than Pamela about superior horseflesh. Averell launched his own string of racehorses in 1922 with his then business partner George Herbert Walker, whose grandson George Herbert Walker Bush became president, and by the end of that decade he had won some of the nation's biggest stakes races and had become a big name in thoroughbred racing.[35]

He also knew, from personal experience, the dangers of riding. Three terrible family accidents guaranteed an otherwise out-of-character readiness to open the purse strings for Pamela. In 1915, Averell's first wife, Kitty Lanier, fell while riding with him along Riverside Drive in New York. The horse crushed her pelvis and, for a while, it was uncertain whether she would walk again.[36]

A second mishap proved worse. His older sister Mary Harriman Rumsey, who had persuaded him to become a Democrat and who had the most influence on him of any woman — and perhaps any man — until Pamela, was killed in 1934 after her horse stumbled when clearing a jump in the very same fields near Middleburg. A third riding accident left a niece permanently disabled.[37]

When Pamela went shopping for horses, she reminded Averell, "So many of your kith and kin have been badly injured by cheap horses." As a result, he did not cut corners when she rode. She, in turn, named her finest jumper The Governor, in his honor.

The wildflower gardens and tall oaks, sycamores, maples and pines are the glory of Willow Oaks. Hiking and riding paths cut through honeysuckle, dogwood, forsythia and lilies-of-the-valley remind Pamela of the grounds of Minterne Magna. She duplicated the breadth of a classic English garden with heather and myrtle along a wilderness walk, a kitchen garden of herbs and flowers, and the area around the house with roses, pyracantha and rhododendron, one of her father's favorite flowers.[38]

Looking over the property, Averell said, "My wife has an unerring eye," one judgment on which her friends and critics alike can agree. Her garden-and-flower eye operates much like the vision she brings to interior decoration. Her secret is in leaving the impression that an object, whether it be a tiny bridge over a creek, a coffee table of gold-painted bamboo, or a clutch of blossoms, looks just right and belongs exactly where she has placed it. As she explains, "However beautiful they are, if flowers are isolated in a spot where you would not come upon them naturally, there's something a bit false about them."[39]

The actual planting and day-to-day maintainance of the gardens were done by four workers under the direction of Bill Hoogeveen, a Dutch-born landscaper whose skills Pamela discovered when living at Birchgrove. He was then working for businessman William Green, chairman of the Clevepak Corporation, whose Bedford estate was known for having one of the loveliest gardens in Westchester County. Judy and Bill Green knew Pamela and Leland, had many of the same friends, and dined at each other's house on occasion.

When Bill Green died, Pamela tried instantly to hire Hoogeveen. She did it in a surreptitious manner, never calling or asking her friend Judy Green her plans, whether Judy intended to keep or sell the estate or whether Hoogeveen might be available. Ruthless in pursuit of something she wants, Pamela wanted Hoogeveen and she wanted him right away. She had to wait. "Bill Hoogeveen's behavior was flawless," said Judy Green.[40] He continued at the Greens' for three more years until the estate was sold, and then he went to work for Pamela. Recognizing his genius with flowers, especially orchids, his new employer even sent him on occasion to Europe to attend horticultural shows.

While Pamela was ordering Averell's life, he introduced her to his. He took her to Arden. The main house had been transformed into a Columbia University study center, but his brother Roland still lived at the nearby Arden homestead. They went on to the capitol at Albany, where he had loved being governor; to Sun Valley, where the simple but elegantly tasteful Harriman Lodge sits separately on the property of the resort he founded; to Fulton, Missouri, where her father-in-law made his Iron Curtain speech and nearby Independence to meet the Trumans; and to the Bethlehem, Pennsylvania, headquarters of the Union Pacific.[41]

In 1974, taking along his daughter Kathleen and Pamela's son Winston, Averell made the first of five trips to the Soviet Union.

He wanted to introduce Pamela to Moscow and show her the sights about which he had written her thirty years before, including the Kremlin rooms where he had met with Stalin and where the loutish Leonid Brezhnev then held sway. As Averell and Brezhnev discussed United States–Soviet relations and arms control issues, Pamela assiduously took notes for her husband.

With input from the specialist or two who invariably accompanied their party, sometimes Peter Swiers, a former State Department aide, they produced highly substantive trip reports which Averell cabled back to Washington for dissemination to White House and State Department officials. Pamela did not speak extensively in these sessions because Averell was notoriously unwilling to allow others to participate substantively in his high-level meetings. But she did ask the occasional solid question and Averell was tremendously proud of her.

On his final visit in 1983, he introduced her to Brezhnev's successor as general secretary of the Communist party, Yuri Andropov. "I am grateful to my wife, Pam, for coming with me," the old statesman told the old Communist. "I hope she will continue my work when I am no longer able to." Andropov, who unbeknownst to the Harrimans was dying himself, wished her well and invited her back.

Pamela was not charmed by the former head of the KGB. "I wouldn't want to play poker with him," she said after the meeting.[42] Experiences like that provided a grounding for her own growing interest in East-West affairs, not to mention unique credentials for her own diplomatic experience in the 1990s.

Two and a half months after they were married, Pamela was sworn in as a U.S. citizen as a belated wedding gift to Averell. "I want to vote and participate in the election," she said. "I think everyone knows which way I will go."[43]

Not if they had known her in the 1950s and 1960s, when she was very conservative. With the exception of her shift leftward while involved with Ed Murrow, all Pamela's instincts have been oriented toward the Republicans or, in broader terms, toward Britain's Tories. All that mattered was that Averell was a Democrat, as Averell's family realized. According to Marie's granddaughter Alida Morgan, "Like Averell, Pam was a pragamatist.

If she had married Nelson Rockefeller, she would have been a Republican; if she had married Frank Sinatra, she'd have been running the gambling lobby."[44]

Their Democratic candidate to topple Richard Nixon in 1972 was Edmund Muskie, the U.S. senator from Maine. Muskie's credentials matched their interests. A former governor, like Averell, Muskie had experience as a member of the Senate Foreign Relations Committee that had given him a solid background in arms control, which was Averell's passion.

The other candidates were of little interest: Hubert Humphrey, Johnson's vice-president, had destroyed his chances by refusing to distance himself from LBJ's Vietnam war policy in 1968, the same policy Averell was backing as LBJ's negotiator in Paris; Senator George McGovern's pledge to pull U.S. troops unilaterally from Vietnam was too dovish for Averell, who believed McGovern's policy, if enacted, would be an admission of weakness to Moscow.

Averell wanted to run as a Muskie delegate from New York, but the party had no interest in slating him, so he tried to run as an independent. Just as she had escorted Randolph to campaign stops in England before the war, Pamela drove Averell thousands of miles around New York State beating the drum for Muskie and Averell's candidacy as his delegate. She loved every exhausting moment. It was fun; it was political action and she was in the middle of it all.

More so than she realized at the time. Good crowds came out wherever Averell arrived, but when the votes were tallied, "The Governor" finished dismally, behind six McGovern candidates, including a nineteen-year-old antiwar activist. It turned out that most of the audiences turned out to see Pamela, whose reputation as a glamour girl and celebrity as Churchill's daughter-in-law had preceded her. After the election, a local group asked her to run for city council. She turned it down but was thrilled to have been asked.

She and Averell went to Miami for the Democratic convention, but the gathering was a terrible anticlimax. They hated McGovern and resented the fact that Muskie and Humphrey never cut a deal to try to deny the South Dakota senator the nomination. The convention itself was such a disaster that the Harrimans and historian Arthur Schlesinger and his wife left early and drove to Hobe Sound to listen to their standard-bearer's acceptance speech, a performance that left them feeling both angry and miserable. All in all, Pamela considered the whole matter a disappointing introduction to Democratic party politics which was made worse by Nixon's landslide reelection in November.

The experience depressed Averell, but Pam looked at the bright side. It was her first up-close look at and involvement with American politics. She, though, tells people otherwise, specifically that she and Leland worked for Bobby Kennedy in his 1964 U.S. Senate campaign in New York, including hosting a fund-raiser for him at Haywire, and that they helped again during his 1968 presidential run.

Robert Kennedy aides do not recall that Pamela or Leland were involved in either campaign. "I was not aware of them being around in 1964 and I'd remember for sure," said Fred Dutton, Kennedy's special assistant. "I know it was not true in 1968. They were in Jackie's social set, but I never saw anything on the political side."[45] Ed Guthman, RFK's press aide in 1964, saw no Hayward involvement that year. Frank Mankiewicz, who held the same job in 1968, said, "I don't have any recollection at all of their participation in the 'sixty-eight campaign."[46]

Because of Averell's closeness to Bobby and her nonpolitical friendship with JFK, it made sense that Pamela would have wanted to claim a pre-Averell connection. But adding to the discrepancy is the fact that Leland's political inclinations were primarily Republican.

He was conservative and promilitary and numbered among his friends not only such solid Republicans as Jimmy Stewart and publisher Walter Annenberg, but also Nancy and Ronald Reagan. Cheray Duchin Hodges, an active RFK volunteer, recalls Pamela being "very anti–Bobby Kennedy." "I remember one of those terrible, terrible jokes about the assassination that came out of Washington and New York that she thought was cute," and told shortly after she met Averell. "Averell turned on her and went absolutely crazy. She was dumbstruck. Her mouth just opened.

She didn't realize how stupid she was to have told Averell, of all people, a very tasteless joke on the Kennedys."[47]

Her connections with Jack Kennedy notwithstanding, Pamela's personal experience with the Robert Kennedy family was anything but good. When operating the Jansen shop in the mid-1960s, she had great difficulty getting Ethel Kennedy to pay bills that ran into the thousands of dollars. Once Pamela settled into marriage to Averell, however — a ceremony which Ethel officially witnessed — Bobby's widow and her clan could do no wrong. Averell was happy to lend them the cottage at Sun Valley for ski trips, but Pamela was appalled to discover that they had crammed up to thirty people in the small cottage and left it filthy, the carpets pitted with cigarette burns. Pamela did not complain, though, because Averell would not have wanted to hear it. Ethel was never a big fan of Pamela's either. She was a friend of Marie's, not Marie's successor as Averell's wife. After Averell died, the two women went their separate ways.

Pamela and Averell felt left out in the early stages of the 1976 presidential race. They favored no special candidate and had no natural ties to Jimmy Carter, a circuit-riding loner who achieved front-runner status outside the structures of the party and its establishment. "How can this man be president?" the eighty-four-year-old Averell muttered during the campaign when the former Georgia governor's polls showed him far ahead of incumbent Gerald Ford. "I don't know him."[48]

Nor did he and Pamela ever like Carter. The relationship grew to be proper but was never close. Little things bothered Pamela: instead of taking pleasure in receiving a note from the president, it annoyed her that he wrote "To Pamela Harriman" instead of "Dear Pamela" or "Dear Mrs. Harriman." As far as she was concerned, Carter had a lot to learn about etiquette.

Regardless of how little he knew Carter the candidate, Averell was determined not to be shut out if a Democrat made it into the White House for the first time in eight years. Through Richard Holbrooke, a foreign service officer and Harriman protégé who worked on the Carter campaign, Averell managed to meet the nominee and offer his services as an intermediary with

Communist party general secretary Leonid Brezhnev, whom he was seeing in the middle of the fall campaign. Carter was open to the offer and met with Averell several times during his presidency, including a session before he flew to Austria in 1979 for a summit with the Russian leader only months before Brezhnev ordered the Soviet invasion of Afghanistan.

As always, Averell's goal was to stay involved. "He was always on the lookout for political influence," said Zbigniew Brzezinski, Carter's national security adviser. "He wanted to be seen as part of the action and he wanted more or less to stage-manage the U.S.–Soviet relationship."[49]

Harriman actively disliked Brzezinski and believed that the Polish-born expert on the Soviets and East-West relations took too hard a line against Moscow. For his part, Brzezinski felt that Harriman was too soft and overly inclined to take at face value Brezhnev's pledges of devotion to peace and disarmament. Determined not to be denied access to the inner councils of the White House, Averell swallowed his differences.

Just as he had forsworn helping Bobby Kennedy campaign in 1968 so that he could stay on in the Johnson administration, Averell did what was necessary to ensure he would be included in the Carter Soviet policy circle. He invited Brzezinski to move into the bachelor apartments set up in the office annex adjacent to the N Street house until he and his wife, Muska, could find a Washington home. Soon after, he covered all bases when he and Pamela invited Cy Vance, his former deputy in Paris and the new secretary of state, whose attitude about the Soviets more closely resembled his own, to move into the guest cottage at Willow Oaks. Marshall Shulman, Vance's special adviser on Soviet affairs, and Richard Holbrooke were also given quarters.

Even then, the Harrimans did not ease off their cultivation of Brzezinski, who was the foreign policy gatekeeper at the White House and could admit or bar Averell from seeing Carter. Pamela sent flowers to Brzezinski's wife, then more flowers, too many, and a Virginia ham, and knickknacks and finally, an offer of a swimming pool cover. "I began to feel a little bit uncomfortable that she was trying to get me in a position where I owed her something," said Muska, who asked Pamela to stop.[50]

In the latter 1970s, her early years of sitting in on East-West discussions, Pamela had little substantive knowledge of United States–Soviet affairs. Until she began traveling to the USSR, her experience was limited to hearing from Averell about his meetings with Stalin and Molotov and the tutoring she received from Winston Churchill Sr. Both statesmen taught her during the war that regardless of personal feelings about the Communists, countries had to cooperate with Russia to get anything done. That was the only way the Allies could beat Germany. Years later, Averell's belief had not changed. Neither had Pamela's.

A decade later, after Averell's death and the collapse of Communism, Pamela returned twice to the former Soviet Union and visited Russia, Ukraine and Central Asia. Back home after the 1992 trip, she commissioned an op-ed page piece written under her name for the *Washington Post* and discussed with Brzezinski her findings, namely that the West had to pay attention to other former Soviet states in addition to Russia. "Her comments were on the ball and quite intelligent," to his surprise, he conceded. "She really was learning something. It wasn't just sight-seeing."[51]

President Carter admired Averell's unrelenting determination. It reminded him of his own approach: inelegant but dogged. Pamela had wondered before the selection of Vance if there were any possibility that Averell might be named secretary of state. The short answer was no, none. But in recognition of Harriman's tenacity and stature, Vance saw to it that he and Pamela were included on a succession of ceremonial delegations around the world. They went to Panama after the negotiation of the Canal Treaty and to Zimbabwe in 1980 to celebrate independence.

They attended more state funerals than Vice-President Walter Mondale: that of Robert Menzies, their wartime blitzmate at the Dorchester, in Australia; in London for IRA bomb victim Earl Mountbatten of Burma, whom Averell first met in the 1920s; Tito's in Yugoslavia.

Anytime a major leader died, especially one with a World War II or East-West connection, the Harrimans were on the shortlist of dignitaries. For one thing, Averell knew most of them personally and Pamela knew a surprising number herself. Also, as a star in the diminishing pantheon of legendary "statesmen," Averell added a touch of history and Pamela some flash to delegations that were sometimes topped out with campaign donors and "personal friends of the president," who were given the trips as a perk.

Enroute overnight to the ceremony for Tito in 1980, a few delegation members slept in bunks that pulled down from the ceiling of the Air Force jet. In the morning, Pamela suddenly looked around frantically. "Where's Averell?" A steward had inadvertently closed him up in his bunk. He was pulled back down, ruffled but unhurt. Coming off the plane in Belgrade in the morning, most of the group looked exhausted and rumpled from sitting up all night. Delegation leader Lillian Carter, the president's mother, emerged in a bulky sweatsuit for the arrival ceremonies.

Not Pamela. Looking as if she had just exited from the beauty parlor, she strode down the ramp in a perfectly tailored, uncreased black suit with a discreet pearl necklace and strode over to the press pen to tell select reporters that "the Governor" was prepared to conduct a background briefing for them at his hotel before their deadlines later that day. "A pretty impressive performance," was *New York Times* reporter R. W. "Johnny" Apple Jr.'s verdict.[52]

It was obvious to anyone who traveled with them on such trips that Pamela was totally devoted to Averell, worrying whether he had taken his medication, ensuring he was comfortable, getting him a blanket if he was cold or helping remove a sweater if he was hot. She was more than a wife, companion or nurse, though. She did her homework before every trip, poring over briefing papers and reading lists put together by their personal coterie of foreign policy advisers, men like Sandy Berger, Richard Holbrooke and Alfred Friendly Jr.

Pamela spent hours in her office reviewing the material, making green-ink jottings in the margins and calling the three specialists and others around town to answer questions or provide amplification. With her own knowledge growing, Pamela briefed Averell on everything from schedules to the substance of meetings when he had increasing difficulty hearing. "In many ways, she became his eyes and ears," said Madeleine Albright, the U.S. ambassador to the United Nations.[53]

Early in 1980, Pamela went with Averell to Capitol Hill to see Senator Edward Kennedy, who was preparing an intraparty challenge to Jimmy Carter for the Democratic nomination. Over a lunch of cold smoked salmon, Teddy asked the Harrimans to support him. Averell was adamant. As in 1968, he could not do it. As long as Carter was president, he intended to support him.

The choice was made easier by the fact that neither Pamela nor Averell believed that Teddy had what it took to be president. Robert Strauss, who was chairing Carter's reelection campaign, cracked to the president's inner circle, "Rose didn't have no triplets." The Harrimans agreed. Ted Kennedy understood their decision, but he had to try. The Carters were grateful that Pamela and Averell didn't jump ship and First Lady Rosalynn Carter called them at Willow Oaks to say thanks.

After a few nervous moments early on, the president easily withstood the Kennedy challenge and recaptured the Democratic nomination. But in November, Carter faced a far more daunting opponent in Ronald Reagan, who buried him in the most savage repudiation of a sitting president since Franklin Roosevelt rolled over Herbert Hoover in the middle of the Great Depression. In the Harrimans' sitting room, no tears were shed for Jimmy Carter. He had come to Washington as an outsider and left the same way, gone like dew on an August morning. They had good friends whom they were sorry to see out of office, but it was good riddance for the anti-establishment Carter.

The results, though, dumped them into the political wilderness, a frustrating wasteland for two similarly ambitious, coldly calculating Washingtonians whose most basic shared trait was a passion for being power players in highest-stake politics. The situation was made worse by the fact that not only had Reagan won the White House, but Republicans took control of the Senate for the first time in twenty-six years and made substantial gains in the House of Representatives. Such Democratic stalwarts and Harriman pals as Idaho's Frank Church and John Culver of Iowa and even Warren Magnuson of Washington, the most senior of all one hundred senators, had been knocked out of Congress.

The situation for Pamela and Averell looked bleak. When

Ronald Reagan was sworn in on January 20, 1981, they had been shunted about as far from the center of power as it was possible to be. She was sixty; he was eighty-nine. Anyone but the most valiant optimist, the most compulsive political animal, would have taken one of the nation's greatest fortunes and retired comfortably to Virginia's horse country or the lush, tropical warmth of Barbados.

CHAPTER SIXTEEN

🖎 🖎

Young Winston

RETIRING to relax or spend time with relatives was the last thing on their minds. Slowing down was out because it would mean drifting away from the key goings-on and family was of minimal interest to both Pamela and Averell. Each was too self-absorbed. Normally, self-absorption does not foster compatibility with a second strong character, but given their common passion for proximity to power, the connection was oddly consistent. To reach and stay at the apex, they needed each other.

Averell had the pedigree, knowledge and connections but was too old and cold to stay in the game on his own. Pamela had vitality and professional charm but lacked the substantive background or money to operate at top level. Each was willing to work hard, but neither was introspective, intellectual or grounded with a core set of beliefs. Both were derivative thinkers and operators.

Those traits may help explain why each felt so confused and despondent, almost desperate, when alone. Averell revealed his dependency whenever he had no presidential assignment and, ultimately, when he lost Marie. Pamela took pride in her independence in fleeing Minterne Magna and living "alone" in France in the 1950s, but she was rarely by herself and has long known that she needs to be with someone with power to thrive.

Individually, they were lacking, but together they made a formidable team. They thrived on mutual nurturing, but that was the extent of their familial instinct. Averell was a distant father to his two daughters; Pamela, an all but nonexistent mother to her son. "My sister has never been maternal," said Sheila Digby Moore.[1]

Only in recent years has Pamela even considered her role as a mother. Until contemplating life after Averell, she simply never gave the subject any thought. The irony is that she made her political reputation as the den mother or godmother or queen mother of the Democratic party. Pamela performed with distinction as an honorary mother. It was as a real mother that she came up short.

To her credit, she recognizes that parenting was not one of her strengths. The disruption of war gets some blame, as it should. But otherwise, she does not try to fake maternal feelings, justify her behavior, agonize over what happened or apologize. She merely presses forward. She did, however, put very little effort into motherhood and, as a result, of all her relationships, the one with her only child, Winston, is her most difficult and complex.

Pamela was able to leave her family and solid base at Minterne Magna because she had both. She and Sheila, Eddy and Jacquetta were raised by governesses and nannies. They did not see much of their parents, who came and went on their own adult schedule and even lived on a separate floor. Nonetheless, the upbringing of the Digby children took place within a reliable context: before the disruption of war and within the framework of happily married parents living in a home that Digbys had inhabited for generations.

Winston faced a much different situation. He was the favored grandchild of the most famous political family in Europe, at the time, probably in the world. Yet Winston grew up without a family life. He was the only child of a loveless marriage that was little more than a frantic prewar coupling. His father was an arrogant drunk and his mother a courtesan to rich men. Winston himself considers it an honor, but being saddled with the twentieth century's most distinguished name has been an even heavier burden than the one his more intelligent father, Randolph, was unable to bear.

Witness simply how he is addressed: past fifty and headed for grandfatherhood himself, his namesake dead for nearly thirty years, he remains widely known as Young Winston, with all the unfortunate reminders of who he is not. Is that fair? It would not be if he had attempted to live his own life, but because he has unwisely tried to imitate his grandfather, he brought much of the onus on himself. His 1989 autobiography, for example, is titled *Memories and Adventures,* after his grandfather's 1932 collection of essays entitled *Thoughts and Adventures.* "My favorite book," Pamela calls the elder Winston's volume.

Pamela considers her son to be a very important part of her life. As she should. Winston has been her ticket. Without him, Pamela Digby might have escaped Dorset. But her lack of education and early professional skills and her almost total lack of any sense of humor make it uncertain that she would have made it far. Ambition, amorality and drive alone would not have moved Pamela Digby anywhere near the men who helped propel Pamela Churchill to her current status.

Hers has been a life of the right contacts, sampled at Leeds Castle but first gained in earnest with the chance meeting of Randolph. Without Randolph's urge to marry and impregnate almost anyone who would have him before he went off to war, she would never have had access to 10 Downing Street. Because the marriage was over almost before it began, it was Young Winston who was her connection to Old Winston and then to the high and mighty, a passport that sliced away barriers to social and political acceptance in France and the United States.

Without her son, she would have no claim to being a Churchill. She not only divorced Randolph, but went the extra torturous step and annulled the marriage in her bid to wed Gianni. An annulment declares a marriage invalid, as if it never happened. Instances when a spouse annuls a marriage but keeps the acquired name are so rare as to be almost nonexistent. Any claim that she kept it for her son's sake would have been spurious.

Young Winston would never have changed his surname when his mother remarried and, in fact, did not.

Yet Pamela always retained the Churchill name because she knew that it was her passport to every drawing room on each side of the Atlantic. She dropped Digby. She dropped Hayward. She is to this day Pamela Churchill Harriman, PCH on her stationery, on her vanity license plates and on all her monograms. According to one of her closest friends: "She has parlayed that Churchill logo into a lifestyle."[2]

She has traded on the name since 1939. She has been able to because as the only son of the only son, Winston heads the sole line to bear the great man's name. Clementine and Winston's daughters Diana and Sarah married and died. Favorite child Mary, the most levelheaded of the Churchill offspring, wed the late Christopher Soames, who had a distinguished political and diplomatic career as governor of Rhodesia, British ambassador to France and leader of the House of Lords. Mary is the youngest and sole surviving child and thus the official family matriarch, but she is Lady Soames and none of her children is named Churchill. She does not discuss Pamela's role in the family and *Clementine Churchill,* her well-received biography of her mother, limits mention of her sister-in-law to the bare fact that Pamela married Randolph.

Mary and Pamela have never been close, but publicly neither speaks ill of the other, careful to mouth only diplomatic niceties to avoid rocking the family ship. "As a young girl, Mary was fat and awkward and used to feel an embarrassment almost to her family, dressed in that dreary A.T.S. uniform," said a close friend of Mary's who knows Pamela well. "Then in would come this raaaavishing Pam, who was anything but nice to her.

"Then years go by and Christopher is ambassador to France and Averell and Pam arrive in Paris on their honeymoon and stay at the Ritz. Mary at last has Pam in a position where she can show off, so she organizes a lunch at the embassy. Christopher invited the most distinguished members of the government and Mary knocked herself silly, getting the flowers just right and the menu perfect. And then, wouldn't you know, everything went wrong.

"Some government crisis came up and the French guests backed out fifteen minutes before lunch. The butler was so nervous, he slipped and dropped the tray with all the drinks. They went in to lunch and the first course, a cheese soufflé, was flat as a pancake. The most infuriating and humiliating part of the whole affair was that Pam was so sweet. She had this big smile and said to Mary, 'We all know how hard it is to keep a house, don't we, dear?' " A vexed Mary concluded, "Pam's a witch."

With no love lost between the family branches and relations proper but otherwise frosty, they usually meet only at required occasions: weddings, funerals and command performances for events honoring Old Winston to whom, it is only fair to say, Pamela has paid every homage.

Family members acknowledge a lingering resentment of Pamela, albeit of lower intensity now than during her playgirl days in France. "She plays up the Churchill thing considerably more than was warranted, since they were not married very long and, after all, she dumped Randolph," said a Churchill family member. "She's taken a lot of limelight for being around such a short time."[3]

Pamela is unapologetic. To her, such talk is pure jealousy. Mary Soames may think she is the head of the family, but to Pamela there is only one Winston Churchill now, only one family line that bears the Churchill name, and it is she who is mother and grandmother to them all.

Given that the name turned out to be her dowry, one might have thought Pamela would have guarded her treasure — Winston — more conscientiously. She had to fight to keep him and did that in a succession of tugging and pulling contests with Randolph, who few argued should have the custody of anyone. While she won enough of those skirmishes to keep her son, she did little to demonstrate that she ever much cared for him, which added to her in-laws' pique, not to mention Winston's. Over most of the past half century, she has devoted little time or effort to Young Winston.

As a child, he was ferried around by her butler, Sam Hudson, who took him to school and soccer matches. He was raised exclusively by nannies, especially Marian Martin, who doubled as

Pamela's housekeeper and message center for suitors for thirty years starting in 1942 at the Grosvenor Square apartment. "Of all those who looked after me during my childhood, it was her whom I loved most dearly," Winston wrote in his autobiography.[4]

During the war he was parked at Cherkley, out of bombs' and his mother's way. At five, he began nursery school near Sloane Square in central London, only a few moments' drive from either the Churchill Club or 49 Grosvenor Square, but even then Pamela did not see much of him. It never occurred to her, for example, to drop him off at school or pick him up. She was rarely around for his vacations during the early years and displayed no interest in his schoolwork. There was no one else for Winston then. Everyone was busy fighting the war.

At the age of eight, the earliest she could dispose of him in boarding school, she did so. When she took up full-time residence in France, The Child was shipped off to Le Rosey in Switzerland and spent the rest of his childhood — fifteen more years — in boarding schools, including Ludgrove prep school, which Princess Diana's and Prince Charles's sons attended, and Eton. A brief stint at the University of Lausanne followed and, finally, there was Oxford.

At school, as in life, it was not easy being Young Winston Churchill. At that age, most children are desperate to avoid being singled out and the embarrassment that inevitably ensues. Winston was no exception, but he was too visible to hide. "At Eton, it was no advantage to be the grandson of the Prime Minister," he recalled. Students were not allowed to be released from school and when Old Winston or Randolph sought exceptions to take him out for the day, Young Winston was embarrassed at being singled out for special treatment. He cringed and burst into tears when his mother came to Eton from Paris one weekend and showed up in a Mercedes. His mother in a German car! Her insensitivity knew no bounds.

He knew that he would pay a price for her lapse, as he always did for the special attention. As one of the smallest boys in his house — Timbralls — with all but a neon sign hanging from his neck and his mother's escapades well known to many of the students' parents and faculty, Winston was a constant victim, regularly caned by masters and bullied by upperclassmen. Trapped in a common room, "My trousers would unceremoniously be removed. They would then take it in turns to beat me with rubber-soled slippers, yelling: 'Take this for being a shit! Take this for being a bastard! And take this for being Winston-bloody-Churchill.' "[5]

If school was a trial, the fact of his parents' separation was not. "This development made no impression on me whatever as, with my father away at war for the first four and a half years of my life, I had no recollection of them ever being together."[6] Once they split up, Winston began to spend more of his holidays with his father and both sets of grandparents.

The senior Churchills and the Digbys doted on their slender, blond, blue-eyed grandchild, more so as they observed the trauma of his parents' relationship. They tried hard to make up what Winston was missing at home and they did a good job. Winston loved the Digbys and absolutely adored his prime minister grandfather, whom he considered the greatest Englishman in history.

His father was another matter. An abusive parent, Randolph often terrified his son. "Being with him as a small boy was like going around hand in hand with a walking volcano. All would be calm, serene and happy one moment; the next, there would be an earthquaking eruption."[7]

Their time together often ended in trouble and tears. At White's, which barred women and children, Winston was kept waiting endlessly in the foyer while his father "finished a drink" or dictated a story to his newspaper's copy desk. Lunch at the nearby Ritz Hotel might end with the dining room stilled as Randolph bellowed abuse at a waiter for slow service or at his child for not having read the editorials in the *Times* that day. "I must confess that I found such episodes traumatic," said Winston.[8]

Randolph had worshipped his father, but for Young Winston, Randolph was no role model. Until he finished university, he avoided his father as much as possible and to this day has shunned his more egregious vices, neither smoking nor gambling and drinking very little, a bit of wine but never whisky.

His relationship with his mother was different, but also uneasy. He was at the age of reason when Pamela moved to France and her dozen years there were especially difficult for him. His good experience with Gianni Agnelli, from the age of eight to twelve was not matched during his mother's years with Elie de Rothschild. The unmarried and friendly Italian accepted and indulged his girlfriend's little boy. The autocratic, chilly and married Frenchman had no use for or interest in the by then teenage son of his mistress.

Leland Hayward, newlywed and smitten by Pam, was a welcome reversion to the Gianni model. He took Winston literally under his wing when his stepson was at Oxford and becoming hooked on racing. Pamela asked Leland to show paternal example and to get Winston interested in something safer than fast cars. The producer, who found Winston easier to deal with than his own children, offered him flying lessons as a twenty-first birthday gift.

It was the perfect present for a boy who loved to go fast from the age of eleven, when he rode a toboggan solo down the Cresta run at Saint Moritz and whose dashing but reckless style earned him the captaincy of the Oxford ski team. Taking Leland up on the offer immediately, Winston soloed after four days of instruction, the start of a lifelong passion for flight that he shared with his new stepfather.

After Oxford, armed with what Randolph advised him was "the greatest byline in journalism," Winston turned what had been a handicap into an advantage, joined the *Times* of London as a foreign correspondent and went off to interview such family friends as the Kennedys and Charles de Gaulle. In later years, he met Ronald Reagan, who was said to have been surprised that Winston Churchill was so young.[9]

The name and such coups made him one of the best-paid journalists on Fleet Street, but just as his grandfather had been a journalist before becoming a politician, journalism would be a warm-up for the grandson as well. His father urged him to become an engineer, but there was too much politics in the Churchill blood to deny the obvious career track.[10]

In 1964, the twenty-three-year-old Winston married Minnie d'Erlanger, the Roman Catholic daughter of Sir Gerard d'Erlanger, who was the board chairman of the British Overseas Airways

Corporation, and the granddaughter of Baron Emile d'Erlanger, a well-known financier from an Anglo-French banking family. On the eve of the wedding, Old Winston sent the groom a check for a thousand pounds, until then the most money he ever had in his life. Young Winston promptly wrote back his thanks and promised that he and Minnie would "do our best to carry the name of Churchill, which you made great, with honour into the future."[11]

It was a near pledge that he would seek a seat in the House of Commons, which he did in 1967 but failed. In 1970, he tried again, and when the Conservative party leader Edward Heath upset Labour prime minister Harold Wilson, Winston took over the former Labour constituency in Stretford, Lancashire, for the Tories. The seat was reconstituted as Davyhulme in 1983, but Winston has held it all along.

Considering that he has had a near quarter century's experience in the Commons, Winston's career has been a disappointment. His Tory party has held office since 1979, but he has never held any government office, much less been named to a Cabinet post despite the large numbers of ministers appointed, chewed up and spat out by Margaret Thatcher during her eleven years in Number 10 and the fact that her successor, John Major, a contemporary of Winston's, picked yet another fresh slate in 1991. Nor is there the slightest expectation in Britain's political circles that he will be tapped anytime soon, or ever, especially to be defense secretary, the job he has long wanted. There are a number of reasons why.

First, Winston is not very bright. His father, for all his failings, was intelligent and boasted a coruscatingly savage wit. Winston did not distinguish himself at school nor university and has not been a standout in debate in the House of Commons. He is a hard worker who can be charming, but he is not particularly articulate and lacks a natural sense of humor, be it bitter or good-natured. In that sense, he is his mother's son. Winston's idea of a joke in his early twenties was to boast to friends that girls told him, "Winston tastes good like a cigarette should." But when Jones Harris, a contemporary who was dating Brooke Hayward, told him he should respond, "like a Marlboro should," a reference to his ducal Marlborough cousins, Winston didn't understand until the joke was explained.[12]

He is a caring politician and likable to those who know him, but those who do not tend to find him pompous. If he is not racist, he is capable of monumental stupidity on matters involving race. At Le Rosey, he introduced a young prince to a visitor as "the black boy." The insensitivity surfaced again at an April 1993 reception at his mother's Georgetown home, where he spoke with General Colin Powell, the New York City–born chairman of the Joint Chiefs of Staff. "If you had come over on another banana boat, you might have landed in Britain instead of Washington," Churchill told the startled general, before asking, "However did you get an education?"[13]

The following month, he drew fire at home from politicians and editorial writers for a speech to a Tory group in which he called for a halt to the "relentless flow of immigrants" which was threatening, he said, Britain's traditional way of life. Prime Minister John Major might believe that in fifty years "spinsters will still be cycling to Communion on Sunday morning," but he believed it more likely that "the muezzin will be calling Allah's faithful to the high street mosque" for Friday prayers. Home secretary Michael Howard immediately criticized back-bencher Churchill for remarks which "could have the effect of damaging race relations." The prime minister agreed with Howard.[14]

Second, Winston is a political loner, almost a pariah within the Conservative party, whose serious members in the House of Commons have little time or use for him. He is not a compromiser and, highly ideological, shows little interest in cutting the kinds of political deals often required for governance. His rigidity, though, has given him a reputation for being thick, arrogant or both. Even physically, he is isolated. Except for captaining the parliamentary ski team, he is little involved in much of the convivial give and take of Westminster politics. Given his own background, family has been important.

He and Minnie produced two sons and two daughters and they try to do everything as a group, or did when the children were young. The effort of creating a solid family has for the most part succeeded, thanks almost exclusively to Minnie's grace and persistence. Churchill family members and friends alike tend to agree that Winston's wife is the backbone of the family and much too good for Winston.

Third, he is a staunch right-winger, at the opposite end of the political spectrum from his liberal Democratic mother; at least, the opposite end since she married Averell. A more centrist Tory on domestic affairs, where he is an advocate for the elderly and has labored diligently for kidney research, in foreign affairs Winston has always been ready to storm the battlements as crusader Churchill: pro–white South Africa, pro-Zionism, an all-out supporter of the Gulf War and Star Wars space-based defense systems, an opponent of defense cuts and an unrelenting hard-liner against the former Soviet Union, all stances that he frequently airs in letters to the editors of Britain's dailies.

Fourth, he has weak political and personal judgment. Maltuned political antennae cost Winston the one job that might have put him in the Cabinet. As a "shadow" defense spokesman in 1978, when the Conservatives were out of power, he had a clear shot at a ministerial job the following year had he backed his party's decision to continue economic sanctions against then white minority-ruled Rhodesia. But Winston, who wanted to ease up on the whites, rebelled and Tory leader Thatcher instantly fired him. He never again came close to higher office, although he might have had he not fumbled his personal affairs.

A year after the Rhodesia fiasco, Winston was discovered to be having an affair with Soraya Kashoggi, the former wife of the notorious international arms dealer Adnan Kashoggi.[15]

Minnie stood by her husband then and in 1992, when Winston's involvement in another affair became public. The second instance involved a striking New York and Newport, Rhode Island, socialite named Jan Cushing Amory. A triple divorcée who had been escorted by Henry Kissinger and Stavros Niarchos, Amory was startled when Winston proposed shortly after meeting her at the glittery Volpi Ball in Venice in the summer of 1991 where, with Minnie in attendance, they all but consumed each other on the dance floor.

"I didn't know he was married," said Amory later. "I certainly didn't think he would be dancing the way we were dancing for four hours if his wife were there. When he told me she was, I was horrified."[16]

("Unlike some men, who are ruled by their head," a family member explained, "Winston's problem is that he is ruled by his cock.")[17]

They began an affair and Amory, who said she fell deeply in love with Winston, was delighted when he proposed marriage during a romantic stay at Cliveden, the former Astor estate outside London, which became a luxury hotel. Winston gave her a beautiful gold-and-diamond chain necklace with a locket, said Minnie had given him permission for a separation, and asked Amory and her eleven-year-old-son, John, to join him on holiday in Florida. The trip never took place.

Pamela, who some friends expected to be upset by her son's behavior, had been quite understanding about Soraya Kashoggi. " 'Like mother, like son,' she once told me,' " said one of Pamela's best pals. "It's the only time she ever said anything even slightly amusing. 'He's a chip off the old block,' she said."[18]

But Pamela put her foot down when Winston told her about his intention to marry Jan Amory. According to Amory, Winston told her that their plans had to be postponed. He had met with his mother, who "turned white" at the news. Pamela told him, Winston informed Jan, that he could "not now" marry Amory because he was facing a parliamentary election and his eldest son was about to be married.

As it turned out, Winston would not marry her later, either. After nine months, Winston broke off the relationship in 1992, when a London photographer caught him kissing Amory outside a Belgravia dining club. When photos of the pair embracing appeared the next day in the *Daily Mail*, Winston called the American, retracted his proposal, and never spoke to her again.

Pamela's reaction to both affairs was pragmatic: she believed the experiences, if not good for her son, at least taught him a lesson about how others lived, including his mother.

Winston, though, understood all too well how his mother has lived and has found the recognition disquieting. After she married Averell in 1971, Winston came for a Christmas visit to what was then still Haywire house. In the first flush of marriage, Averell had turned overwhelmingly generous. At the insistent prodding of Pamela, who was worried about Winston flying around in a single-engine plane, Averell gave his new stepson an eighty-five-thousand-dollar twin-engine aircraft as a Christmas present. Averell had not completely flipped. He slipped back into character with his gift for Marie's godson, Peter Duchin: a lovely silk tie. Winston left Haywire to deliver the gift to Cheray and Peter, who were close to his age and who lived twenty minutes away.

"He was really sad," said Peter. "He had come by himself to say hi and deliver a few gifts and it was clear that he was really moribund. So I said, 'What's wrong?' "

Christmas troubled him because it raised memories of how past Christmases with his mother, even at such glamour spots as Saint Moritz, had always centered around her boyfriends. "She was too busy whoring around" to have much time for him, he lamented, according to separate conversations with each Duchin.[19] He only wished she could have been like everybody else's mother, not the kind who picked him up in a Mercedes or took him cruising on Stavros Niarchos's yacht.

He appeared embarassed by Pamela, although by that stage, she was working hard to make up for past omissions by trying to insinuate him into Averell's life. She had tried to make him part of Leland's and it had worked to a limited extent, although she overplayed her hand when she had Winston read a lesson at Leland's funeral but froze out Leland's own children. Brooke and Bill were permitted to attend, but Pamela did not allow them to participate.

Leland was a good influence on Winston and if he had been younger and healthier, he might well have been a more enduring role model. That was Pamela's hope, but it was not particularly realistic. By the time his mother had taken over Leland's life,

Winston was in his early twenties, had finished Oxford and was more interested in his own father.

It was ironic that Winston felt embarrassed in the 1950s by his mother, because his father was no less difficult in those years than he had been during the war. Randolph had returned to journalism and writing, but a stint as a war correspondent in Korea ended quickly when he suffered a minor flesh wound in a leg.

Randolph's critical book on his father's successor — *The Rise and Fall of Sir Anthony Eden* — was so intemperate that it caused a rift within the family. The Churchills were embarrassed and angered by Randolph's repeated references to the architect of the 1956 Suez Crisis as "Jerk Eden." Randolph's cousin Clarissa Churchill, who had married Eden in 1947, was thoroughly alienated.[20]

Randolph was drinking and smoking heavily — a bottle and a half of whisky a day and five packs of cigarettes, purchased with cash loans from visitors. As Young Winston explained, his father's "finances were precarious in the extreme." Bill collectors continued to line up at his door.[21]

June Osborne Churchill could not stand the life any longer and left him, taking with her their infant daughter, Arabella. Her departure was less problematic than had been Pamela's, who departed with the irreplaceable namesake. Relations between Randolph and Pamela actually improved slightly. On occasion, they met for lunch. "All he really needed now," she said, "was a spot of genuine success to give him something to be proud of."[22]

The success Randolph sought was to write his father's official biography. By burnishing the legend, he could redeem himself and fill his own depleted bank account. But years went by, Winston retired in 1955 from Downing Street for the second time, and nothing happened. Finally, in 1960, a telegram arrived at Randolph's home in Suffolk, where he had moved after abandoning London.

"He's asked me," Randolph shouted. "He's asked me at last."[23] Elated by his father's request, he dug into the project and fended off all but two interruptions.

The first was a 1964 lung operation for what was thought to

be cancer. A biopsy determined the tissue was nonmalignant, which prompted Evelyn Waugh to comment, "Trust those damn fool doctors to cut out the only part of Randolph that wasn't malignant."[24]

Another pause came in 1967, when Randolph and Young Winston teamed up to write a quickie book on the Arab-Israeli Six Day War, which Young Winston had covered as a Middle East correspondent. The collaboration could have been a disaster, given the intrinsic difficulty of working with Randolph on anything, but the project turned out well. As they labored, past discomfitures receded and the bond between father and son grew stronger. A year later, Randolph died at the age of fifty-seven. He had completed two good volumes of Sir Winston's biography, a project which was then assumed by one of his researchers, Martin Gilbert.

Their productive time together prompted Winston to revise his thinking about his father. "I was thrilled, above all, to have the opportunity of working in such close harness with my father."[25] Until then, he had seen far more of Randolph's prodigious temper than his writing talent. By the time his father died, Winston was twenty-eight, old enough and wiser — having also been subjected to the stresses of being a Churchill, having labored as a journalist and having failed in a parliamentary election — to better comprehend what Randolph had endured and accomplished.

He had greater appreciation for the parent he once considered a "walking volcano" and less for his mother. She had cut and run mid-war on Randolph and then abandoned England, a homeland for which Winston feels immeasurable pride and love. Winston's opinion of his mother was not helped by her affair with Elie de Rothschild, whom he disliked, or by what he heard about her from his father.

The postdivorce relationship between Randolph and Pamela may have become more cordial, but Randolph was always capable of the uncontrollable outburst. In 1961, when Randolph visited Pamela and Leland at 1020 Fifth Avenue, Randolph called her "a whore" to her face, to the astonishment of an onlooker.[26]

Overwhelmed by her behavior during his earlier years, Winston has been underwhelmed by his mother's political success, although he was proud of her nomination as U.S. ambassador to France. He disagreed, though, with the many Washingtonians who consider Pamela a political pro. "My mother's not a politician," he averred. "She married a politician."[27] Because she never stood for office, he believed, she was not one herself no matter how much she would like to be considered one. "I don't see she'd have ever carved out a political role on her own," he said.[28]

A man of firm convictions himself, it troubles Winston that his mother has no strongly held beliefs beyond expediency. "She is a bit of a chameleon," in his analysis, and yet, he added, "She has always known what she wanted."[29]

Some relatives and friends believe the relationship is very uncomfortable. Some friends in both England and the United States feel that Winston hates his mother. That is too severe, simplistic and emotional an assessment. There is, however, an undeniable tension underlying the family ties. That should not be surprising. There is strain in all Pamela's relationships, whether with kin or friends.

It bothers Pamela that Winston does not appear to appreciate her as much as she would like. When they are together one on one, they get along reasonably well. Apart or in a group, the strain is more palpable. She was hurt that he made her such a minor character in his autobiography: there are eighteen rather impersonal references to her on 58 pages of text, compared with forty-one vastly more detailed references to Randolph on 183 pages. As she read the galley proofs, it did not appear to her that he had a mother.

The treatment was especially annoying because she sees a lot of herself in Winston, every bit as much as Randolph. That is an arguable claim, but there are certainly similarities. One is Winston's apparent willingness to be influenced by money, a financial hold over him that Pamela has exercised with great skill since marrying Averell and finally gaining access to a serious supply of cash.

Winston lives high on few resources of his own. Old Winston gave him the foreign rights of his *History of the English-Speaking Peoples*, a patrimony which allowed him and Minnie to buy their first home.[30] Minnie's family has provided a modest legacy. Winston's parliamentary pay is a meager thirty-one thousand pounds sterling a year, about forty-seven thousand dollars. Most of the rest has come from Pamela, who does not let him forget it.

She loves her four grandchildren and has paid for all their education. (She also paid for the education of two of Bill Hayward's children, for whom she felt sorry after he left them and their mother for another woman.) When they were old enough to drive, she gave each of her grandchildren a car. In an exceptional example of generosity, she even gave a Fiat 600 to David Sulzberger, the son of her friend Marina and Cy Sulzberger, the Paris-based foreign affairs columnist for the *New York Times*, when he went off to Harvard. "She told him nobody could go off to college without a car. You must take this Fiat," said his sister, Marina Berry. "David has been her slave ever since" and has provided occasional escort service when she traveled alone overseas.[31]

She also provided Winston's children with their own apartment in the Pimlico section of London, not far from the Tate Gallery. Every year she gives ten thousand dollars, the maximum allowable to avoid gift taxes, to each child, plus Winston and Minnie, a total of sixty thousand dollars. She also gave the family an apartment in Klosters, Switzerland, where they ski.

Another apartment, on Portugal's Algarve coast, was financed from the proceeds of the twin-engine plane that Averell gave Winston in 1971. Winston used the plane for several years to run an air taxi service from Gatwick Airport, south of London. The business was never much of a success and when Winston sold the plane, he was allowed to keep the net receipts and put the cash into the beach place.

That was all Winston's good fortune. He has been less fortunate to have been a member, or "Name" as they are called, at Lloyd's, the three-hundred-year-old London insurance underwriting firm, which began hemorrhaging money in 1988. For 1988 and 1989, losses at Lloyd's as a result of hurricanes, air crashes, oil rig explosions and a deluge of unforseen American asbestos and pollution claims, totaled $4 billion. Losses for 1990 and 1991 —

Lloyd's closes its books with a three-year lag to allow for claims — were projected to reach $6 billion, while more recent hurricanes and floods hold out the prospect of much more red ink.[32]

To become a Name, investors pledged their assets "down to the last pair of cuff links," but did not have to put up any cash. In return, for years they were virtually guaranteed an annual return of about 10 percent on their investment.[33] Winston has been a Name since 1976 and did well until the market soured. At that point, he began to roll up losses, nearly eighty thousand dollars in 1991 alone, and raised the fearsome prospect for Pamela that she might have to help bail him out with cash infusions many times that amount.

Going nowhere politically. Acting stupid maritally. Going backwards financially. At Pamela's beck and call because of her firm grip on the family's pocketbook and the expectation that, eventually, he may inherit much of her estate as long as he behaves.

Winston does not enjoy being in thrall to Mummy, as he calls her, and dislikes it even more when she treats him as a child, which Pamela is wont to do. But he has little alternative. By securing her position throughout the 1970s with Averell, Pamela succeeded in organizing the family situation just the way she wanted.

Winston understood his duties. Brooke and Bill Hayward were isolated. Bill even dropped his lawsuit against Pamela over Leland's will as soon as she married Averell, knowing that he could not sue her once she was backed by the Harriman fortune. The Duchins were pushed aside. Marie Harriman's family and friends were out. There was no need to worry about family or to relax with them in the 1980s. Pamela had already taken care of everything.

CHAPTER SEVENTEEN

Clark, Bob and Janet

FOR PAMELA, the 1980 Reagan landslide was a replay of 1945, when Winston Churchill was swept out of office. Not that she confused Jimmy Carter with her former father-in-law. Certainly not. Pamela and every other voter in America knew months before the election that a weak economy, fifty-four Americans held hostage in Iran for more than a year, and a president who was a fine, pious moralizer, but an unimpressive national leader made it highly possible, if not likely, that the Democrats would lose.

It was the overwhelming magnitude of their defeat that was so haunting. In 1945, the Conservatives did not just lose, they were annihilated. Churchill's party held 397 seats going into the election and emerged with only 213 seats. Everyone Pamela had known at Number 10 and in Churchill's Cabinet had been tossed out like stale bread.

Now, thirty-five years later, she was witnessing at close hand another drubbing. So many of her and Averell's Democratic friends were defeated. In addition to Frank Church and John Culver, the Senate also lost leading liberals like Birch Bayh of Indiana and Wisconsin's Gaylord Nelson. In the House of

Representatives, twenty-six incumbent Democrats lost, including majority whip John Brademas, an eleven-term veteran, and Al Ullman of Oregon, the powerful chairman of the Ways and Means committee.

"It's the most crushing rejection of a President and his party in Congress since Herbert Hoover," said Michigan's Guy Vander Jagt, chairman of the National Republican Congressional Committee. "Democratic leaders who managed to survive had the bejesus scared out of them."[1]

Some Democrats wanted to blame the whole disaster on Jimmy Carter and his politics of indecision and national malaise, but the party's problems went much deeper than its standard-bearer. Long before the 1980 vote, even before the McGovern debacle of 1972, Democrats had lost their discipline and philosophical coherence. Depleted as well as defeated, with a vision stuck on Franklin Roosevelt's New Deal, Democrats could not stop touting their past as their future.

Republicans painted them into corners as tax-and-spend Democrats, a party that would raise taxes, cut defense spending, then give the money away for social programs, boosting welfare payments and pushing a so-called liberal agenda: pro-minorities, pro-abortion, pro—gay rights, pro-union and soft on crime.

As Americans moved south and west to the Sunbelt and better jobs, often in nonunion businesses, those who stayed behind in the Rustbelt Northeast and industrial Midwest were mostly Democrats. By the mid-1970s, the party seemed to be comprised mainly of urban poor, blacks, Hispanics, people on welfare, the sick or troubled. John Kennedy's party had lost its "vigah."

Democratic Big Government seemed less likely to protect citizens than to rip them off, hiking taxes and spending the money on Big Bureaucracy. Ronald Reagan's triumph had mangled the old Democratic coalition. The party had so lost its way that its very core — Jews, labor union members, ethnic whites, middle-class-and-above city dwellers — crossed over and voted for a Republican who had been considered by many Americans to be too old, too conservative and, with his background as an actor, too frivolous.

Democrats had hit bottom. "This is a party with no sense [of] what it's about, what it should be about, where it's going, where it should go," said Larry Hansen, an aide to Illinois senator Adlai Stevenson III after the election. "There is no vision."[2]

Nor was there a clear idea where any vision might be spotted. The party leaders who survived were all old-style liberals: Walter Mondale, Carter's vice-president; Thomas P. "Tip" O'Neill, the House Speaker; Senate minority leader Robert Byrd, the "King of Pork." They were old tax-and-spend Democrats and a big part of the problem.

The think tanks were not the answer. They are filled with talented academics, theoreticians and dreamers. Followers, not leaders. There was no forum to be found in the states. They were too far from the center of what power was left and besides, Democrats had tumbled out of governors' mansions as well.

"People were just floundering," said Stuart Eizenstat, domestic policy adviser in the Carter administration. "We Democrats were devastated, thrown out on our heels and left with a president with the most conservative agenda of any president in our lifetime. We were looking at a wasteland, a desert."[3]

Enter Pamela, whose timing with the Democrats was as exquisite as her timing with men. The party was lost and she was at loose ends herself. Averell was despondent, muttering about "that dismal event" in November 1980. She could only go to Moscow so many times with a husband as old as Averell. Sure, they would see Brezhnev, although he was a walking corpse by 1980, even if he was still presiding in name over what democratic Russians would later call the "era of stagnation."

They might meet Andrei Gromyko, the dean of foreign ministers, or some of his senior advisers, to discuss the Strategic Arms Limitation Treaty or the Soviets' 1979 invasion of Afghanistan. But rarely did much *happen* in these meetings. Their significance was that they took place and that Averell was still taken seriously, in Moscow if not in Washington. "You know how it is — you get older, you're not in the swim," said Kitty Carlisle Hart, one of Pam's best friends. Then, "Pam got him to Russia and the Russians gave him all those lovely awards and he began to enjoy it all again."[4]

Otherwise, the Moscow trips were a lot less glamorous than

they sounded. In 1975, for example, Averell led a United States delegation to Moscow for ceremonies marking the thirtieth anniversary of the end of World War II. The group included General Lyman Lemnitzer, the former Supreme Commander of allied troops in Europe, John Eisenhower, the son of the former president, and two Avis Bohlens, the widow and daughter of Charles "Chip" Bohlen, the former U.S. ambassador to the USSR and France.

Pie Friendly, whose husband, Alfred, was then the *Newsweek* bureau chief in Moscow and whose father had worked with Averell during the Marshall Plan in Paris, sent the Harrimans a note asking them over if they had a free moment. Pamela immediately called. "Free moment. We haven't got a damned thing to do. We've got one laying of the wreath, but otherwise we're sitting up in these guest houses in Lenin Hills with American Kleenex in the bathrooms and nothing to do."[5]

Even the sightseeing trips to Georgia and Suzdal and shopping expeditions to hard-currency *beriozkas* proved ultimately to be of limited appeal. On one of her last trips with Averell, Pamela asked where she might pick up some sable. Instead of inviting her to the wholesale fur auctions in then Leningrad, officials recommended she try Maximiliam's on New York's Fifth Avenue.

If she were not going to die of boredom, Pamela needed a project. She hated all the hand-wringing. She had seen the Conservatives go through that from 1945 until 1951, when Churchill returned for a second term. Lamentations and second-guessing frustrated her. She wanted to *do* something.

One of her great talents has been the ability to spot an opening and supply what is missing, whether it be an antique porcelain vase in the proper spot or a value-added bonus to her men, each of whom needed something that she could provide. Randolph wanted a presentable dam to produce a son; Averell in war, a girlfriend and entrée to the Churchill circle; Ed wanted glamour; Gianni, a postwar seal of approval; Elie, a woman with style who shared his interests; Leland, a nanny; Averell in marriage, a partner in politics and diplomacy.

They and other men wanted or needed more, of course. They all needed support and she was the ultimate supportive partner.

She would do what little things she could, she said when Jimmy Carter won office. "Everybody needs help."[6] Four years later, the Democrats were needier than all her men combined and she was ready.

The party's general need was a new approach, a new program of fresh ideas. The press hammered home the question every day. Democrats from the highest national to the lowest state office asked each other the same question constantly: Got any new ideas?

In 1980, the Republicans outspent the Democrats six to one on Congressional races — $109 million to $19 million — but, however much it might have appeared to be critical, money was not the party's top priority. Money was in the need-to-have-to-win category, not must-have-to-even-be-considered. Any party in the age of paid television advertising always needs more cash, but the Democrats were far from broke. They did not need cocktails or dinners either. There was nothing to celebrate and nobody was interested in meeting the Hollywood crowd, rich donors or chatting up a bunch of fresh, unknowing faces.

"What the party desperately wanted to do then was talk and to try to find its balance," said Chris Matthews, a top aide to Speaker Tip O'Neill and a Carter White House speechwriter turned columnist. "Pamela said, 'Come on over. Have a few drinks and we'll talk about the future of the Democratic party and what it stands for.' It was the perfect offer. The perfect seduction at the right moment."[7]

More than timing was involved. Pamela was the right person. She had all the tickets, beginning with experience. From being an observer at Leeds Castle to gathering the politicians, generals, diplomats and journalists throughout the war in her London flat, she had done it all before. Incapable of long-term pessimism, she had the right temperament.

Furthermore, she was attractive, had the right bloodlines and connections, the right sponsor in Averell, the right drawing room with the right art on the walls; even the right designer clothes — Blass and Givenchy — classy, not flashy. It mattered that she was positive but not a cheerleader. A tub-thumper would have been an irritant on the long Sisyphean haul the Democrats faced and never would have made the distance. Pamela was serious, but far from leaden, and probably more organized than anyone in the capital.

The power game was also her game. "Pamela likes power,"said Bob Strauss, the former Democratic party chairman. "She is not a couch potato. She is a player. She wants to be a participant, not an observer. And, since she's in Washington, a town of power and politics, she wants to be a player in power and politics."[8]

Equally significant was what Pamela was not — a Washington hostess. There have been many of those. Perle Mesta and Marjorie Merriweather Post were the best known, wealthy matrons who gave six-course meals on gold plates and hosted costume balls. The John Sherman Coopers of Kentucky gave an annual dance party for hundreds, while Katharine Graham hosted parties for sixty to eighty of her friends, many of them serious political people. But those gatherings were primarily social or designed to provide a setting for men to do business.

Alice Roosevelt Longworth, Evangeline Bruce and Susan Mary and Joe Alsop gave serious lunches and dinners at which Washington's governing elite gathered to discuss the issues of the day. The ultimate thrill for any of them was to have a guest summoned to take a phone call from the White House or State Department, then return to the table to tell everyone the very latest developments.

Still, with the possible exception of Mrs. Longworth's, none quite qualified as a salon because, as Vangie Bruce explained: "In a salon, you can't be ponderous, egocentric. Anything other than a lucid, witty, graceful style is simply not allowed. That doesn't sound like Washington, does it?"[9]

No, Washington was filled with big egos that needed constant stroking by any means, grace and wit being no prerequisite. New York was more fecund ground for enlightened salons. Among the greatest hosts there was lifelong real Democrat Marietta Tree, the ambassador-rank patrician who, night after night in the 1960s, opened her house for serious, table-wide conversations with politicians like Democratic nominee Adlai Stevenson, Asian diplomats, Oxford dons, editors and playwrights, baffling her husband, who often had no idea who his visitors were.[10]

As the guests mingled before dinner, ogling the eighteenth-century furniture the Trees brought to New York when they sold Ditchley Park, the estate near Oxford which Churchill used during the war, Marietta was usually able to discern what was on everyone's agenda that night, and often how her fellow U.N. delegates intended to vote in the next day or so.[11]

Pamela knew Marietta and admired her technique, proof if any were needed that what had worked for her in London, and to a less political extent in Paris, ought to work in the United States. Attempting it in Washington had special appeal because Pamela had tried being a social hostess in the 1970s without much success. "I hate that word 'hostess,' " she said.[12]

Socializing with other women held no interest for her. She dutifully led the women upstairs and away from the dining room table, leaving the men to their brandy and cigars because that was how one entertained in proper British fashion, but she felt a certain sympathy for Sally Quinn one night when the writer and wife of *Washington Post* editor Benjamin Bradlee insisted on staying with the men and Averell threw her out of the house for impertinence.

"It's my house," Averell snapped. "You go. You cannot stay here."

Quinn walked out. Pamela had no intention of stepping into the imbroglio. She could do nothing, so she said nothing and took no stand. "Pamela was bemused," said Bradlee, who waited a few minutes before making his excuses and joining Quinn. "No feminist she." No, she was not. Never had been.

Averell, as the Quinn incident suggested, was not much himself for displaying grace or ease in social situations. Marie had been good at those, all wise-ass irreverent. "My God, what's the matter, Averell?" she cracked once when Averell arrived at the table. "You look like a million dollars. You must be sick."

Pamela was good at ensuring that guests were comfortable, but she was not good at poking fun or juggling conversations of non sequiturs, particularly after she married Averell. His bad hearing made dinner parties, with chitchat to the left and right, which he hated, difficult. His preferred evening's pastime was a game of bridge, which he had played well since his Yale days. Pamela loyally took bridge lessons and played whenever The Governor wished, but, just as when she played bezique with Winston Churchill, it was a labor of love. She did not like cards and such games were never one of her strengths.

Because Averell was serious to the point of ponderousness, Pamela became more serious and single-minded about his interests: Democratic politics and Soviet affairs. Years before political correctness undergirded every public pronouncement, she explained why women in general and she in particular had lost interest in hostess duties: "Women aspire to be political leaders, not social leaders."[13]

Pamela did not want to be a political leader in the sense of running for elective office herself. Nor did the concept of designing a particularly brilliant political strategy excite her. But she did want clout to remain an insider.

She has always been fascinated by being with interesting people in situations where she could make a difference. She is most engaged when dealing with personalities rather than an overall campaign. Saving the spotted owl or loggers' jobs, for example, has never been her approach. Her preference was to travel in the American West with a tall, handsome environmentalist senator such as Colorado's Tim Wirth, who escorted her on fact-finding missions.

In such a nexus, combined with the fact that she was not asking for anything for herself, there was broad opportunity for Pamela. "She has a remarkable record of doing things for people in the Democratic party without seeking any payback except being in the know," said Alfred Friendly Jr., a Russian and Soviet affairs expert who helped her prepare speeches and articles. "It's been very helpful to the party to have a Broadway angel like that."[14]

Offstage or not, she had no intention of playing down her role. She was very ambitious and tired of being labeled the reflection of her man of the moment. It was time she received some recognition on her own. "She did not want to be a fixture, just the wife of," said Stuart Eizenstat. "She saw this opening as an opportunity to carve her own niche. She had a deep interest in resuscitating the Democratic party and felt she could make a contribution in her own right. This wasn't going to be Pam-

Harriman-wife-of-Averell's project, but Pam Harriman's project."[15] If Averell keeled over, she did not want the phones to stop ringing.

At that moment, what she really wanted was a project. She knew — it was in the press every day and that's all the pros were talking about — that Democrats needed to discover who they were intellectually and politically. If the party had been robust or confident, it would not have worked. The leadership would not have needed her. As it turned out, said Chris Matthews, "she became a host of ideas, giving an intellectual focus to the evening and bringing the Georgetown party to its ultimate level."[16]

The concept of holding a continuing series of "issues dinners" did not spring fully formed from her brain. Because of Averell and the effort she was making to re-create herself for him and ultimately herself, Pamela had become involved during the Carter administration with the White House Preservation Fund, which was created to raise money to pay for the purchase and restoration of antique furniture and fine arts for the executive mansion's public rooms.

Walter Shorenstein of San Francisco, one of the party's biggest fund-raisers, headed the group and also used the fund's Lafayette Square office as an East Coast base to raise money for Democratic Senate and House races. With her expertise in antique furniture and period objects plus her political and financial connections, Pamela was an obvious choice to join Shorenstein on the board of directors and chair several fund-raising dinners.

They worked hard, but the key to the operation was a tough Texan named Janet Howard, the fund's executive director and one of Washington's most energetic and best-informed political insiders from earlier work on Capitol Hill. Introduced to state, national and Beltway politics in the 1960s by Senator Ralph Yarborough, Howard helped Shorenstein beat the bushes nationally for money. Along the way she arranged for the Women's National Democratic Club to name Pamela Outstanding Democratic Woman in 1980, when it was widely expected that Joan Mondale, wife of the campaigning vice-president, would receive the award.

That summer, the White House was hit with allegations that rides on Air Force One to a major West Coast fund-raising dinner

were being offered to ten-thousand-dollar-contributors. No criticism was directed at Janet, but in August, shortly after the imbroglio broke, she left the Preservation Fund office and, armed
with the files detailing her fund-raising network and a forty-
thousand-dollar salary from the Harrimans, moved into a rent-
free apartment in the N Street office building to become Pamela's
political brain trust.

In early December 1980, at two postelection dinners at the
Harriman house, a Howard-guided Pamela pressed guests to produce a coherent plan for the party. At one for eighty-five labor
leaders, Jesse Calhoon, president of the Marine Engineers Ben-
eficial Association, which was the merchant mariners union, told
Pamela that if she felt as strongly as she sounded, she ought to
organize her own political action committee and call it PamPAC.
Calhoon was half joking, but Pamela and Janet were 100 percent
serious first thing the next morning when they began exploring
the possibilities of establishing a PAC.

PACs had been a factor on the political landscape for barely a
half dozen years, spawned by the reform mood which seized
Washington, Congress and the country after Watergate. In 1974,
Congress amended the federal election laws to limit the impact
on campaigns of wealthy contributors and to stop under-the-table
payoffs to candidates and incumbents by corporations, unions
and interest groups. By limiting donations to one thousand dollars
from individuals and five thousand dollars from a political action
committee to a candidate's primary and general campaign, the
law intended that PACs would be a regulated channel of financial
support.

But just as no good deed goes unpunished, the reforms were
perverted. Instead of cleaning up campaign financing, PACs made
the money morass worse. Rabbits couldn't proliferate as fast as
PACs, which multiplied from 113 committees which dispensed
$9 million to congressional candidates in 1972 to 2,551 handing
out nearly $60 million in 1980.[17] (For 1991–92, Federal Election
Commission records showed that 4,643 PACs gave nearly $189
million to Senate and House candidates, up 19 percent over the
1989–90 election cycle.)[18]

Critics charge that PACs, and specifically the money they throw into a race, corrupt the democratic process by upsetting the balance between the public good and private interests through vote buying. PAC contributions also drove up the cost of campaigning — from an average of $50,000 for a House race in 1974 to $150,000 in 1980.[19] The fact remained, however, that PACs were perfectly legal, and refusing to accept PAC money — as fewer than a dozen congressmen did in the early 1980s — almost inevitably put a candidate at a serious financial disadvantage.

Because the bottom line for any PAC is access to power, the thought of creating her own had tremendous appeal for Pamela. She and Janet spent little time discussing whether to start up and concentrated instead on how to get underway. It was their baby, although as many as 80 percent of the political calls were made by Janet.

Averell was uninvolved beyond offering moral and financial support. "It's all her show," he said. "I'm just part of the supporting cast."[20] Nearly ninety, he was cooperating with *Los Angeles Times* reporter Rudy Abramson on his biography. He no longer had Pamela's energy, but he was thrilled to see her so excited and engaged and was pleased that her PAC would keep them up-to-the-minute on what was happening inside the party.

Averell discussed her plans with Bob Strauss, the chairman of the Democratic National Committee from 1972 to 1977, and John White, a fellow Texan who followed Strauss at the head of the party during the Carter years in the White House.

"I'm a lot older than Pamela and I want her to have interests after I'm gone," Averell told Strauss.[21]

"Averell said that she had great enthusiasm and commitment and wanted to get involved in the party," added White. "He hoped that we could give her some guidance and help so she wouldn't step in any puddles."[22]

No two could have done it better. Strauss took special care to follow The Governor's request. Since arriving in Washington from Dallas in 1970 as Democratic party treasurer, lawyer Strauss within a decade had become the ultimate power broker and consummate Washington insider. He knew everybody, had been everywhere and done everything a professional politician could do except hold elective office.

He was so well wired that there wasn't a national committee-man or committeewoman he didn't know, not a top party operative or union boss or businessman in either party who hadn't drunk vodka with him, not a senior political journalist who hadn't been to his house for firehouse three-alarm chili. As former House Speaker Jim Wright once toasted Strauss at a private dinner, "It's an honor to have with us a close friend of the next President of the United States — *whoever* the hell he may be."[23]

Strauss had been Carter's U.S. special trade representative, then the president's personal envoy for Middle East negotiations and had chaired the Carter-Mondale re-election campaign. What Davis and Blanchard were to the great Army football teams of the 1940s — Mr. Inside and Mr. Outside — Strauss was to the Democrats in the 1970s. In 1991, Republican president George Bush crossed party lines to name Strauss U.S. ambassador to the collapsing Soviet Union and then to Russia, in the hope that the Russians could learn deal making from a master.

Strauss had known Pamela from the moment she married Averell. In 1977, when he took the administration's top trade job, he was forced to give up his seat on several corporate boards, including that of the Dallas-based Braniff Airways. At the same time, Averell was contemplating another aspect of Pamela's future.

"You know," he told Strauss, "Pamela's going to have money. She has some now. She's going to have more to be responsible for. I wish she had some business experience, on a board or something."

"Averell, I just left the board of Braniff," the Texan replied. "You and Pamela both know [Braniff chairman] Harding Lawrence. She'd be a great director for him."

Strauss took the matter up with Lawrence, who was more than willing. Lawrence knew Pamela's natural connections with flight dated back to the Eighth Air Force during the war, not to mention Leland's and Young Winston's passion for flying. Leland had even been a member of the board of Wells, Rich and Green, the advertising agency started by Lawrence's wife, Mary Wells. The Lawrences also shared Pamela's affinity for the south of

France. Their spectacular Palladian mansion, La Fiorentina, was a Cap Ferrat neighbor of La Léopolda.

Averell was thrilled when the formal invitation arrived asking Pamela to join the airline board. The tightfisted multimillionaire had only two questions for Strauss. Did he get to fly free? Yes, when he traveled with Pamela. And what was the director's fee? "Pam is so naive about business she didn't even ask what the fee was," said Averell. Strauss could not recall. "Well, I believe you're worse than she is," the old diplomat declared. That, however, was not Harding Lawrence's judgment. "Mrs. Harriman was an excellent Braniff director," said Lawrence. "She is a quick study, studious, sincere, hard working and a very pleasant person with whom to work."[24]

Which must have been helpful, since Pamela's four years on the board came at a tough time for the airline. The 1978 onset of deregulation caused Braniff to lose $44 million in 1979 and $128.5 million in 1980, the start of a tailspin that led to its collapse in 1989. For outside director Pamela, whose only previous business exposure had been the Jansen shop, the Braniff experience was an invaluable lesson in high-stakes finance, which dovetailed neatly with the launch of PamPAC.

It wasn't really called PamPAC, of course, although Pamela never minded the nickname. Nor "Pammy's PAC," as some Washingtonians snickered, anticipating that it was little more than a self-indulgence for a glamorous hostess which would soon go the way of most political start-ups — quietly into the night.

"Democrats for the 80's" was the name and it was up and running by December to take full advantage of 1980 tax year write-offs. One of its early formal meetings was held January 21, 1981, the night after Ronald Reagan's inauguration. Pamela greeted the guests with Averell but made no formal presentation and quickly turned the evening over to Clark Clifford. "She didn't want to get up and say, 'I have a marvelous new idea,' " said a participant. "She just let it unfold."

As the PAC's first executive director, Pamela hired Peter Fenn, the chief of staff and campaign manager for defeated Idaho senator Frank Church. Fenn knew Pamela and Janet, had been at Pamela's house for some fund-raisers and was flattered. But he had another job offer as a political consultant and was not interested in working with a bunch of limousine liberals.

"I wouldn't be real good at cocktail parties," he told Pamela. "My interest is in winning elections."

"So is mine," she replied. "That's why I want you."[25] A little more talk with her and some checking with other influential Democrats and Fenn was convinced.

They joined the fray immediately. Their first step was to spend twenty thousand dollars on a radio campaign to back liberal Maryland senator Paul Sarbanes, who had been attacked by the National Conservative Political Action Committee. "We were just so outraged by these ads against Sarbanes that we decided to do our bit," Pamela told an April 1981 news conference. "I regret that this is necessary. Democrats for the 80's was not organized to counter the right wing. It was organized to make a positive contribution to the revitalization of the Democratic party. And that remains its central purpose. It has become increasingly clear, however, that the political process itself is being threatened by a maverick organization that scorns both parties and makes a travesty of civility, fair play and accountability."[26]

Fenn told the news conference that Pamela's PAC had raised $150,000 in its first four months and planned to spend $1 million during the year. The overall goal was to rejuvenate the party, to "strengthen the party in funding, ideas and organization . . . generating new ideas and helping provide the support system" of candidate training, computers, direct mail, polling, issue research and media, all areas where the Republicans had a distinct advantage.

With the PAC up and rolling, what struck Fenn was how he had misjudged Pamela. "She had a very solid, very tough political mind. She wasn't milquetoasty at all. It was real obvious right away that this wasn't some kind of hobby or toy. This was serious business and she got right into the nitty-gritty."[27]

One of her first efforts came on June 9, 1981, when she held a twenty-five-dollar-a-head garden party. The price was deliberately kept low to draw young Democrats, many of whom had lost policy jobs when Reagan entered office. Pamela had no idea whether thirty or three hunded would show up. As it turned out, more than six hundred waited in a line that snaked down N Street, a show of support that made the party an annual event. Pamela greeted every arrival individually. "My boss asked me to tell you," said Mike Stafford, an aide to Hawaiian congressman Cec Heftel, "that you are the first person he has spoken with who seems to have grasped the nature of the problem and knows what to do."[28]

"Issues dinners" became the focus of the PAC. Very quickly they evolved from being solely a means of bringing people together to discuss ideas to a method of attracting money from people inside and outside Washington who wanted the thrill of being in a Georgetown living room with big-name political players. Not a salon in the normal sense because their focus was so one-dimensional, the ninety-one dinners eventually held were instead a special breed of political salon.

They were a unifying force for the party, a unique morale-raising and money-raising technique. Pamela was not modest in describing how she made the difference. "If an individual has a fund-raiser at a hotel, he can raise $50,000," she said matter-of-factly. "But if he has it at my house, he can raise $150,000."[29] "Her home," said lobbyist Tony Podesta, "became the gathering place for the party in exile."[30]

What made the difference was the quintuple twist Pamela put on the "typical" Georgetown dinner: legendary hosts, historic setting, specific topic, all-star cast and major money. Aided by Janet, Fenn and policy specialists Stuart Eizenstat on domestic policy and Samuel "Sandy" Berger on foreign affairs, Pamela would decide on an issue for the evening, such as energy, the environment or international trade — the dinners never focused on any particular political contest — then charge outsiders heavily to come as her personal guest for what was showcased as a political cause in the public good.

"She treated every guest as an honored friend," said a regular attendee. "The only difference was that as you came in, there was a card table in the front hall and you would be asked to sign the guest book and, if the money had not arrived, to sign the check right then and there. It was a thousand dollars and Pamela did not take chits."[31]

The invitations went out around the country every month in Pamela's name, advising that the speaker would be Senator Edmund Muskie or Congressman Richard Gephardt or somesuch and that the moderator would be Clark Clifford, the party's silky éminence grise before his indictment in the BCCI banking scandal, or Bob Strauss or former Lyndon Johnson aide Harry McPherson. After accepting, said a frequent guest, this is what happened:

"So Mr. Smith from Nashville, Tennessee, would arrive at seven P.M. with his thousand dollars and be taken down the hall facing van Gogh's *White Roses*, and major domo Michael Kuruc and two hired butlers in black tie would greet him with a tray of drinks. He'd walk down two steps past the Degas sculpture of *The Dancer* and the Derain and the Matisse on the wall into this beautiful, softly lit room with bouquets of fresh flowers placed just right and there would be Governor Harriman in pinstripes and Pamela in a perfectly tailored Bill Blass suit and diamond earrings greeting you with exquisite grace.

"It didn't matter if you were a car dealer from Ohio or the king of England, you got the same treatment. And there, seriously, would be several of the Senate or House leaders, because Pamela only went straight to the top, and a smattering of younger House members who she thought should have a higher profile. There would be ten people standing there who you would give your right arm to meet under *any* circumstances.

"There would be thirty to thirty-eight people total, never more than forty, and you'd schmooze around drinking and nibbling molded canapés of ham or tuna with mayonnaise on little toast bits or thick, iced carrot rounds. After one full drink, everyone would sit down and Pamela would say, 'Averell and I are so thrilled to have you in our drawing room.' Then The Governor would say hello and turn it over to Clark, who would introduce the big banana of the night, maybe Senator [George] Mitchell, and he would make twenty minutes of remarks.

"Then Michael would announce dinner and you would sit at round tables on the sun porch overlooking the terraced gardens and in the dining room, eight to ten at a table, with the Digby ostrich place cards with the green border, always everything green, written by the secretary with the best finishing-school penmanship. You would be served a beautiful dinner, entirely prepared by Pamela's cook, Gretchen, and her sous chef, beginning with smoked trout or creamed lobster. Absolutely first class.

"It was exactly as if you had come to Pamela's for an exclusive private dinner. That was the secret. That you had just signed a check for a thousand dollars had nothing to do with the fact that you were being totally enveloped in this beautiful world. There would be six decorative ladies to keep the tables from being too male, as well as wives along with the schnooks from Wisconsin or wherever.

"Then it was filet and fiddle ferns and a salad course with cheese and English water biscuits, three wines. Dessert was a bombe of some sort, then champagne and coffee. Pamela would clink her glass and make a little toast about how necessary it was to get the party's juices flowing, then ask everyone to go back into the library, where little gold chairs had been brought in.

"There the discussion was opened up to everyone. Stuart or Sandy would make some remarks to get things started and by ten-thirty everybody would go home. It was more pseudointellectual than intellectual, but it was fabulous. Of course, it got a little tiring after three or four years, and how she hung in there for ten, I don't know. But if you came from West Wherever or even just once in a while from Washington, those dinners were something else."[32]

They certainly went a long way toward disabusing participants of the notion that Democrats were the party of the poor and dispossessed. "We get the best of both worlds," joked Massachusetts Senator John Kerry. "We eat like Republicans and think like Democrats."[33]

More important than the food or the subject matter was the guest mix. "This was the only forum where insiders and outsiders, investment bankers and labor union leaders could all be exposed to one another and interact," said Eizenstat. "It gave people a sense that there were still some Democrats in the world and that we had some usable thoughts."[34]

It was actually Pamela's absence at one early dinner that put her gatherings onto the national political map. In the fall of 1981, Pamela was kicked by a horse and hospitalized with three broken ribs, long enough to miss a September 15 dinner at N Street. Felix Rohatyn, the New York investment banker, was the evening's speaker on the issue of the Reagan economic plan, specifically how he believed it would divide the country along regional and class lines with the rich getting richer and the poor poorer. Multimillionaire Rohatyn recommended the creation of a New Deal intervention because if something wasn't done, "Society's going to blow up."

Among those present were Senators Alan Cranston of California, Dale Bumpers of Arkansas and former Senator Frank Church, along with Congressman Gephardt, lawyer and diplomatic negotiator Sol Linowitz, Strauss and Clifford. In a pluperfect example of inside-the-Beltway mutual stroking, all agreed that Rohatyn was brilliant, but no one was very certain about how to take on the new president.

Clifford was soothing as always. Soon, he predicted, the country would recognize that Ronald Reagan was "an amiable dunce" whose policies were destined to be "a hopeless failure."[35]

The problem was that the evening's off-the-record conversation had been taped and a transcript made so the absent Pamela would not miss anything. When the *Wall Street Journal* put the story by its top political writer, Jim Perry, on page one, the "amiable dunce" remarks reverberated around the country. Pamela was angered that the sanctity of the private evening had been violated. "I am just mortified," she said. "Obviously, taping will never be done again."[36]

It did not have to be. No one ever suggested that the leak had been orchestrated from inside and there was a day or two of embarrassing awkwardness about Clifford's choice of words. But no other PAC ever rated such publicity. "She was on the map," said Strauss.

The headline FOR THE DEMOCRATS PAM'S IS THE PLACE FOR THE ELITE TO MEET seared PamPAC into the national political consciousness. If you were a Democrat and hadn't been to Pam's, you were a nobody. Soon the rush was on.

Between December 18, 1980, and December 31, 1982, Democrats for the 80's raised $1,273,130.09 of which $894,850.88 were net dollars. More than half a million went directly to candidates, primarily to regain the Senate, but also because the upper body was the more patrician chamber and thus had more appeal for Pamela. A smaller amount was set aside for the House, which was already controlled by the Democrats. The issues dinners provided the largest chunk of income — $330,100 taken in and less than $11,000 spent on expenses, not much more than the rental cost of a decent ballroom.

Pamela's evenings were not only special, but cost effective. No other fund-raisers showed such a high ratio of net receipts to gross; no other PAC turned over such a high ratio directly to the field. Pamela and Averell gave the maximum allowable each year and she and Janet monitored every penny. The only area where the PAC lost any money — fifty thousand dollars taken in, and eighty-five thousand spent — was in publishing a fact book, the one project which, after the dinners, defined Democrats for the 80's.

The Democratic National Committee should have published such a book, and had done so years before, but dropped it for being too costly and time consuming. The thought of reviving the book came from Eizenstat, who had produced one for Jimmy Carter when he was governor of Georgia. When he made the suggestion to Pamela, she immediately recognized another opening.

The idea was to provide incumbents and candidates for Congress, state houses, city halls and state legislatures with a non-academic critique of Reagan administration policies and to offer a platform of fresh, alternative ideas on which Democrats at all levels could run. Study groups were established, team leaders picked and young policy people solicited to submit ideas with the intent of engaging a younger generation of Democrats as well as just possibly picking up a few new thoughts. Ten thousand copies of the 375-page book were published in a hard-cover office model and a loose-leaf version that could be used on the stump. Pamela called it "a portable research staff."[37]

If a candidate went to a meeting of teachers, he or she could flip to the education section, pull out the pages and pop them in a binder. There were sections on defense, foreign policy, social security, health care, tax policy and more, all prepared by the party's best minds. "God, it was a lot of work," said Fenn, grimacing at the recollection. Pamela did not write anything, but she and Janet combed the drafts repeatedly, looking for holes. "She stayed right with it the whole way. With her, you work every minute."[38] "An indefatigable worker," echoes Senate minority leader Byrd.[39]

The work began to pay dividends in the 1982 off-year election, when the Democrats solidified their hold on the House by picking up twenty-six more districts, captured seven more governorships to bring their total to thirty-four and controlled both houses of thirty-four legislatures, six more than they held when voters entered the polling booths. Republicans held their fifty-four to forty-six margin in the Senate, but with Reagan not running, the change in the race margins was dramatic.

Democratic incumbents won big and if they had picked up a total of forty-three thousand votes in five states, the party would have won back the upper chamber. According to Kentucky's Wendell Ford, chairman of the Democratic Senatorial Campaign Committee and a frequent visitor in Pamela's living room: "The Democrats came within a whisker of having a landslide."[40]

Peter Fenn left after the election. To replace him Pamela hired Sven Holmes, a smart young lawyer who had run David Boren's successful 1974 campaign for the governorship of Oklahoma. Holmes had no experience in Washington politics. He had never met Pamela, who barely knew freshman senator Boren. By early 1983, Democrats for the 80's was a hot operation and there was considerable jostling for the director's job with all manner of Democratic factions pitching candidates. Pamela eventually had enough of the infighting. While she is competitive, conflict makes her uncomfortable and she was getting upset at having to break what had turned into applicant gridlock.

When she picked an unknown on the basis of an hour's conversation and another hour of furious phone calls to consult Clifford, McPherson, Berger and Eizenstat, the Washington insider crowd was mystified. But it made perfect sense to Pamela. Very instinctive, she had discovered all she needed to know about her new hire. "I may have thought it was a dialogue, but she's probably the most able person in the world to find out everything

there is to know about someone in the course of a conversation,"
said Holmes. "She left me wearing a barrel."[41]

Holmes handled the day-to-day operation of the PAC for the
1983–84 election cycle. In the two years, Democrats for the 80's
raised nearly $1.178 million, published a second, more detailed
fact book and jumped into polling and research. It shared with
the Democratic Senatorial Campaign Committee and the AFL–
CIO the fifteen-thousand-dollar cost per state of polls conducted
by Peter Hart, and cosponsored with the Democratic National
Committee fifteen-thousand dollars' worth of research for Senate
Democratic challengers.

Another sixteen issues dinners raised nearly ten thousand dollars apiece and the N Street meetings began to take on the look
of the headquarters of a government-in-exile. By the end of 1983,
the mailing list numbered 8,522 contributing members. From its
origins as drawing room farce, PamPAC had become serious
drama. "Pamela's is the most unique political emergence that I
have seen," said Truman administration veteran Clark Clifford.[42]

Pamela dashed around the country, attending as many meetings as she could fit in, fund-raisers and conferences from North
Carolina to Minnesota to Texas. Averell was by then almost totally
deaf and quite crippled. At the age of ninety-two, he had been
strolling on the beach at Mango Bay in Barbados on Christmas
Eve with Pamela when a wave knocked them down and broke
his leg. The leg healed slowly, but Averell began to slip.

Because the Georgetown house and office had more stairs, she
parked him out at Willow Oaks, which also made it easier to
satisfy the Virginia residency requirements. She did not want to
leave him alone so, as she had when Leland became ill, Pamela
arranged every day for her chauffeur to pick up a friend or several
in Washington and drive them to the country house for lunch
and bring them home. Middleburg neighbors and friends filled
in at dinner so District residents would not have to make the
two-hour round-trip drive after dark.

Pamela made every effort to avoid being gone overnight. Her efforts, combined with his dwindling resistance, eventually sold Averell on buying her the twin-engine, eight-seat jet as a sixty-fourth
birthday present in March 1984, complete with a personalized

tail number: N, signifying a U.S.–registered plane, 84PH.

The 1984 election was too much for the Democrats at almost every level. At the top of the ticket, Ronald Reagan trounced Walter Mondale. The president carried forty-nine states and rolled up a 525 to 13 electoral vote margin, second only in modern times to Franklin Roosevelt's 523 to 8 drubbing of Alf Landon in 1936. Pamela was not involved at all with Mondale during the campaign, "not even semi-close," said one of the former vice-president's top aides.[43]

"She wouldn't give me or [campaign manager] Jim Johnson the time of day," said another senior manager of the Mondale effort. "The only time she was effusive was after Mondale won the first debate. She was all over us, blowing kisses and saying how wonderful it was and wasn't this great. But, basically, she didn't think we were going to win, that the action was in the House and Senate and that was where she was going to spend her time and money."[44]

Which is precisely what she did. She let presidential candidates John Glenn, Gary Hart, Ernest Hollings and Mondale all hold meetings in her house, but $457,700 in Democrats for the 80's contributions went to Senate, House and various state candidates.

Still, just because she thought it was a lost cause and did not get involved in the presidential race did not mean that Pamela was prepared to be left out. Mondale was the nominee of the Establishment and she was angry with his tight team for stranding her — by that time Mrs. Establishment — on the sidelines.

She was bitter that the former vice-president's staff was paying insufficient attention to the top party satraps, the big fund-raisers. She was right, but they were playing hardball. The feeling in the Mondale camp was that Pamela had not made the Long March for their man, so the hell with her. Campaign manager Jim Johnson later became a friend of Pamela's but it took him years to erase the resentment she felt in 1984.

The only bright note in the campaign for Pamela came when she was asked to address the San Francisco nominating convention. She was nervous and, the day before she was scheduled to speak, rehearsed diligently with the TelePrompTer crew. They told her that Mario Cuomo had just finished six hours of practice, laboring over every inflection. Gary Hart had been in too but spent less than thirty minutes and never read his remarks in their entirety.

Pamela made a mental note about each man. A perfectionist herself, she was pleased when Cuomo came across brilliantly the next day. As for Hart, she liked him, but she was not surprised then or later when his political career collapsed. One always paid a price for sloppiness, she believed.

Her own performance pleased her tremendously. Gloria Steinem introduced her as "the woman who proved that all feminists don't have to wear combat boots." Steinem either did not know or did not care about what Pamela really thought about feminists. It didn't matter. New York congresswoman Geraldine Ferraro was Mondale's choice as his vice-presidential running mate, so the whole convention became a feminist celebration.

Pamela's best line — "I am an American by choice and a Democrat by conviction" — was crafted by political consultant Bob Shrum, one of her regular writers, and delighted the delegates. Unlike the credibility of some overhyped political statements, this had the virtue of being at least half true.

When the dust cleared in November, there was not much good news for Democrats, who had once more tried and failed to stitch together either the old New Deal or new New Deal coalition. Not only had Reagan thrashed Mondale, but the Republicans picked back up in the House of Representatives thirteen of the twenty-six seats they lost in 1982. There was widespread gloom about the future of the party, which had lost four of the five previous presidential elections. But not at PamPAC.

"Every time there's been a landslide, people say the party that lost is through," said Clark Clifford, recalling that four years after the Democratic rout of 1964, the Republicans took back the White House and that four years after the Republican rout of 1972, the Democrats were again sitting in 1600 Pennsylvania Avenue. "Well, it doesn't happen that way and it won't this time."[45]

The Democrats for the 80's could afford modest bluster because the results in the Senate, where the PAC had concentrated its efforts, offered the only hint of blue sky on an otherwise dark political horizon. The Republicans retained control of the Senate but lost a net two seats from their preelection fifty-five to forty-five majority. Five new Democratic senators came from the eight challenger states that Pamela's PAC had targeted, prompting her to predict, "We're on our way to recapturing a majority in 1986."[46]

With that goal uppermost in mind, her political work was almost all-consuming in 1985 when PamPAC raised $901,030, one of its best single-year totals. Almost consuming, but not quite. There was an important bit of unfinished business that required Pamela's close attention. Averell was ninety-four, in dreadful shape, and the matter of his will was of paramount concern.

When Averell's father, E. H. Harriman, died in 1909, he left a ninety-one-word will which gave his entire $100 million estate to his wife, Mary, whom he also named executor. "Honest Ave the Hair-Splitter," the statesman whose most rewarding professional moments were spent negotiating minute details of treaty language, was not about to deal in such cavalier fashion with his fortune. He began reworking his will after his brother Roland died in 1978. Their two sisters had died in 1948 and 1966, so Averell was the sole survivor.

He worked closely on the document with William Rich, head of the Harriman family office in New York, with lawyer-fixer Clark Clifford and with Pamela, who had learned a thing or two about wills the hard way from her experience with Leland. "Claaahhk," as Pamela called him, and Averell had played poker together with Harry Truman and had known each other almost forty years. Clifford was also Lyndon Johnson's defense secretary and, like Strauss, knew everyone in national politics.

As a mainstay of Democrats for the 80's, he became as close to Pamela as he had been to Averell. She spoke to him every day, sometimes several times. Clifford once told Averell that "marrying Pamela was one of the best decisions you ever made." Averell smiled and said, "No, not one of the best. It was *the* best."[47]

Unlike her experience with Leland's lawyer, Sol Rosenblatt, Pamela's interests this time could not have been better represented. In return, when Clifford's BCCI troubles hit, Pamela remained staunch even when his dwindling band of supporters suffered such outspoken defections as Strauss, who said in 1992,

"I worry about being tempted in the same way my old friend Clark Clifford became tempted. And I am not saying Clark did it for money, although he was always greedy as hell."[48]

Taking Clark's advice, Averell completed a will on September 12, 1984, and updated it on August 7, 1985. The document was fifty pages long, but in essence it was no different than the single paragraph prepared by his father. Pamela had devoted herself to Averell, met every need of a difficult man at all stages of their relationship, given him a new lease on life after Marie's death and kept him totally involved throughout their marriage. When they married in 1971, Marina Sulzberger had written a "Pam darling" letter, predicting, "You will make Averell the happiest of men. How clever of him to snatch you up."[49] She had been prescient. "Pamela never gave up on him," said broadcast journalist John Chancellor, a Birchgrove neighbor and Mango Bay visitor. "I've never seen anyone work so hard to keep an ancient oak alive."[50]

Averell loved her for all of it. At his ninetieth birthday party — which Pamela turned into a $220,000 fund-raiser for the PAC — Averell told the audience, "The happiest years of my life have been those with Pam." From a table that held some longtime friends of Marie Harriman came a brief, unmistakable hiss that the guest of honor did not hear.

Averell was not just saying it. For most of their marriage, whenever Pamela entered the room, Averell lit up like the lights on a Christmas tree. Near the end, he told Clayton Fritchey, a Washington friend who, in earlier years, had escorted Pamela, "I would not have wanted to live the last ten years of my life, if not for Pam."[51] The will was final proof how much he meant what he said. Pamela was to get everything and was also named executrix.

When Marie died in 1970, Averell gave, in her memory, twenty-three paintings to the National Gallery in Washington. The remainder of the art collection that he had assembled with Marie, Averell had given to Pamela on their tenth anniversary in 1981 with the understanding that she pass on the works to the National Gallery on her death.

The collection was valued at $50 million to $100 million depending on the state of the market. In the frenzied 1980s, art dealers estimated that van Gogh's *White Roses* alone might bring as much as $60 million if sold at auction. Van Gogh's *Irises* was sold in November 1987 for $53.9 million, which broke an auction record of $39.9 million set earlier that year for his *Sunflowers*. *White Roses*, which Averell and Marie had bought in 1930 for $72,000 was, according to National Gallery of Art director J. Carter Brown, "as good as any van Gogh that's been sold."[52]

Pamela was also to receive all the homes: Georgetown, Willow Oaks, Sun Valley and Birchgrove, which had been hers anyway. Each of his six grandchildren, whose schooling he had paid for, was to receive $100,000. A $6 million trust was established to be distributed to the grandchildren after twenty-five years.

In the meantime, Pamela was to receive the interest on the trust for the remainder of her life as well, in addition to the rest of the fortune. Its value was not made public, but sources close to the family estimated it at up to $145 million, depending on the value of Union Pacific stock, one of Averell's major assets.

For all intents and purposes, the rest of the family was cut out, but for four thousand dollars to each of his two daughters. "I have intentionally refrained from making substantial provision for my beloved daughters Kathleen Lanier Harriman Mortimer and Mary Averell Harriman Fisk in this will not from any lack of love and affection for them but because I know them to be otherwise well provided for."[53]

Indeed they were. Since 1947, Kathleen had been married to Stanley G. Mortimer Jr., the former husband of Barbara "Babe" Cushing, who divorced him in 1946 and married Bill Paley. Mortimer came from an aristocratic and wealthy family. His father was a descendant of John Jay, the first chief justice of the United States; his mother's father was a founder of Standard Oil of California. Averell's elder daughter, Mary, in 1940 had married Dr. Shirley Fisk, a respected New York internist who had also served in the 1960s in the Defense Department under Robert McNamara as a deputy assistant secretary of defense for manpower, health and medicine. Both families were well off and certainly comfortable.

They were also more than slightly surprised later to discover that Pamela got everything. "Upset?" said a grandchild. "Talk about an understatement. Damn right they were upset."[54]

But none ever considered disputing the will. It was not only that Pam's pockets were deep enough to withstand any challenge. The relatives also knew that the will represented Averell's wishes. It was clear to them that he was devoted to Pamela and that, while he had been collapsing physically and mentally in his final years, he had not lost his sensibilities about his money. No one accused Pamela of having twisted his arm. It had not been necessary.

By 1986, the will was resolved and Pamela was in the midst of a full-court press for the November midterm elections. That spring, seventeen events and fund-raisers were held at the Georgetown house and at Willow Oaks, almost all of them aimed at winning back the Senate for the Democrats.

On July 4, Pamela hosted an Independence Day party at the Virginia estate. It was a hot, steamy day and Averell was unwell. Feeling very weak, he stayed inside and was visited only by Paul Warnke, an old friend who was Jimmy Carter's strategic arms negotiator and Clifford's law partner. Pamela knew that the end was near and that Averell wanted to die in New York State.

They took the jet north to Westchester County airport and drove to Birchgrove, where Leland had died fifteen years before. Averell's doctor was away on a cruise and the local doctors were nervous that the statesman might die on their watch. Pamela did not want Averell kept alive mechanically. She had been allowed to bring Leland home at the end and she wanted Averell to depart in peace and dignity as well. The doctors insisted that a decision not to prolong his life could not be made without the concurrence of Averell's full family. So Pamela cabled Kathleen and Mary, who were vacationing in Alaska, and they returned in time.

Averell was alert enough for Kathleen to read him *Air Force Spoken Here*, James Parton's just-published biography of another old friend, General Ira Eaker, and his days in wartime Britain at the head of the Eighth Air Force. On July 26, Averell died with his two daughters, Pamela and Young Winston by his bedside.[55]

The next two days were a blur for Pamela, who swallowed her

grief and scarcely slept while she and Janet worked in a controlled frenzy to plan every detail of Averell's funeral. On the third day, the ceremony drew 750 of the country's top politicians and diplomats to St. Thomas's Episcopal church in Manhattan, where his mother had worshipped.

Among the dignitaries were Walter Mondale, former secretaries of state Henry Kissinger, Cyrus Vance and Edmund Muskie, and Vernon Walters, the U.S. ambassador to the United Nations who had worked with Harriman at the Paris peace talks. Three New York governors and four New York City mayors attended along with Clark Clifford, former attorney general Nicholas Katzenbach and ambassador and economist John Kenneth Galbraith.

Peter Duchin, Young Winston and five grandsons carried the coffin to the hearse which, escorted by motorcycle riders, transported Averell's remains across the George Washington bridge and back to Arden. Some sixty relatives and friends — Harrimans, Churchills, Mortimers, Kennedys, Vances and Schlesingers — followed the cortege on the hour-long drive to the grave site on the knoll overlooking St. John's Church. Arden caretaker Lionel Bond and a work crew dug the open grave next to Marie Harriman's final resting place. Averell would be the eighth Harriman buried in the pine-shaded row, just down from his mother and father and beloved sister Mary.

Episcopal bishop Paul Moore Jr. led the prayers and poured sand on the casket. When the ceremony was over, the onlookers left for a reception. When some returned for a final look before heading back to New York City, the grave had been filled and a mound covered the site.

The only problem was that unbeknownst to nearly everyone there, including the bishop and most of the family, Averell had not been buried. When the mourners left, his body was returned to the Frank Campbell Funeral Home in New York and refrigerated for two months while an alternate burial site was prepared.

Averell told long-time retainer Michael Kuruc that he wished to be buried between Marie and Pamela, but Pamela had other ideas. Her adviser William Rich explained that several years before, Averell had decided to be buried on the shore of Forest Lake, four miles away from the family plot. The site is tucked away down an embankment off a dirt road in the depths of the Arden estate. Averell's stone monument with a chiseled inscription, "Patriot, Public Servant, Statesman," is off-center on the patch of ground, presumably to leave room for Pamela to join him one day. The spot is enclosed by a modest fence, but in the summer of 1992, the space was heavily overgrown by unkempt grass and weeds, an incongruously isolated final resting place for the last of the Harrimans and for a couple who hated being left outside of anything.

The official explanation was that Pamela had picked out the site earlier in the summer, but the lakeside was mostly granite and the blasting work required to prepare the grave had not been completed in time for the funeral. There had been no rush to finish the site, Rich explained, because, although Averell was ninety-four, Pamela had expected him to recover.[56]

"The thing was that everyone had come to New York from various places for the funeral and they had blocked out the day. There was no intention to deceive anyone," said Robert C. Fisk, the eldest of the six Harriman grandchildren. "You couldn't just leave the body in the church . . . [Pamela] thought the most dignified thing was to go ahead with the normal conclusion of the Episcopal ceremony."[57]

Which still failed to explain the hole in the ground and the fact that few except Pamela and the funeral home officials knew what was happening. "It was a complete shock," said Nancy Lutz, Marie Harriman's daughter. "I think she's jealous for some reason of my mother, though I can't for the life of me imagine why, since my mother had been dead for fifteen years. But there's no question she did not want Averell beside Mum."[58]

No, she did not, although Pamela's decision to isolate Averell was not aimed personally at Marie, whom she had never met. There was a more basic reason: In life, Pamela had always been forced to share her men. She was damn well not going to share Averell in death.

CHAPTER EIGHTEEN

Bill and Al

WHEN AVERELL DIED, Pamela came into her own in every sense.

Financially, she had finally made it. For most of her life, and especially after her terrifying financial experiences with Randolph, she had been driven by a near pathological obsession about money and a deeply inbred fear of never having enough. Now, with a fortune in the $100 million range, she had become one of the world's wealthiest widows.

Politically, she was her own power, with her own checkbook, source list, lines to every influential Democrat and, above all, her own identity.

Familially, she had total control — from who could use the Sun Valley ski cottage to who might one day inherit the estate from her. Would it be Winston and his children? Might Kathy and Mary's offspring receive more if they behaved about her? Or might she instead withhold the millions from them and endow something with her name on it?

Pamela was the puppet master.

Socially, she could have her choice.

Psychologically, she was free.

She never complained publicly, but Averell had been a tremendous burden in his final years, enormously frustrated that he could no longer see, could barely hear even with the most advanced hearing aids and could move only on a walker or with the assistance of a nurse who hauled him from the soothing heat of his pool. A Soviet film crew came in 1985 on the fortieth anniversary of the end of World War II to record his thoughts but found his mental capacity sorely diminished. It was difficult for Pamela, trying her hardest but also attempting to maintain some semblance of a life for herself. "Those final eighteen months were rough," said Bob Strauss. "Very stressful," Pamela acknowledged.

There was understandable tension between Averell and his wife, occasional flare-ups that visitors had witnessed. They never resulted in shouting, but in shut doors and an icy, silent treatment that left Averell sitting alone in his room, staring off into space. "She would rush home," said Michael Kuruc, "then ignore him."

Pamela was busy with a political schedule that had her up every day at 5 A.M. and there was a limit to how long she could sit around alone with him herself. She tried to anticipate his needs, to ensure his comfort and to keep him well supplied with company and distractions. Averell had been used to superb health and was angry and understandably upset in his nineties that he had so many needs and was attempting desperately to maintain the dignity that was so important to him.

She loved him and grieved for her benefactor, but his death was also a relief, a huge weight off her shoulders, which had literally begun to hunch like his. Her once-shimmering auburn hair had turned mousey brown. She had deep lines in her face, bags under her eyes and a double chin; her childhood tendency toward plumpness had returned with a vengeance. Some friends wondered why she had let herself go.

Others thought they understood the reason. "She has extraordinary self-control and could have dieted or had a face-lift, but she did not want to," one woman friend explained. "Averell was fading and she did not want to remind him that he was on the way out by looking too good. She kicked herself for mishandling the Leland estate and she was not going to make the same mistake twice."[1]

By the time Averell died, Pamela was chunky, matronly and exhausted. She hardly slept while planning the minute details of his funeral and an even larger memorial service seven weeks later in Washington's National Cathedral which drew dignitaries from the Truman, Kennedy, Johnson, Carter and Reagan administrations plus Supreme Court Justices Thurgood Marshall and Byron White and every major Democrat on Capitol Hill.

She also had a terrible fright immediately after Averell's funeral. Her assistant, Janet Howard, began hemorrhaging and Pamela, near exhaustion, raced her from Arden to a hospital in New York City. There, instead of being helped right away, they sat like many emergency room patients, ignored in a grotesque waiting room for what seemed like forever, fearing that Janet was slipping away.

Pamela could not help but wonder if she were about to lose within the same few days the two most important people to her, a status that Janet had attained through a combination of total devotion, extraordinary efficiency and a willingness to tolerate Pamela's perfectionist demands.

Janet recovered and, having assumed the PAC's directorship in 1985, she pressed ahead with Pamela toward winning the Senate in November, only three months away. Pamela had special stationery printed with a letterhead showing the Capitol building and the slogan "Senate Majority '86." "We can take the Senate this year," she wrote in an appeal for funds that summer. "We are within striking distance. From Alaska to Florida, from North Dakota to Alabama, Republican seats are ripe to be taken. One vote, one contribution, one year: This is it." Adding a personal touch, she scrawled across the bottom, "It's been a long road back from the Reagan landslide of 1980, but we're almost there."[2]

The Democrats' chances looked reasonable. The Republicans were defending twenty-two of the thirty-four seats up for reelection, including those of sixteen vulnerable freshman Republicans who had been carried into office in the 1980 Reagan tide that had lifted all GOP boats. There was a problem, though. The president was fighting hard for his candidates to preserve the "Reagan Revolution."

In the most vigorous midterm effort ever by a president, he campaigned that fall in sixteen states for freshmen and veterans alike. But when the votes were counted on November 4, the Teflon president turned out to have Teflon coattails: only half of the first-term Senate Republicans were reelected and only four of those he had campaigned for had won. A 53 to 47 Republican majority had been replaced by a 55 to 45 Democratic majority. The Democrats also gained five more seats in the House.[3] Everything Pamela had worked for had come to pass.

All those issues evenings: Energy and Natural Gas policy with majority leader Jim Wright and congressman Al Gore Jr. and moderator Bob Strauss; Recovery and Industrial Policy with Senator Lloyd Bentsen, congressman Lee Hamilton and moderator Harry McPherson. All those "Evenings with . . ." Governor Mario Cuomo or congressman Dan Rostenkowski or Senator Fritz Hollings. All the endless arm-twisting and fund-raising appeals which she loathed. The battles for money with other PACS and for influence with dozens of other special interest groups.

Some of her worst moments had been disputes with Democratic "friends," notably in the Jewish community. She discovered that pro-Israel activists played the roughest hardball, ready to slit the throat of any Democrat of suspect loyalty, just as they had eviscerated Ohio senator John Glenn when he voted in favor of the United States selling AWACS radar planes to Saudi Arabia.

All that endless, torturous backroom work had paid off. Some close friends and advisers admitted they had been wrong. Bob Strauss voiced doubts to Pamela at the outset about the usefulness of Democrats for the 80's. "I said, 'Pam, it's a very good idea, but you ought to remember that you're limited to how much it's going to amount to. This organization will be useful but never a big deal because people want to give money directly to the party or the candidate themselves. They don't want to filter it through you.' "

After years of watching her be more than a pretty face, of seeing her roll up her sleeves and dig in to the party rebuilding process from the foundation up, Strauss admitted, "I totally misjudged it. It became a hell of a lot more important than I ever thought it would be."⁴ According to New York governor Mario Cuomo, "Democrats for the 80's is the most effective political organization I know of within our party."

The $1.8 million raised at N Street dinners in 1985 and 1986, a third fact book costing $103,000 to publish — all appeared to have had an impact. "This is not the outcome we sought," President Reagan conceded. "What happened this week creates a minority mentality for the Republicans and a majority mentality for the Democrats," said Ed Rollins, the president's first-term political adviser and manager of his 1984 campaign. "The Democrats will now be more aggressive and we might be less so."⁵ Six years of gathering Republican momentum had stalled and few had more right to crow than Pamela.

"There was an enormous sense of exhilaration," said Stuart Eizenstat, "a sense that we had resuscitated the party and that the dark, dark days were behind us."⁶ Pamela was ecstatic: "Democrats are on the march again and we won't stop until we reach the White House in 1988."⁷

If they made it, there would be something in it for her — deserved recognition that she was a woman of substance, an understanding that her role had evolved a long way from her days as a hostess or courtesan or rich man's amusement. With 1988 in mind, she committed to keeping the PAC going for another two years and, with a fresh sense of vindication and total independence, began to spread her wings, a much merrier widow.

She did not talk about it openly, but she had her eye on an ambassadorship. Embassies were the traditional payoff for big contributors. But Pamela was not interested in just any embassy. She had not yet targeted a specific capital, but it would have to be a substantial and worthwhile post, no piddling Caribbean or African dumping ground of a thank you like Shirley Temple Black's appointment to Ghana. She considered herself a major league player and expected to be treated like one.

To secure a proper post, however, she needed to establish credentials that went beyond domestic politics and fund-raising. Moving quickly to pick up Averell's diplomatic mantle, she threw herself into the world of foreign policy — as distinct from foreign affairs — with a 1987 blitz that had her looking every bit like an ambassador-at-large-in-training.

She visited China that summer, accepting an invitation that had been extended to Averell, but which they had to let lapse when the old statesman became ill. After his death, Averell protégé and Pamela courtier Richard Holbrooke, an Asia specialist, let it be known that the widow and independent force in the Democratic party would like to accept the invitation if the Chinese government remained interested.

It was, and Pamela embarked with her own delegation, which included historian Arthur Schlesinger and his wife, Averell's grandson David Mortimer, and her pod of foreign policy advisers: Sandy Berger and Holbrooke, supplemented by Harry Harding, a China scholar from the Brookings Institution, a Washington think tank.

Beijing made clear that if she wanted to bring a delegation, that was fine, but they were paying for her. Pamela picked up the tab for her guests, some of whom discharged their debt by "helping" her write on her return a *New York Times* op-ed piece on China's attitude toward Mikhail Gorbachev's economic reforms in the Soviet Union. Her conclusion: China wanted Gorbachev to succeed because "an economically preoccupied Soviet Union poses less of a security threat to China's northern border, freeing China to concentrate more on its pressing economic agenda."[8]

She was fascinated by China and especially delighted with the semiofficial treatment she received, being feted at endless banquets, put up in official guest houses, and hosted in meetings by a Chinese vice-premier and U.S. ambassador Winston Lord. She clambered up the Great Wall only to run into CNN boss Ted Turner, but the trip was far from an idle jaunt.

It was just what she wanted, a substantive mission replete with lengthy roundtable discussions on China's politics and economy, agrarian reform, health care, relations with the United States and the likely impact on China and the rest of the Communist world of Gorbachev's twin policies of *glasnost* and *perestroika,* or openness and restructuring.

Pamela was fairly comfortable discussing Russia, but China was virgin territory. She had prepped for the trip, reading papers by Harding and Holbrooke and talking late into the night with both men, but nothing substituted for being there. By the time it was over, she felt a surge of confidence about an entirely new area of foreign policy.

Holbrooke that same year helped her join the New York–based Council on Foreign Relations, the unofficial headquarters for the predominantly Democratic and Northeast foreign policy establishment. Membership requirements include intellectual expertise, experience in international affairs, standing among peers and potential contributions to the Council's work.

Pamela's meetings with foreign dignitaries, including Soviet leaders on her trips to Moscow with Averell, plus her involvement in issues dinners on foreign policy, arms control and defense matters were deemed sufficient qualification. Some members muttered about favoritism, but Pamela was better apprised, at least superficially, of global developments through her brain trust and her own increasingly sophisticated firsthand experiences than most of the Council's then two thousand members. She was also better-heeled than most to contribute financially, and did: according to Harriman Foundation tax records, she gave nothing in 1987 but donated five thousand dollars in 1989, and twenty-five thousand each in 1990 and 1992.

She had been a member for two years of the Atlantic Council, a bipartisan policy center based in Washington, which in recent years has received fifty thousand dollars annually from Harriman trusts — twenty-five thousand from W. Averell and Pamela C., the remainder from Marie W., Pamela's predecessor.

In November 1987, she traveled as a member of one of their delegations to Istanbul. She made no formal presentation, but she listened well and asked direct, pertinent questions in discussion periods. On her return, after discussing with her advisers her trip notes and whether she had the credentials to go public with her thoughts, she submitted another op-ed piece for the *Times*, titled TURKEY DESERVES PRIORITY ATTENTION.

"Turkey is exposed to pressures from its historic rival the Soviet Union, to the north, and the new wave of Islamic fundamentalists to the east and south," she wrote with expert help. "It is too little exposed to Americans. We need to tune in more closely to its progress at home and abroad."[9]

As she did in her China article, she picked a noncontroversial topic loosely linked to the main area where she had been building knowledge, the Soviet Union, and presented a cogent, conventional argument in keeping with the Atlantic Council briefing papers and the discussions she attended in Turkey. It was a smart, fault-free strategy.

The apex of a year in which she conscientiously stretched herself took place in December, when Raisa Gorbachev came to Washington for her husband's meeting with Ronald Reagan. Raisa had infuriated Nancy Reagan the year before when she showed up unexpectedly at the Reykjavik summit and stole much of the media attention. Home alone in Washington, she thought by mutual agreement, Mrs. Reagan fumed.

Now, a year later, Nancy was angry again. Raisa had ignored for two weeks the First Lady's invitation to tea and a White House tour during the latest summit, but at the urging of Soviet ambassador Anatoly Dobrynin, who knew the Harrimans well, she had sought and quickly accepted an invitation to Pamela's house, the first time a Soviet leader's spouse had visited a private American home. "I was offended," sniped Mrs. Reagan.[10]

Pamela was elated. She assembled five distinguished American women for a power-packed colloquy: Justice Sandra Day O'Connor, the first woman to serve on the U.S. Supreme Court; Senators Barbara Mikulski, a feisty Maryland Democrat, and Nancy Kassebaum, a Kansas Republican; University of Chicago president Hanna Holborn Gray; and Katharine Graham.

Raisa arrived with a box of Russian chocolates and a book on Soviet icons for Pamela. When she emerged an hour and a quarter later, in sharp contrast to her frosty exchanges with Nancy, Raisa and Pamela were smiling broadly and holding hands. Raisa praised Averell, saying that he "always believed that our peoples can be together." To the clustered reporters, Pamela responded diplomatically in kind, commending the Russian First Lady for "doing a fine job."

In between arrival and departure, the group sipped tea, and

met Pamela-style: purposefully around the dining room table, which was set with pads and pens for serious conversation about collaborative efforts to combat cancer and alcoholism, prospects for university and cultural exchanges and how to improve nutrition and housing for low-income families in both countries. All strong characters, the women had no hesitation about speaking up. Pamela helped steer the conversation but let the others do most of the talking. Her role, as it had long been, was to facilitate and few did it better.

The meeting was an unqualified success. It was bipartisan, serious, substantive, classy — and in every newspaper, newsmagazine and television news broadcast in America. "If First Ladies could be elected on a separate ticket," wrote Carter foreign policy adviser David Aaron in the *New York Times*, "Governor Harriman's widow would now be the front runner."[11]

On April 27, 1988, a week after Michael Dukakis won the New York primary and revved up his bandwagon for the Democratic nomination that July, "the only Washington hostess with her own foreign policy," as the *Washington Post* described her, gave a speech at Georgetown University.[12]

In an address titled "Where Is the Water's Edge? The President and Congress in U.S. Foreign Policy," Pamela called for improving collaboration between the Reagan White House and Democratic-controlled Capitol and deplored the ideological and partisan wrangling between the two which has "weakened respect for America and its government here and abroad."

It was a good ghost-written speech, sensible and, as always, noncontroversial, with some nice anecdotes about Harry Hopkins, FDR and Churchill. Her opening lines included just the right grace note. She would be doing "a disservice," she explained, "if I pretended this evening to professional expertise" in foreign policy. Instead, she preferred "offering some thoughts on the making of our foreign policy from the perspective of an American active in our national politics."

Despite her introduction by former senator and secretary of state Edmund Muskie, the forty-five-minute speech indeed did not cast her as an expert. But with the single exception that she was not wearing ostrich feathers — she had on a short, tight,

black silk cocktail dress — the appearance constituted her diplomatic debut every bit as much as her debutante presentation to
King George VI precisely fifty years earlier marked her formal
introduction to British society.

"I think it's important from her perspective to be seen as something other than a major fund-raiser, something other than a
social figure," said Stuart Eizenstat. "This establishes her credentials in that area."[13]

The event, which was attended by three hundred political
friends and career diplomats and followed by a reception paid for
by Pamela, did not happen by chance.

The forum was the Eighth Samuel D. Berger Memorial Lecture,
a production of the Institute for the Study of Diplomacy, which
is part of Georgetown University's School of Foreign Service. A
four-page program on thick bond paper listed Pamela's biography,
including her graduation from Downham College and "postgraduate work" at the Sorbonne, and her memberships in such
groups as the Board of Friends of the Kennan Institute for Advanced Russian Studies, which is reserved for donors, and the
Advisory Council of the W. Averell Harriman Institute for Advanced Soviet Studies, which does not exclude a widow of the
chief patron.

A longer biography of Samuel D. Berger (no relation to Sandy
Berger) identified him as a distinguished envoy, who had served
in the Lend-Lease program in Britain in 1942 (with Averell), later
as ambassador to Korea (with Averell his boss as assistant secretary of state for East Asian and Pacific Affairs), a stint as deputy
assistant secretary of state for that same department (while Averell
was negotiating at the Paris peace talks).

It should, therefore, have been of little surprise to scanners of
the program notes to read that the Berger lecture series "owes its
establishment to the generosity of the Honorable W. Averell Harriman." In previous years, the lecture had been delivered by such
celebrated diplomats as Roy Jenkins, Britain's chancellor of the
exchequer and cofounder of the Social-Democratic party; Leonard
Woodcock, president of the United Auto Workers and U.S. ambassador to China; Philip Habib, ambassador to Vietnam and
Korea and presidential envoy to the Middle East and Central

America; and David Abshire, the U.S. permanent representative to NATO.

It was heady company for one not pretending expertise. After Pamela spoke in 1988, one more Berger lecture was delivered, the following year by Deputy Secretary of State Lawrence Eagleburger. After that, the Berger lecture series was scrapped. "Funding stopped," explained a staffer at the Institute for the Study of Diplomacy. The forum had served Pamela's purpose. She was launched.

She was not, however, affiliated early with Michael Dukakis, who would be the one to fix her orbit if he won. "I didn't hear from her," said Dukakis campaign manager John Sasso. Nor did Susan Estrich, who succeeded him when Sasso was forced to resign early in the campaign for leaking a tape revealing the origins of an alleged campaign plagiarism by Senator Joseph Biden.

Pamela's candidate was Albert Gore Jr., the freshman senator from Tennessee whose campaign she and PamPAC backed in 1984. A quintessential young Establishment politician who grew up in Washington, D.C., where his father, Albert Sr., represented Tennessee for three influential terms in the Senate, Gore was a Super Tuesday star in March 1988. By late April, however, his campaign had collapsed and he did not seem in contention for a shot at the vice-presidential slot.

Coming out for Gore marked the first time Pamela supported a specific presidential candidate since she and Averell had campaigned for Muskie in 1972. That experience had been sufficiently painful to eliminate all temptation to step back into the presidential primary maelstrom. In 1984, Pamela did not campaign for him, but she later staged a $250-a-head fund-raiser for Gary Hart complete with a tent, rock and roll entertainment and hundreds of donors to help him retire his $3.2 million debt. "I don't know if I was 'her guy,' but she sure raised money for me," said Hart. "It was a spectacular event."

What drew her to Hart was his interest in modernizing the Democratic party, which matched her goal, and his strong focus on foreign policy, especially East–West affairs, Averell's specialty. "She and Averell believed that I and people like me had a kind of vision for the party's future that was going to be required to win," said the former Colorado senator. "We all agreed that you couldn't just keep repeating the New Deal litany."[14]

Hart sought Pamela's support again in 1987, but everyone was looking for her patronage then and she made no commitment, to him or anyone else. When the *Monkey Business* scandal linking him to model Donna Rice forced him out of the race that May, Hart never heard from Pamela again.

In early 1988, she decided to back the politically patrician Gore. Senators were always her favorites. She has little time for women, because most — Kay Graham being an obvious exception — lack power. But Pamela loved Gore's wife, Tipper, an ebullient and independent woman who supported herself as a photojournalist before marriage and who holds a master's degree in psychology. Pamela had supported her husband since 1981, when she sent the then Tennessee congressman a $500 PAC check. She considered him well-behaved, suitably deferential, deadly serious and she admired his strongest suit: his strong sense of the dangers and potentials in the United States–Soviet relationship. For Pamela, Gore seemed the only candidate with any qualifications on defense and foreign policy. Averell was dead, but his policy priorities lived on.

Personally, she liked Jesse Jackson tremendously. He was almost hypnotic, very engaging, with just the right touch of roguish flirtation that she found appealing. But Jesse was not going to be the nominee. In fact, she worried that he might go from being a pain in the party's side to actually hurting its chances. But he was smart enough, she was certain, to avoid being too disruptive.

Massachusetts governor Dukakis was not Pamela's type at all. He felt like another Jimmy Carter to the N Street drawing-room set. He was a Washington outsider with neither national credentials nor foreign policy experience, had little or no charisma, was an uninspiring speaker and, if that were not enough, was physically unimpressive. He was "sort of a fluke" as the party's leading candidate, she decided.[15]

Still, when he sewed up the nomination, she was ready to host his introduction to Washington and to all the establishment pooh-bahs. The Dukakis staff advanced the visit and informed Pamela and Janet that their five-foot-eight candidate needed a platform on which to stand. An eighteen-inch riser was built and placed by the fireplace in the living room right in front of *White Roses*. When it came time for his remarks, Pamela barely heard a word Dukakis said. She was terrified throughout that he was about to topple off the platform and fall straight through her zillion-dollar canvas.

He was charming up close, though, and made a good impression on the thirty top Democrats she had assembled for him, but the good will quickly evaporated. Instead of calling or dropping a note to each of the guests later, thanking them for their interest in his campaign and giving them a special telephone number where they might record and leave ideas or helpful suggestions, Dukakis never followed up. No one was ever asked to do anything.

All it would have taken was a little TLC, or tender loving care, Pamela's stock in trade, but the Dukakis team was too inept to react to the Republicans' vigorous negative campaign, let alone adopt such minor, professional touches. The next time around, she made a mental note that she would sit down early with each of the candidates for some basic training in how to behave in a national campaign.

George Bush made such gestures better than anyone. The hand-written note was his trademark and almost succeeded in disguising the fact that his administration had no domestic policies. Proper etiquette was one Republican trait that she wished her Democrats would appropriate. Although it prompted a discouraged sigh, her disappointment in how Dukakis dealt with her guests did not mean that wild horses could have kept Pamela away when the Massachusetts governor made his first major foreign policy speech that June at the Atlantic Council. There was Pamela, smiling silkily, beside him on the dais. In the audience, two retired career foreign service officers, both Georgetown neighbors of Pamela, conferred. Ambassador to the United Nations, they decided, was what she wanted.

She certainly would have considered that or any other serious offer, but when the results came in on November 7, the Democrats were once again on the receiving end of a mini-landslide, courtesy of Bush and Dan Quayle. The electorate preferred that Reaganism be extended, at least if the alternative were Dukakis's liberalism.

The party had lost five of the past six presidential elections and had begun to look like Charlie Brown, the sad-sack character in the comic strip "Peanuts" who, whenever he tried to kick a football, saw it snatched away at the last second by Lucy and fell on his fanny.

"The humor, of course lies in Charlie Brown's earnest belief that despite the implacable evidence of history, this time will somehow be different and the pigskin will finally go sailing through the uprights," wrote *Time* magazine's Walter Shapiro. "So, too, for the Democrats. They begin each presidential cycle convinced that they have at last redefined their ideology, risen above the folly of faction and rediscovered the magic formula to create a national majority."[16]

Although they had bombed again at the top of the ticket, the Democrats were doing fine everywhere else. The Senate, House, governorships — the majorities of each were all in Democratic hands, and Democrats for the 80's and Pamela in particular could rightly claim a place in the front row of the pantheon of those responsible. The PAC had given the maximum in 1987–88 to each Senate contest and participated in nineteen House and six governors' races, handing out a total of $864,360.95.

In October 1988, it had sponsored a two-hundred-thousand-dollar generic get-out-the-vote campaign with a sixty-second radio spot broadcast nationwide on CBS and Mutual Broadcasting for the four days before the election and several thirty-second spots in key states with close races. Pamela had also chaired the 1988 Annual Fall Dinner of the Democratic Senate Campaign Committee, which raised another $1.5 million.

In addition, when the party needed three hundred thousand dollars to install a satellite hookup to allow Democrats better exposure through direct communication with their local TV stations, Pamela staged a thousand-dollar-a-plate dinner at Washington's Ritz Carlton and raised $610,000 for the system, which was installed on Capitol Hill in a facility gratefully named the Harriman Communications Center.

She had done all she could. It was not her fault that the party's presidential nominees kept coming up short. Where she was involved, the party did fine. But there did not seem to be much else that she could do. PamPAC had accomplished its mission by 1986 and in 1988 ensured that there was no backsliding. She had plowed every fund-raising furrow. It was time to close up shop. Pamela was tired. She felt as though she had been running full tilt ever since Averell died. It was time to spend some time on herself.

"I've decided that this, the final year of Democrats for the 80's, the PAC should act only as a financial vehicle," she wrote to the group's board members on January 31, 1989, eleven days after George Bush had taken his oath of office. "Our goal will be to raise $330,000 ($10,000 per race) in federal funds for the Senate races in 1990. I will be making the major commitment of time to the Democratic Senatorial Campaign Committee and will work jointly with other organizations on polling, generic media and development of an absentee ballot program for our party."[17]

Pamela found it impossible to withdraw completely from the political salon business. She cut back but still held eight candidate receptions at home in 1989. By 1990 and the off-year elections, she had tailed off to four. Her big splash that year was a June extravaganza at the Kennedy Center, a "Party of the Decade" featuring Dana Carvey, Roberta Flack and Crosby, Stills and Nash. Once House Speaker Tom Foley promised that there would be no political speeches, twenty-five hundred people bought tickets and raised $1.2 million for various Democratic committees.

The party picked up one Senate seat and eight in the House in November, but Pamela was suffering burnout. Early that year, the PAC had been renamed Democrats for the 90's, but her heart was no longer in it. Halfway through his term, George Bush was building an international coalition to go to war against Iraq for invading Kuwait and his poll numbers were soaring. It did not look as though 1992 would be much different from 1988.

On December 7, 1990, Pamela wrote each member of her board to inform them that she was closing the PAC. "This does not represent any lessening of my own commitment to the Democratic cause," she said, adding, "I am determined to be involved in electing a Democratic President in 1992." Until then, she wrote,

"I intend to refocus my political endeavors — and given that decision, I can no longer personally devote the time I have in the past to the PAC."[18]

What began as a joke had become one of the most successful political action committees ever, having raised, by her accounting, nearly $12 million from all sources in a decade. Publicly, she was more concise: "I've paid my dues."[19]

She had given literal refuge to Democrats in their hour, make that years, of need. She had brought together disparate elements of the party to reconcile differences for the greater good of the greater number in an environment that bespoke conciliation and consensus, not quarreling. It was difficult to feel despair amid priceless French Impressionists, Chinese porcelains, museum-quality ormolu furniture, pots of fresh roses and tulips and in the presence of the party's most powerful leaders.

She had lavished care and attention on the Democratic party just as she had lavished attention on her men. The party had her total focus. She fed it, housed it, arranged for its education and entertainment, and, in what was no less than a twelve-year seduction, brought millions to its coffers. The power players she brought together in Georgetown in the 1980s and 1990s were the same kinds of political and business movers and doers who had gathered forty years before at 49 Grosvenor Square in London. There had been a challenge then to beat the Germans and win the war just as the goal now was to whip the Republicans and win the White House. And here she was again at the elbow of power, just as she had been at Downing Street with Winston Churchill. There was a remarkable quality of déjà vu to the whole picture.

If the setting looked familiar, it was Pamela who had changed the most. She was still a facilitator, just as she had been in wartime London. She was still putting people together — Bill Clinton and Speaker Tom Foley — just as she had once linked up Averell Harriman and Fred Anderson with Lord Beaverbrook. She had been more carefree then, more open to easy influence. A postwar life of unlimited opportunities lay ahead.

But the intervening four decades, for all their glamour and learning experiences, had been filled with disappointments and heartbreak, been far rougher than most people thought. Averell had left her, then Ed, then Gianni. Women mistrusted her and tried to lock their husbands away from her. She had been seriously ill with cancer and was estranged from her Digby family, although the separation was self-imposed. She loved Leland but had a miserable time with his children and felt rejected in death by what she considered his failure to provide for her.

She finally got what she wanted with Averell — a combination of security and easy access to power — but by the time it all came together, he was nearly ninety. By the time she inherited his estate, she was sixty-six, past retirement age for most people. Whatever others thought, she did not think her life had been a bowl of amaryllis. But it could be now.

She had done her bit, she told politicians who lamented her departure from the day-to-day battles, the same phrase Churchill used when he stepped down from his second term in 1955. She would never sit back and do nothing. She did not even like to sit quietly and read for pleasure. Pamela has too much energy to stay still and always needs a project.

Her first venture after Averell died was to whip herself into shape with closer attention to her diet, more exercise now that she was on her own, and a face-lift. "The best face-lift in the entire world," said an envious socialite who has known Pamela since her days with Leland. "Her face is unbelievable. She's much prettier today than she was ten years ago."[20]

Dr. Sherrell Aston, a Park Avenue cosmetic surgeon, performed the operation. Pamela lost her double chin and the bags under her eyes and had her strong jaw defined — all with no visible scars. "Unless you catch her coming out of the water in that strong Barbados light," said one who had, with a smile. It is not a subject she talks about. When an acquaintance called her office to ask if Pamela could recommend a good cosmetic surgeon, the reply was no, Mrs. Harriman had no experience in such matters and had no idea whom to suggest.

She began dieting rigorously. She was not happy with the way she looked in clothes. In 1977, she had been named by a group of designers and fashion editors to the international best-dressed list, along with sculptor Louise Nevelson, actress Mary Tyler

Moore and Olympe de Rothschild, who, had things worked out differently, might have been an in-law.[21]

Pie Friendly thought that she would laugh off the honor as a frivolous accolade. "Pamela, aren't you just going to die of shame?" she teased when they met at a dinner right after the announcement. Pamela drew herself up, glared and replied ponderously, "I have worked for this for twenty years," meaning ever since Babe Paley became a list fixture, and refused to speak to her younger friend for the next two years.[22]

By the beginning of the 1990s, Pamela was no anorexic social x-ray, but she was thoroughbred-lean and looking anything but dowdy. She was not compulsive about her diet, but she was careful. Gretchen Johnson, the cook, prepared grilled fish and lightly steamed vegetables at home with lots of fresh-fruit desserts. Pamela's preference is to eat at home, where she can control the environment.

When she did go to a restaurant, her favorite in Washington was Galileo, which serves the capital's best Italian food. The Jockey Club, with its dark woods and leather banquettes, which had been the in place during the Kennedy administration, was her backup choice. Fare aboard her jet came in hampers and included cold grilled chicken, fresh fruit, cheeses, English water biscuits and fine wines bought by the case from a Sun Valley wholesaler.

Sport and programmed exercise were not her thing, but she loved swimming — more on weekends in the country or at Mango Bay than in the pool at the Georgetown house. She continued to ride into her seventies, but hiking in the country was her favorite exercise and she walked for hours at a time in knee-deep snow or shimmering heat along trails in Sun Valley and Middleburg. Fair-complexioned, she is careful in the sun. In winter, she will wear a knit ski cap pulled down to the frames of dark glasses and a scarf pulled up over her nose; in summer, she has a penchant for broad-brimmed straw hats.

While pushing herself into shape, she got the post-Averell house operating to her own exacting specifications. The Parish-Hadley interior design firm oversaw the renovation of several rooms, including her upstairs study, which involved the application of eighteen coats of striated high-gloss paint that gave a porcelain glaze—like depth to the walls of her favorite room.

Majordomo Michael Kuruc left after nearly thirteen years' service. He had been devoted to Averell, who had told him that he and the rest of the personal house staff were covered by a pension-and-benefits plan. Averell's father, E. H. Harriman, had such a plan for servants at the Arden estate, which Averell had discussed with Michael, and so had Mrs. Cornelius Vanderbilt, Kuruc's employer before he joined the Harriman staff in 1974. There had been no problem while Averell was alive. Averell had even put Kuruc's daughter Michele through law school at the University of Wyoming.

When Averell died, Pamela gave Janet Howard fifty thousand dollars in Union Pacific stock in memory of her husband. Kuruc, who had worked there six years longer, was given thirteen thousand dollars' worth of stock and decided he had better double-check just how different life might be around the Harriman homes with Pamela in charge and Janet ascendant.

"I approached Mrs. Harriman and asked what benefits she intended to provide. She said there were no benefits," he said. "I felt crushed. I told her I would have to rethink my future if I wasn't going to have any pension. I had wasted more than twelve years."

"She said, 'When are you leaving?' "

Right away, as it turned out, in September 1986.[23]

Just as Pamela shut out Marie Harriman's friends after her death, she wanted a staff devoted totally to her. Michael, a former policeman, was thoroughly professional but not in awe of Pamela, whose personality can turn mercurial when things do not go her way. "You must understand," he once wryly told a friend of Pamela's who was seeking to understand why her temperament could shift so dramatically and quickly from composure to rage, "Mrs. Harriman does not like to be inconvenienced."[24]

In the house, Pamela consulted Gretchen on all menus, which, like those of the duchess of Windsor, were prepared in French in a daily menu book presented on her 6 A.M. breakfast tray. Wines were reviewed with Kuruc's replacement, Clive Whittingham, a gracious, all-around manservant who maintained wine books in each house indicating what was in stock and the preferences of noted guests.

The floral arrangements in the Georgetown and Willow Oaks houses come from the gardens of the Virginia estate. Pamela has been known to claim responsibility for the arranging, but a retainer, who was also responsible for the in-town yardwork, should get the credit. Until her full-time gardener Bill Hoogeveen constructed three greenhouses on the Willow Oaks property, Pamela purchased cut flowers — up to forty thousand dollars' worth a year — from a florist in the nearby Cleveland Park neighborhood of Washington. Once Hoogeveen's operation came on line, she bought flowers only to send as gifts. Dry cleaning was flown to Windsor in Queens, New York. Before the jet, Pamela had it Fedexed. Any bills which arrived in Washington were also sent by overnight packet to Bill Rich, the financial chief at the Harriman family office in Manhattan.

New York was a favorite destination, where Pamela stayed on the East Side with Kitty Carlisle Hart, one of her closest friends, who is the energetic chairman of the New York State Council on the Arts, and whose late husband, playwright Moss Hart, had been a Broadway pal of Leland's.

She loves visiting Bill Blass, her favorite designer, who charges her wholesale. Kenneth does her hair in New York, sometimes in an all-day session. It is no longer red, nor even auburn, but a light, golden-honey color. In Washington, Eivind left his Georgetown salon and lugged two suitcases of professional hair equipment to N Street whenever Pamela called. Makeup was pedestrian, bought off the counter at Saks.

Next door at the office, complete control was in the hands of Janet, who lived in the building and thought nothing of working until 3 A.M. All paperwork of the two junior secretaries and occasional intern went through Janet, who, in drill-sergeant fashion, ensured that Pamela's orders were carried out precisely, including the assembly of the staff in the foyer in Victorian English fashion whenever Madame departed on or returned from a trip. Attendance of Gretchen, the cook, Clive, the butler, and Iris, Pamela's personal maid, was mandatory while driver Habib wrestled with luggage and handled one of two maroon Mercedes.

Other requirements: incoming phone calls, which Pamela monitored and sometimes taped, especially if they were from Berger, Holbrooke or Shrum with substantive advice, were answered on the first ring. "The staff goes through contortions to insure that happens," said Kris Bauer, a former secretary. "Life in that house is always on the edge. If anything goes awry, there's trouble."[25] Not all the office staff has been up to the tasks. Janet ran through assistants at nearly the rate cars go through the Holland Tunnel. One quit after suffering a nervous breakdown that she felt was brought on by the demanding routine.

There was no noticeable trouble in Pamela's social life, where a variety of powerful and interesting men were happy to squire her around. Pamela continued to see Gianni Agnelli, particularly when he came to New York, but also in Europe, the continuation of a friendship which never ended.

(In 1990, Pamela was at the Agnelli apartment in New York having drinks with Gianni and designer Oscar de la Renta, who calls her "the enchantress of the Western world" because "she had seduced more powerful men than anyone else. It's because she has the power of making a man, every man, feel wonderful. She doesn't put pressure on men and she totally concentrates on them. They fall for her like trees."[26]

That day, de la Renta was not offering encomiums, but only chatting with Gianni and Marella Agnelli, when in walked Liliane de Rothschild, invited by Marella, who had not realized that Pamela would be there. Spotting Pamela, Liliane froze, then ran out of the room and hid in Marella's bedroom until Pamela left.)

Admiral Noel Gaylor, a former director of the National Security Agency, was an escort for a while. Policy adviser Holbrooke occasionally walked Pamela. Property developer Mallory Walker and writer Alfred Friendly Jr., both well married to women friends of Pamela's, happily took her to the movies.

One of Pamela's favorite men in the world is Speaker of the House Tom Foley, who is cultured, approachable and superb company for women and men alike. There was nothing romantic about the friendship, but the two often ended up at the same functions throughout the 1980s, delighting the courtly congressman, who is one of Washington's biggest Anglophiles and is occasionally mentioned as a potential ambassador to Britain.

The Speaker has much in common with Pamela: despite his title and power, he is essentially an inside operator, respected in Congress for taking care of the concerns of representatives in a direct, pragmatic manner. Like Pamela, he is not ideological, but a facilitator and consensus builder who tries to get things done with a minimum of fireworks.

Foley and his wife and unpaid-chief-of-staff, Heather, who unlike many women was neither a threat to nor threatened by Pamela, were frequent visitors to Mango Bay. They brought their bicycles and, mindful of House ethics rules, turned down Pamela's repeated offers to fly down with her and took care to pay for their own housing and transportation. Foley had to be extra careful: Pamela was not a lobbyist because she never asked for anything. But he was the Speaker, his predecessor Jim Wright had been ousted on questions of ethical impropriety, and Pamela was the country's best-known fund-raiser.

There were widespread stories in Washington and elsewhere that Pamela's relationship with Bob Strauss went beyond the professional. It is true that she likes Strauss tremendously and often talked to him by phone, even when he moved to Moscow, where she also visited him. It is also true that Strauss is a world-class flirt, albeit nonthreatening, who proposes to most women he meets. There is no evidence that their relationship went beyond friendship. Strauss denies that it did and credibly: his more than 50-year marriage to Helen Strauss has epic stature among his colleagues and their friends.

The serious man in Pamela's life after Averell for several years was J. Carter Brown, the Rhode Island aristocrat who was for twenty-three years, until his retirement in 1992, the director of the National Gallery of Art in Washington, D.C.

A brilliant intellectual and scholar, Brown is also the art impresario who brought to the nation's capital the great traveling exhibits "The Splendors of Dresden" and "Circa 1492," a suitable extravaganza for a museum career finale which incorporated some of the world's greatest pieces from Renaissance Europe, the

Americas and the Far East all at the time of the discovery of the New World.[27]

Pamela, who is fourteen years older than Brown, or Carter, as he is universally known, disavowed a romantic link. "Just because we go to a lot of the same social gatherings doesn't mean anything more than a long-term friendship."[28]

At the time they began showing up together, Carter was living two blocks away from Pamela in Georgetown, under the same roof with his second wife, who is also named Pamela, while they worked on a separation agreement. But Pamela Harriman was being disingenuous.

Some Washingtonians who did not know Carter well presumed that he was strictly a walker. But any woman who danced with Carter or accepted a ride home from him knew that he was intensely physical with women. Pamela and he shared a romantic relationship which played out in Willow Oaks, Mango Bay, on the Orient Express and on a yacht cruising off the coast of Turkey. On her bedside table in Barbados, next to photos of Young Winston and Averell, was a picture of Carter. Not only was the relationship romantic, but Pamela displayed strong signs of jealousy.

"I've known Carter for a very long time and we always chat and there we were at this Italian embassy dinner, just talking, and up came Pamela and very ostentatiously put her arm through his, claiming her territory," said one of Pamela's Washington friends. "It amused me, but she is very possessive, very territorial. If you belong to her, you belong to her."[29]

Chicago socialite and novelist Sugar Rautbord, a bright and lively blonde who knows Carter, described with admiration Pamela's response when another woman drew near them. "Her reaction depends entirely on how one approaches. If I approach her and Carter in a décolleté dress and I'm pouring out raging pheromones, she's Mother Superior, very scornful and rejecting. If I approach very demurely, or solicitously, perhaps as a major donor, I'm immediately taken into the circle. But the reaction is always based on an instant assessment that she makes with the most incredibly fine-tuned antennae. She can be an impenetrable iceberg or little-girl vulnerable. It's a highly practiced technique found in great actresses, supreme courtesans and, of course, fine diplomats."[30]

Because Carter is highly complex and intellectual and Pamela is single-minded and unintellectual, they seemed to many who knew them a less than obvious match. But in many ways, they were a perfect pairing, each bringing something to the relationship that the other wanted. Carter has first-class tastes and loves to live and travel well. It's near impossible to live or travel better than with Pamela, who was also generous to his children, taking them in on weekends, opening her pool to them and flying them to Barbados.

For Pamela, who is uncomfortable without a man at her side, Carter was the perfect escort. Not only was he handsome, sophisticated and stimulating, they shared many friends in Washington, New York, Paris and London.

It was almost incidental that he provided her first real introduction to painting. For all the flaunting of the Sorbonne and the Harriman collection, her knowledge of drawing, painting and sculpture was superficial at best and never a passion. "Pamela understands art about as well as she understands nuclear fusion," said a longtime friend, who was more matter-of-fact than critical.[31]

The Harriman collection had been assembled by Marie; even Averell was not thoroughly versed in what he owned, although artist Walt Kuhn tutored him. Pamela could be stimulating about English country houses, which were the subject of one of Carter's and the National Gallery's great shows, "The Treasure Houses of Britain" exhibit in 1986. Carter's knowledge, on the other hand, was as deep as it was broad.

No one could facilitate gifts to the gallery better than Carter, including those from Pamela, who gave the gallery twenty thousand dollars in 1986 and again in 1987. In 1989, in mid-affair, she announced that she would give *White Roses* to the gallery for its fiftieth anniversary exhibit in 1991. When press stories suggested that her relationship with Carter was behind the gift, she insisted that it had nothing to do with her decision.

"My husband had already given the Gallery quite a number

of Impressionist paintings. When he gave me the van Gogh *Roses*, he said he hoped I would leave it there too, because naturally one wants one's collection kept together. The fiftieth anniversary seemed a good moment to indicate my gift, that's all. It was really very, very simple."[32]

The National Gallery was delighted because *White Roses* became the centerpiece of the anniversary drive and helped prompt the donations of dozens of pieces of art from some of the nation's great private collections. Privately, Pamela seethed at the implication that the gift was inspired more by latter-day passion than Averell's well-intended generosity.

(The gift had considerable tax implications. Donors were allowed to deduct current market value of artworks until tax reform in 1986 limited deductions to the amount paid for a work, in this case seventy-two thousand dollars. The ruling took effect in 1987 and had such a harsh impact on gifts that museums squealed for relief. Arts advocate Senator Daniel Moynihan of New York — where the Metropolitan, Museum of Modern Art, Guggenheim, Whitney and others were hard hit — pushed for a return to the old tax break. Congress balked at a complete rollback, but allowed a one-year window for, what a coincidence, 1991. Pamela turned over twenty percent of *White Roses* that year, entitling her to a theoretical $12 million tax break if the picture were appraised at $60 million — the figure bandied about in the frenzied art market of 1989. The remaining 80 percent of the painting stayed in her estate to be taxed at the prevailing rates at the time of her death. Bill Clinton's 1994 budget, however, which was steered through a congressional conference committee by the new chairman of the Senate Finance Committee — none other than Senator Moynihan — abrogated the pertinent provisions of the 1986 legislation and reopened the window indefinitely. Pamela's lawyers said that she made a commitment "to complete the gift through her will," suggesting that she would give no more of the painting until she died, but that was before the 1993 legislation passed. Under Clinton's law, she is entitled to deduct additional portions of *White Roses*, or of any other Harriman paintings, each year to offset her taxes.)

Some friends especially loved to be around Pamela when she was with Carter because he had eclectic interests, was articulate and could display wonderful, wicked flashes of humor, enlivening what could sometimes be single-minded, solemn gatherings featuring arcane discussions about Kremlin politics or the role of NATO in the Gulf War. Traveling with Carter was a treat, especially in Europe, because he knew the scholarly and anecdotal history of almost every site, be it Greek, Roman, Norse, Persian or Pharaonic. But Pamela seldom participated.

When friends traveling with her visited a Greek temple or shrine under Carter's guiding hand, Pamela showed little interest, walking off alone for exercise rather than sightseeing. "She is completely circumscribed by her own interests," said a friend of more than twenty years. "For all the time I have spent with her, she has no idea what I do or what my interests are. She has never asked me. She is totally self-centered and narcissistic. She is wonderfully generous about having you visit because she is very lonely, but if you had trouble, Pamela is not the person you would call because your problem would be an inconvenience to her. But if she has a problem, she calls all the time."[33]

Visiting Pamela is a mixed treat. The service is wonderful, the environment sublime, but as one regular visitor pointed out, "You have to do what she wants to do." Visitors to Sun Valley are expected to hike with her, but not to go off and fish because she doesn't fish. One does not leave the room to read if a video is the evening's entertainment. A guest is expected to sit and view it with her even if he or she has already seen it.

When one prominent visitor with a bad back visited Mango Bay and asked Pamela, who was sitting on the couch, if they could exchange seats so the visitor could stretch out, Pamela stood up and wordlessly went to her bedroom for the remainder of the evening.

At meals, Pamela guides the discussion, invariably to politics or Russia. "The conversation is controlled, which means that if you want to talk about museums or books or anything which isn't in her orbit, you cannot do it," said one. "There's a wonderful Turkish proverb: the guest is the donkey of the host. At Pamela's, for so many bright people, there are a lot of donkeys."[34] According to another visitor, "Visiting Pam is all business. Every day you have to sing for anything you put in your stomach."

When the PAC closed in early 1991, Pamela was free, but she was also at loose ends. She had lost her focus. By March, the Gulf War was over and George Bush's approval ratings were moving toward a stratospheric 90 percent. There seemed hardly any Democrats even willing to challenge the president that spring.

Former Massachusetts senator Paul Tsongas had announced his candidacy, but few outside his immediate family at that point took his bid seriously and some of them wavered. The nagging question was whether any other candidates would even try. The usual suspects — Mario Cuomo, Richard Gephardt, Al Gore, Bill Bradley — were all holding back.

At the annual Democratic National Committee gala that fall, West Virginia senator Jay Rockefeller had stolen the show with a barrage of witty, self-deprecating one-liners: "Mayor Dinkins and I both grew up in New York playing with blocks; mine were Forty-eighth and Forty-ninth Street."

Long known as a sincere and decent, but also boring and unfocused, politician, Rockefeller seemed to have a fresh aura of confidence and a new quiver of sharpened skills. He had plenty of qualifications: he was a popular former governor of his state; he was six feet seven and looked presidential; he had the name to convince voters that he would not consciously wreck the United States economy; he had good liberal credentials and an expertise in health care issues; and he was married to perhaps the only other person in West Virginia who could defeat him for public office, the former Sharon Percy, daughter of a liberal Republican U.S. senator from Illinois and herself the president of Washington's WETA public television and radio stations.[35]

On May 7, Rockefeller told an audience in Cleveland that he was thinking of running. Pamela signed on almost immediately. Jay was her kind of candidate, especially for what looked like a lost cause. He was a senator and a patrician at that. He was serious and a solidly conservative liberal; no wild-eyed radical he. She liked him personally, thought Sharon was wonderful and their four kids divine. They were American thoroughbreds with perfect bloodlines. "I think he's got leadership quality," Pamela declared. "People get excited about him and think of him as a future president — which he probably is."[36]

Unfortunately, Rockefeller's future was not due to arrive in 1992. On August 7, 1991, he announced that he was "not ready" and took himself out of the race. Pamela was disappointed — she took to her bed for two days — and angry at being let down. He had gone too far to crawl away the way he did. Saying he "wasn't ready" was foolish. Who was ever ready to be president? There had never been a real cutting edge to him, but she was surprised that he did not have more backbone. All that talk about concern for his family and their needs was just cover. It was all Jay and he simply did not have the fire in the belly.

Once he had failed her, Pamela decided not to back any other candidate for the time being. She drifted from June through November, which is when she considered and dropped the idea of her autobiography. There were distractions. People like Neil Rudenstine, the new president of Harvard University, sought her counsel about fund-raising. She was happy to give it, but in actual fact, Pamela hates fund-raising, hates asking people for money and hates being considered "a fund-raiser." Still, she and Janet were good at it and there was something satisfying about the man who controlled the world's largest university endowment asking her for advice.

The Senate Judiciary Committee hearings in September on the nomination of Clarence Thomas to replace the retired Thurgood Marshall on the Supreme Court got Pamela's juices boiling when law professor Anita Hill accused the conservative U.S. circuit court judge of sexual harassment. Calls about the contentious hearings poured into her N Street office from women's groups and Court activists seeking her support. She watched hours of the hearings live on CNN, worked the phones and lobbied Democratic senators to reject the appointment, livid at what she considered committee chairman Joseph Biden's weak leadership.

When Senators Bob Graham of Florida, Lloyd Bentsen of Texas and Georgia's Sam Nunn called for her views, she told them all to think hard about chauvinism and get on the right side of the issue. As soon as the 52 to 48 full Senate vote was over on October

15, confirming Thomas by the lowest margin of any justice this century, Pamela scanned the voting sheets to assess, with a practiced eye, how the vote broke. The eleven Democratic senators who gave Thomas his slim victory, she promised, would get no fund-raising help from her, not a dime.[37]

She reserved her strongest ire for her own Virginia senator, Charles Robb, whom she found hard to respect. His vote for Thomas came on the heels of a sex-and-drugs scandal in which Robb, the son-in-law of President Lyndon Johnson, was alleged to have had an affair with a former Miss Virginia and to have been present at Virginia Beach parties where drugs were available. A grand jury was also investigating a nasty feud between Robb and Virginia governor Douglas Wilder which involved allegations of illegal wiretapping.

Robb avoided indictment, but when she considered his Thomas vote, Pamela concluded that he was hurting the party, especially fund-raising efforts, and should step down from his post as head of the Democratic Senatorial Campaign Committee. She hated bashing a fellow Democrat, but where Robb was concerned, she felt that she had to speak up. To no avail, however. The more criticism Robb heard, the harder he dug in his heels.

The Thomas fight and the bitter acrimony it generated toward George Bush suggested to Pamela well before it became conventional wisdom that the president might not be as invincible as he looked. Bob Shrum told her that the White House was becoming hysterical about the early November election in Pennsylvania to replace Senator John Heinz, who had been killed in a plane crash. When Bush's former attorney general Richard Thornburgh squandered a forty-point lead and lost the race to Democrat Harris Wofford, who campaigned on a wave of anti-Washington populism and the country's lack of affordable health care, Pamela realized that the president was downright vulnerable and that it was time to get back in the game.

She had strong feelings about each of the candidates, noncandidates and possible candidates, but none of her feelings involved much optimism.

Iowa Senator Tom Harkin was an old friend, but his prairie populism frightened her in a presidential candidate. He was an excellent speaker and had a real gift as a campaigner, which made it possible that his candidacy might take off. But he was too liberal for Pamela, too reminiscent of a latter-day George McGovern. Dangerous, was her assessment.

Doug Wilder was her governor, but not her candidate for anything higher. She had no problem with the fact that he was an African American. What troubled her was that Wilder was disruptive, a loose cannon who refused to be a team player. Wilder was for Wilder and that was not good enough.

Mario Cuomo, the governor of New York, had been wonderful when Averell died and she, like many Democrats, considered him very talented. But she had had enough of his endless public pondering about his future. Would he or wouldn't he? He had done it too often. She had given up on Mario.

Bob Kerrey, the Nebraska senator and former governor, was winning support from some of her friends, but not from Pamela. He was a conservative Democrat and she found him interesting but too flaky, a total oddball. He was reluctant to join in any Democratic National Committee events and seemed far too much a loner. Not as bad as "Governor Moonbeam," former California governor Jerry Brown, who was simply too loony for Pamela, but she could not see Kerrey running anything. Jesse Jackson had not joined the 1992 race and she doubted that he would.

Which left Bill Clinton. She liked Clinton very much for his brains, charm, confidence and omnivorous interest in policy. His stamina impressed her too: one evening in the early 1980s, he and Kerrey came over and stayed until 3 A.M. talking politics, went home and slept till 5 A.M. and flew back to the Midwest. Clinton's two years in England as a Rhodes scholar gave them an extra link. When he lost his reelection bid as Arkansas governor in 1980, she asked him to join the first board of Democrats for the 80's and found he was tremendously impressive in small meetings. "He has a very organized mind."

Clinton could talk issues for hours, down to the arcane details of welfare reform or international trade legislation, and draw out the best from other participants by incisive questioning. She even liked the fact that he had lost his first bid for reelection. "It's very important in life to have success, but it's even more important to have failure, and to know how to handle it," she said of Clinton, perhaps thinking of her own history as well.[38]

But Clinton also seemed terribly immature. His infamous nominating Speech That Would Not End at the 1988 Atlanta Democratic convention had been more than an embarrassment. With the crowd of delegates fidgeting and hollering for him to shut up and sit down, Clinton's insistence on droning on to the bitter end of his nineteen-page text, despite flashing red lights and signals from the chairman to stop, had shown insensitivity and an amazing lack of judgment. Afterward, Pamela and Sandy Berger took him to dinner and tried to ease the hurt of a stupid, self-inflicted wound which he began to heal the next day when he admitted, "It wasn't my finest hour. It wasn't even my finest hour and a half."[39]

Four years later, Clinton was good, but he was far from perfect. Nor did he project a presidential aura. His problems with women were another issue that gave Pamela pause. With the public in such a censorious mood, as exemplified by the Gary Hart precedent and the more recent Thomas-Hill hearings, the press had a good chance of destroying his candidacy. Still, in a weak field, Clinton looked like the best candidate to her. She would not commit to anyone in the fall of 1991, but she was glad Sandy Berger was joining Clinton's team. He could be her mole.

In the meantime, she would be glad to give any advice the candidate wanted. When he was trying to find a campaign manager, Clinton called several times to run names by her and ask for suggestions. When he debated whether to accept PAC money, she sent him a memo explaining why he would be foolish to turn it down. When he answered the Gennifer Flowers allegations on national television in January, he showed the spine Pamela respected. She was happy to jump on board.

Once she did, there was no holding back her enthusiasm. In a bit of revisionism, she portrayed Clinton as having been her candidate all along. Whether they were serious or only joking, no one could say anything ill of Bill in her presence.

"All of a sudden, Clinton could do no wrong," said a Democratic party activist. "Even suggest that he was perhaps not infallible, and she'd cut you dead. Just turn on her heel and walk away." From advocate, Pamela became a complete devotee.

Television and print commentators called Clinton an ersatz Kennedy for his tendency to minic the gestures and voice patterns of the late president. For Pamela, the comparison was all wrong. "Where Jack Kennedy was born to power, Bill Clinton got there all by himself," she told a Virginia audience. "The Kennedy script was written in advance. The Clinton story was written as he went. It was the great American story of enduring a tough childhood in a small corner of his country, facing adversity, learning its lessons and moving beyond."[40]

When he had the nomination sewn up, Pamela flew to Russia to burnish her diplomatic credentials, just in case anyone might soon be checking them out. She stopped in Moscow to see Ambassador Strauss, of course, then flew on to Tashkent in Uzbekistan and to Kiev, the capital of Ukraine.

On her return, she had another sensible op-ed message. "For us to see Moscow any longer as the single focal point of this entire Eurasian expanse would be both foolish and perilous," she wrote in the *Washington Post*. "It is time to recognize and respond to the rest of the former Soviet Union."[41]

Less than three weeks later, Clinton picked Al Gore to be his running mate. No one was more enthusiastic about the choice than Pamela, who had arrived for the five-day convention in New York City with invitations to 150 separate parties. Staring down at Bill and Al on the Madison Square Garden podium, she could see how they complemented one another. Suddenly, the two looked like a dream ticket.

Hillary and Tipper were on stage dancing to Fleetwood Mac, but it was Pamela, standing at her seat applauding and swaying elegantly to the beat of "Don't Stop Thinking About Tomorrow," who felt like the belle of the ball. She was seventy-two, but across her face was the grin of a twenty-two-year-old. After staying the course for twelve long years, waiting for that tomorrow, finally she felt she was backing a winner.

In June 1991, she had held the Middleburg Meeting at Willow Oaks, a day-long campaign planning session for all the likely candidates and several major donors. President George Bush could not resist a gibe about the Democrats meeting "at Pamela Harriman's farm, that bastion of democracy."[42] But Pamela was only warming up. In September 1992, she opened up the Virginia estate again for a ten-thousand-dollar-a-head Day in the Country for Clinton and Gore and raised $3.2 million. There were no caustic remarks from the White House this time.

The president was not only surprised, but rightly jealous. Money dried up for the Republicans down the homestretch of campaign 1992 while the taps opened up for the Democrats. According to Federal Election Commission records, the Democratic National Committee raised $69 million in the final six months of 1992, a full $20 million more than pulled in by their Republican counterparts and the first time in a generation that a Democratic presidential candidate raised more than his opponent.

It was the Willow Oaks fund-raiser that got the ball rolling. No one would have been prouder of her than Averell. He would have loved seeing her put their estate to such good partisan use.

At the start of the 1992 campaign, Pamela thought Clinton had made a mistake by keeping his headquarters in Little Rock and told him so, but she was happy to be proved wrong when she flew to the Arkansas capital to join the inner circle watching the returns come in the night of November 3. Clinton's 43 percent plurality in the popular vote, compared with 38 percent for Bush and 19 percent for Ross Perot, was solid if not spectacular. In a year when "incumbent" had become a dirty word, Pamela was thrilled that most of her congressional friends made it back and that the Democrats had even picked up one more seat in the Senate.

She was exhilarated when she returned to Washington to plan her November 20 reception at home for the Clintons and ninety of their closest friends. When that Georgetown party and schmoozing and self-congratulations were all done, Pamela walked the president-elect to his new armored limousine. "Thank you, Pamela, for all your help and for a wonderful night," he told her, leaning over to kiss her cheek. "I'll talk to you soon."

CHAPTER NINETEEN

🐚 🐚

Madame Ambassador

THE PRESIDENT-ELECT was as good as his word and did telephone Pamela after her November 20 dinner. When he wasn't calling her at the Georgetown house or at Willow Oaks in Middleburg, she was ringing him in Little Rock. She and Clinton talked two or three times *a day* throughout December, she told friends, not all of whom believed her. "That's what she's telling people, but I'm quite sure she doesn't," said one. "He hasn't told her what she wants to hear, namely what he intends to give her. It's the old Washington thing: she wants to create a perception."

The perception — that she and Clinton were very close — was no illusion. The odd detail might have been suspect but there was no questioning the underlying facts of the relationship. Not only did they honestly like and appreciate each other, but Pamela had introduced Clinton to the Washington power circuit and she had helped organize and pay for the overhaul of the Democratic party. The president-elect owed her a big one.

She knew that he realized he had a debt and would deliver, but knowing something and having it happen was not the same thing. Pamela worried that, after making it this far, she could be washed out in the crosscurrents suddenly whipping over and around the new president. From her days in Downing Street, she understood how bright, ambitious and jealous subordinates battled to press their views on a leader. Stress was always highest in the start-up phase, when a government was put together and the lines of command were drawn. All too often, friendship and loyalty went by the boards and the weak found themselves squeezed out and dropped without pity by the wayside. It was not going to happen to her.

The first weeks of a new administration were no better than a vicious rugby scrum of flying knees and elbows and twisted ears as the victor's campaign staff expanded at warp speed to meet the broader demands of running the country, sucking in and spitting out would-be candidates for White House advisers, Cabinet officials and key ambassadors. The old saw "If you want a friend in Washington, buy a dog" endured because it held inherent truth. Pamela understood that no matter her friendship with Clinton, she would have to fight for what she wanted.

She might not look the type who would be comfortable in such a brawl, but she was. Her exquisite manners and refined tastes belied a hustler's inner steel. Externally, she was a sleek party fat cat with no obvious blemishes; internally, a lifetime of scrambling to keep a place at the head table had left her looking like another kind of cat, a scarred and tough alley Tom. By then a two-decade veteran of America's political wars, she knew what had to be done and threw herself into the free-for-all.

She was not worried about being abandoned by Bill Clinton. And she was confident that Vice-President Al Gore would go to bat for her in an instant if need be. But she was concerned that in the crush of putting together a new administration, the president-elect's youth brigade of inner-circle advisers might not accord loyal, old-line Democrats their just due. "If you're someone like Pamela Harriman, it's easy to have detractors," said Bob Strauss. "Easy to be the object of jealousy."[1]

Even as the calls and letters of congratulations flooded into her Georgetown office, praising her unstinting commitment to the party and how her faith had contributed to its resurrection, Pamela could not shake an overwhelming anxiety.

"She is very tense," explained a friend who saw and spoke with her regularly. "She's having trouble sleeping and hardly eats a thing. She tries to laugh it off, but you can hear the strain in her voice and see it in her eyes. You don't often see so many bloodshot lines."

"I'm suddenly feeling older than I even am," Pamela admitted in a moment of candor, adding correctly that "Washington can be a cruel town."[2]

She was right to fret. "If you're not nervous in the shakeout, you're a damn fool," said Strauss.[3] Some of Clinton's top campaign advisers wanted to keep the president's distance from the rich establishment. She knew from longtime pals like Sandy Berger, who had been at the center of the campaign, that several non-Washingtonians in the inner circle had little or no use for the Old Guard.

Some younger advisers recalled the prediction of Jimmy Carter's campaign mastermind Hamilton Jordan in 1976 that if establishment veterans Cyrus Vance and Zbigniew Brzezinski became secretary of state and national security adviser, as they did, New Democrat Carter would be doomed. Several Clinton aides worried that the president would link himself to smooth establishment types like Pamela and Vernon Jordan, the two post-election dinner hosts.

"Oh God, not those old fossils," said one appalled adviser when told how Clinton intended to enter Washington through their homes on successive nights. "Totally wrong image." Pamela, her political antennae in a constant state of quivering alert, picked up the warning signals immediately and determined to move fast to clinch her reward.

Hillary Rodham Clinton was another factor in determining Pamela's fate. "She has met her match in Hillary," said a friend of Pamela's who closely tracks the Washington political scene. "Pamela and Hillary do not get along at all." The First Lady and the until-then First Lady of the Democratic Party were more than acquaintances, but never close friends. They knew each other from Bill Clinton's 1980 membership on the board of Democrats for the 80's and his ever-expanding role in party circles leading up to the 1992 election. They sometimes saw each other at party conferences or conventions and whenever the Clintons came to-gether to Washington, they stopped by. But such contact was infrequent. More often, Bill Clinton was alone during the 1980s when he saw Pamela.

Despite their surface similarities as determined, successful women married to powerful, political men, Hillary and Pamela were different in almost every area except ambition, a charac-teristic both possessed in large measure. Hillary came from a comfortable, middle-class background, made it on her own, was educated as a professional, a lawyer and feminist, was close to her parents and only child and held strong convictions, stronger than those of her politician husband. Pamela shared none of those traits. Ideologically, they were near opposites.

As a result, Pamela had nothing approaching the rapport with Hillary that she shared with Tipper Gore, who was a neighbor from nearby Arlington, Virginia, and a more traditional "wife of" type that Pamela better understood and with whom she was used to dealing.

Part of the problem was generational. Pamela had no difficulty dealing with professional political women with their own power base, such as Democratic senator Dianne Feinstein of California or even Republican senator Nancy Kassebaum of Kansas or TV anchor Diane Sawyer.

Her quandary arose when she confronted a powerful woman attached to a more powerful man. When that happened, all her synapses automatically snapped onto the man and the woman was cut out and often left feeling angry or jealous. In Hillary's case, Pamela knew her throughout the 1980s as a successful law-yer, but not as a woman to whom she related.

Whenever Hillary did come to Washington or they met at party functions, Pamela was unfailingly courteous, but it was always Bill, the man with clout and an insatiable appetite for political minutiae, on whom she focused her attention and charm.

"Everything is always geared to the husband," said the wife of a prominent Washingtonian who has known Pamela for many years and who took a long time coming to terms with her ap-proach. "I have spent quite a bit of time soothing the ruffled feathers of angry wives because she really treats them as if they did not exist."⁴ When Pamela calls friends to invite them to dinner, she always tells them that Bob or Stu or Sandy will be there, never Bob and Helen, Stu and Fran or Sandy and Susan. The same held true with Bill until the 1992 campaign.

To be sure, Hillary's arrival in Washington as First Lady was not comparable to Marie Harriman's scheduled postwar arrival in London to join Averell, a plan that forced Pamela to flee the capital for a transatlantic posting. No one seriously suggested in 1992, as they had in 1946, that Pamela should again pack her bag because the town was not big enough for the two women. Clearly Washington was, not least because there was no sexual relationship between Pamela and the president as there had been between Pamela and the ambassador.

Yet, the arrival of Hillary inevitably meant a diminishing of Pamela's role as party savior. Rosalynn Carter had sat in on Cabinet meetings during her husband's presidency, but it was clear that Hillary Rodham Clinton, as she chose to be known, would play a much larger part in the new Democratic administration. Within days of his inauguration, Bill Clinton announced that Hillary would oversee the government's health care reform package, the legislation on which the success or failure of his presidency might well ride. Suddenly, First Lady was more than a title. Hillary was going to be huge.

Some party insiders and a few friends felt that Pamela might have difficulty accepting a reduced role in Washington, but she gave no outward indication that that was true. On the contrary, she put the best face on the situation. She had no intention of leaving town, she replied, when asked after the election if she wanted to be an ambassador. "I haven't worked this hard for twelve years to elect a Democratic president only to leave Washington," she said. The response was disingenuous, but it had the ring of truth and bought her time while she and the president figured out what she would do.

The prospect of a reduced role in Washington was not the problem; the problem was avoiding a nonsubstantive role. For years she had immersed herself in party policy and had made tremendous progress toward remaking her image from gold digger to woman of substance. It was more than image. She had made the transformation. Perle Mesta and Brooke Astor and Mercedes Bass did not have private meetings with top Russian and Chinese officials on request. They could never summon the congressional leadership to their living rooms to discuss energy policy at the snap of their well-manicured fingers. Only Pamela could do that and she had no intention of retiring.

But if she stayed in Washington with a new generation in power, what would she do? She did not want to backslide. She could go in and out of the White House and attend whatever state dinners she wanted, but so what? Her ornament days were behind her. "Issues dinners" were history. Who would come to her house anyway, now that the real thing, the White House, was available a mile away? The last thing she wanted was to get stuck on some rubber-stamp presidential board or commission or to run out to Andrews Air Base as chief of protocol to greet every visiting minister of trade or opposition parliamentarian. Those jobs would be a nightmare.

Some backers, including Stuart Eizenstat, who was himself named U.S. ambassador to the European Community, believed that appointing her secretary of commerce or U.S. ambassador to the Court of St. James's would be appropriate.

The first was Averell's old Cabinet job during the Truman administration, but nostalgia aside, Pamela had no qualifications for the post, which went to lawyer-lobbyist Ron Brown, chairman of the Democratic National Committee. Nor was she suited for any other Cabinet job, including that of U.S. ambassador to the United Nations, which was mentioned but was also too substantive. Potential friction with Hillary and the staff problem with "fossils" ruled out anything in the White House.

The rumor mill worked overtime on the second option, the London embassy, which seemed to many unaware of Pamela's full story to offer a neat, historic closing of the circle: baron's daughter and Sir Winston's daughter-in-law returns home in glory. There were, however, several obstacles to her taking a post in London. Her former British citizenship, the fact that her brother sat — quietly — in the House of Lords and her son sat — controversially — in the House of Commons were credentials, and also potential conflicts of interest, that made her a shade too close to Britain.

More important was the less well known history that made her too distant: the continued resentment of many Britons in political circles of Pamela's "excessive fraternization" during the war and their tendency to mock her active social life in France in the late 1940s and 1950s. Appointment to London would have had the British tabloid press in baying pursuit throughout her posting.

The panting began in London in 1988 when even the staid *Times* wondered in a four-column headline whether there was A CHURCHILL CONNECTION FOR GROSVENOR SQUARE? The paper's Ben Macintyre noted then that Pamela "is being tipped as a possible choice for U.S. Ambassador to Britain" and pointed out quickly that "the list of her former liaisons reads like an extract from Who Was Who."

Four years later, in October 1992, the tabloid *Evening Standard* asked IS POWER-BROKER PAMELA SET TO RETURN AND CONQUER? According to the *Standard*'s Peter Bradshaw, "Diplomatic circles here are alive with the rumour that the queenly 72-year-old Harriman is poised to come over to London as the United States Ambassador to the Court of St. James's." He went right out and interviewed "one friend of the Churchill family" who told him, "She's been swinging and power-broking around the world and now she's ready to return in triumph. It's just like a Judith Krantz novel." Concluding, "Indeed it is," Bradshaw licked his chops at the prospective appointment. "There is something slightly brash and Eighties about the unstoppable rise of Pamela Harriman," he wrote, before giving an abbreviated version of her social past.

But the biggest impediment of all to Pamela's returning to Britain was that she still cannot tolerate Britain or most Britons. She dislikes the country, its pessimism and compulsion to look to the past, and the empty-headed arrogance of too many men in high position and their attitude about her. She spent her adult life avoiding the place. Clinton might well have overridden the objections of the State Department, where officials felt strongly that she should not be given the post in Britain, had Pamela pushed for the job. But she was not interested.

The U.S. embassy in Paris, on the other hand, was a perfect choice. She had lived in France for a dozen years, through the Churchills knew President Charles de Gaulle, the architect of postwar political France, maintained good cultural and social contacts, spoke the language and knew well — and adored — Paris itself. Returning to France *en triomphe* was the circle she wanted to close. The post met her standards: it was big, luxurious, in the middle of Europe and, in the post–Cold War shakedown, plenty substantive.

There was an added attraction. If she were given the job, it would be no small irony that the stunning official residence she would move into at 41 rue du Faubourg Saint-Honoré was a Rothschild house until World War II, the home of Elie's great-uncle Baron Edmond, known as the "Father of Israel" for his philanthropy in Palestine, and later of his son Maurice, Elie's cousin. She would be the mistress of a Rothschild mansion after all or, perhaps more accurately, the master.

For her dozen years of work for Democrats, $12 million raised for the party's coffers, and a faith in him that dated to 1980, the president was prepared to give Pamela whatever she wanted within reason. Paris qualified and she asked for it. But he was too busy in December 1992 picking his new Cabinet to focus on embassy jobs. Week after week, Pamela waited for some definitive word, becoming more and more tense by the day. On December 22, Sandy Berger was named deputy national security adviser, which cemented her ties to the new foreign policy pod. The hopes of her social-climbing adviser, Richard Holbrooke, had typically ranged as high as secretary of state, but he was stiff-armed from any position for months, which added to her anxiety.

At Christmas, she flew to Barbados to spend the holidays with friends and Winston and Minnie and their children at Mango Bay. She loves her grandchildren dearly and she was pleased that her son and daughter-in-law had smoothed over the worst scars of Winston's fling with Jan Cushing Amory. But what should have been a happy, relaxed vacation, was anything but.

"There was a great deal of tension," said a visitor. "Pamela is obsessed with everything Clinton is doing and is very uptight about what is happening to her."[5] She told a different visitor that she did not want anything from Clinton, but she was being economical with the truth. As this well-connected friend noted later, "She knew then that her job was in the works."[6]

The deal was not finally closed until after Clinton's inauguration on January 20, 1993. By the end of that month, Pamela was assured that Paris was hers, the first time a major embassy would be headed by a woman since 1976, when President Gerald Ford sent Texan Anne Armstrong to London as ambassador. While there would be no announcement of the nomination until late March, she began immediately and quietly to prepare for the assignment and her Senate confirmation hearings.

Pamela approached the task with the kind of meticulous, leave-no-detail-to-chance organization one might expect of a person whose secretaries maintained five matching appointment calendars and produced daily a computer-generated schedule modeled after the president's that included her expected dress at appointments and the names of those who would greet and introduce her.

As she had for the previous twenty years, she did her homework. In some cases using intermediaries to prevent leaks, she collected briefing papers on everything about France from its Bosnia policy to its stance on oil-seed subsidies from the State Department, the Council on Foreign relations, the Atlantic Council and the Senate Foreign Relations Committee, headed by her friend Claiborne Pell, the aristocratic Democrat from Rhode Island. She met for hours with former ambassadors and political officers who served in France, including her immediate predecessor, Walter Curley, who had been nominated by George Bush, and Arthur Hartman, a foreign service professional whom Jimmy Carter sent to Paris and Ronald Reagan named ambassador to Moscow.

"She had immersed herself in her homework and was looking at all the right issues," said Hartman. "She put her finger on trade as the one area where she knew there'd be trouble between the U.S. and France. I told her not to worry, that there were others who could deal with trade details. What was important was that she become close to the French elite, the key officials and players, admire their culture, get them into the embassy and dig in. That's the key to success in France and it's something she'll do superbly.

And, as far as explaining the Clinton administration to the French, she's in great shape."[7]

Pamela asked Nicholas Wahl, director of the Institute of French Studies at New York University, to conduct a day's seminar focused on trade and economic issues for her. "She also asked, 'Who in the present French government will be friends? Who is interested in the U.S.?' " said Wahl. "She is tough-minded, with a real sense of where niches are where you can get in and get things moving."[8] All day she asked questions and took laborious notes with her green-ink fountain pen.

She was equally methodical in rearranging her personal affairs. For two years she had been considering the sale of Mango Bay. There was no mortgage on the property, but maintaining the estate was expensive. The weather took a toll on the oceanfront house and extensive gardens which were cared for by a staff of four. Even with the jet, she only managed to get to Barbados two or three times a year from Washington and rentals of the property at ten thousand dollars a week had been too few and far between despite her best efforts to push the merits of holidays there on acquaintances. Going to Paris made the decision easy. She put the estate on the market for $3.5 million and sold it for only slightly less.

Soon after, she put her beloved Westwind jet up for sale and began preparations for closing her houses. After Averell's death in 1986, the second time a spouse had died there, Pamela sold Birchgrove in Westchester county. The house and nearly sixty acres, which a quarter century earlier had cost ninety thousand dollars, had been offered for sale in 1978 by Sotheby Parke Bernet Realty for $750,000, but Pamela had taken it off the market.[9] Eight years later, skyrocketing real estate prices during the Reagan era had pushed the property's value into the millions.

She intended to keep the cottage in Sun Valley, which was maintained by the Sun Valley Lodge. The Georgetown house and office were to be kept but closed up and the staff released. Janet Howard would come to Paris as her personal executive assistant. Gretchen Johnson, the cook, and Clive Whittingham, the butler, were hired by Representative Michael Huffington, a multimillionaire Republican freshman from Santa Barbara, California.

She had an ingenious solution for the Willow Oaks property in Middleburg, Virginia. Patsy and Lewis Preston, friends from Westchester when he chaired Morgan Guaranty Bank, moved to Washington in 1991 after he was appointed head of the World Bank. Pamela had turned over the comfortable, roomy stone cottage on the estate to them for weekend use. She did not want to push them out or close the property, which remained her legal residence and where she would stay whenever she returned to Washington.

Rather than let the main house sit vacant, she offered it to Peter Tarnoff. A one-time career diplomat who was a top assistant to Cyrus Vance when he was secretary of state, Tarnoff was the former head of the Council on Foreign Relations in New York and a good friend. More important to Pamela in her current situation was that Bill Clinton had appointed him under secretary for political affairs, the number three job in the State Department. Tarnoff would oversee at close hand her work at the Paris embassy. As tenant of her beautiful home, he could be counted on to protect her diplomatic and political flanks among the professionals in Foggy Bottom.

She spent part of February and March preparing a detailed personal biography and dealing with an FBI background check which involved her appearing for a face-to-face, two-hour interview and producing, as demanded of every appointee, a urine specimen to detect possible drug use. She and Harriman office director Bill Rich spent hours reviewing her holdings for inclusion in what would be a twenty-two-page financial disclosure report submitted to the Office of Government Ethics.

News of her appointment began leaking in late February and was made official by a presidential statement on March 23, 1993. "Anyone who has been involved with the Democratic Party for any length of time is certainly familiar with Mrs. Harriman's talent for diplomacy," the president said in reference to her ability to bring warring parties together in her house and force them to hammer out pragmatic compromises. "Her many years of dedicated service to the United States and her unceasing devotion to the cause of world peace are only two of the many qualifications that she will bring with her to Paris."

Pamela was ecstatic. She made no public statement about the announcement but said the right thing — how she was "deeply honored" — whenever asked for her reaction. Finally, she could begin to relax and get some rest.

The tension that had begun to create dark circles under her eyes receded. She makes and receives dozens of calls a day and loves discussing the most minute details of political gossip or intrigue on the phone but felt constrained after the election from discussing her own situation in any detail with all but her closest advisers. "Free at last," she told one with a smile of relief.

Reaction to the nomination was, for the most part, very positive. "An excellent choice," said Benoit d'Aboville, France's consul general in New York. "She knows France, is certainly well-connected to the Clinton administration, and will be, I am certain, a spendid representative."[10]

"At 73, the most powerful kingmaker of the Democratic Party has retained the allure and the charm that made her, in half a century, a legend on both sides of the Atlantic," said the conservative *Le Figaro* newspaper in a front-page article. "A veritable heroine from a novel."

PAMELA L'ENSORCELEUSE, bannered *Paris Match* in a two-inch-high headline. "Pamela, the Enchantress," the magazine gushed, "this woman of exceptional destiny."[11]

L'Express was more evocative, calling her "a cross between Lady Hamilton and Moll Flanders." The first was the legendary early nineteenth-century mistress of Horatio Nelson, a liaison conducted while she was married to Britain's ambassador to Naples; the latter, one of the literary world's most fascinating characters: Daniel Defoe's seventeenth-century English adventuress who relied on her beauty and wits to support herself in luxury by marrying a succession of husbands and amassing a sizable fortune.[12]

Le Point cast a cool eye on the policy aspects of the appointment. Calling the nomination "Clinton's gift to Pamela," the conservative weekly said that Pamela "fills all the requisite conditions for becoming the U.S. Ambassador in France but for one: she is not a diplomat. It's baffling at a time where from GATT [the global trade negotiations] to the reform of NATO, not to mention the options for dealing with the civil war in Yugoslavia, one might believe that a touch of professionalism would not hurt in this post. But, just as has been true for the majority of her predecessors, she is a friend of the American President. She herself contributed munificiently to financing his campaign." Americans, it noted, "ignored all, or nearly all, of her past."[13]

A few catty remarks in the same vein could be heard in Washington and New York. "What an insult to France," sniffed a Washington doyenne who had been too often ignored by Pamela. "What kind of government names a courtesan as ambassador to one of its most important allies?"[14]

"How is she any different from Joy Silverman?" asked a New York Republican, a reference to the wealthy New Yorker whose 1989 nomination by George Bush to be ambassador to Barbados was rejected by the dominant Democrats on the Senate Foreign Relations Committee. Democratic Senator Paul Sarbanes led a revolt against her appointment on the grounds that fund-raiser Silverman had no policy experience and had been named solely because she had given $180,000 to various Republicans, including Bush, during his 1988 presidential campaign.

There was no comparison. Pamela had been dipping her toe into policy waters ever since she married Averell until the point in the late 1980s where she had immersed herself quite thoroughly.

Her depth on the intricacies of Franco-American relations was not all that it might be compared with career professionals, but she had far more foreign policy experience than the president who nominated her. She was going to do just fine in Paris. She had over her lifetime honed a political dexterity that no career diplomat could touch.

Furthermore, to compare her credentials unfavorably with those of her immediate predecessors was a lamentable sexist joke. Bush's envoy Curley was a clubby investment banker selected in part because he was a Yale University friend of the president's older brother. He was a nonentity within the Bush administration and an envoy with virtually no clout in France. "Curley passed completely unnoticed," said Dominique Dhombres, the Americas editor at *Le Monde*, France's most prestigious daily.[15]

Curley's predecessor was even less impressive. Joe Rodgers was a Nashville, Tennessee, construction magnate before Ronald Reagan appointed him ambassador in 1985. Rodgers was Reagan's top fund-raiser in 1984, but he had no experience in France and promised the Senate that one of his top priorities was to "learn the beautiful French language" while in the embassy.[16]

When it came to credentials, Pamela was in a different league altogether. According to Marie-France Toinet, a U.S. specialist at France's National Foundation for Political Science, "Mrs. Harriman will be seen as someone who has political influence and can get the President's attention."[17] Even Susan Mary Alsop, Pamela's occasionally critical contemporary in Paris and Washington, applauded the appointment. "I think the French will be crazy about her."[18]

Certainly the Senate Foreign Relations Committee, which had to pass on her nomination, was crazy about her. Rarely has a nominee had such a warm welcome. The hoary, staid, policy-intensive body received her the way La Scala hails Pavarotti, the Meadowlands greets Bruce Springsteen or, a more pertinent simile for this situation, the way his Swiss banker greets Saudi Arabia's King Fahd. Star-struck senators, including the normally dour Republican Jesse Helms, all but fell over each other when she arrived for her hearing seventeen minutes early at 2:13 P.M. on May 4, 1993.

Eleven photographers jostled to capture Pamela's entrance in a lush green tailored suit with a simple gold brooch, a double strand of pearls, a white silk scarf, freshly sprayed, champagne-colored hair and a tense, but determined, smile. With the exception of Janet Howard, who was at her elbow, Pamela's advisers and closest friends are all men, but only women friends showed up to support her in the cavernous hearing room on the fourth floor of the Dirksen Senate Office Building: Lady Renwick, wife of the British ambassador; Patsy Preston; Joan Challinor, a Democratic party activist, and Ina Ginsburg, a politically attuned socialite and writer.

Pamela was the scheduled second of four nominees to be quizzed. Harry Gilmore, nominated to become ambassador to Armenia, took one look at the anxious senators, journalists and spectators jammed in to watch her and politely offered that she go ahead of him to spare everyone the wait. Several senators stepped down from the raised semicircular platform on which they sit to the well of the hearing room to greet Pamela. Senator Charles Robb, the Virginia Democrat whose resignation as a lead Senate fund-raiser Pamela had sought, gave her a big kiss. He was a member of the Foreign Relations Committee but was present specifically to introduce his good friend to his distinguished colleagues.

"An extraordinary lady that could have chosen — given her obvious wit, charm, intellect, grace — simply to be an observer to some of the most important events and meetings with some of the most important people of the twentieth century," Robb began. "But she clearly chose to be an active participant and in almost everything she has done throughout her very distinguished career, has managed to play an important role and indeed help to shape events. Given the opportunities that she had, she could have been certainly the most gracious of those who host events and important people from around the world, but she chose instead to make virtually every gathering an important, intellectual exercise in trying to deal with some of the difficult policy choices that face us.

"Usually, in naming ambassadors to particularly important posts, a president tries to get someone who has one of several important nexes to the country . . . but it is not often that you find someone that comes with all of the credentials that Pamela Harriman brings to this particular post. I would suspect that there are many world leaders who would envy the career that Pamela Harriman has had."

Pamela looked serious throughout the formal introduction, which is always a paean of praise, but a slight smile began to play around the corners of her mouth after several other Democratic pals hit the same notes. "She will do a superb job," said Illinois senior senator Paul Simon, whose 1990 re-election campaign received a thousand dollars from Pamela in March 1989 and five thousand more from her PAC in June that year.

Committee chairman Claiborne Pell, to whom Pamela had given five thousand dollars for his 1984 campaign and another thousand for his 1990 race, was in Moscow. He sent a message that "if there ever were an individual who combines all the qualities of true diplomats, it is you."

The fact that Christopher Dodd of Connecticut had not received any contributions did not stint his support. "This is truly a fine appointment," he said. "I don't think the administration could have made a better choice." Harlan Mathews of Tennessee did not run for office but was appointed to take the seat of Al Gore — five thousand dollars in 1983; a thousand in 1988 — when he became vice-president. Because he had not campaigned, Mathews had not been the direct beneficiary of Pamela's largesse either, but he was as effusive as Dodd. "The president has made a lot of outstanding choices," he said, "but I do not know of any that is as outstanding and as super as this one. If she does half the job [in France] that she does in every other assignment she has, our nation will be well represented."

Senator Paul Sarbanes agreed. The Maryland Democrat was one of the first big recipients of help from Democrats for the 80's. In 1981, when he was challenged by the National Conservative Political Action Committee, PamPAC gave him $20,104 to fight back. A battle-tested friend of Pamela's ever since, he called the nomination "a very fine appointment" and said that Pamela brought "very serious qualifications to the post" besides being an active fund-raiser.

The praise was not unexpected, although it was the most lavish since General Norman Schwarzkopf reported to Congress in 1991 after winning the Gulf War. Pamela deserved credit even if she had not been a substantial donor to almost every Democrat on the committee. John Kerry of Massachusetts and Harris Wofford of Pennsylvania were also members of the panel's Democratic majority. Pamela gave Kerry a thousand dollars in 1988 and another thousand in 1990. Wofford received a thousand in 1991 and an additional thousand the following year.

Delaware's Joseph Biden, who chaired the hearings in Pell's absence, gave Pamela a dream welcome, praising her for capturing the confidence of Democrats and Republicans alike. "I cannot think of a nomination that is country specific as this is that is better suited by way of education, temperament, background, knowledge and, I think, interest, than Ms. Harriman is to be our ambassador to France." Pamela could not withhold a broad grin then which cracked into outright laughter later when Senator Jesse Helms, the ranking Republican member, read a list of Democrats to whom Pamela had given money. Biden's name was not on it.

"Where is Biden?" the Delaware senator asked in mock dismay. "I am going to have to reconsider my position here."

"You did not ask, Senator," Pamela replied.

The spectators joined the chortling, unaware that, of course, Biden had asked and Pamela had delivered. Twice. Pamela had made certain that Democrats for the 80's on December 7, 1983, gave Biden five thousand dollars for his 1984 campaign and another check for five thousand on June 14, 1989, for his successful 1990 effort to win a fourth term.

Never before had so much charm been exerted and influence purchased strategically in advance by a nominee before the august Senate Committee on Foreign Relations.

All the good will and camaraderie in the room could not disguise the fact that Pamela's own statement on her nomination was well-crafted and, despite an initial nervous quaver, well delivered down to the deliberately reminiscent echoes of her former father-in-law. "I come before you today conscious of one great difference between us and one great similarity," she said, stretching out every syllable. "Unlike you, I was not born in this country. I am an American by choice. But, like all of you, I have a deep love for this land that has long been my home and I am proud to serve it in any way I can."

She sketched her foreign policy experience, her credentials for the job: vice-chairman of the Atlantic Council, active member of the Council on Foreign Relations, involved with the Kennan Institute for Advanced Russian Studies, the Harriman Institute, the English-Speaking Union and the Brookings Institution (recipient of a $325,000 donation from her in 1992), her speeches and articles on foreign affairs issues and her "many meetings" with foreign leaders.

"My own firsthand knowledge of France goes back to 1936 to 1938, when I studied at the Sorbonne in Paris. Then, during the Second World War, I watched a leader of indomitable will and extraordinary courage, Charles de Gaulle, fight for the fate of France. After the war, I spent many years in France, 1948 to 1959, and I was there when NATO and the Marshall Plan were born — which, although we could not know it then, set the course that two generations later ended in the collapse of the Soviet empire."

She noted the Franco-American bonds that stemmed from the Treaty of Paris which ended the Revolutionary War and confirmed U.S. independence and declared that 210 years later, "the fundamental ideals and interests that unite the United States and France remain far stronger than any issues that may divide us." She would, however, speak for the U.S. in areas of disagreement too and, in a line which reflected Congress's current budgetary concerns, promised "to represent our domestic interests as well as our foreign policy interests — to promote our economic well-being at home by seeking fair and equitable economic and trade relations abroad. This obligation, you may be assured, will at all times be uppermost in my mind.'"

What she did not say, but the senators understood implicitly, was that she would have the best grasp of U.S. domestic policy and politics of any ambassador to France since Lyndon Johnson sent Sargent Shriver to Paris twenty-five years earlier.

The performance was bravura and the senators all but leaped to their feet and applauded when she finished her four-minute statement at 2:50 P.M. Pamela sat back in her chair, flashed a broad smile and crossed her trim legs under the witness table. The questions that followed came only from Biden and Helms and were uniformly gentle.

Senator Biden wanted to know what she thought of the new government headed by Conservative Premier Edouard Balladur and any changes he might make in France's approach to resolving the agricultural subsidies issue that held up resolution of a world trade agreement. Pamela pointed out that Balladur promised to continue the foreign policies of the former Socialist government but that there could be "perhaps even a bettering of our relations." On the trade issues, she was encouraged that "they wish to move to diplomacy of movement rather than diplomacy of obstruction."

When asked whether the Balladur government would support European unity, she responded that the new prime minister campaigned for the Maastricht Treaty, which promoted union.

Biden would never embarrass her, but Pamela uncrossed her legs, took a deep breath and leaned forward in her chair when Jesse Helms reached for the microphone. She had strongly opposed Helms's bid for a third term in 1984 and saw to it that Democrats for the 80's gave the maximum five thousand dollars to his opponent that year, North Carolina governor James Hunt. Helms won anyway after a bitter campaign and when he came up for a fourth term in 1990, Pamela took out her own checkbook and wrote a check for a thousand dollars, the maximum for an individual, to his opponent, Harvey Gantt, a black liberal, but again to no avail.

The Senate's most outspokenly conservative member, Helms is anathema to partisan Democrats and has made a career out of vilifying liberalism, big government and anyone he considered soft on the Soviet Union or in favor of abortion or homosexual rights. Throughout the 1980s, he combined a mastery of arcane Senate procedures with a mule-like stubbornness to hold up or block the nominations of ambassadors he considered insufficiently anti-Communist or simply "too liberal." Pamela knew that if he so chose, Helms could be trouble.

As it happened, he chose instead to declare that Winston Churchill was his hero, that he had fifty books on the prime minister, "and I have read them all." He described a pilgrimage to Sir Winston's grave and his surprise at finding no eternal flame, no great monument. "Just a little block saying 'Winston Churchill' with the year of his birth and death. I stood there thinking, this man does not need a monument. His monument was his life." He would not even inquire about all her financial contributions, he said. "I believe you are going to do a good job." Staring at him, Pamela gave a startled little jump. Her eyes widened, her shoulders relaxed and her lightly glossed, rose-red lips parted in surprise.

"But you do acknowledge the enormous amount of help you gave to political candidates was, at least in part, responsible for this nomination. Do you not believe this to be so?"

"Yes, Senator. I think that was part of it," she replied. "I do not think it was the whole."

"If it were the whole, W-H-O-L-E, I would oppose your nomination. But I think you are going to do a good job."

"Thank you, Senator."

"I hope that we can put aside this business of rebuking people because they took an active part in politics. You happen to be much more affluent than a lot of Americans. You had more to contribute and you contributed it."

"Yes, Senator."

"There were two or three campaigns I wish you had not contributed to."

"And vice-versa, Senator."

"But I never doubted your sincerity."

He noted that France was worried that its soldiers on the ground in Bosnia could become victims if the United States launched military actions against Serbia and asked her opinion. Pamela ducked, saying that Secretary of State Warren Christopher was in Europe at that moment discussing "this very delicate subject" which she considered "too sensitive" to handle. Naturally, she was prepared to support any position her country took.

In reviewing her résumé, Helms saw that Pamela was involved with the Monet society and asked whether she shared the idealism for an integrated Europe as conceived by the French political economist Jean Monnet, spiritual founder of the European Community. Pamela looked as if she had been hit by a brick, stunned and baffled.

"Senator, I do not think I am involved in the Monet Society. I have never heard of it, frankly."

"I believe the information submitted says that. Is that not correct?"

Pamela spun around in confusion, looking for help. Janet Howard leaped from her chair and whispered in Pamela's ear. A relieved look spread over her face.

"Ooohh, it is Claude Monet, the painter, the artist. I have given a contribution to Giverny, where he lived and painted, to help restore his home."

The hearing room erupted in laughter. In the 1930s in Paris, she had learned the difference between a Monet and a Manet. It had never occurred to her that six decades later she would have to distinguish a Monet from a Monnet for the Senate's chief scourge of federal funding of avant-garde art. A few of Helms's softballs followed: did she see her ambassadorial role as a "social mission" and "You're not just going to pour tea?" No, her interests and language ability ensured that she would be substantively involved. Was she ready to supplement her ambassadorial salary with her own money?

"Yes, Senator. Whatever is necessary."

"It will be necessary."

Suddenly, the hearing was over. Forty-three minutes from start to finish and Pamela was home free. All that remained was the committee's unanimous endorsement and, three days later on May 7, consideration by the full Senate. Vice-president Gore, who presides over the Senate with the power to break ties, joked that "if it comes to a tie, you can count on my vote."[19]

Neither was worried and when the moment came Friday afternoon, the few senators on the floor gave a voice vote of unanimous consent to confirm Pamela. Just before, GOP leader Bob Dole acknowledged that he too was "a longtime admirer of Mrs. Harriman" and that as far as Republicans were concerned, "obviously, we had no intention of interfering with this nomination."

Pamela had done it. Madame Ambassador. In her own right. She had overcome the advantages of her birth. She had pursued her twin goals of wealth and high-stakes action with unflagging determination, used every available tool to clamber over disappointments and past the kind of lower-level successes that would have satisfied others less driven until she grabbed the golden ring. Averell had given her the means and Bill Clinton had given her the final boost. But the will had been her own.

The legendary Jane Digby ended her days in a Bedouin tent in the Syrian desert. Pamela was capping her career with a presidential appointment, confirmed unanimously by the U.S. Senate, to one of the most prestigious positions in the United States government, a job held by Benjamin Franklin and by Thomas Jefferson. The legendary Jane? She was no longer even the top-ranked legend in her own family.

Epilogue

PAMELA had kept a low profile throughout the winter and early spring of 1993 preparing for her hearing, but as her planned departure neared, she was anxious to head to France in style. The first to toast her, before the French embassy in Washington arranged a party and a week before the Senate confirmed her, were British ambassador Sir Robin Renwick and his wife, Annie, who is French. As befit the embassy with the best political connections in the capital and a guest with better political ties than the president, the dinner and dance were an A-list smash.

Among the guests in the residence designed by Edward Lutyens, father of Pamela's old admirer Robert, were a host of Cabinet secretaries, senators, congressmen and congresswomen, senior White House and State Department officials, top media executives, the chief of the Federal Reserve, the governor of the Bank of England and the chancellor of the Exchequer.

In a brilliant vermillion party dress, and looking like a movie star twenty years younger than her actual seventy-three, Pamela arrived on the arm of Richard Holbrooke, her romance with Carter Brown having tapered off with his retirement from the

National Gallery and her concentration on the Paris job. Each was moving into a new phase. While they would remain friends, neither had the same need for the other as when both were drifting in private life, wondering what to do after Averell's death and the breakup of Carter's second marriage.

Pamela spoke to the ten tables of ten after dinner, describing her nights bunking with Sir Winston during the Blitz, and reading a wartime letter to her from Charles de Gaulle, who had been sending a children's book for young Winston. Two things surprised a number of guests: Pamela never discussed France and, in reciting DeGaulle's note, her French was very poor, an awkward, upper-class schoolgirl rendition in an artificial baritone that had eyebrows arching into hairlines around the room.

British journalist Christopher Hitchens said she "sounded like the young Margaret Thatcher."[1] Andrei Kolosovski, the Russian chargé d'affaires, leaned toward his dinner partner, a Georgetown grande dame, and whispered, "What a pity she hasn't had more time for lessons." Pamela does claim fluency in French, and it is quite good, but prior to her returning to France, her accent was also very rusty. No one who knew her doubted that, once in Paris, she would quickly regain her old facility.

Other parties came thick and fast — Nancy Dickerson and John Whitehead's at the Hay-Adams Hotel, Katharine Graham's at home in Georgetown and, eventually, a gathering at the French embassy hosted by Ambassador Jacques Andreani, a bright professional, but an envoy who left the impression that he would rather be almost anywhere but in America.

All were star-studded with political, social and journalistic luminaries, but none was as exclusive as the small May 17 dinner hosted by the Clintons in the yellow oval room — a Stephane Boudin creation for Jackie Kennedy — in the White House family quarters. That was for Pamela and her friends in The Leadership, as she constantly refers to House Speaker Tom Foley and Senate Majority Leader George Mitchell and a few others, including the Gores, Jordans, Bergers and Wren and Tim Wirth, the former Colorado senator and now State Department counselor who was one of Pamela's advisers on environmental affairs.

Young Winston was also there, having flown in from London

for his mother's swearing-in earlier that day at the State Department. The elegant paneled and chandeliered state reception rooms on the eighth floor are named appropriately for Thomas Jefferson and Benjamin Franklin and are filled with priceless American antiques. Most swearing-ins draw a few dozen guests at most, department colleagues and friends of the appointee who turn out in response to what is often an invitation by telephone. Not Pamela's.

She ordered — and paid for — engraved invitations, champagne, smoked salmon and French eclairs. More than three hundred people showed up to watch Young Winston hold the family bible given to Old Winston in 1908 on his marriage to Clementine Hozier by his American mother, Jennie Jerome Churchill, herself one of the great Victorian courtesans, who numbered King Edward VII among her many lovers.[2]

Vice-president Gore administered the oath. Secretary of State Warren Christopher delivered remarks. Pamela had the last word. "Now my home in Paris will be your home. Please come — but not all at once."

When she said "my home," Pamela meant just that. The magnificent property adjacent to the British embassy and just down the street from the Elysée Palace did not belong to her, of course. The Nazis seized the residence from the Rothschilds in 1940 and turned it into quarters for senior Luftwaffe officers during the Occupation. When Paris was liberated in 1944, the classical three-story columned mansion and its two-and-a-half-acre garden became a Royal Air Force Club. The U.S. government purchased the property for $2,111,783 in 1948, a steal at that price even then.[3]

But she would make it her home, with her own special touches that she would again bring "on my back like a turtle," just as she had for every other home, no matter how temporary.

The most striking touch was shipping the art collection she inherited from Averell to Paris. Traditionally, the Art in Embassies program of the State Department allows ambassadors to select paintings and sculptures by American artists for shipment to their post. But with the exception of Walter Annenberg, the publisher and philanthropist whom Richard Nixon posted to Britain in

1969, no other American diplomat in recent memory has had a personal art collection to rival what Pamela inherited.

"It caused some consternation when I said I was bringing my own collection and that they were not all American pictures," she said.[4] The anxiety passed, replaced by the packing and speedy dispatch of the van Gogh *White Roses*, two Cézannes, a Matisse, a Renoir, a Rousseau, a Picasso, a Sargent and a bronze bust of Jack Kennedy.

Charles Moffett, director of the Phillips Collection in Washington, flew to Paris to help install the twenty works of art Pamela sent over to create her home. Decorator Mark Hampton personalized her private quarters by toning down the bright peach-colored walls she inherited.

Pamela arrived at the end of May and hit the ground running. Jetting in on an overnight flight from Washington, she came off the plane just after dawn as fresh and crisp as if she had just stepped from her dressing room. Bedraggled tourists stumbled off after her, but Pamela showed not a crease in her tailored suit, no bloodshot lines in her eyes — shades of her Belgrade arrival for Tito's funeral — and immediately set to work, leaving no doubt that hers would be an action-packed tenure.

The morning she landed was set aside for meetings with her senior staff, with her first courtesy call received that afternoon and a working dinner. The following day she lunched with an ambassador, hosted a reception, made her own first courtesy call on her next-door neighbor, British ambassador Sir Christopher Mallaby, and gave a speech for a retiring member of the U.S. embassy staff.

Her first week she hosted receptions and dinners for three visiting Cabinet members from Washington — treasury secretary Lloyd Bentsen, commerce secretary Ron Brown and trade representative Mickey Kantor — who were in Paris for economic and trade meetings, and also hosted a separate lunch for George Shultz, secretary of state under Ronald Reagan.

There was little idle chitchat. Shultz discussed the dangers of protectionism. Douglas Warner, president of Morgan Guaranty Trust, voiced his views on the U.S. economy. Pamela engaged in an urgent dialogue in French with her lunch partner, former

French president Valéry Giscard d'Estaing. "I enjoyed that lunch because the talk was substantive," said Shultz. "It's true she provides the spark and the sparkle."[5]

In her first month in Paris, before she presented her credentials to President François Mitterrand on June 30, Pamela hosted five U.S. Cabinet ministers and an endless number of meetings, briefings and gatherings. One day, a working breakfast began at 5 A.M.; dinner that night for 140 ended at midnight. The next day she invited in the Anglo-American Press Association for cocktails.

On July 4, she opened her new home to celebrate the 217th birthday of the United States. As an Army Reserve band from Idaho set up on the marble veranda and played the "Star-Spangled Banner," "God Bless America" and a selection of rousing Sousa marches, some fifteen hundred French and American citizens — actress Lauren Bacall among them — ogled the paintings, ate, drank and strolled through the city center garden with its 150 varieties of flowers, plants and trees, including sequoias and magnolias from the U.S. and maples and dogwood from China and Japan.

The main attraction was Pamela. "Scintillation personified," said Paris-based writer Suzanne Lowry. The embassy staff of eleven hundred was already exhausted by her breakneck pace, but not their boss. "It's a rhythm," the new ambassador said. "You get into it."[6]

Some rhythm. At seventy-three, how does she do it? How does she cope with a schedule that would cripple a forty-three-year-old? Discipline — professional and personal organization — is one answer. Meetings start and end on time, sooner if the decisions for which she constantly presses can be reached quickly.

Sleeping only five hours a night, with a supplemental afternoon nap, she frequently hears friends urge that she husband her strength and energy. She watches her diet carefully, preferring simple grilled fish with fresh lemon and dill, undercooked seasonal vegetables and fruits. She loves white wine and does not shy away from drinking at lunch, a legacy of her earlier years in France, but she is abstemious about the amount she drinks and is always careful to drink plenty of mineral water, no matter what else she is imbibing.

Adrenaline and a nervous vitality aimed at ensuring she does everything perfectly help maintain the pace. A fascination for the job and the substance involved also keeps her going. She is challenged by how much she has to learn, but she will not let the substantive material beat her down. She feels she can absorb as much, if not a great deal more, than her predecessors. When she does have a problem, she does not hesitate to call on her old team — Sandy Berger in the White House, Peter Tarnoff at the State Department, Stuart Eizenstat, U.S. ambassador to the European Community, and Richard Holbrooke, who was named ambassador to Germany.

That she had such allies and old friends as Eizenstat and Holbrooke so close by in Brussels and Bonn was a tremendous relief and boon to Pamela. Together, they could help her handle such complex issues as the Franco–German relationship, the most important and trickiest in Europe, plus military, defense and NATO policy, and international trade and financial issues.

Her own drive and determination would also keep policy from getting the best of her. That fierce ambition that her siblings saw in her in childhood remains a salient element. Also, Pamela maintains that she is not deterred by criticism, that it rolls off her back like water off a duck.

That, of course, is nonsense. She is well aware that countless critics — in politics, in diplomatic and social circles, in the press — are waiting for her first missteps, ready to hammer her for being a hostess who is in over her head. She will run herself into the ground before she affords any of them the satisfaction.

Finally, Pamela is able to do it because she has a superb number two at the embassy, deputy chief of mission Avis Bohlen, a career officer who has some of the best political contacts in France. Bohlen's assignment to her new ambassador is replete with irony.

Her late father, Charles E. "Chip" Bohlen, was a legendary professional diplomat, a younger contemporary of Averell Harriman's, who was U.S. ambassador to Moscow when Nikita Khrushchev succeeded Stalin, and, under John Kennedy and Lyndon Johnson, ambassador to Paris, where young Avis visited on vacations from high school and Radcliffe. Averell and Chip had been Soviet policy colleagues under Roosevelt, and both worked the Teheran and Yalta conferences and meetings in Moscow. A half century later, another Harriman-Bohlen team was working together, a female version.

Pamela has long known the younger Avis but never expected the kind of close relationship they have in Paris. Given Pamela's well-known preference for working with men — a partiality that she declares openly — each woman was uncertain about how the relationship would work. Pamela, who considered seeking a male replacement, thought the better of it after a wide variety of advisers told her that she would be foolish to lose such a talented deputy.

Foreign service professionals and journalists, she was told, would have a field day if she ousted a woman with so much experience in France. Every political instinct telling her that they were right, Pamela agreed. After several months of working together, the two women were sufficiently comfortable with one another that Bohlen asked that her assignment be extended for yet another year.

By the time Bill Clinton marked his first anniversary in the White House, Pamela was hitting her stride in Paris. She was giving television and radio interviews in French on military and trade issues and speeches to the Ministry of Economics and Finance and before the French Senate Foreign Affairs Commission on investment and European security. With the United States the biggest foreign investor in France, putting together bilateral business groups became a priority. "Face-to-face," she noted, "is better than fax-to-fax."[7]

She went everywhere — from private meetings in the Elysee Palace with Mitterrand to Normandy, Bordeaux, Marseilles and an aircraft carrier in the Mediterranean. She did everything — from GATT negotiations and wine-harvesting ceremonies to benefits for AIDS or various schools. She talked to everyone — including those back home. Almost every night, beginning at midnight, or 6 P.M. on the East Coast, she worked her bedroom phone for an hour or more, calling the White House, State Department, pals and political cronies. Checking in, keeping posted.

Pamela was her own woman, with her own style. "The iron lady in the silk suit," as *France Soir* described her. But she never stopped honing the skill that helped propel her to the Paris embassy, taking special care of her man. "Give President Clinton a chance," she snapped to her dinner partners, the right-wing financiers Sir James Goldsmith and Conrad Black, one evening at Taillevent when she could no longer bear listening to their fond recollections of Ronald Reagan.

"He is a young, talented president with the breadth of intellect, personal courage and long-term vision to face up to the historic choices before us," she gushed to a luncheon meeting of the American Club of Paris. "He is fulfilling that indispensable requirement of leadership — which is to tell people not what they want to hear, but what they need to know."[8] Her own talent to tell both, she might have added, got her to Paris — and everywhere else.

Notes

INTRODUCTION

1 Enid Nemy, *New York Times*, 6/27/93, section 9, p. 9.
2 R. W. Apple Jr., *New York Times*, 11/21/92.
3 Elizabeth Mehren, *Los Angeles Times*, 4/5/93, p. F1.

CHAPTER ONE

1 Hardy, *The Woodlanders*, p. 57; Beningfield and Zeman, *Hardy Country*, p. 65.
2 Khoi Nguyen, *Tatler*, June 1993, p. 111.
3 Manchester, *The Last Lion: Visions of Glory*, p. 93.
4 Schmidt, *Passion's Child*, p. 7, quoting John Aubrey's *Brief Lives*.
5 Petersson, *Sir Kenelm Digby, 1603–1665*, p. 16.
6 Clive Aslet, *Country Life*, 2/21/80.
7 Blanch, *The Wilder Shores of Love*, p. 140.
8 Manchester, *Visions of Glory*, p. 88.
9 Ibid., pp. 89–91.
10 Blanch, p. 142.
11 Schmidt, p. 4.
12 Blanch, p. 153.
13 Draper and Fowles, *Hardy's England*, p. 103.
14 Aslet, *Country Life*, 2/28/80, p. 576.

CHAPTER TWO

1 Stevenson, *British Society, 1914–1945*, p. 95.
2 Ibid., p. 92.
3 Ibid., p. 31.
4 Margetson, *The Long Party: High Society in the Twenties and Thirties*, pp. 56–57.
5 Ibid., p. 16.
6 Ibid., p. 184.
7 Stevenson, p. 132.
8 Martha Duffy, *Time*, 7/5/93, p. 46.

9 Sampson, *Anatomy of Britain*, p. 9.
10 Winston S. Churchill, *Memories and Adventures*, p. 71.
11 Marie Brenner, *Vanity Fair*, July 1988, p. 79.
12 *The Economist*, 7/31/93, p. 53.
13 Perrott, *The Aristocrats*, p. 175.
14 Duke of Devonshire to author, October 1992.
15 Duffy, p. 44.
16 I sought comment from Sheila, widow of Charles Moore, but Pamela asked her family not to speak to me about her for this book. Despite the fact that they have been estranged nearly all their lives, Sheila complied. Friends of both women confirm the chasm between them.
17 Brenner, p. 79.
18 Thomas, *Hunting England*, p. 13.
19 Graves, *The Long Week-End*, p. 119.
20 Ibid., pp. 355–356.
21 Ibid., p. 227.
22 Brenner, p. 81.

CHAPTER THREE

1 Lambert, *1939: The Last Season of Peace*, p. 41.
2 History of Down Hall. The Downham School property, originally known as Down Hall, is currently a hotel. Down Hall Hotel publication, November 1992.
3 Marquis, *Who's Who in America, 1992–93*, vol. 1, p. 1452.
4 Ibid.
5 *Sunday Times Magazine* (London), 10/31/82, p. 14.
6 Interview, confidential source, January 1993.
7 Lambert, p. 43.
8 Braudy, *This Crazy Thing Called Love*, p. 46.
9 Amory, *Who Killed Society?* p. 12.
10 Braudy, p. 59.
11 Ibid.
12 Lambert, p. 43.

13 *New York Times*, 3/2/77.
14 Interview, Sarah Norton Baring, February 1993.
15 Lambert, pp. 8, 83.
16 Lambert, p. 14.
17 *Sunday Times Magazine* (London), 10/31/82, pp. 14–15.

CHAPTER FOUR

1 Lord Geoffrey Lloyd, *Leeds Castle*, p. vi.
2 Cleggett, *History of Leeds Castle and Its Families*, pp. 153–159.
3 Hampton, *Legendary Decorators of the Twentieth Century*, p. 168.
4 Ibid., p. 170.
5 Cleggett, p. 155.
6 Hampton, p. 177.
7 James, *Chips: The Diaries of Sir Henry Channon*, p. 20.
8 Colville, *Fringes of Power*, p. 745.
9 Interview, Douglas Fairbanks Jr., 12/1/92.
10 Hampton, p. 179.
11 Interview, Alan Pryce-Jones, 11/19/92.
12 Interview, confidential source.
13 Interview, Sarah Norton Baring, 2/15/93.
14 Interview, Sarah Norton Baring.
15 Brenner, *Vanity Fair*, July 1988.
16 Reynolds, *A London Diary*, p. 266.
17 Geoffrey Lloyd, p. 22.
18 Smith, *In All His Glory*, p. 178.
19 Leslie, *Cousin Randolph*, p. 47.
20 Winston S. Churchill, *Memories and Adventures*, p. 7n.

CHAPTER FIVE

1 Mollie Panter-Downes, "*The New Yorker*," 9/9/39, in The New Yorker *Book of War Pieces, London, 1939 to Hiroshima, 1945* (New York: Schocken Books, 1947).
2 Interview, Sarah Norton Baring, 2/15/93.
3 Churchill, *Memories and Adventures*, p. 7.

4 Interview, Julian Amery, 10/15/92.

5 Otto Friedrich, *Time*, 9/4/89, p. 20.

6 Pearson, *The Private Lives of Winston Churchill*, p. 163.

7 Ibid., p. 215.

8 Halle, *Randolph Churchill: The Young Unpretender*, pp. 23–25.

9 Colville, *Winston Churchill and His Inner Circle*, p. 29.

10 Manchester, *Visions of Glory*, p. 135.

11 Martin, *Jennie: The Life of Lady Randolph Churchill*, p. 247.

12 Pearson, pp. 18–19.

13 Gilbert, *Winston S. Churchill*, vol. 5, p. 422n.

14 Churchill, *Memories and Adventures*, p. 3.

15 Interview, Sarah Norton Baring, 2/15/93.

16 Churchill, *Memories and Adventures*, p. 8.

17 *Sunday Times Magazine* (London), 10/31/82, p. 15.

18 Gilbert, *Winston S. Churchill*, vol. 6, 9/29/39, citing Churchill papers.

19 Soames, Mary, *Clementine Churchill: The Biography of a Marriage*, p. 315.

20 Interview, Lord Norwich, 10/14/92.

21 Gilbert, vol. 6, Sept. 29, 1939. Churchill papers 19/2.

22 Roberts, *Randolph: A Study of Churchill's Son*, p. 189, citing Tree, *When the Moon Was High*, p. 94.

23 Interview, Piers Dixon, 10/14/92.

24 Churchill, *Memories and Adventures*, pp. 7–8.

25 Ibid., p. 9.

26 Ibid., p. 10.

27 Ibid., p. 11.

28 Otto Friedrich, *Time*, 9/4/89, p. 22.

29 Hough, *Winston and Clementine*, p. 457.

30 Sherwood, *Roosevelt and Hopkins*, p. 241.

31 Manchester, *The Last Lion: Alone*, p. 10.

32 Interview, Douglas Fairbanks, Jr., 12/1/92.

33 Colville, *Fringes of Power*, p. 177.

34 Pamela Harriman, "Churchill's Dream," *American Heritage*, Oct./Nov. 1983, p. 84.

35 Churchill, *Memories and Adventures*, pp. 14–15.

36 Roberts, p. 193.

37 Diana Mitford Mosley, *A Life of Contrasts*, p. 203.

38 Soames, p. 464.

39 Harriman, *American Heritage*, pp. 84–86.

40 Churchill, *Memories and Adventures*, p. 17.

41 Roberts, p. 196, citing Cooper, *Trumpets from the Steep*, p. 62.

42 Cowles, *Winston Churchill*, p. 326.

43 Churchill, *Memories and Adventures*, p. 20.

44 Hough, p. 544.

45 Waugh, *Diaries of Evelyn Waugh, 1976*, cited in Churchill, *Memories and Adventures*.

46 *The Economist*, 7/10/93, p. 55.

47 Waugh, *The Letters of Evelyn Waugh*, Feb. 23, 1941.

48 Churchill, *Memories and Adventures*, p. 26.

49 Hough, p. 475.

50 Chisholm and Davie, *Beaverbrook*, p. 444.

51 Bryan and Murphy, *The Windsor Story*, p. 119.

52 Clark, *Another Part of the Wood*, p. 216.

53 Clark, p. 219.

54 Bryan and Murphy, p. 120.

55 Margetson, p. 89.

CHAPTER SIX

1 Elizabeth Bumiller, *Washington Post*, 6/12/83, p. L1.

2 James, *Chips*, p. 318.

3 Bumiller, 6/12/83.

4 Murray Marder, *Washington Post*, 7/27/86.

5 Isaacson and Thomas, *The Wise Men*, p. 103.

6 Abramson, *Spanning the Century,* p. 236.
7 Isaacson and Thomas, p. 42.
8 Abramson, p. 177.
9 Ibid., pp. 262–3.
10 Smith, p. 111.
11 Isaacson and Thomas, p. 103.
12 Abramson, p. 267.
13 Gilbert, vol. 6, 5/18/40.
14 Dimbleby and Reynolds, *An Ocean Apart,* pp. 142–143.
15 Sherwood, p. 230.
16 Harriman and Abel, *Special Envoy,* pp. 3–20.
17 Harriman and Abel, p. 22.
18 Bumiller, 6/12/83.
19 Pearson, p. 301.
20 Abramson, p. 304, citing Lash, *Eleanor and Franklin,* p. 659.
21 *Dictionary of American Biography,* 1946–50, p. 899.
22 Interview, James Parton, 11/10/92.
23 Chisolm and Davie, *Beaverbrook,* p. 403.
24 Abramson, p. 171.
25 David Pryce-Jones, *Evelyn Waugh and His World,* p. 149.
26 Smith, *In All His Glory,* p. 217, citing Marie Brenner interview with William S. Paley.
27 Dimbleby and Reynolds, p. 129.
28 Ibid., p. 137.
29 Interview, Tex McCrary, 2/2/93.
30 Ibid.
31 Brenner, p. 82.
32 Isaacson and Thomas, p. 603.
33 Sherwood, p. 247.
34 Adams, *Harry Hopkins,* foreword by Averell Harriman, pp. 15–16.
35 Dimbleby and Reynolds, p. 151.
36 Sherwood, *The White House Papers of Harry L. Hopkins* (London, 1948), p. 233.
37 Harriman and Abel, p. viii.
38 Abramson, p. 305, citing Harriman papers.
39 Amory, *Letters of Evelyn Waugh,* p. 514.
40 Abramson, p. 306.
41 Churchill, *Memories and Adventures,* p. 27.
42 Roberts, *Randolph,* p. 204.

43 Ibid., p. 211.
44 Leslie, *Cousin Randolph,* p. 59.
45 Churchill, *Memories and Adventures,* p. 29.
46 Abramson, p. 313.
47 Ibid.
48 Harriman and Abel, p. 111.
49 Lash, *Roosevelt and Churchill,* p. 490.
50 Pamela Harriman, *Washington Post,* op-ed article, 12/7/91.
51 Dimbleby and Reynolds, p. 149.
52 Roberts, p. 214.
53 James, p. 313.
54 *Sunday Times Magazine* (London), 10/31/82, p. 15.
55 Interview, Lord Norwich.
56 Roberts, p. 231.
57 Nicolson, *Harold Nicolson: The War Years,* vol. 2, p. 208.
58 Roberts, *Randolph,* p. 229.
59 Ibid., p. 231.
60 James Bowman, *Wall Street Journal,* 11/25/92, reviewing *Evelyn Waugh: The Later Years: 1939–1966,* by Martin Stannard.
61 Gilbert, vol. 7, p. 101.
62 *Sunday Times Magazine* (London), 10/31/82.

CHAPTER SEVEN

1 *Time* London cable #2071, from Mary Welsh to David Hulburd, 4/14/41.
2 Abramson, p. 315.
3 David Pryce-Jones, *Evelyn Waugh and His World,* p. 142.
4 Fitzroy Maclean, "Randolph as Commando," in *Randolph Churchill,* compiled by Kay Halle, p. 90.
5 Churchill, *Memories and Adventures,* p. 36.
6 Barrow, *Gossip: A History of High Society from 1920 to 1970,* p. 131.
7 Interview, confidential source.
8 Colville, *Winston Churchill,* p. 733.
9 *New York Times,* 9/6/43, p. 16.
10 Clark, *The Other Half,* p. 57.
11 Ibid., p. 58.
12 Elborn, *Edith Sitwell,* p. 172, cit-

ing John Lehmann, *Am I My Brother?* (Longmans, 1960).

13 Interview, Lewis Powell, 7/21/92.

14 Interview, Elie Abel, 8/17/92.

15 Brenner, *Vanity Fair*, July 1988, p. 82.

16 Interview, Larry LeSueur, 7/1/92.

17 Interview, Mary Lutyens, 11/10/92.

18 Interview, Peter Duchin, 9/11/92.

19 Verne W. Newton, director, Franklin D. Roosevelt library, letter to author, 8/12/93.

20 *Times* (London), 10/1/92, p. 15.

21 Interview, James Parton.

22 Interview, Larry LeSueur.

23 *Current Biography*, 1944, p. 12.

24 Interview, Tex McCrary, 2/2/93.

25 Sherwood, p. 442.

26 Dimbleby and Reynolds, pp. 154–155.

27 Ibid., p. 169.

28 Interview, James Parton.

29 Blake and Nichols, *Dictionary of National Biography, 1971–80*, p. 685.

30 Smith, *In All His Glory*, p. 109.

31 Paley, *As It Happened*, p. 144.

32 Ibid., p. 150.

33 Ibid., p. 151.

34 Smith, p. 217, citing Marie Brenner interview with William S. Paley.

35 Morgan, *Edwina Mountbatten*, p. 333.

36 Kahn, *Jock: The Life and Times of John Hay Whitney*, xiii passim.

37 Ibid., p. 81.

38 Ibid., p. xvi.

39 Interview, Tex McCrary.

CHAPTER EIGHT

1 John Gilbert Winant, quoted in Edward R. Murrow FBI file, NY 161–148, 2/9/61.

2 Paley, p. 151.

3 Sperber, *Murrow: His Life and Times*, p. 36.

4 Ibid., p. 35.

5 Ibid., p. 59.

6 Sevareid, *Not So Wild a Dream*, p. 83.

7 Halberstam, *The Powers That Be*, p. 132.

8 Sperber, p. 179.

9 Kendrick, *Prime Time: The Life of Edward R. Murrow*, p. 206.

10 Murrow, *This Is London* (August 18, 1940), pp. 145–146.

11 Kendrick, p. 208.

12 Murrow, pp. 146–147.

13 Kendrick, p. 203.

14 *Time*, 9/30/57, p. 49.

15 Paley, p. 152.

16 Ibid.

17 Kendrick, p. 206.

18 Ibid.

19 Ibid., p. 231.

20 Ibid., p. 224.

21 Robert Landry, "Edward R. Murrow," *Scribner's* magazine, December 1938, cited in Sperber, p. 132.

22 Interview, Richard C. Hottelet, 6/26/92.

23 Interview, Larry Le Sueur, 7/1/92.

24 Sevareid, pp. 176–177.

25 Sperber, p. 108.

26 Interview, William Shirer, 7/1/92.

27 Interview, Richard C. Hottelet.

28 Interview, William Shirer.

29 Smith, p. 217.

30 Janet Murrow, letter to author, 9/7/92.

31 Sperber, p. 244.

32 Ibid., pp. 244–245.

33 Ibid., p. 246.

34 Ibid.

35 Janet Murrow letter.

36 Churchill, *The Second World War*, vol. 4, p. 583.

37 Kendrick, p. 288.

38 Cholly Knickerbocker, *New York Journal-American*, 2/22/47.

39 Janet Murrow letter.

CHAPTER NINE

1 Abramson, pp. 406–407.

2 Dimbleby and Reynolds, pp. 182–184. Bevin quote cited from Alan Bullock, *Ernest Bevin: Foreign Secretary, 1945–51*, p. 132.

3 Harriman and Abel, p. 553.
4 Pamela Churchill, *Evening Standard* (London), 1/14/47.
5 Brenner, p. 80.
6 Ernest Hemingway, *88 Poems*, no. 83, p. 156.
7 *Evening Standard* (London), 3/12/93.
8 Blair and Blair, *The Search for JFK*, p. 557.
9 Ibid., pp. 558–559.
10 Longford, *Kennedy*, p. 5.
11 Blair and Blair, p. 559.
12 Reeves, *A Question of Character*, p. 93, citing Blair and Blair, pp. 587–589, 603–605.
13 Slater, *Aly*, p. 132.
14 Young, *Golden Prince: The Remarkable Life of Prince Aly Khan*, p. 145.
15 Georgina Howell, *Vanity Fair*, June 1988, p. 108.
16 Slater, p. 9.
17 Ibid., p. 6.
18 Ibid., p. 91.
19 Ibid., p. 239.
20 Howell, p. 108.
21 Slater, p. 50.
22 Ibid., p. 127.
23 Ibid., p. 123.
24 Howell, p. 173.
25 Slater, p. 139.
26 Collier and Horowitz, *The Kennedys*, p. 169.
27 Slater, p. 152.
28 Morella and Epstein, *Rita: The Life of Rita Hayworth*, p. 118.

CHAPTER TEN

1 Friedman, *Agnelli: Fiat and the Network of Italian Power*, p. 49.
2 Interview, confidential source.
3 Interview, confidential source.
4 *Fortune*, 9/7/92, p. 102.
5 "Prime Time," 9/12/91.
6 Friedman, p. 33.
7 Sally Bedell Smith, "Agnelli: The Rules of the Game," *Vanity Fair*, July 1991, p. 147.
8 *Time*, 1/17/69, p. 61.
9 Pochna, *Agnelli, L'Irresistible*, p. 234.

10 Stadiem, *Too Rich: The High Life and Tragic Death of King Farouk*, p. 302.
11 Friedman, p. 43.
12 Smith, p. 147.
13 Friedman, p. 53, citing Biagi.
14 Childs, *Britain Since 1945*, p. 36.
15 Ziegler, *Diana Cooper*, p. 267.
16 Bryan and Murphy, *The Windsor Story*, p. 493.
17 Interview, Susan Mary Patten Alsop, 2/16/92.
18 Pearson, p. 358.
19 Friedman, p. 50.
20 Interview, Taki Theodoracopulos, 10/15/92.
21 Ibid.
22 *New York Journal-American*, 8/26/58, p. 8.

CHAPTER ELEVEN

1 Interview, Alan Pryce-Jones, 11/19/92.
2 Interview, confidential source.
3 Cowles, *The Rothschilds*, p. 234.
4 Hebe Dorsey, *International Herald Tribune*, 10/2/72.
5 Ben Macintyre, *New York Times Review of Books*, 9/20/92, reviewing *The Bride of the Wind: The Life and Times of Alma Mahler-Werfel*, by Suzanne Keegan (New York: Viking, 1992).
6 Interview, Susan Mary Patten Alsop, 2/26/92.
7 Interview, Peter Viertel, 1/13/93.
8 Interview, confidential source.
9 Interview, confidential source.
10 Interview, confidential source.
11 Interview, confidential source.
12 Morton, *The Rothschilds*, pp. 288.
13 Interview, confidential source.
14 Bryan and Murphy, p. 421.
15 Interview, Gerald Van Der Kemp, 10/12/92.
16 Interview, Zozo de Ravenel, 10/14/92.
17 Interview, Odette Pol Roger, 10/13/92.
18 Interview, Zozo de Ravenel.
19 Interview, Andre de Staercke, 10/12/92.

20 Churchill, *Memories and Adventures*, p. 119.
21 Interview, Susan Mary Patten Alsop.
22 White, *In Search of History*, p. 263.
23 Flanner, *Paris Journal*, p. 83.
24 Interview, Ben Bradlee, 7/8/92.
25 Buchwald and Buchwald, *Seems Like Yesterday*, p. 43.
26 Shnayerson, *Irwin Shaw*, p. 132.
27 Interview, Marian Shaw, 11/19/92.
28 Shnayerson, p. 95.
29 Whelan, *Robert Capa*, p. 177.
30 Interview, Ben Bradlee.
31 Interview, confidential source.
32 Whelan, p. 259.
33 Interview, confidential source.
34 Interview, confidential source.
35 Charmley, *Duff Cooper*, p. 221.
36 Ziegler, *Diana Cooper*, p. 24.
37 James, *Chips*, p. 21.
38 Cooper, *Autobiography*, p. 709.
39 Ziegler, p. 243.
40 Cooper, *Autobiography*, p. 172.
41 Ziegler, p. 143.
42 Ibid., p. 241.
43 Buchwald and Buchwald, p. 31.
44 Ziegler, p. 241.
45 Beaton, *The Happy Years*, p. 36.
46 Alsop, *To Marietta from Paris*, p. 187.
47 Jullian and Phillips, *Violet Trefusis*, p. 114.
48 Alsop, p. 283.
49 Doris Lilly, *Those Fabulous Greeks*, p. 270.
50 Sally Bedell Smith, *Vanity Fair*, August 1992, p. 182.
51 Interview, Jan Cushing Amory, 12/16/92.
52 Brenner, *Vanity Fair*, December 1991, p. 214.
53 Ziegler, p. 242.
54 Bryan and Murphy, p. 421.
55 Martin, *The Woman He Loved*, p. 446.
56 Martin, p. 448.
57 Ibid., p. 449.
58 Bryan and Murphy, p. 576.
59 Morton, *The Rothschilds*, p. 283.

CHAPTER TWELVE

1 Interview, confidential source.
2 Interview, Peter Viertel, 1/13/93.
3 Mitford, *The Blessing*, p. 30.
4 Michael Gross, *New York* magazine, 1/18/93, p. 31.
5 Interview, confidential source.
6 Keith and Tapert, *Slim*, p. 183.
7 Ibid., p. 183.
8 Brenner, *Vanity Fair*, July 1988, p. 123.
9 Interview, Brooke Hayward, 9/10/92.
10 Interview, confidential source.
11 Keith and Tapert, p. 182.
12 Interview, Susan Mary Patten Alsop, 2/16/92.
13 Churchill, *Memories and Adventures*, p. 137.
14 Keith Munroe, *Life*, 9/20/48, p. 128.
15 Interview, James Michener, 11/25/92.
16 Michener, *The World Is My Home*, pp. 291–292.
17 Logan, *Josh: My Up and Down, In and Out Life*, p. 348.
18 Munroe, p. 128.
19 Margaret Case Harriman, *Take Them Up Tenderly*, p. 222.
20 *Time*, unpublished interview, 6/20/55.
21 *Theater Arts*, July 1955, p. 90.
22 Hepburn, *Me*, pp. 183–184, 189.
23 Jack Gould, *New York Times*, 3/6/77.
24 Interview, William Hayward, 8/19/92.
25 Keith and Tapert, p. 127.
26 John Leonard, *New York Times*, 2/28/77.
27 Keith and Tapert, pp. 86–87.
28 Interview, Brooke Hayward, 9/10/92.
29 Interview, Brooke Hayward.
30 Keith and Tapert, p. 191.
31 Hayward, *Haywire*, pp. 229–230.
32 Ibid., p. 274.
33 Interview, confidential source.
34 *Architectural Digest*, June 1984, p. 111.

35 Churchill, *Memories and Adventures*, p. 142.
36 Laura Foreman, *New York Times*, 3/2/77, p. C14.
37 *New York Times*, 6/28/65, p. 20.
38 Berman, *The Crossing*, p. 256, citing Leland Hayward letter to Dr. Saul Fox, 12/31/58.
39 Berman, p. 272, citing Hayward letter to Kurnitz, 6/5/63.
40 *Variety*, 2/2/60.
41 Gould, *New York Times*, 2/1/60.
42 Interview, Brooke Hayward.
43 Interview, Paul Manno, 12/9/92.
44 *Vogue*, 2/15/64, p. 124.
45 Valentine Lawford, *Vogue*, 2/15/64, p. 130.
46 Ibid., pp. 127–130.
47 Foreman, *New York Times*.
48 Nadine Brozan, *New York Times*, 5/26/93.
49 Interview, Paul Manno.
50 Interview, Jones Harris, 12/16/92.
51 Logan, *Movie Stars, Real People and Me*, p. 183.
52 Berman, p. 279.
53 *New York Times*, 7/28/65.
54 Gould, *New York Times*, 10/30/64.
55 *Variety*, 10/15/64.
56 Interview, David Frost, 11/10/92.

CHAPTER THIRTEEN

1 Cholly Knickerbocker, *New York Journal-American*, 11/19/59.
2 Interview, Brooke Hayward.
3 Ibid.
4 Hayward, *Haywire*, p. 21.
5 Interview, William Hayward.
6 Interview, Brooke Hayward.
7 Ibid.
8 Interview, William Hayward.
9 Ibid.
10 Rodriguez, *Dennis Hopper*, p. 46.
11 Susan Watters and Patrick McCarthy, *W* newspaper, 11/30/87, p. 21.
12 Knickerbocker, *New York Journal-American*, 6/1/59.
13 Clarke, *Capote*, p. 316.
14 Ibid., p. 274.
15 Truman Capote, "La Côte Basque 1965," *Esquire*, November 1975, p. 113.
16 Interview, Gerald Clarke, 7/28/92.
17 Capote, p. 113.
18 Julie Baumgold, *New York* magazine, 11/26/84, p. 61.
19 Clarke, p. 486.
20 Ibid.
21 Interview, confidential source.
22 Interview, confidential source.

CHAPTER FOURTEEN

1 Cahan, *No Stranger to Tears*, p. 211.
2 Interview, confidential source.
3 Interview, Cheray Duchin Hodges, 11/4/92.
4 Ibid.
5 Elizabeth Bumiller, *Washington Post*, 6/12/83.
6 Hayward, p. 100.
7 Kelley, *His Way*, p. 388.
8 Ibid., pp. 439–400.
9 *Sunday Express* (London), 5/6/71.
10 *Daily Mirror* (London), 8/28/71.
11 Interview, confidential source.
12 Interview, confidential source.
13 Interview, Bill Hayward.
14 *Washington Post*, 6/12/83.
15 Interview, Brooke Hayward.

CHAPTER FIFTEEN

1 Ambrose, *Eisenhower*, vol. 2, p. 281.
2 Interview, Rudy Abramson, 7/27/92.
3 Interview, Ellen Barry, 7/7/92.
4 Interview, Luke Battle, 12/2/92.
5 Interview, Timothy Dickinson, 2/10/93.
6 Interview, confidential source.
7 Jacob Heilbrunn, *New Republic*, 6/27/92, p. 58.
8 Daniel Patrick Moynihan, 11/14/91.
9 Abramson, p. 577.
10 Arthur Schlesinger Jr., *A Thousand Days*, p. 149.
11 Alsop with Platt, "*I've Seen the Best of It,*" p. 272.
12 Abramson, p. 672.

13 Ibid., p. 676.
14 Interview, confidential source.
15 Interview, Ethel Kennedy, 10/27/93.
16 Interview, Peter Duchin, September 1992.
17 Abramson, p. 414.
18 Joseph A. Califano Jr., *The Triumph and Tragedy of Lyndon Johnson*, p. xx, cited in *Washington Post Bookworld*, 10/20/91, p. 10.
19 Maxine Cheshire, *Washington Post*, 9/17/71.
20 Abramson, p. 685.
21 Charlotte Curtis, *New York Times*, 9/28/71, p. 35.
22 George F. Kennan, *Memoirs: 1925–1950*, p. 231.
23 William Walton, *Architectural Digest*, June 1984, p. 112.
24 Interview, Hugh Newell Jacobsen, 10/29/92.
25 Interview, confidential source.
26 Interview, confidential source.
27 Interview, confidential source.
28 Interview, Nancy Lutz, 12/5/92.
29 Interview, Alida Morgan, 12/9/92.
30 Interview, Nancy Whitney, 12/2/92.
31 Interview, Cheray Duchin Hodges, 11/4/92.
32 Interview, confidential source.
33 William Walton, *Architectural Digest*, January 1984, and author visit.
34 Elaine B. Steiner, *Architectural Digest*, October, 1982, p. 113.
35 Abramson, p. 170.
36 Ibid., p. 110.
37 Ibid., p. 257.
38 Steiner, p. 115.
39 Ibid., p. 112.
40 Interview, Judy Green, 5/4/93.
41 Abramson, p. 685.
42 Brenner, July 1988, p. 125.
43 *New York Times*, 12/14/71.
44 Interview, Alida Morgan.
45 Interview, Fred Dutton, 11/6/92.
46 Interviews, Ed Guthman, 11/19/92; Frank Mankiewicz, 11/5/92.
47 Interview, Cheray Duchin Hodges.
48 Interview, confidential source.
49 Interview, Zbigniew Brzezinski, 7/25/92.
50 Interview, Emilie Benes Brzezinski, 7/25/92.
51 Interview, Zbigniew Brzezinski.
52 R. W. Apple Jr. to author, 3/9/93.
53 Interview, Madeleine Albright, 9/9/92.

CHAPTER SIXTEEN

1 Brenner, July 1988, p. 124.
2 Interview, confidential source.
3 Interview, confidential source.
4 Churchill, *Memories and Adventures*, p. 48.
5 Ibid., pp. 112–113.
6 Ibid., pp. 54–55.
7 Ibid., p. 55.
8 Ibid., p. 57.
9 Pearson, p. 426.
10 Ibid., p. 410.
11 Churchill, *Memories and Adventures*, p. 246.
12 Interview, Jones Harris.
13 Interview, confidential source.
14 William Schmidt, *New York Times*, 6/1/93, p. 2.
15 Dunne, *The Mansions of Limbo*, p. 96.
16 Interview, Jan Cushing Amory, 10/28/92.
17 Interview, confidential source.
18 Interview, confidential source.
19 Interviews, Peter Duchin 9/11/92, and following; Cheray Duchin Hodges, 11/4/92, and following.
20 Pearson, p. 385.
21 Churchill, p. 337.
22 Pearson, p. 385.
23 Ibid., p. 408.
24 Churchill, p. 347.
25 Ibid., p. 317.
26 Interview, confidential source.
27 Donnie Radcliffe, *Washington Post*, 11/6/92, p. D2.
28 Joy Billington, *Sunday Times Magazine* (London), 10/31/82, p. 17.
29 Ibid., p. 17.

30 Churchill, p. 149.
31 Interview, Marina Berry, 10/9/92.
32 Helen Gibson, *Time*, 5/3/93, pp. 56–58.
33 William Tuohy, *Los Angeles Times*, 4/30/93.

CHAPTER SEVENTEEN

1 *Time*, 11/17/80, p. 61.
2 Lance Morrow, *Time*, 11/17/80, p. 44.
3 Interview, Stuart Eizenstat, 8/25/92.
4 Brenner, July 1988, p. 125.
5 Interview, Pie Friendly, July 1992.
6 *New York Times*, 3/2/77, p. C4.
7 Interview, Chris Matthews, 9/4/92.
8 Interview, Robert S. Strauss, 9/17/93.
9 Barbara Gamarekian, *New York Times*, 5/11/84.
10 Brenner, December 1991, p. 214.
11 Ibid., p. 218.
12 Bill Peterson, *Washington Post*, 2/11/81, p. C8.
13 Gamarekian, 5/11/84.
14 Interview, Alfred Friendly Jr., 11/3/92.
15 Interview, Stuart Eizenstat.
16 Interview, Chris Matthews.
17 Walter Isaacson, *Time*, 9/25/82, p. 20.
18 *Washington Post*, 5/4/93, p. A19.
19 Isaacson, *Time*, 9/25/82, p. 21.
20 Muriel Bowen, *Sunday Times* (London), 3/11/84.
21 Interview, Robert S. Strauss.
22 Interview, John White, 7/23/92.
23 Stanley W. Cloud, *Time*, 3/14/88, p. 60.
24 Harding Lawrence, letter to author, 2/2/93.
25 Interview, Peter Fenn, 9/2/92.
26 Pamela Harriman statement, dated 4/30/81.
27 Interview, Peter Fenn.
28 Jacqueline Trescott, *Washington Post*, 6/10/81, p. B3.
29 Evan Thomas, *Newsweek*, 6/15/87, p. 32.

30 Mehren, p. E1.
31 Interview, confidential source.
32 Interview, confidential source.
33 Thomas, *Newsweek*, p. 32.
34 Interview, Stuart Eizenstat.
35 James Perry, *Wall Street Journal*, 10/8/81, p. 1.
36 Bumiller, 10/9/81, p. C1.
37 Pamela Harriman, news conference introducing 1986 fact book, 6/26/86.
38 Interview, Peter Fenn.
39 Lynn Rosellini, *New York Times*, 10/1/82, p. 22.
40 Walter Isaacson, *Time*, 11/15/82, p. 12.
41 Interview, Sven Holmes, 8/5/92.
42 Bumiller, 10/9/81, p. L3.
43 Interview, confidential source.
44 Interview, confidential source.
45 Kurt Anderson, *Time*, 11/19/84, p. 64.
46 Democrats for the 80's, Annual Report 1984, p. 2.
47 Myra MacPherson, *Washington Post*, 9/17/86, p. A18.
48 Marie Brenner, *The New Yorker*, 12/28/92–1/4/93, p. 156.
49 Sulzberger, *Marina: Letters and Diaries of Marina Sulzberger*, p. 412.
50 Interview, John Chancellor, 11/13/92.
51 Clayton Fritchey to author, 9/27/93.
52 Elizabeth Kastor, *Washington Post*, 5/21/89, p. A1.
53 Will on file, Loudoun County, Va., recorder's office, Leesburg, Va; *Washington Post*, 9/23/86.
54 Interview, confidential source.
55 Abramson, p. 697.
56 Mary Battiata, *Washington Post*, 9/19/86, pp. D1, D4.
57 Ibid.
58 Interview, Nancy Lutz, 12/5/92.

CHAPTER EIGHTEEN

1 Interview, confidential source.
2 Senate Majority '86, fund-raising letter, 6/27/86.

3 Jacob Lamar Jr., *Time*, 11/17/86, p. 38.
4 Interview, Robert S. Strauss, 9/17/93.
5 Laurence I. Barrett, *Time*, 11/17/86, p. 39.
6 Interview, Stuart Eizenstat, 8/25/92.
7 Pamela Harriman, Democrats for the 80's appeal, 1/31/87.
8 Pamela Harriman, *New York Times*, 8/19/87.
9 Pamela Harriman, *New York Times*, 2/20/88.
10 Kitty Kelley, *Nancy Reagan*, p. 497.
11 David Aaron, *New York Times*, 12/14/87.
12 Stephanie Mansfield, *Washington Post*, 4/28/88, p. C1.
13 Ibid.
14 Interview, Gary Hart, 1/14/93.
15 Donnie Radcliffe, *Washington Post*, 11/6/92, p. D2.
16 Walter Shapiro, *Time*, 11/21/88, p. 58.
17 Pamela Harriman, memo to board members, Democrats for the 80's, 1/31/89.
18 Pamela Harriman, letter dated 12/7/90.
19 Chuck Conconi, *Washington Post*, 12/11/90, p. D3.
20 Interview, confidential source.
21 *New York Times*, 2/14/77.
22 Interview, Pie Friendly.
23 Interview, Michael Kuruc, 10/12/93.
24 Interview, confidential source.
25 Interview, Kris Bauer, 6/12/92.
26 Susan Watters and Patrick McCarthy, *W* newspaper, 11/30/87, p. 20.
27 John Sedgwick, *Connoisseur*, December 1991, p. 119.
28 Ibid., p. 42.
29 Interview, confidential source.
30 Interview, Sugar Rautbord, 11/25/92.
31 Interview, confidential source.
32 Sedgwick, p. 116.
33 Interview, confidential source.

34 Interview, confidential source.
35 Barbara Matusow, *Washingtonian*, February 1992.
36 Pamela Harriman, *People*, 5/20/89.
37 Priscilla Painton, *Time*, 10/28/91, p. 26.
38 Donnie Radcliffe, *Washington Post*, 11/6/92, p. D2.
39 *Time*, 8/1/88, p. 21.
40 Ibid.
41 Pamela Harriman, *Washington Post*, 5/26/92.
42 Elizabeth Mehren, *Los Angeles Times*, 4/5/93, p. B11.

CHAPTER NINETEEN

1 Donnie Radcliffe, *Washington Post*, 11/6/92, p. D2.
2 Ibid.
3 Robert S. Strauss to author, 9/17/93.
4 Interview, confidential source.
5 Interview, confidential source.
6 Interview, confidential source.
7 Interview, Arthur Hartman, 10/13/93.
8 Martha Duffy, *Time*, 7/5/93, p. 44.
9 Albin Krebs, *New York Times*, 4/28/78, p. A18.
10 Benoit d'Aboville to author, March 1993.
11 *Paris Match*, 7/22/93, p. 62.
12 Frank Magill, *Cyclopedia of Literary Characters*, p. 732.
13 *Le Point*, 4/3/93, p. 62.
14 Interview, confidential source.
15 Sharon Waxman, *Washington Post*, 3/26/93, p. G7.
16 Charles Bremner, *Times* (London), 3/28/93, p. 11.
17 *Wall Street Journal*, 3/12/93, p. 9.
18 Anne Gowen, *Washington Times*, 3/24/93.
19 Susan Watters, *W* newspaper, May 24–31, 1993.

EPILOGUE

1 Christopher Hitchens, *Vanity Fair*, August 1993, p. 46.

2 William Manchester, *Visions of Glory*, p. 137.
3 *La Résidence des Ambassadeurs Americains à Paris*, 1985.
4 Suzanne Lowry, *Daily Telegraph*, 6/25/93, p. 15.
5 Marthy Duffy, *Time*, 7/5/93, p. 44.
6 Lowry, p. 15.
7 John L. Davidson, " 'New Ties' Hailed by Pamela Harriman," *Commerce in France*, Fall 1993.
8 Pamela Harriman speech 9/29/93 to the American Chamber of Commerce and the American Club of Paris.

Bibliography

Abramson, Rudy. *Spanning the Century*. New York: William Morrow, 1992.

Adams, Henry H. *Harry Hopkins*. New York: G. P. Putnam's Sons, 1977.

Addison, Paul. *The Road to 1945*. London: Jonathan Cape, 1975.

Alsop, Joseph W., with Adam Platt. *"I've Seen the Best of It."* New York: W. W. Norton, 1992.

Alsop, Susan Mary. *To Marietta from Paris, 1945–1960*. New York: Doubleday, 1974.

Ambrose, Stephen E. *Eisenhower*. Vol. 2: *The President*. New York: Simon and Schuster, 1984.

Amory, Cleveland. *Who Killed Society?* New York: Harper, 1960.

Amory, Mark. *The Letters of Evelyn Waugh*. New York: Ticknor and Fields, 1980.

Bacall, Lauren. *By Myself*. New York: Alfred A. Knopf, 1979.

Barnett, Correlli. *The Collapse of British Power*. Gloucester, England: Alan Sutton, 1987.

Barrow, Andrew. *Gossip: A History of High Society from 1920 to 1970*. New York: Coward, McCann and Geoghegan, 1979.

———. *International Gossip. A History of High Society, 1970–1980*. London: Hamish Hamilton, 1983.

Beaton, Cecil. *The Happy Years: Diaries, 1944–48*. London: Weidenfeld and Nicolson, 1972.

———. *The Restless Years: Diaries, 1955–63*. London: Weidenfeld and Nicolson, 1976.

Begbie, J. *Walking in Dorset*. London: Maclehose, 1936.

Beningfield, Gordon, and Anthea Zeman. *Hardy Country*. London: Cameron, 1983.

Berman, Sonia. *The Crossing. Adano to Catonsville: Leland Hayward's Producing Career.* New York: Columbia University, 1980.

Blair, Joan, and Clay Blair Jr. *The Search for JFK.* New York: Berkley/G. P. Putnam's Sons, 1976.

Blake, Lord, and C. S. Nicholls. *The Dictionary of National Biography, 1971–1980.* London: Oxford University Press, 1986.

Blanch, Lesley. *The Wilder Shores of Love.* New York: Simon and Schuster, 1954.

Bliss, Edward Jr. *In Search of Light: The Broadcasts of Edward R. Murrow, 1938–1961.* New York: Alfred A. Knopf, 1967.

Braudy, Susan. *This Crazy Thing Called Love.* New York: Alfred A. Knopf, 1992.

Bryan, J. III, and Charles J. V. Murphy. *The Windsor Story.* New York: William Morrow, 1979.

Buchwald, Ann, and Art Buchwald. *Seems Like Yesterday.* New York: G. P. Putnam's Sons, 1980.

Buchwald, Art. *How Much Is That in Dollars?* Cleveland: World, 1961.

Buckle, Richard. *Self-Portrait with Friends: The Selected Diaries of Cecil Beaton, 1926–1974.* New York: Times Books, 1979.

Butcher, Captain Harry C. *My Three Years with Eisenhower.* New York: Simon and Schuster, 1946.

Cahan, William G., M.D. *No Stranger to Tears.* New York: Random House, 1992.

Califano, Joseph A. Jr. *The Triumph and Tragedy of Lyndon Johnson: The White House Years.* New York: Simon and Schuster, 1991.

Cannadine, David. *The Decline and Fall of the British Aristocracy.* New Haven: Yale University Press, 1990.

———. *The Pleasures of the Past.* London: Collins, 1989.

Carroll, Gordon. *History in the Writing.* New York: Duell, Sloan and Pearce, 1945.

Charmley, John. *Duff Cooper.* London: Papermac, 1987.

Childs, David. *Britain Since 1945.* London: Methuen, 1979.

Chisholm, Anne, and Michael Davie. *Beaverbrook.* London: Hutchinson, 1992.

Churchill, Randolph S. *Twenty-One Years.* Boston: Houghton Mifflin, 1965.

———. *The Rise and Fall of Sir Anthony Eden.* London: Macgibbon and Kee, 1959.

Churchill, Winston Spencer. *Thoughts and Adventures.* London: Mandarin, 1990.

———. *The Second World War.* 6 vols. London: Cassell, 1948–54.

Churchill, Winston S. *Memories and Adventures.* London: Coronet, 1990.

———. *First Journey.* New York: Random House, 1965.

Clark, Kenneth. *Another Part of the Wood: A Self-Portrait.* New York: Harper and Row, 1971.

———. *The Other Half.* New York: Harper and Row, 1977.

Clarke, Gerald. *Capote: A Biography.* New York: Simon and Schuster, 1988.

Cleggett, David A. H. *History of Leeds Castle and Its Families.* Maidstone, Kent, England: Leeds Castle Foundation, undated, but signed by author, November 1990.

Clifford, Clark, and Richard Holbrooke. *Counsel to the President.* New York: Random House, 1991.

Collier, Peter, and David Horowitz. *The Kennedys: An American Drama.* New York: Summit, 1984.

Colville, John. *The Fringes of Power: Downing Street Diaries, 1939–1955.* Vol. 1. London: Hodder and Stoughton, 1985; Vol. 2. October 1941–1955. London: Sceptre, 1985.

———. *Winston Churchill and His Inner Circle.* New York: Wyndham Books, 1981.

Cooper, Artemis. *The Letters of Evelyn Waugh and Diana Cooper.* New York: Ticknor and Fields, 1992.

Cooper, Diana. *The Rainbow Comes and Goes.* Boston: Houghton Mifflin, 1958.

———. *Trumpets from the Steep.* Boston: Houghton Mifflin, 1960.

———. *Diana Cooper: Autobiography.* New York: Carroll and Graf, 1985.

Cowles, Virginia. *The Rothschilds.* New York: Alfred A. Knopf, 1973.

———. *Winston Churchill: The Era and the Man.* New York: Harper and Brothers, 1953.

Cullingford, Cecil N. *A History of Dorset.* Chichester, Sussex, England: Phillimore, 1984.

Curtis, Charlotte. *The Rich and Other Atrocities.* New York: Harper and Row, 1976.

Davie, Michael. *The Diaries of Evelyn Waugh.* Boston: Little, Brown, 1976.

Davis, John H. *The Kennedys.* New York: S.P.I. Books, 1992.

Dimbleby, David, and David Reynolds. *An Ocean Apart.* New York: Random House, 1988.

Donaldson, Frances. *Edward VIII.* New York: J. B. Lippincott, 1975.

Draper, Jo, and John Fowles. *Thomas Hardy's England.* Boston: Little, Brown, 1984.

Dunne, Dominick. *The Mansions of Limbo.* New York: Bantam, 1992.

Edsall, Thomas Byrne, with Mary D. Edsall. *Chain Reaction: The Impact of Race, Rights and Taxes on American Politics.* New York: W. W. Norton, 1991.

Elborn, Geoffrey. *Edith Sitwell: A Biography.* New York: Doubleday, 1981.

Flanner, Janet (Genêt). *Paris Journal, 1944–1965.* New York: Atheneum, 1965.

Fleming, Kate. *The Churchills.* New York: Viking, 1975.

Fonda, Afdera, with Clifford Thurlow. *Never Before Noon.* New York: Weidenfeld and Nicolson, 1986.

Ford, Hugh. *Nancy Cunard: Brave Poet, Indomitable Rebel, 1896–1965.* Philadelphia: Chilton, 1968.

Freeman, Anne Hobson. *The Style of a Law Firm.* Algonquin Books of Chapel Hill, 1989.

Friedman, Alan. *Agnelli: Fiat and the Network of Italian Power.* New York: New American Library, 1989.

Friedman, Lawrence J. *Menninger: The Family and the Clinic.* Lawrence: University Press of Kansas, 1990.

Gardiner, Dorothy. *Companion into Dorset.* London: Methuen, 1937.

Geoffrey-Lloyd, Lord. *Leeds Castle.* Maidstone, Kent, England: Leeds Castle Foundation, 1976.

Gilbert, Martin. *Winston S. Churchill.* Vol. 5, *The Prophet of Truth, 1922–1939.* Boston: Houghton Mifflin, 1977.

———. *Winston S. Churchill.* Vol. 6, *Finest Hour, 1939–1941.* Boston: Houghton Mifflin, 1983.

Grafton, David. *The Sisters.* New York: Villard, 1992.

Graves, Robert, and Alan Hodge. *The Long Week-End. A Social History of Great Britain, 1918–1939.* W. W. Norton, 1963.

Green, Stanley. *The World of Musical Comedy.* A. S. Barnes and Company, 1974.

Grobel, Lawrence. *Conversations with Capote.* New York: New American Library, 1985.

Halberstam, David. *The Powers That Be.* New York: Knopf, 1979.

Halle, Kay, compiler. *Randolph Churchill: The Young Unpretender.* London: Heinemann, 1971.

Hampton, Mark. *Legendary Decorators of the Twentieth Century.* New York: Doubleday, 1992.

Harriman, W. Averell, and Elie Abel. *Special Envoy to Churchill and Stalin, 1941–1946*. New York: Random House, 1975.

Harriman, Margaret Case. *Take Them Up Tenderly*. New York: Books for Libraries Press, Alfred A. Knopf, 1972.

Hardy, Thomas. *The Woodlanders*. New York: Harper and Brothers, 1923.

Hart, Moss. *Act One*. New York: Signet, 1959.

Hastings, Selina. *Nancy Mitford*. London: Papermac, 1986.

Hayward, Brooke. *Haywire*. New York: Alfred A. Knopf, 1977.

Hemingway, Ernest. *88 Poems*. Edited by Nicholas Gerogiannis. New York: Harcourt Brace Jovanovich, 1979.

———. *Selected Letters, 1917–1961*. New York: Scribner's, 1981.

Hepburn, Katharine. *Me: Stories of My Life*. New York: Alfred A. Knopf, 1991.

Hornblow, Leonora. *The Love-Seekers*. New York: Random House, 1957.

Hotchner, A. E. *Papa Hemingway*. New York: Random House, 1966.

Hough, Richard. *Winston and Clementine*. London: Bantam, 1991.

Isaacson, Walter, and Evan Thomas. *The Wise Men*. London: Faber and Faber, 1986.

James, Robert Rhodes. *Chips: The Diaries of Sir Henry Channon*. London: Weidenfeld and Nicolson, 1967.

Joesten, Joachim. *Onassis: A Biography*. New York: Abelard-Shuman, 1963.

Jullian, Philippe, and John Phillips. *Violet Trefusis*. London: Methuen, 1986.

Kahn, E. J. Jr. *Jock: The Life and Times of John Hay Whitney*. New York: Doubleday, 1981.

Keith, Slim, with Annette Tapert. *Slim*. New York: Warner, 1990.

Kelley, Kitty. *His Way*. New York: Bantam, 1987.

———. *Jackie Oh!* New York: Ballantine, 1978.

Kennan, George F. *Memoirs, 1925–1950*. New York: Pantheon, 1983.

Kendrick, Alexander. *Prime Time: The Life of Edward R. Murrow*. Boston: Little, Brown, 1969.

Kennedy, Rose Fitzgerald. *Times to Remember*. New York: Doubleday, 1974.

Kidd, Charles, and David Williamson. *Debrett's Peerage and Baronetage*. London: Macmillan.

Kluger, Richard. *The Paper: The Life and Death of the New York Herald Tribune*. New York: Alfred A. Knopf, 1986.

Lacey, Robert. *Majesty*. London: Sphere, 1986.

Lambert, Angela. *1939: The Last Season of Peace*. London: Weidenfeld and Nicolson, 1989.

Lankford, Nelson Douglas. *OSS against the Reich. The World War II Diaries of Col. David K. E. Bruce*. Kent, Ohio: Kent State University Press, 1991.

Lash, Joseph P. *Roosevelt and Churchill, 1939–1941*. New York: W. W. Norton, 1976.

Leslie, Anita. *Cousin Randolph*. London: Hutchinson, 1985.

Lilly, Doris. *Those Fabulous Greeks: Onassis, Niarchos and Livanos*. New York: Cowles, 1970.

Littlewood, Joan. *Baron Philippe: The Very Candid Autobiography of Baron Philippe de Rothschild*. New York: Crown, 1984.

Logan, Joshua. *Josh: My Up and Down, In and Out Life*. New York: Delacorte, 1976.

———. *Movie Stars, Real People and Me*. New York: Delacorte, 1978.

Longford, Lord. *Kennedy*. London: Weidenfeld and Nicolson, 1976.

Lutyens, Mary. *Edwin Lutyens*. London: Black Swan, 1991.

Lysaght, Charles Edward. *Brendan Bracken*. London: Allen Lane, 1979.

Magill, Frank. *Cyclopedia of Literary Characters*. New York: Harper and Row, 1963.

Manchester, William. *The Last Lion. Winston Spencer Churchill: Alone, 1932–1940.* Boston: Little, Brown, 1988.

Margetson, Stella. *The Long Party: High Society in the Twenties and Thirties.* Farnborough, England: Saxon House, 1974.

Martin, Ralph G. *The Woman He Loved.* New York: Simon and Schuster, 1973.

Martin, Ralph S. *Jennie: The Life of Lady Randolph Churchill.* New York: New American Library, 1972.

McCrary, Captain John R. (Tex), and David E. Scherman. *First of the Many.* Robson, 1981.

McJimsey, George. *Harry Hopkins: Ally of the Poor and Defender of Democracy.* Cambridge: Harvard University Press, 1987.

Mee, Arthur. *Dorset.* London: Hodder and Stoughton, 1967.

Michener, James. *The World Is My Home.* Random House, 1992.

Mitford, Nancy. *The Blessing.* London: Penguin, 1957.

———. *The Pursuit of Love in a Cold Climate.* New York: Modern Library, 1982.

Morgan, Janet. *Edwina Mountbatten.* San Francisco: HarperCollins, 1991.

Morella, Joe, and Edward Z. Epstein. *Rita: The Life of Rita Hayworth.* New York: Delacorte Press, 1983.

Morton, Frederic. *The Rothschilds: A Family Portrait.* New York: Atheneum, 1962.

Mosley, Charlotte, editor. *Love from Nancy: The Letters of Nancy Mitford.* Boston: Houghton Mifflin, 1993.

Mosley, Diana. *The Duchess of Windsor.* London: Sidgwick and Jackson, 1980.

———. *A Life of Contrasts: An Autobiography.* New York: New York Times Books, 1977.

Murrow, Edward R. *This Is London.* New York: Simon and Schuster, 1941. Reprint, New York: Schocken, 1989.

Nicolson, Nigel. *Harold Nicolson: The War Years, 1939–1945.* New York: Atheneum, 1967.

Nunnerley, David. *President Kennedy and Britain.* New York: St. Martin's Press, 1972.

O'Donnell, Kenneth P., and David F. Powers, with Joe McCarthy. *"Johnny, We Hardly Knew Ye."* Boston: Little, Brown, 1972.

Ogrizek, Doré. *Paris.* London: McGraw-Hill, 1955.

Paley, William S. *As It Happened: A Memoir.* New York: Doubleday, 1979.

Panter-Downes, Mollie. *London War Notes, 1939–1945.* New York: Farrar, Straus and Giroux, 1971.

Parmet, Herbert S. *The Presidency of John F. Kennedy.* Norwalk, Conn.: Easton Press, 1983.

Parton, James. *Air Force Spoken Here: Gen. Ira Eaker and the Command of the Air.* Bethesda, Md.: Adler and Adler, 1986.

Pearson, John. *The Private Lives of Winston Churchill.* New York: Touchstone, 1991.

Perrott, Roy. *The Aristocrats.* London: Weidenfeld and Nicolson, 1968.

Petersson, R. T. *Sir Kenelm Digby, 1603–1665.* Cambridge: Harvard University Press, 1956.

Phillips, Gene D. *Evelyn Waugh's "Officers, Gentlemen and Rogues."* Chicago: Nelson-Hall, 1975.

Pochna, Marie-France. *Agnelli, L'Irresistible,* Paris: Edition Jean-Claude Lattès, Expansion Hachette, 1989.

Pryce-Jones, David. *Evelyn Waugh and His World.* Boston: Little Brown, 1973.

Reeves, Thomas C. *A Question of Character: A Life of John F. Kennedy.* New York: The Free Press, 1991.

Reynolds, Quentin. *A London Diary.* New York: Random House, 1941.

Robbins, Jhan. *Everybody's Man: A Biography of Jimmy Stewart.* New York: G. P. Putnam's Sons, 1985.

Roberts, Allen, and Max Goldstein. *Henry Fonda: A Biography.* London: McFarland, 1984.

Roberts, Brian. *Randolph: A Study of Churchill's Son.* London: Hamish Hamilton, 1984.

Roberts, Nickie. *Whores in History: Prostitution in Western Society.* London: HarperCollins, 1992.

Rodriguez, Elena. *Dennis Hopper: A Madness to His Method.* New York: Thomas Dunne/St. Martin's Press, 1988.

Roll, Eric. *Crowded Hours.* London: Faber and Faber, 1985.

Rothschild, Guy De. *The Whims of Fortune: The Memoirs of Guy De Rothschild.* New York: Random House, 1985.

Russell, A. L. N. *The Churchill Club: The Story of Ashburnham House.* London: Ashburnham House, 1943.

Sampson, Anthony. *Anatomy of Britain.* London: Hodder and Stoughton, 1962.

Schlesinger, Arthur M. Jr. *A Thousand Days.* Boston: Houghton Mifflin, 1965.

Schmidt, Margaret Fox. *Passion's Child: The Extraordinary Life of Jane Digby.* New York: Harper and Row, 1976.

Secrest, Meryle. *Kenneth Clark.* New York: Holt, Rinehart and Winston, 1984.

Sevareid, Eric. *Not So Wild a Dream.* New York: Atheneum, 1976.

Shaw, Christine, and Graham Shaw. *The Dorset Garden Guide.* Wimborne, Dorset, England: Dovecote, 1991.

Sherwood, Robert E. *Roosevelt and Hopkins: An Intimate History.* New York: Harper and Brothers, 1948.

Shirer, William L. *Twentieth Century Journey.* Vol. 3, *A Native's Return.* New York: Bantam, 1992.

Shnayerson, Michael. *Irwin Shaw: A Biography.* New York: G. P. Putnam's Sons, 1989.

Sidey, Hugh. *John F. Kennedy, President.* New York: Atheneum, 1964.

Skilling, M. R. *Walk Round Dorchester (Casterbridge) with Hardy.* Dorset, England: Thomas Hardy Society, 1975.

Slater, Leonard. *Aly: A Bibliography.* New York: Random House, 1965.

Smith, R. Franklin. *Edward R. Murrow: The War Years.* Kalamazoo, Mich.: New Issues Press, Western Michigan University, 1978.

Smith, Sally Bedell. *In All His Glory.* New York: Touchstone, 1991.

Soames, Mary. *Clementine Churchill: The Biography of a Marriage.* London: Cassell, 1979.

Sperber, A. M. *Murrow: His Life and Times.* New York: Freundlich, 1986.

Stadiem, William. *Too Rich: The High Life and Tragic Death of King Farouk.* New York: Carroll and Graf, 1991.

Stannard, Martin. *Evelyn Waugh: The Later Years 1939–1966.* New York: Norton, 1992.

Stevenson, John. *British Society, 1914–1945.* London: Penguin, 1984.

Sulzberger, C. L. *A Long Row of Candles: Memoirs and Diaries, 1934–1954.* New York: Macmillan, 1969.

———. *Marina: Letters and Diaries of Marina Sulzberger.* New York: Crown, 1978.

Sykes, Christopher. *Evelyn Waugh: A Biography.* Boston: Little, Brown, 1975.

Teale, Edwin Way. *Springtime in Britain.* New York: Dodd, Mead, 1970.

Teichmann, Howard. *Fonda: My Life.* New York: New American Library, 1982.

Thomas, Tony. *A Wonderful Life: The Films and Career of James Stewart.* Secaucus, N.J.: Citadel Press, 1988.

Thomas, Sir William Beach. *Hunting England*. New York: Charles Scribner's, 1936.

Viertel, Peter. *Dangerous Friends*. New York: Nan A. Talese, Doubleday, 1992.

Wade, J. H. *Rambles in Dorset*. London: Methuen, 1931.

Whalen, Richard J. *The Founding Father: The Story of Joseph P. Kennedy*. New York: New American Library, 1964.

Whelan, Richard. *Robert Capa: A Biography*. New York: Alfred A. Knopf, 1985.

White, Theodore H. *In Search of History*. New York: Harper and Row, 1978.

———. *Fire in the Ashes: Europe in Mid-Century*. New York: William Sloane, 1953.

Williams, Emrys. *Bodyguard: My Twenty Years as Aly Khan's Shadow*. London: Golden Pegasus Books, 1960.

Wills, Garry. *The Kennedy Imprisonment*. Boston: Atlantic Monthly Press, 1981.

Wright, William. *All the Pain that Money Can Buy*. London: Victor Gollancz, 1991.

Young, Gordon. *Golden Prince: The Remarkable Life of Prince Aly Khan*. London: Robert Hale, 1955.

Young, Philip, and Charles W. Mann. *The Hemingway Manuscripts: An Inventory*. Pennsylvania State University Press, 1969.

Ziegler, Philip. *Diana Cooper*. London: Hamish Hamilton, 1981.

———. *King Edward VIII: A Biography*. New York: Alfred A. Knopf, 1991.

Acknowledgments

P ART OF ME feels sorry that Pamela Harriman and I were unable to complete our planned collaboration. A larger part is much happier with the final outcome. Whatever its flaws, which are my responsibility, this is a more objective and realistic portrait of a remarkable woman than, as became clear, would have been produced in an authorized memoir.

I could not have completed this work without the help of many people in the United States, Britain, France, Italy, Belgium, Switzerland and Barbados. I owe them all a great debt of gratitude, including a large number — among them some of Mrs. Harriman's closest friends and associates — who have chosen to remain anonymous during her lifetime.

I am grateful to Mrs. Harriman for the opportunity to observe her at close range in Washington, D.C., in New York City, at Willow Oaks in Middleburg, Virginia, and on long walks in the hills around Sun Valley, Idaho. Thank you, Richard Holbrooke, U.S. ambassador to Germany, for initiating our original collaboration.

When Mrs. Harriman broke that off, several top editors at *Time*, notably John Stacks and Dick Stolley, guided me into the secure hands of Bill Phillips at Little, Brown, which is part of the Time Inc. publishing family. He did me a big favor by teaming me up with Frederica Friedman, my editor.

Quite simply, Fredi Friedman is a marvel, one of those rare talents who sees the big and little pictures, improves what's there, spots what's missing, and whose intelligence, high standards and charm cannot but encourage a writer. Her editorial assistant, Eve Yohalem, shepherded the manuscript at every stage with skill, understanding and unfailing good cheer.

Throughout a considerable portion of the process, Mrs. Harriman's lawyers made threatening noises about suing me and/or Little, Brown in an effort to halt publication. I relied on the counsel of several attorneys. Alan Gelfuso of Gelfuso and Lachut in Cranston, Rhode Island, is my lifelong friend as well as personal lawyer. He devoted countless hours to giving me superb advice. Richard Kurnit of Frankfurt, Garbus, Selz and Klein in New York City proved a master of literary law. Carol Ross of Time Warner also deserves great thanks.

Primary sources, of course, are the key ingredient for any biography and in this regard I was very fortunate.

Mrs. Harriman's brother, Lord Digby, graciously welcomed me to Minterne Magna in Dorset, gave me a tour of the house, an explanation of the family's history and the run of the estate. As a child, I spent part of 1952 in Britain and was taken to Downing Street to wave to Prime Minister Winston Churchill. I covered his grandson, Young Winston, in the House of Commons while serving as *Time*'s London bureau chief from 1985–89, then dined with him in Washington, D.C., in 1991 where I talked with his wife, Minnie.

Some of the many sources who helped me better understand Mrs. Harriman's life in Europe, or who provided other assistance, included, in alphabetical order: Sir Antony Acland, Susan Mary Alsop, Lord Amery, Mrs. Sarah Norton Baring, Anthony Beevor, Logan Bentley, Sir Isaiah Berlin, Marina Sulzberger Berry, Joy Billington, Artemis Cooper, Fleur Cowles, the Duke of Devonshire, Piers Dixon, Maurice Druon, Douglas Fairbanks Jr., David Frost, Richard C. Hottelet, Julia Langdon, Larry LeSueur, Mary Lutyens, Janet Murrow, Lord Norwich, Geoffrey Parkhouse, James Parton, Roland Petit, Odette Pol Roger, Alan Pryce-Jones, the Marquise de Ravenel, Sir Robin Renwick, Liliane de Rothschild, Marian Shaw, William Shirer, Andrei de Staercke, Taki Theodoracopulos, Gerald Van Der Kemp, Peter Viertel, William Walton, W. A. A. Wells.

Among those who provided guidance about Mrs. Harriman's life in the United States from 1960 on were, also in alphabetical order: Elie Abel, Rudy Abramson, Madeleine Albright, Jan Cushing Amory, Kenneth Banta, Ellen Barry, Luke Battle, Robert Beckel, Samuel "Sandy" Berger, Michael Berman, Ben Bradlee, Muska Brzezinski, Zbigniew Brzezinski, Art Buchwald, Joan Challinor, John Chancellor, Margaret Chapman, Gerald Clarke, Heather Cohane, Paul Costello, TImothy Dickinson, Fred Dutton, Albert Eisele, Stuart Eizenstat, Susan Estrich, Peter Fenn, Alfred Friendly, Jr., Jean Friendly, Pie Friendly, Joan Gardner, Ina Ginsburg, Peter Gold, Judith Green, Ed Guthman, Joyce Haber, Jones Harris, Gary Hart, Catherine Hirsch, Sven Holmes, Townsend Hoopes,

Barbara Howar, Mary Hoyt, Hugh Jacobsen, Robert G. Kaiser, Judith Kipper, Joseph Krakora, Joseph Laitin, Harding Lawrence, Robert E. Lee, Nancy Lutz, Roger Mandle, Frank Mankiewicz, Thomas Mann, Paul Manno, Tex McCrary, Christopher Matthews, James Michener, Richard Moe, Alida Morgan, Sylvia Morris, Elva Murphy, Lewis Powell, Marjorie Quinn, Gerald Rafshoon, Sugar Rautbord, Susan Reynolds, Marie Ridder, Mary Russell, John Sasso, Michael Shnayerson, Greg Schneiders, Frank Sieverts, Billy Shore, Lee Solters, Timothy Stanley, Robert Strauss, David Sulzberger, Lady Carolyn Townshend, Diana Walker, Mallory Walker, Stanley Wellborn, John White, Axcie Whitney, Nancy Whitney, Burke Wilkinson.

I am especially grateful for the extensive help given me by Peter Duchin, Brooke Hayward, Bill Hayward, and Cheray Duchin Hodges. Each proved as delightful as helpful.

Bruce Nelan and Michael Duffy, two exceptional colleagues at *Time*, read the manuscript and offered excellent editorial advice. Two Michael Ogdens, my father and my son, also made very helpful fixes and suggestions.

Cassie Furgurson provided superb assistance with research in Washington, D.C., as did Anne Moffett, Lissa August, Galit Zolkower and Joan Connelly. My reporting in Europe could not have been accomplished without the help of my *Time* colleagues Michael Brunton in London nor on the Continent without Victoria Foote-Greenwell in Paris. Thanks also to Mairi Ben Brahim, Claire Senard, Susanna Schrobsdorff, Robert Kroon, and Garry Clifford.

Photo research was fun and even easy, thanks to Sahm Doherty-Sefton, a longtime friend and London-based *Time* colleague, Ellen Graham, Cindy Joyce and Beth Zarcone of the Time-Life Picture Collection, Eve Pellegrino of Bettmann Archives and Nat Andriani of Wide World Photos, Inc.

Thank you, Betty Power of Little, Brown, for a keen copyeditor's eye and pen.

My editors at *Time* were generous in their support for this book and the leeway they allowed me from weekly magazine writing. None deserves more thanks than Karsten Prager, although Joe Ferrer, Chris Redman and George Russell were wonderful in juggling assignments. My thanks also to Washington bureau chief Dan Goodgame and to Jef McAllister, for help far beyond the call of collegiality.

My biggest thank you goes to Deedy, my wife, and Michael and Margaret, our children, who have had to put up with so much over the past three years. They endured this process and supported me with understanding, enthusiasm, grace and a special love that makes this work worth doing. Thanks, guys, you were, and are, fabulous.

Washington, D.C.
February, 1994

Index